James Beattie

Essays on the Nature and Immutability of Truth

Vol. I.: In Opposition to Sophistry and Scepticism....

James Beattie

Essays on the Nature and Immutability of Truth
Vol. I.: In Opposition to Sophistry and Scepticism....

ISBN/EAN: 9783337025298

Printed in Europe, USA, Canada, Australia, Japan

Cover: Foto ©Thomas Meinert / pixelio.de

More available books at **www.hansebooks.com**

A N

E S S A Y

ON THE

NATURE and IMMUTABILITY

O F

T R U T H,

IN OPPOSITION TO

SOPHISTRY and SCEPTICISM.

A NEW EDITION,

REVISED AND CAREFULLY CORRECTED.

Nunquam aliud Natura, aliud Sapientia dicit.   JUVENAL.

E S S A Y S

ON THE

NATURE AND IMMUTABILITY

OF

T R U T H,

IN OPPOSITION TO SOPHISTRY AND SCEPTICISM;

ON

POETRY AND MUSIC,

AS THEY AFFECT THE MIND;

ON

LAUGHTER, AND LUDICROUS COMPOSITION;

AND, ON THE

UTILITY OF CLASSICAL LEARNING.

BY JAMES BEATTIE, LL. D.

PROFESSOR OF MORAL PHILOSOPHY AND LOGIC IN THE
MARISCHAL COLLEGE AND UNIVERSITY OF ABERDEEN.

IN TWO VOLUMES.

VOL. I.

DUBLIN:
PRINTED FOR C. JENKIN, (No. 58) DAME-STREET.
M,DCC,LXXVIII.

C O N T E N T S.

I.

An Essay on the nature and immutability of Truth, in opposition to Sophistry and Scepticism.

All reasoning terminates in first principles.
All evidence ultimates intuitive. Common

THE CONTENTS.

P A R T   II.

C H A P.   I.

Confirmation of this doctrine, from
    the practice,

CHAP.

THE CONTENTS.

C H A P. II.

C H A P. III.

P A R T III.

C H A P. I.

THE CONTENTS.

Chap. II.

Chap. III.

PREFACE

PREFACE.

THIS Edition will, it is hoped, be found lefs faulty than any of the former. Several inaccuracies are now removed, unneceffary words and fentences expunged, a few erroneous paffages either cancelled or rectified, and fome new-modelled in the ftyle, which before feemed too harfhly or too ftrongly expreffed.

In regard to the reafonings and general principles of this Effay, I have not as yet feen caufe to alter my opinion; though I have carefully attended to what has been urged againft them by feveral ingenious authors. Some objections will perhaps be found obviated by occafional remarks and amendments interfperfed in this Edition. I once intended to have offered a more compleat vindication, and had actually prepared materials for it: but, finding them fwell to a confiderable bulk, and recollecting, that difputes of this nature, when once begun, are not foon terminated, and are apt to become lefs ufeful as they grow more voluminous, I was eafily prevailed with to lay afide that defign, at leaft till Providence fhould be pleafed to grant me better health. Even then, the profecution of this controverfy may not perhaps be thought requifite. To the wife a word is faid to be enough. If the principles of this Book

be

be good, they need no further fupport; if erroneous or bad, they deferve none. All I fhall add at prefent on this head, is, that after a long examination of thefe matters, it appears, not to me only, but to many other perfons of far fuperior underftanding, that my principles are founded on right reafon, and on that way of thinking and judging, which has in every age been moft familiar to the human mind. To advance paradoxes, or to be an innovator in philofophy, was never my defign. I hate paradoxes; I am no friend to innovation. If I cannot reconcile myfelf to fome modern theories of the underftanding, it is for this reafon, among others, becaufe I look upon them as paradoxical, and inconfiftent with thofe dictates of Rationality, which feem to me to be as old and as extenfive as human nature. It is poffible I may have thrown a little light on fome points relating to Moral Science; but to difcover in the human mind any thing which was never difcovered before, would require a degree of fagacity which I am certain I do not poffefs.

A complete theory of evidence is not to be expected in this Book. The attentive reader will fee I never intended one. That is a very copious and difficult fubject; and I have not profecuted it further than my argument feemed to require. It is with great pleafure I take this opportunity to declare, that the beft Theory of Evidence I have ever feen, is delivered by my excellent Friend Dr. Campbell, in that moft ingenious and learned performance, *The Philofophy of Rhetoric.* His principles and mine, though
they

they differ fomewhat in the arrangement, (in which I am inclined to think that his have the advantage), will not be found to differ in any thing material.

I have been blamed for borrowing fome hints, without acknowledgement, from Dr. Price, Dr. Ofward, and Buffier. I beg leave to fay, that I am to this hour totally unacquainted with that work of Dr. Price which is alluded to; and that, when I publifhed the firft Edition of the Effay on Truth, I was totally unacquainted with the writings of Buffier and Dr. Ofwald. I had heard indeed, that the French Philofopher ufed the term *Common Senfe* in a way fimilar to that in which I ufe it; but this was only hear- fay; and I have fince found, that though be- tween his fundamental opinions and mine there is a ftriking refemblance, his application of that term is not entirely the fame. I fhould not have mentioned this, if I did not think, that it fupplies an argument in favour of our com- mon principles.

I had finifhed all thefe papers for the prefs, when a friend at London fent me an *Ad- vertifement*, which had juft then appeared pre- fixed to a new Edition of Mr. Hume's Effays; and which, in juftice to that Au- thor, I fhall here infert, fubjoining a few re- marks in juftice to myfelf.

" Moft of the principles and reafonings con- " tained in this Volume were publifhed in a " work in three volumes, intituled, *A Treatife of* " *Human Nature:* a work, which the author " had projected before he left the college, and " which he wrote and publifhed not long after.

B 2

" But

" But not finding it fuccefsful, he was fenfible
" of his error in going to the prefs too early,
" and he caft the whole anew in the following
" pieces; where fome negligences in his former
" reafoning, and more in the expreffion, are,
" he hopes, corrected. Yet feveral writers,
" who have honoured the author's philofophy
" with anfwers, have taken care to direct all
" their batteries againft that juvenile work,
" which the author never acknowledged; and
" have affected to triumph in any advantages
" which, they imagined, they had obtained
" over it: a practice very contrary to all rules
" of candour and fair-dealing, and a ftrong in-
" ftance of thofe polemical artifices, which a bi-
" gotted zeal thinks itfelf authorifed to employ.
" Henceforth the author defires, that the fol-
" lowing pieces may alone be regarded as con-
" taining his philofophical fentiments and prin-
" ciples." Thus far Mr. Hume.

I do not think it was with an evil purpofe,
that any of thofe who attacked this author's
philofophy directed their batteries againft the
Treatife of Human Nature. In regard to myfelf,
the cafe was briefly this.

Ever fince I began to attend to matters of this
kind, I had heard Mr. Hume's philofophy mentioned as a fyftem very unfriendly to religion
both revealed and natural, as well as to fcience;
and its author fpoken of as a teacher of fceptical
and atheiftical doctrines, and withal as a moft
acute and ingenious writer. I had reafon to believe, that his arguments, and his influence as a
great literary character, had done harm, by fubverting or weakening the good principles of fome,

and

and countenancing the licentious opinions of others. Being honoured with the care of a part of the Britifh youth; and confidering it as my in-difpenfable duty (from which I truft I fhall ne-ver deviate) to guard their minds againft impiety and error, I endeavoured, among other ftudies that belonged to my office, to form a right efti-mate of Mr. Hume's philofophy, fo as not only to underftand his peculiar tenets, but alfo to per-ceive their *connection* and *confequences.*

In forming this eftimate, I thought it at once the fureft and the faireft method to begin with the *Treatife of Human Nature*, which was allowed, and is well known to be, the ground-work of the whole; and in which fome of the principles and reafonings are more fully profecuted, and their connection and confequences more clearly feen by an attentive reader, (notwithftanding fome inferiority in point of ftyle), than in thofe more elegant republications of the fyftem, that have appeared in the form of *Effays.* Every found argument that may have been urged againft the paradoxes of the *Treatife*, particularly againft its firft principles, does, in my opinion, tend to difcredit the fyftem; as every fuccefsful attempt to weaken the foundation of a building does in effect promote the downfal of the fuperftructure. Paradoxes there are in the *Treatife*, which are not in the *Effays*; and, in like manner, there are licentious doctrines in thefe, which are not in the other: and therefore I have not directed *all* my batteries againft the firft. And if the plan I had in view when I publifhed this book, had been completed, the reader would have feen, that, though I began with the *Treatife of Human Na-*

B 3   *ture,*

ture, it was never my intention to end with it. In fact, the Essay on Truth is only one part of what I had projected. Another part was then in so great forwardness, that I thought its publication not very remote, and had even made proposals to a bookseller concerning it; tho' afterwards, on enlarging the plan, I found I had not taken so wide a view of the subject as would be necessary. In that part my meaning was, to have applied the principles of this Book to the illustration of certain truths of morality and religion, to which the reasonings of Helvetius, of Mr. Hume in his *Essays*, and of some other modern philosophers, seemed unfavourable. That work, however, I have been obliged, on account of my health, to lay aside; and whether I shall ever be in a condition to resume it, is at present very uncertain.

For these eighteen years past, (and before that period I knew nothing of this author's writings), I have always heard the *Treatise of Human Nature* spoken of as the work of Mr. Hume. Till after publishing the Essay on Truth, I knew not that it had ever been said, or insinuated, or even suspected, that he either did not acknowledge that Treatise, or wished it to be considered as a work which he did not acknowledge. On the contrary, from his reprinting so often, in *Essays* that bore his name, most of the principles and reasonings contained in it; and never, so far as I had heard, disavowing any part of it; I could not but think, that he set a very high value upon it. By the literary people with whom I was then acquainted it had been much read; and

by

by many people it was much admired. And, in general, it was confidered as the author's chief work in philofophy, and as one of the moft curious fyftems of human nature that had ever appeared. Thofe who favoured his principles fpoke of it as an unanfwerable performance. And whatever its fuccefs might have been as an article of fale, (a circumftance which I did not think it material to inquire into), I had reafon to believe, that as a fyftem of licentious doctrine it had been but *too fuccefsful*; and that to the author's reputation as a philofopher, and to his influence as a promoter of infidelity, it had contributed not a little.

Our author certainly merits praife, for thus publicly difowning, though late, his *Treatife of Human Nature*; though I am forry to obferve, from the tenor of his declaration, that he ftill feems inclined to adhere to " moft of " the reafonings and principles contained in " that Treatife." But if he has now at laft renounced any one of his errors, I congratulate him upon it with all my heart. He has many good as well as great qualities; and I rejoice in the hope, that he may yet be prevailed on to relinquifh totally a fyftem, which I fhould think would be as uncomfortable to him, as it is unfatisfactory to others. In confequence of his Advertifement, I thought it right to mitigate in this Edition fome of the cenfures that more efpecially refer to the *Treatife of Human Nature :* but as that Treatife is ftill extant, and will probably be read as long at leaft as any thing I write, I did not think it expedient to make any material change in the reafoning or in the plan of this performance. *Aprl* 30, 1776.

INTRODUCTION.

To thofe who love learning and mankind, and who are more ambitious to diftinguifh themfelves as men, than as difputants, it is matter of humiliation and regret, that names and things have fo oft been miftaken for each other; that fo much of the Philofopher's time muft be employed in afcertaining the fignification of words; and that fo many doctrines, of high renown, and of ancient date when traced to their firft principles, have been found to arife from verbal ambiguity. If I have any knowledge of my own heart, or of the fubject I intend to examine, I may venture to affure the reader, that it is no part of the defign of this book, to encourage verbal difputation. On the contrary, it is my fincere purpofe to avoid, and to do every thing in my power to check it; convinced as I am, that it never can do any good, and that it has been the caufe of much evil, both in philofophy and in common life. And I hope I have a fairer chance to efcape it, than fome who have gone before me in this part of fcience. I aim at no paradoxes; my prejudices (if certain inftinctive fuggeftions of the underftanding may be fo called) are in favour of truth, virtue and Chriftianity; and I have no principles to fupport, but fuch as feem to me to have influenced the judgment of the rational attachment to hypothefis and party; profefs to ftudy men,,and things, as well as books and words; and affert, with the utmoft vehemence of proteftation, our love of truth, of candour, and of found philofophy. But let us not be deceived by appearances. Neither Moral Philofophy, nor the kindred fciences of Logic and Criticifm, are at prefent upon the moft defirable footing. The rage of parodox and fyftem has transformed thefe, which of all fciences ought to be the fimpleft and the cleareft, into a mafs of confufion, darknefs, and abfurdity. One kind of jargon is laid afide; but another has been adopted, more fafhionable indeed, but not lefs frivolous. Hypothefis, though verbally difclaimed, is really adhered to with as much obftinacy as ever. Words have been defined; but their meaning ftill remains indefinite. Appeals have been made to experience; but with fuch mifreprefentation of fact, and in fuch equivocal language, as plainly fhow the authors to have been more concerned for their theory, than for the truth. All fciences, and efpecially Moral Philofophy,, ought to regulate human practice: practice is regulated by principles, and all principles fuppofe conviction: yet the aim of fome of our celebrated moral fyftems is, to diveft the mind of every principle, and of all conviction; and, confequently, to difqualify man for action, and to render him ufelefs, and wretched. In a word, SCEPTICISM is now the profeffion of our fafhionable inquirers into human nature; a fcepticifm that is not confined to points of mere fpeculation, but has been ex

tended

tended to practical truths of the higheft importance, even to thofe of morality and religion.

I faid, that my prejudices are all in favour of truth and virtue. . To avow any fort of prejudice, may perhaps ftartle fome readers. If it fhould, I muft here entreat all fuch to paufe a moment, and afk of their own hearts thefe fimple queftions.—Are virtue and truth ufeful to mankind? Are they matters of indifference? Or are they pernicious?—If any one finds himfelf difpofed to think them pernicious, or matters of indifference, I would advife him to lay my book afide; for it does not contain one fentiment in which he can be interefted; nor one expreffion with which he can be pleafed. But he who believes that virtue and truth are of the higheft importance, that in them is laid the foundation of human happinefs, and that on them depends the very exiftence of human fociety, and of human creatures,—that perfon and I are of the fame mind; I have no prejudices that he would wifh me not to have: he may proceed: and I hope he will proceed with pleafure, and encourage, by his approbation, this honeft attempt to vindicate truth and virtue; and to overturn that pretended philofophy, which fuppofes, or which may lead us to fuppofe, every dictate of confcience, every impulfe of underftanding, and every information of fenfe, queftionable and doubtful.

This fceptical philofophy (as it is called) feems to me to be dangerous, not becaufe it is ingenious, but becaufe it is fubtle and obfcure. Were it rightly underftood, no confutation would be neceffary; for it does, in fact, confute itfelf,

as

as I hope to demonſtrate. But many, to my certain knowledge, have read it, and admitted its
tenets, who do not underſtand the grounds of
them; and many more, ſwayed by the faſhion
of the times, have greedily adopted its conclu-
ſions, without any knowledge of the premiſes,
or any concern about them. An attempt therefore to expoſe this pretended philoſophy to public view, in its proper colours, will not, I hope,
be cenſured as impertinent by any whoſe opinion I value: if it ſhould, I ſhall be ſatisfied with
the approbation of my own conſcience, which
will never reproach me for intending to do good.

I am ſorry, that in the courſe of this inquiry, it
will not always be in my power to ſpeak of ſome celebrated names with that deference, to which ſuperior talents and ſuperior virtue, are always intitled.
Every friend to civil and religious liberty, every lover of mankind, every admirer of ſincerity and ſim-
ple manners, every heart that warms at the recollection of diſtinguiſhed virtue, muſt conſider
Locke as one of the moſt amiable, and moſt illuſt-
rious men, that ever our nation produced. Such he
is, ſuch he will ever be, in my eſtimation. The
parts of his philoſophy to which truth obliges
me to object, are but few, and, compared with
the extent and importance of his other writings,
extremely inconſiderable. I object to them, becauſe I think them erroneous and dangerous;
and I am convinced, that their author, if he
had lived to ſee the inferences that have been
drawn from them, would have been the firſt to
declare them abſurd, and would have expunged
them from his works with indignation.—Berkeley was equally amiable in his life, and equally
a friend

a friend to truth and virtue. In elegance of compofition he was perhaps fuperior. I admire his virtues: I can never fufficiently applaud his zeal in
the caufe of religion: but fome of his reafonings on the fubject of human nature I cannot admit, without renouncing my claim to rationality.—There is a writer now alive, of whofe philofophy I have much to fay.   By his philofophy,
I mean the fentiments he has publifhed in a book
called, *A Treatife of Human Nature*, in three volumes, printed in the year 1739; the principal
doctrines of which he has fince republifhed again
and again, under the title of, *Effays Moral and
Political*, &c. Of his other works I fay nothing;
nor have I at prefent any concern with them.
Virgil is faid to have been a bad profe-writer; Cicero was certainly a bad poet: and this author,
though his philofophy of human nature be in
many things exceedingly reprehenfible, may yet
be a profound politician, and a learned, elegant,
and accurate hiftorian.   His high merit in thefe
characters is indeed generally allowed: and if my
fuffrage could add any thing to the luftre of his
reputation, I fhould here, with great finçerity
and pleafure, join my voice to that of the public, and make fuch an encomium on the author
of *the Hiftory of England* as would not offend
any of his rational admirers.   But why is this
author's character fo replete with inconfiftency!
why fhould his principles and his talents extort
at once our efteem and deteftation, our applaufe
and contempt! That he, whofe manners in private life are faid to be fo agreeable, fhould yet, in
the public capacity of an author, have given fo
much caufe of juft offence to all the friends
                                                        of

of virtue and mankind, is to me matter of afto-
nifhment and forrow, as well as of indignation.
That he, who fucceeds fo well in defcribing the
fates of nations, fhould yet have failed fo egre-
gioufly in explaining the operations of the mind,
is one of thofe incongruities in human genius,
for which perhaps philofophy will never be-able
fully to account. That he, who has fo impartially
ftated the oppofite pleas and principles of our
political factions, fhould yet have adopted the moft
illiberal prejudices againft natural and revealed religion: that he, who on many occafions
has difplayed a profound erudition, fhould fometimes, when intoxicated with a favourite theory,
have fuffered affirmations to efcape him, which
men of no great learning might perceive to be
ill founded: and, finally, that a moral philofopher, who feems to have exerted his utmoft ingenuity in fearching after paradoxes, fhould yet
happen to light on none but fuch as are on the
fide of licentioufnefs and fcepticifm :—thefe are
inconfiftencies equally inexplicable. And yet,
that this author is chargeable with all thefe inconfiftencies, will not, I think, be denied by
any perfon of fenfe and candour, who has read
his writings with attention.. His philofophy has
done great harm. Its admirers, I know, are
numerous; but I have not as yet met with one
perfon, who both admired and underftood it.
We are prone to believe what we wifh to be true:
and moft of this author's philofophical tenets are
fo well adapted to what I fear I may call the
fafhionable notions of the times, that thofe who
are ambitious to conform to the latter, will hardly be difpofed to examine fcrupuloufly the evidence

dence of the former.—Having made this declaration, which I do in the ſpirit of an honeſt man, I muſt take the liberty to treat this author with that plainneſs, which the cauſe of truth, and the intereſts of ſociety, ſeem to me to require. The ſame candour that prompts me to praiſe, will alſo oblige me to blame. The inconſiſtency is not in me, but in him. Had I done but half as much as he, in labouring to ſubvert principles which ought ever to be had ſacred, I know not whether the friends of truth would have granted me any indulgence; I am ſure they ought not.

If it ſhall be acknowledged by the candid and intelligent reader, that I have in this book contributed ſomething to the eſtabliſhment of old truths, I ſhall not be much offended, though others ſhould pretend to diſcover, that I have advanced nothing new. Indeed I would not wiſh to ſay any thing on theſe ſubjects, that has not often occurred to the rational part of mankind. In Logic and Ethics, we may have new treatiſes, and new theories; but we are not now to expect new diſcoveries. The principles of moral duty have long been underſtood in theſe enlightened parts of the world; and mankind, in the time that is paſt, have had more truth under their conſideration, than they will probably have in the time to come. Yet he who makes theſe ſciences the ſtudy of his life, may perhaps collect particulars concerning their evidence, which, though known to a few, are unknown to many; may ſet ſome principles in a more ſtriking light than that in which they have been formerly viewed; may deviſe methods of confuting new errors, and expoſing new paradoxes; and may hit upon a

C

more

more popular way of difplaying what has hitherto been exhibited in too dark and myfterious a
form.

It is commonly allowed, that the fcience of
human nature is of all human fciences the moft
curious and important. To know ourfelves, is
a precept which the wife in all ages have recommended, and which is enjoined by the authority
of revelation itfelf. Can any thing be of more
confequence to man, than to know what is his
duty, and how he may arrive at happinefs? It
is from the examination of his own heart, that
he receives the firft intimations of the one, and
the only fure criterion of the other.—What
can be more ufeful, more delightful, and more
fublime, than to contemplate the Deity? It is in
the works of nature, particularly in the conftitution of the human foul, that we difcern the
firft and moft confpicuous traces of the Almighty;
for without fome previous acquaintance with our
own moral nature, we could not have any certain knowledge of His.—Deftitute of the hope
of immortality, and a future retribution, how
contemptible, how miferable is man! And yet,
did not our moral feelings, in concert with what
reafon difcovers of the Deity, evidence the probability of a future ftate, and that it is neceffary to the full vindication of the divine government, we fhould be much lefs qualified, than
we now are, to judge rationally of that revelation, by which life and immortality have been
brought to light.

How then is this fcience to be learned? In
what manner are we to ftudy human nature?
Doubtlefs by examining our own hearts and
feelings,

feelings, and by attending to the conduct of other men. But are not the writings of philo-sophers useful towards the attainment of this science? Most certainly they are: for whatever improves the sagacity of judgement, the sensibi-lity of moral perception, or the delicacy of taste; whatever renders our knowledge of moral and intellectual facts more extensive; whatever im-presses our minds with more enlarged and more powerful sentiments of duty, with more affecting views of God and Providence, and with greater energy of belief in the doctrines of natural religi-on;—every thing of this sort either makes us more thoroughly acquainted, or prepares us for be-coming more thoroughly acquainted with our own nature, and with that of other beings, and with the relations they and we bear to one ano-ther. But I fear we shall not be able to improve ourselves in any one of these respects, by reading the modern systems of scepticism. What ac-count then are we to make of those systems and their authors? The following essay is partly de-signed as an answer to this question. But it has a further view: which is, to examine the foun-dations of this scepticism, and see whether these be consistent with what all mankind acknowledge to be the foundations of truth; to inquire, whe-ther the cultivation of scepticism be salutary or pernicious to science and mankind; and whether it may not be possible to devise certain *criteria*, by which the absurdity of its conclusions may be detected, even by those who may not have leisure or subtlety, or metaphysical knowledge, suffici-ent to qualify them for a logical confutation of all its premises. If it be confessed, that the pre-

sent

fent age has fome tendency to licentioufnefs, both
in principle and practice, and that the works of
fceptical writers have fome tendency to favour
that licentioufnefs; it will alfo be confeffed,
that this defign is neither abfurd nor unfeafona-
ble.

A celebrated writer * on human nature has
obferved, that " if truth be at all within the
" reach of human capacity, it is certain it muft
" lie very deep and abftrufe:" and a little after
he adds, " that he would efteem it a ftrong
" prefumption againft the philofophy he is going
" to unfold, were it fo very eafy and obvious."
I am fo far from adopting this opinion, that I
declare, in regard to the few things I have to
fay on human nature, that I fhould efteem it a
very ftrong prefumption againft them, if they
were not eafy and obvious. Phyfical and mathematical truths are often abftrufe; but facts
and experiments relating to the human mind,
when expreffed in proper words, ought to be
obvious to all. I find that thofe poets, hiftorians, and novelifts, who have given the moft lively difplays of human nature, and who abound
moft in fentiments eafily comprehended, and readily admitted as true, are the moft entertaining,
as well as the moft ufeful. How then fhould
the philofophy of the human mind be fo difficult?
Indeed, if it be an author's determinate purpofe
to advance paradoxes, fome of which are incredible, and others beyond comprehenfion; if he
be willing to avail himfelf all he can of the natural ambiguity of language in fupporting thofe
paradoxes; or if he enter upon inquiries too refined

* Treatife of Human Nature, vol. 1. p. 3. 4.

fined for human underftanding; he muft often
be obfcure, and often unintelligible. But my
views are very different. I intend only to fuggeft
fome hints for guarding the mind againft error;
and thefe, I hope, will be found to be deduced
from principles which every man of common
capacity may examine by his daily experience.

It is true, that feveral fubjects of intricate fpeculation are treated of in this book. But I have
endeavoured, by conftant appeals to fact and experience, by illuftrations and examples the moft
familiar I could think of, and by a plainnefs and
perfpicuity of expreffion which fometimes may
appear too much affected, to treat of them in a
way, that I hope cannot fail to render them intelligible, even to thofe who are not much converfant in ftudies of this kind. Truth, like virtue, to be loved, needs only to be feen. My
principles require no difguife; on the contrary,
they will, if I miftake not, be moft eafily admitted by thofe who beft underftand them. And I
am perfuaded, that the fceptical fyftem would
never have made fuch an alarming progrefs, if
it had been well underftood. The ambiguity of
its language, and the intricacy and length of
fome of its fundamental inveftigations, have unhappily been too' fuccefsful in producing that
confufion of thought, and indiftinctnefs of apprehenfion, in the minds both of authors and
readers, which are fo favourable to error and
fophiftry.

Few men have ever engaged in controverfy,
religious, political, or philofophical, without
being in fome degree chargeable with mifconception of the adverfary's meaning. That I have

never

never erred in this way, I dare not affirm. But I am confcious of having done every thing in my power to guard againft it. The greater part of thefe papers have lain by me for feveral years. They have been repeatedly perufed by fome of the acuteft philofophers of the age, whom I have the honour to call my friends, and to whofe advice and affiftance, on this, as on other occafions, I am deeply indebted. I have availed myfelf all I could of reading and converfation; and endeavoured, with all the candour I am mafter of, to profit by every hint of improvement, and to examine to the bottom every objection, that others have offered, or myfelf could devife. And may I not be permitted to add, that every one of thofe who have perufed this effay, has advifed the author to publifh it; and that many of them have encouraged him by this infinuation, to him the moft flattering of all others, That by fo doing, he would probably be of fome fervice to the caufe of truth, virtue, and mankind? In this hope he fubmits it to the public. And it is this hope only that could have induced him to attempt polemical difquifition : a fpecies of writing, which in his own judgement, is not the moft creditable; which he knows, to his coft, is not the moft pleafing; and of which he is well aware that it will draw upon him the refentment of a numerous, powerful, and fafhionable party. But,

Welcome for thee, fair Virtue! all the paft;
For thee, fair Virtue! welcome even the laft.

If

If thefe pages, which he hopes none will condemn who have not read, fhall throw any light
on the firft principles of moral fcience; if they
fhall fuggeft, to the young and unwary, any cau-
tions againft that fophiftry, and licentioufnefs
of principle, which too much infect the converfations and compofitions of the age; if they
fhall, in any meafure, contribute to the fatisfaction of any of the friends of truth and virtue; his purpofe will be completely anfwered:
and he will, to the end of his life, rejoice in the
recollection of thofe painful hours which he
paffed in the examination of this moft important
controverfy.

January, 1770.

AN

AN

ESSAY

ON THE

NATURE and IMMUTABILITY

OF

TRUTH,

IN OPPOSITION TO

SOPHISTRY and SCEPTICISM.

I PURPOSE to treat this fubject in the following manner.

FIRST, I fhall endeavour to trace the feveral kinds of Evidence and Reafoning up to their firft principles; with a view to afcertain the Standard of Truth, and explain its immutability.

SECONDLY, I fhall fhow, that my fentiments on this head, however inconfiftent with the genius of fcepticifm, and with the practice and principles of fceptical writers, are yet perfectly confiftent with the genius of true philofophy, and with the practice and principles of thofe who are allowed to have been the moft fuccefsful in the inveftigation of truth: concluding with fome inferences or rules, by which the more important fallacies of the fceptical philofophy may be detected by every perfon of common fenfe, even though he fhould not poffefs acutenefs or meta-

phyfical

phyſical knowledge ſufficient to qualify him for a logical confutation of them.

THIRDLY, I ſhall anſwer ſome objeſtions; and make ſome remarks, by way of *Eſtimate of ſcepticiſm and ſceptical writers.*

I divide my diſcourſe in this manner, chiefly with a view to the reader's accommodation. An exaſt arrangement of parts is neceſſary to confer elegance on a whole; but I am more ſtudious of utility than of elegance. And though my ſentiments might have been exhibited in a more ſyſtematic order, I am apt to think, that the order in which they firſt occurred to me is the moſt natural, and may be the moſt effeſtual for accompliſhing my purpoſe.

PART I.

OF THE STANDARD OF TRUTH.

THE love of truth has ever been accounted a good principle. Where it is known to prevail, we expeſt to find integrity and ſteadineſs; a temper of mind favourable to every virtue, and tending in an eminent degree to public utility. To have no concern for the truth, to be falſe and fallacious, is a charaſter which no perſon who is not utterly abandoned would chuſe to bear; it is a charaſter from which we expeſt nothing but levity and inconſiſtence. Truth ſeems to be conſidered by all mankind as ſomething fixed, unchangeable and eternal; it may therefore be thought, that to vindicate the permanency of truth is to diſpute without an adverſary. And indeed, if theſe queſtions were

propoſed

propofed in general terms,--Is there fuch a thing
as truth ? Are truth and falfehood different and oppofite ? Is truth permanent and eternal ?—few
perfons would be hardy enough to anfwer in
the negative. Attempts, however, have been
made, fometimes through inadvertence, and
fometimes (I fear) from defign, to undermine
the foundations of truth, and to render their
ftability queftionable ; and thefe attempts have
been fo vigoroufly forwarded, and fo often renewed, that they now conftitute a great part of
what is called *the philofophy of the human mind.*

It is difficult, perhaps impoffible, to give a
definition of Truth. But we fhall endeavour
to give fuch a defcription of it, as may make
others underftand what we mean by the word.
The definitions of former writers are not fo
clear, nor fo accurate, as could be wifhed.
Thefe therefore we *shall* overlook, without
feeking either to explain or to correct them ;
and fhall fatify ourfelves with taking notice of
fome of the mental phenomena that attend the
perception of truth. This feems to be the faf-
eft way of introducing the fubject.

C H A P T E R   I.

Of the perception of Truth in general.

ON hearing thefe propofitions,—I exift,
Things equal to one and the fame thing
are equal to one another, The fun rofe to-
day, There is a God, Ingratitude ought to be
blamed

blamed and punifhed, The three angles of a triangle are equal to two right angles, &c.—I am confcious, that my mind admits and acquiefces in them. I fay, that I believe them to be true; that is, I conceive them to exprefs fomething conformable to the nature of things. *
Of the contrary propofitions I fhould fay, that my mind does not acquiefce in thm, but difbelieves them, and conceives them to exprefs fomething not conformable to the nature of things. My judgement in this cafe, I conceive to be the fame that I fhould form in regard to thefe propofitions, if I were perfectly acquainted with all nature, in all its parts, and in all its laws †.

If I be afked, what I mean by *the nature of things*, I cannot otherwife explain myfelf, than by faying, that there is in my mind fomething which induces me to think, that every thing exifting in nature, is determined to exift, and to exift after a certain manner, in confequence of eftablifhed laws; and that whatever is agreeable to thofe laws is agreeable to the nature of things, becaufe by thofe laws the nature of all things is determined. Of thofe laws I do not pretend to know any thing, except fo far as they feem to be intimated to me by my own feelings, and by the fuggeftions of my own underftanding. But thefe feelings and fuggeftions are fuch, and affect me in fuch a manner, that I cannot help receiving them, and trufting in them, and believing that their intimations

are

---

* —ὥσθ' ἕκαςον ὡς ἔχει τῦ ἶναι, οὕτω καὶ τῆς ἀληθίας.

Arifto. Metaph. lib. 2. cap. 1.

† This remark, when applied to truth in general, is fubject to certain limitations; for which fee part 2. chap. 1. fect. 3.

are not fallacious, but such as I should approve if I were perfectly acquainted with every thing in the universe, and such as I may approve, and admit of, and regulate my conduct by, without danger of any inconvenience.

It is not easy on this subject to avoid identical expressions. I am not certain that I have been able to avoid them. And perhaps I might have expressed my meaning more shortly and more clearly, by saying, that I account That to be *truth* which the constitution of our nature determines us to believe, and That to be *falsehood* which the constitution of our nature determines us to disbelieve †. Believing and disbelieving are simple acts of the mind; I can neither define nor describe them in words; and therefore the reader must judge of their nature from his own experience. We often believe what we afterwards find to be false; but while belief continues, we think it true; when we discover its falsity, we believe it no longer.

Hitherto I have used the word *belief* to denote an act of the mind which attends the perception of truth in general. But truths are of different kinds; some are certain, others only probable: and we ought not to call that act of the mind which attends the perception of certainty, and that which attends the perception of probability, by one and the same name.
Some

† I might have said more explicitly, but the meaning is the same, " That I account that to be *truth* which the constitution " of human nature determines man to believe, and that to be " *falsehood* which the constitution of human nature determines " man to disbelieve.

Some have called the former *conviction*, and the latter *aſſent*. All convictions are equally ſtrong: but aſſent admits of innumerable degrees, from *moral certainty*, which is the higheſt degree downward, through the ſeveral ſtages of *opinion*, to that ſuſpenſe of judgement which is called *doubt*.

We may, without abſurdity, ſpeak of probable truth, as well as of certain truth. Whatever a rational being is determined, by the conſtitution of his nature, to admit as probable, may be called *probable truth*; the acknowledgement of it is as univerſal as that rational nature, and will be as permanent. But, in this inquiry, we propoſe to confine ourſelves chiefly to that kind of truth which may be called certain, which enforces our *conviction*, and the belief of which, in a ſound mind, is not tinctured with any doubt or uncertainty.

The inveſtigation and perception of truth is commonly aſcribed to our rational faculties; and theſe have by ſome been reduced to two; Reaſon and Judgement; the former being ſuppoſed to be converſant about certain truths, the latter chiefly about probabilities. But certain truths are not all of the ſame kind; ſome being ſupported by one ſort of evidence, and others by another: different energies of the underſtanding muſt therefore be exerted in perceiving them; and theſe different energies muſt be expreſſed by different names, if we would ſpeak of them diſtinctly and intelligibly. The certainty of ſome truths, for inſtance, is perceived intuitively; the certainty of others is perceived not intuitively, but in conſequence of a proof. Moſt
of

of the propofitions of Euclid are of the latter
kind; the axioms of geometry are of the former.   Now, if that faculty by which we perceive truth in confequence of a proof, be called
Reafon, that power by which we perceive felf-
evident truth, ought to be diftinguifhed by a
different name.   It is of little confequence
what name we make choice of, provided that in
chufing it we depart not from the analogy of
language; and that in applying it, we avoid
equivocation and ambiguity.*   Some philofophers of note † have given the name of *Common Senfe* to that faculty by which we perceive
felf-evident truth; and, as the term feems proper enough, we fhall adopt it.   But in a fubject of this kind, there is great danger of our
being impofed upon by words; we cannot
therefore be too much upon our guard againft
that fpecies of illufion.   We mean to draw
fome important inferences from this doctrine
of the diftinction between Reafon and Common Senfe.   Now thefe words are not always
ufed in the ftrict fignification we have here affigned them: let us therefore take a view of all
the fimilar fenfes in which they are commonly
ufed, and let us explain more particularly that
fenfe in which we are to ufe them; and thus
we fhall take every method in our power to fecure ourfelves againft the impropriety of confounding our notions by the ufe of ambiguous
and indefinite language.   Thefe philological dif-
cuffions

* We might call the one *Reafon* and the other *Reafoning*; but
the fimilarity of the terms would frequently occafion both obfcurity in the fenfe, and harfhnefs in the found.

† Dr. Reid, &c.

cuffions are indeed no part of philofophy; but
they are very neceffary to prepare us for it.
" Qui ad interpretandum naturam accefferit."
fays Bacon, " verborum mixtam naturam, et
" juvamenti et nocumenti imprimis participem,
" diftinĉte fciat*."

This diftinĉtion between Common Senfe and
Reafon is no modern difcovery †. The ancient geometricians were all acquainted with it.
Ariftotle treats of felf evident principles in many parts of his works, particularly in the fourth
book of his Metaphyfics, and in the firft book of
his latter Analytics.   He calls them, *Axioms* or
Dignities,

---

* De interpretatione Naturæ, fent. 9.

† The κοινονονμοσύη of the Greek Stoics feems to mean that
benevolent affeĉtion which men owe to fociety and to one another.   Some modern moralifts have called it the *Public Senfe.*
But the notion or idea we mean to exprefs by the term *Common
Senfe* is quite different.
The *Senfes Communis* of the Latins hath feveral fignifications.
1. It denotes this *Public Senfe*, or κοινονονμοσύη. *See Shaftefbury's Effays on the freedom of wit and humour, part 3. feĉt.
1. Note.* 2. It denotes that experience and knowledge of
life which is acquired by living in fociety.   Thus Horace feems
to ufe it, *lib. 1. fatir. 3. lin. 66.* And thus Quintilian, fpeaking of the advantages of a public education : " Senfum ipfum
qui communis dicitur, ubi difcet, cum fe a congreffu, qui non ho-
minibus folum, fed mutis quoque animalibus naturalis eft, fegre-
garit ;" *lib. 1. cap. 2. 3.* It feems to fignify that inftinĉtive
perfuafion of truth which arifes from intuitive evidence, and is the
foundation of all reafoning :

> " Corpus enim per fe communis deliquat effe
> " Senfus : quo nifi prima fides fundata valebit,
> " Haud erit occultis de rebus quo referentes
> " Confirmare animi quicquam ratione queamus."
> *Lucretius, lib. 1. ver. 423.*

Dignities, Principles and *Common Sentiments** ;
and fays of them, " That they are known by
" their own evidence † ; that except fome firft
" principles be taken for granted, there can
" be neither reafon nor reafoning ‡ ; that it
" is impoffible that every truth fhould admit
" of proof, otherwife proof would extend *in in-*
" *finitum,* which is incompatible with its na-
" ture ‖ ; and that if ever men attempt to

---

* Ἀξιώματα, Ἀρχαὶ, Κοιναὶ δόξαι.—Λέγω δὲ ἀποδεικτικὰς, καὶ τας
κοιναὶ δόξας, ἐξ ὧν ἅπαντες δεικνύουσι οἶον, ὅτι πᾶν ἀναγκαῖον ἤ φαναι,
ἤ ἀποφάναι· καὶ ἀδύνατον ἅμα εἶναι καὶ μὴ εἶναι.
                                        Metaphyf. lib. 3. *cap.* 2.

† *Analytic, lib.* 2. *cap.* 16.——Of thefe firft principles, a
French Peripatetic, who wrote about the beginning of the laft
century, expreffes himfelf thus : " Ces principes portent le nom
" de communs, non feulement parce qu'ils fervent à plufieurs fci-
" ences, mais auffi parce que *l'intelligence en eft commune à tous.*
" On les appelle auffi *dignitez* et *notions communes :* à fçavoir, dig-
" nitez, quafi comme dignes entre toutes les autres qu'on y adi-
" oufte foy, à caufe de la grande excellence de leur clarté et evi-
" dence ; et notions communes, pour ce qu'ils font fi connus, qu'
" auffi toft que la fignification des termes dont ils font compofez
" eft entenduë, fans difcourir ny argumenter davantage deffus,
" chacun entend naturellement leur verité ; fi ce n'eft quelque
" hebeté privé de raifon ; lequel je revoye à Ariftote, qui pro-
" nonce, que ceux qui doutent, qu'il faut reverer les Dieux, ou
" aymer les parents, meritent d'eftre punis ; et que ceux qui dou-
" tent que la nege eft blanche ont befoin de fens ; et à Averroes,
" qui dit, que ceux qui ne fçauroient diftinguer ce qui eft connu
" par foy d'avec ce qui ne l'eft pas, font incapables de philofo-
" pher ; et que ne pouvoir connoiftre ces principes, procede de
" quelque defaut de nature, ou de peu d'exercife, ou d'une mau-
" vaife accouftumance enracinée.

D   " prove

Corps de toute la Philofophie de Theophrafte Bouju, p. 79.

‡ Μηδὲν γὰρ τιθέντις, ἀναιροῦσι το διαλέγεσθαῖ, καὶ ὅλως λογον·
                                        Ariftot. Metaphyf. lib. 2. *cap.* 6.

‖ Ὅλως μὲν γὰρ ἁπάντων ἀδύνατον ἀπόδειξιν εἶναι· εἰς ἄπειρον γὰρ ἂν
βαδίζοι· ὥστε μηδ' οὕτως εἶναι ἀπόδειξιν·
                                        Ariftot. Metyphyf. lib. 4. *cap.* 4.

" prove a firſt principle, it is becauſe they are
" ignorant of the nature of proof *."

The word *Reaſon* is uſed in different ſenſes.
1. It is uſed to ſignify that quality of human
nature which diſtinguiſhes man from the inferior animals. Man is called a *reaſonable* being,
and the brutes are ſaid to be *irrational*. But
the faculty of reaſon, taking the word in a ſtrict
ſenſe, is perhaps not more characteriſtical of the
nature of man, than his moral faculty, or his
imagination, or his power of artificial language, or his riſibility. Reaſon, in this acceptation, ſeems to be a general name for all the
intellectual powers, as diſtinguiſhed from the
ſenſitive part of our conſtitution. 2. Every
thing that is called truth is ſaid to be perceived by reaſon : by reaſon, we are ſaid to perceive,
that the three angles of a triangle are equal to
two right angles : and we are alſo ſaid to perceive, by reaſon, that it is impoſſible for the
ſame thing to be, and not to be. But theſe
truths are of different kinds ; and therefore
the energies of underſtanding to which they are
referred, ought to be called by different names.
3. The power of invention is ſometimes aſcribed to reaſon. LOCKE tells us, that it is reaſon
which *diſcovers* and *arranges* the ſeveral intermediate proofs in an argument ; an office
which, according to the common uſe of words,
is to be referred, not to reaſon, but to imagination.

---

* Αξιουσι δι και τυτο αποδηκνυιχι τινες δι απαιδιυσιαν· ιστι γαρ
απαιδιυσια, το μη γινωσκειν τινων δει ζητει ι αποδειξιν, και τινων ου δει.
Ariſt. Metaphyſ. lib. 4. *cap.* 4.

I cite theſe authorities, that I may not be ſuppoſed to affect either an uncommon doctrine, or uncommon modes of expreſſion.

nation. 4. Reafon, as implying a faculty not marked by any other name, is ufed by thofe who are moft accurate in diftinguifhing, to fignify that power of the human mind by which we draw inferences, or by which we are convinced, that a relation belongs to two ideas, on account of our having found, that thefe ideas bear certain relations to other ideas. In a word, it is that faculty which enables us, from relations or ideas that are known, to inveftigate fuch as are unknown; and without which we never could proceed in the difcovery of truth a fingle ftep beyond firft principles or intuitive axioms. And it is in this laft fenfe we are to ufe the word *Reafon* in the courfe of this inquiry.

The term *Common Senfe* has alfo feveral different fignifications. 1. Sometimes it feems to be fynonymous with prudence. Thus we fay, that a man has a large ftock of common fenfe, who is quick in perceiving remote confequences, and thence inftantaneoufly determines concerning the propriety of prefent conduct. 2 We often meet with perfons of great fagacity in moft of the ordinary affairs of life, and very capable of accurate reafoning, who yet, without any bad intention, commit blunders in regard to decorum; by faying or doing what is offenfive to their company, and inconfiftent with their own character: and this we are apt to impute to a defect in common fenfe. But it feems rather to be owing to a defect in that kind of fenfibility, or fympathy, by which we fuppofe ourfelves in the fituations of others, adopt their fentiments, and in a manner perceive their thoughts; and which

is

is indeed the foundation of good breeding*. It
is by this fecret, and fudden, and (to thofe
who are unacquainted with it) inexplicable,
communication of feelings, that a man is enabled
to avoid what would appear incongruous or offenfive. They who are prompted by inclination, or obliged by neceffity, to ftudy the art
of recommending themfelves to others, acquire
a wonderful facility in perceiving and avoiding
all poffible ways of giving offence; which is a
proof, that this kind of fenfibility may be improved by habit: although there are, no doubt,
in refpect of this, as well as of fome other mo-
difications of perception, original and conftitutional differences in the frame of different minds.
3. Some men are diftinguifhed by an uncommon
acutenefs in difcovering the characters of others:
they feem to read the foul in the countenance,
and with a fingle glance to penetrate the deepeft
receffes of the heart.   In their prefence, the hypocrite is detected, notwithftanding his fpecious outfide; the gay effrontery of the coxcomb
cannot conceal his infignificance; and the man
of merit appears confpicuous under all the dif-
guifes of an ungainly modefty. This talent is
fometimes called *Common Senfe*; but improperly.
It is far from being common; it is even exceedingly rare: it is to be found in men who are not
remarkable for any other mental excellence;
and we often fee thofe who in other refpects are
judicious enough, quite deftitute of it.   4. Neither ought every common opinion to be referred
to common fenfe.   Modes in drefs, religion,
and converfation, however abfurd in themfelves,
may

* See Smith's Theory of moral fentiments, fect. 1.

may fuit the notions or the tafte of a particular people: but none of us will fay, that it is agreeable to common fenfe, to worfhip more gods than one; to believe that one and the fame body may be in ten thoufand different places at the fame time *; to like a face the better becaufe it is painted, or to diflike a perfon becaufe he does not lifp in his pronunciation. Laftly, The term *Common Senfe* has been ufed by fome philofophers to fignify that power of the mind which perceives truth, or commands belief, not by progreffive argumentation, but by an inftantaneous and inftinctive impulfe; derived neither from education nor from habit, but from nature; acting independently on our will, whenever its object is prefented, according to an eftablifhed law, and therefore not improperly called *Senfe*; and acting in a fimilar manner upon all mankind, and therefore properly called *Common Senfe*. It is in this fignification that the term *Common Senfe* is ufed in the prefent inquiry.

That there is a real and effential difference between thefe two faculties; that common fenfe cannot be accounted for, by being called the perfection of reafon, nor reafon, by being refolved into common fenfe, will perhaps appear from the following remarks. 1. We are confcious, from internal feeling, that the energy of underftanding which perceives intuitive truth, is different from that other energy which unites a conclufion with a firft principle, by a gradual chain of intermediate relations. We believe the truth of an inveftigated conclufion, becaufe

we

* Tranfubftantiation.

we can affign a reafon for our belief: we believe
an intuitive principle, without being able to affign any other reafon but this, that we know it
to be true; or that the law of our nature, or
the conftitution of the human underftanding,
determines us to believe it, 2. We cannot difcern any *neceffary* connection between reafon and
common fenfe; they are indeed generally connected; but we can conceive a being endued
with the one who is deftitute of the other.
Nay, we often find, that this is in fact the cafe.
In dreams, we fometimes reafon without common fenfe. Through a defect of common fenfe,
we adopt abfurd principles; but fuppofing our
principles true, our reafoning is often unexceptionable. The fame thing may be obferved in
certain kinds of madnefs. A man who believes
himfelf made of glafs, fhall yet reafon very
juftly concerning the means of preferving his
fuppofed brittlenefs from flaws and fractures.
It deferves alfo to be remarked, that a diftinction
fimilar to the prefent is acknowledged by the
vulgar, who fpeak of mother-wit as fomething
different from the deductions of reafon, and the
refinements of fcience. When puzzled with argument, they have recourfe to their common
fenfe, and acquiefce in it fo fteadily, as to render
all the arts of the logician ineffectual. " I am
confuted, but not convinced," is an apology
fometimes offered, when one has nothing to oppofe to the arguments of the antagonift, but the
original undifguifed feelings of his mind. This
apology is indeed very inconfiftent with the dignity of philofophic pride; which, taking for
granted that nothing exceeds the limits of human

man capacity, profeſſes to confute whatever it
cannot believe, and which is ſtill more difficult,
to believe whatever it cannot confute : but this
apology may be perfectly conſiſtent with ſincerity and candour; and with that principle of
which Pope ſays, that " though no ſcience it
" is fairly worth the ſeven."

Thus far I have endeavoured to diſtinguiſh
thoſe two powers of our rational nature, to
which I give the names *Reaſon* and *Common
Senſe*. Their connection and mutual dependence, and the extent of their reſpective juriſ-
dictions, I now proceed more particularly to in-
veſtigate. — I ought perhaps to make an apology for theſe, and ſome other metaphorical
expreſſions. And indeed it were to be wiſhed,
that in all matters of ſcience, they could be
laid aſide; for the indiſcreet uſe of metaphor
has done great harm, by leading philoſophers to
miſtake verbal analogies for real ones; and often, too, by giving plauſibility to nonſenſe, as
well as by diſguiſing very plain doctrines with
an affected pomp of high-ſounding words and
gaudy images. But in the philoſophy of the human mind, it is impoſſible to keep clear of metaphor; becauſe we cannot ſpeak intelligibly
of immaterial things, without continual alluſi-
ons to matter, and its qualities. All I need to
ſay further on this head is, that I mean not
by theſe metaphors to impoſe upon the reader;
and that I ſhall do my utmoſt to prevent their
impoſing upon myſelf.

It is ſtrange to obſerve, with what reluc-
tance ſome people acknowledge the power of
inſtinct. That man is governed by reaſon,

the

the brutes by inftinct, is a favourite topic with certain philofophers; who like other froward children, fpurn the hand that leads them; and defire, above all things, to be left at their own difpofal. Were this boaft founded on truth, it might be fuppofed to mean little more, than that man is governed by himfelf, and the brutes by their Maker *, But, luckily for man, it is not founded in truth, but in ignorance and inattention. Our inftincts, as well as our rational powers, are far fuperior, both in number and dignity, to thofe which the brutes enjoy; and it were well for us, on many occafions, if we laid our fyftems afide, and were more attentive to thefe impulfes of nature wherein reafon has no part. Far be it from me to fpeak with difrefpect of any of the gifts of God; every work of his is good; but the beft things, when abufed, may become pernicious. Reafon is a noble faculty, and, when kept within its proper fphere, and applied to ufeful purpofes, proves a means of exalting human creatures almoft to the rank of fuperior beings. But this faculty has been much perverted, often to vile, and often to infignificant purpofes; fometimes chained like a flave or malefactor, and fometimes foaring in forbidden and unknown regions. No wonder, then, if it has been frequently made the inftrument of feducing and bewildering mankind, and of rendering philofophy contemptible.

In

---

* And Reafon raife o'er Inftinct as you can,
  In this 'tis God directs, in that 'tis man.
  Pope's Effay on Man, Ep. 3. *ver.* 99.

In the science of body, glorious discoveries have been made by a right use of reason. When men are once satisfied to take things as they find them ; when they believe nature upon her bare declaration, without suspecting her of any design to impose upon them ; when their utmost ambition is to be her servants and interpreters; then, and not till then, will philosophy prosper. But of those who have applied themselves to the science of human nature, it may truly be said, (of many of them at least), that too much reasoning hath made them mad. Nature speaks to us by our external, as well as by our internal, senses; it is strange, that we should believe her in the one case, and not in the other; it is most strange, that supposing her fallacious, we should think ourselves capable of detecting the cheat. Common sense tells me, that the ground on which I stand is hard, material and solid, and has a real, separate, independent existence. BERKELEY and HUME tell me, that I am imposed upon in this matter : for that the ground under my feet is really an idea in my mind; that its very essence consists in being perceived ; and that the same instant it ceases to be perceived, it must also cease to exist; in a word, that *to be* and *to be perceived*, when predicated of the ground, the sun, the starry heavens, or any corporeal object, signify precisely the same thing. Now, if my common sense be mistaken, who shall ascertain and correct the mistake ? Our reason, it is said. Are then the inferences of reason in this instance clearer, and more decisive than the dictates of common sense ? By no means : I still trust

to

to my common fenfe as before; and I feel
that I muft do fo. But fuppofing the inferences of the one faculty as clear and decifive
as the dictates of the other; yet who will affure me, that my reafon is lefs liable to miftake than my common fenfe ? And if reafon be
miftaken, what fhall we fay ? Is this miftake to
be rectified by a fecond reafoning, as liable to
miftake as the firft ?—In a word, we muft deny
the diftinction between truth and falfehood,
adopt univerfal fcepticifm, and wander without
end from one maze of uncertainty to another;
a ftate of mind fo miferable, that Milton makes
it one of the torments of the damned;—or
elfe we muft fuppofe, that one of thefe faculties is of higher authority than the other; and
that either reafon ought to fubmit to common
fenfe, or common fenfe to reafon, whenever a variance happens between them : — in other words,
that no doctrine ought to be admitted as true
that exceeds belief, and contradicts a firft principle.

I has been faid, that every enquiry in philofophy ought to begin with doubt; — that nothing is to be taken for granted, and nothing
believed, without proof. If this be admitted, it
muft alfo be admitted, that reafon is the ultimate judge of truth, to which common fenfe
muft continually act in fubordination. But
this I cannot admit; becaufe I am able to
prove the contrary by inconteftable evidence.
I am able to prove, that " except we believe
" many things without proof, we never can
" believe any thing at all; for that all found
" reafoning muft ultimately reft on the prin-
                                    " ciples

" ciples of common fenfe; that is, on princi-
" ples intuitively certain, or intuitively proba-
" ble; and confequently, that common fenfe is
" the ultimate judge of truth, to which rea-
" fon muft continually act in fubordination." —
This I mean to prove by a fair induction of
particulars.

C H A P.   II.

*All reafoning terminates in firft principles. All
evidence ultimately intuitive. Common Senfe
the Standard of Truth to Man.*

IN this induction,, we cannot comprehend all
forts of evidence, and modes of reafoning; but
we fhall endeavour to inveftigate the origin of
thofe which are the moft important, and of
the moft extenfive influence in fcience, and common life*; beginning with the fimpleft and
clearest,

* That the induction here given is fufficiently comprehenfive,
will appear from the following analyfis.
All the objects of the human underftanding may be reduced to
two claffes, viz. *Abftract Ideas*, and *Things really exifting*.
Of *Abftract Ideas, and their Relations*, all our knowledge is *certain*, being founded on MATHEMATICAL EVIDENCE *(a)*;
which comprehends, 1. Intuitive Evidence, and, 2. the Evidence of ftrict demonftration.
We judge of *Things really exifting*; either, 1. from *our own
experience*; or, 2. from *the experience of other men*.
1. Judging of *Real Exiftences* from *our own experience*, we attain either *Certainty* or *Probability*. Our knowledge is *certain*
when fupported by the evidence, 1. Of SENSE EXTERNAL *(b)*
    (a) Sect 1. ,   *(b)* Sect. 2.

or

cleareft, and advancing gradually to thofe which are more complicated, or lefs perfpicuous.

S E C T I O N   I.

Of Mathematical Reafoning.

THE evidence that takes place in pure mathematics, produces the higheft affurance and certainty in the mind of him who attends to, and underftands it; for no principles are admitted into this fcience, but fuch as are either felf evident, or fufceptible of demonftration. Should a man refufe to affent to a demonftrated conclufion, the world would impute the refufal, either to want of underftanding, or to want of honefty; for every perfon of underftanding feels, that by mathematical demonftration he muft be convinced whether he will or not. There are two kinds of mathematical demonftration.

or INTERNAL *(c)*; 2. Of MEMORY *(d)*; and, 3. Of LEGITIMATE INFERENCES OF THE CAUSE FROM THE EFFECT *(e).*— Our knowledge is *probable,* when, *from* facts already experienced, we argue, 1. *to* fact OF THE SAME KIND *(f)* not experienced; and, 2. *to* facts OF A SIMILAR KIND *(g)* not experienced.

2. Judging of *Real Exiftences* from *the experience of other men,* we have the EVIDENCE OF THEIR TESTIMONY *(h).* The mode of underftanding produced by that evidence is properly called *Faith;* and this faith fometimes amounts to *probable opinion,* and fometimes rifes even to *abfolute certainty.*

(*c*) Sect. 3.   (*d*) Sect. 4.   (*e*) Sect. 5.   (*f*) Sect. 6.
(*g*) Sect. 7.   (*h*) Sect. 8.

demonftration. The firft is called *direct*; and
takes place when a conclufion is inferred from
premifes that render it neceffarily true: and
this perhaps is a more perfect, or at leaft a fimpler, kind of proof, than the other; but both
are equally convincing. The other kind is called *indirect*, *apagogical*, or *ducens ad abfurdum*;
and takes place, when, by fuppofing a
propofition falfe, we are led into an abfurdity,
which there is no other way to avoid, than by
fuppofing the propofition true. In this manner it is proved, that the propofition is not, and
cannot be, falfe; in other words, that it is a
certain truth. Every ftep in a mathematical
proof, either is felf evident, or muft have been
formerly demonftrated; and every demonftration does finally refolve itfelf into intuitive or felf-
evident principles, which it is impoffible to prove,
and equally impoffible to difbelieve. Thefe firft
principles conftitute the foundation of mathematics: if you difprove them, you overturn the
whole fcience; if you refufe to believe them,
you cannot, confiftently with fuch refufal, acquiefce in any mathematical truth whatfoever.
But you may as well attempt to blow out the
fun, as to difprove thefe principles: and if you
fay, that you do not believe them *, you will be
charged either with falfehood or with folly; you
may as well hold your hand in the fire, and fay
that you feel no pain. By the law of our nature,

* Si quelque opiniaftre les nie de la voix, on ne l'en fçauriot
empefcher; mais cela ne luy eft pas permis interieurement en fon
efprit, parce que fa lumiere naturelle y repugne, qui eft la partie
où fe rapporte la demonftration et le fyllogifme, et non aux pa-
roles externes. Au moyen de quoy s'il fe trouve quelqu'un qui ne
les puiffe entendre, cettuy-là eft incapable de difcipline.
Dalectique de Boujou, liv. 3. ch. 3.

ture, we muſt feel in the one caſe, and believe
in the other; even as, by the ſame law, we
muſt adhere to the earth, and cannot fall head-
long to the clouds.

But who will pretend to prove a mathematical axiom, That a whole is greater than a
part, or, That things equal to one and the ſame
thing are equal to one another? Every proof
muſt be more evident than the thing to be proved. Can you then aſſume any more evident
principle, from which the truth of theſe axioms
may be conſequentially inferred? It is impoſſible; becauſe they are already as evident as any
thing can be †. You may bring the matter to
the teſt of the ſenſes, by laying a few halfpence
and farthings upon the table; but the evidence
of

† Different opinions have prevailed concerning the nature of
theſe geometrical axioms. Some ſuppoſe, that an axiom is not
ſelf-evident, except it imply an identical propoſition; that therefore this axiom, *It is impoſſible for the ſame thing at the ſame time,
to be and not to be*, is the only axiom that can properly be called
intuitive; and that all thoſe other propoſitions commonly called
axioms, ought to be demonſtrated by being reſolved into this fundamental axiom. But if this could be done, mathematical truth
would not be one whit more certain than it is. Thoſe other axioms produce abſolute certainty, and produce it immediately,
without any proceſs of thought or reaſoning that we can diſcover.
And if the truth of a propoſition be clearly and certainly perceived by all men without proof, and if no proof whatever could
make it more clear or more certain, it ſeems captious not to allow that propoſition the name of *Intuitive Axioms.*—Others ſuppoſe, that though the demonſtration of mathematical axioms is
not abſolutely neceſſary, yet that theſe axioms are ſuſceptible of
demonſtration, and ought to be demonſtrated to thoſe who require
it. Dr. Barrow is of this opinion. So is Apollonius; who a-
greeably to it, has attempted a demonſtration of this axiom, That
things equal to one and the ſame thing are equal to one another.—
But whatever account we make of theſe opinions, they affect not
our doctrine. However far the demonſtration of axioms may be
carried, it muſt at laſt terminate in *one* principle of common ſenſe,
if not in *many*; which principle we muſt believe without proof,
whether we will or no.

of fenfe is not more unqueftionable, than that
of abftract intuitive truth; and therefore the
former evidence, though to one ignorant of the
meaning of the terms, it might ferve to explain
and illuftrate the latter, can never prove it.
But not to reft any thing on the fignification
we affix to the word *proof*; and to remove every
poffibility of doubt as to this matter, let us fuppofe, that the evidence of external fenfe is more
unqueftionable than that of abftract intuitive
truth, and that every intuitive principle in mathematics may thus be brought to the teft of
fenfe; and if we cannot call the evidence of
fenfe a proof, let us call it a confirmation of the
abftract principle : yet what do we gain by this
method of illuftration ? We only difcover, that
the evidence of abftract intuitive truth is refolvable into, or may be illuftrated by, the evidence
of fenfe. And it will be feen in the next fection, that we believe in the evidence of external
fenfe, not becaufe we can prove it to be true,
but becaufe the law of our nature determines us
to believe in it without proof. So that in
whatever way we view this fubject, the point
we mean to illuftrate appears certain, namely,
" That all mathematical truth is founded in
" certain firft principles which common fenfe,
" or inftinct, or the conftitution of the human
" underftanding, or the law of rational nature,
" compels us to believe without proof, whether
" we will or not."
Nor would the foundation of mathematics be
in the leaft degree more ftable, if thefe axioms
did admit of proof, or were all refolvable into
one primary axiom expreffed by an identical propofition.

pofition. As the cafe now ftands, we are abfolutely certain of their truth; and abfolute
certainty is all that demonftration can produce.
We are convinced by a proof, becaufe our conftitution is fuch, that we muft be convinced by
it: and we believe a felf-evident axiom, becaufe our conftitution is fuch, that we muft believe it. You afk, why I believe what is felf-
evident? I may as well afk, why you believe
what is proved? Neither queftion admits of an
anfwer; or rather, to both queftions the anfwer
is the fame, namely, Becaufe I muft believe it.

Whether our belief in thefe cafes be agreeable to the eternal relations and fitneffes of things,
and fuch as we fhould entertain if we were perfectly acquainted with all the laws of Nature,
is a queftion which no perfon of a found mind
can have any fcruple to anfwer, with the fulleft
affurance, in the affirmative. Certain it is, our
conftitution is fo framed, that we muft believe
to be true, and conformable to univerfal nature, that which is intimated to us, as fuch,
by the original fuggeftions of our own underftanding. If thefe are fallacious, it is the Deity
who makes them fo; and therefore we can never
rectify, or even detect, the fallacy. But we
cannot even fuppofe them fallacious, without vio-
lating our nature; nor, if we acknowledge a
God, without impiety; for in this fuppofition it
is implied, that we fuppofe the Deity a deceiver.
Nor can we, confiftently with fuch a fuppofition, acknowledge any diftinction between
truth and falfehood, or believe that one inch
is lefs than ten thoufand miles, or even that we
ourfelves exift.

I am

I am inclined to think, though I have not as
yet fo thoroughly examined the notion as to be
able to prove it, that all mathematical truth is
refolvable into identical propofitions. But yet
I do not fee, that there is any impropriety in faying,
(according to my ufe of the terms), that mathematical truth refts on certain principles (or
fome one principle) of common fenfe, which the
law of our nature (or of rational nature) determines us to believe: For, might we not have
been fo framed, as not to perceive the coincidence of the predicate, with the fubject, of an
identical propofition ?   And if fo, is not our
power of perceiving that coincidence a part of
the conftitution of our nature ?   All beings endued with reafon have this power as well as we;
for we cannot conceive underftanding or reafon
to be, where this power is not.   But the exiftence of rational creatures is an effect of that
conftitution of things, which the good providence
of God has been pleafed to eftablifh *.

SECT.   II.

Of the evidence of External Senfe.

ANother clafs of truths producing conviction,
and abfolute certainty, are thofe which depend
upon the evidence of the external fenfes; Hearing, Seeing, Touching, Tafting, and Smelling.
On this evidence is founded all our knowledge
of external or material things; and therefore all
conclufions in natural philofophy, and all thofe

E   prudential

* See part 2. chap. 1. fect. 3.

prudential confiderations which regard the prefervation of our body, as it is liable to be affected
by the fenfible qualities of matter, muft finally
be refolved into this principle, That things are
as our fenfes reprefent them.   When I touch a
ftone, I am confcious of a certain fenfation,
which I call a *fenfation of hardnefs*. But this fenfation is not hardnefs itfelf, nor any thing like
hardnefs: it is nothing more than a fenfation or
feeling in my mind; accompanied, however,
with an irrefiftible belief, that this fenfation is
excited by the application of an external and
hard fubftance to a certain part of my body.
This belief as certainly accompanies the fenfation, as the fenfation accompanies the application
of the ftone to my organ of fenfe. I believe,
with as much affurance, and as unavoidably,
that the external thing exifts, and is hard, as I
believe that I receive, and am confcious of, the
fenfation of hardnefs; or, to fpeak more ftrictly,
the fenfation which by experience I know to be
the fign of my touching a hard body*.   Now,
why do I believe that this fenfation is a real fenfation, and really felt by me?   Becaufe my
conftitution is fuch that I muft believe fo. And
why do I believe, in confequence of my receiving this fenfation, that I touch an external object, really exifting, material, and hard?   The
anfwer is the fame: the matter is incapable of
proof: I believe, becaufe I muft believe. Can
I avoid believing, that I really am confcious of
receiving this fenfation? No. Can I avoid
believing, that the external thing exifts, and has
a certain quality, which fits it, on being applied

to

---

* See Dr. Reid's Inquiry into the human mind, chap. 5. fect. 3.

to my hand, to excite a certain feeling or fenfation in my mind? No; I muft believe this,
whether I will or not. Nor could I diveft myfelf of this belief, though my life and future
happinefs depended on the confequence.—To believe our fenfes, therefore, is according to the
law of our nature; and we are prompted to
this belief by inftinct, or common fenfe.
I am as certain, that at prefent I am
in a houfe, and not in the open air; that I fee
by the light of the fun, and not by
the light of a candle; that I feel the ground
hard under my feet; and that I lean againft a
real material table,—as I can be of the truth of
any geometrical axiom, or of any demonftrated
conclufion; nay, I am as certain of all this as
of my own exiftence. But I cannot prove by
argument, that there is fuch a thing as matter
in the world, or even that I myfelf exift: and
yet I know as affuredly, that I do exift, and
that there is a real material fun, and a real
material world, with mountains, trees, houfes,
and animals, exifting feparately, and independently on me and my faculties; I fay, I know
all this with as much affurance of conviction,
as the moft irrefragable demonftration could
produce. Is it unreafonable to believe in thefe
cafes *without* proof? Then, I affirm, it is
equally unreafonable to believe in any cafe *with*
proof. Our belief in either cafe is unavoidable,
and according to the law of our nature; and if
it be unreafonable to think according to the law
of our nature, it muft be equally unreafonable
to adhere to the earth, to be nourifhed with food,
or to die when the head is feparated from the body. It is indeed eafy to affirm any thing, provided a man can reconcile himfelf to hypocrify and

falfehood.

falſehood.   A man may affirm, that he ſees with
the ſoles of his feet, that he believes there is
no material world, that he doubts of his own
exiſtence.   He may as well ſay, that he believes
one and two to be equal to ſix, a part to be greater than a whole, a circle to be a triangle; and
that it may be poſſible for the ſame thing, at the
ſame time, to be and not to be.

But it is ſaid, that our ſenſes do often impoſe
upon us; and that by means of reaſon we are
enabled to deteƈt the impoſture, and to judge
rightly even where our ſenſes give us wrong information; that therefore our belief in the evidence of ſenſe is not inſtinƈtive or intuitive, but
ſuch as may be either confuted or confirmed by
reaſoning.   We ſhall acknowledge that our ſenſes do often impoſe upon us: but a little attention will convince us, that reaſon, though it
may be employed in correƈting the preſent fallacious ſenſation, by referring it to a former ſenſation, received by us, or by other men, is not
the ultimate judge in this matter; for that all
ſuch reaſoning is reſolvable into this principle of
common ſenſe, That things are what our external ſenſes repreſent them.   One inſtance will
ſuffice at preſent for illuſtration of this point *.

After having looked a moment at the ſun, I
ſee a black, or perhaps a luminous, circle ſwim-
ming in the air, apparently at the diſtance of two
or three feet from my eyes. That I ſee ſuch a circle,
is certain; that I believe I ſee it, is certain; that I
believe its appearance to be owing to ſome cauſe,
is alſo certain:—thus far there can be no impoſture, and there is no ſuppoſition of any.
                                        Suppoſe

* See part 2. chap. 1. ſeƈt. 2.

Suppofe me from this appearance to conclude, that a real, folid, tangible or vifible, round fub-ftance, of a black or yellow colour, is actually fwimming in the air before me; in this I fhould be miftaken. How then come I to know that I am miftaken? I may know it in feveral ways. 1. I ftretch out my hand to the place where the circle feems to be floating in the air; and having *felt* nothing, I am inftantly convinced, that there is no *tangible* fubftance in that place. Is this conviction an inference of reafon? No; it is a conviction arifing from our innate propenfity to believe, that things are as our fenfes repre-fent them. By this innate or inftinctive pro-penfity I believe that what I touch exifts; by the fame propenfity I believe, that where I touch nothing, there nothing tangible does exift. If in the prefent cafe I were fufpicious of the ve-racity of my fenfes, I fhould neither believe nor difbelieve. 2. I turn my eyes towards the op-pofite quarter of the heavens; and having ftill obferved the fame circle floating before them, and knowing by experience, that the motion of bodies placed at a diftance from me does not follow or depend on the motion of my body, I conclude, that the appearance is owing, not to a real, external, corporeal object, but to fome diforder in my organ of fight. Here rea-foning is employed; but where does it terminate? it terminates in experience, which I have ac-quired by means of my fenfes. But if I believ-ed them fallacious, if I believed things to be otherwife than my fenfes reprefent them, I fhould never, by their means, acquire experience at all. Or, 3. I apply, firft to one man, then to ano-

E 3   ther,

ther, and then to a third, who all affure me, that they perceive no fuch circle floating in the air, and at the fame time inform me of the true caufe of the appearance. I believe their declaration, either becaufe I have had experience of their veracity, or becaufe I have an innate propenfity to credit teftimony. To gain experience implies a belief in the evidence of fenfe, which reafoning cannot account for; and a propenfity to credit teftimony previous to experience or reafoning, is equally unaccountable *.—So that although we acknowledge fome of our fenfes, in fome inftances, deceitful, our detection of the deceit, whether by the evidence of our other fenfes, or by a retrofpect to our paft experience, or by our trufting to the teftimony of other men, does ftill imply, that we do and muft believe our fenfes previoufly to all reafoning†.

A human creature born with a propenfity to difbelieve his fenfes, would be as helplefs as if he wanted them. To his own prefervation he could contribute nothing; and, after ages of being, would remain as deftitute of knowledge and experience, as when he began to be.

Sometimes we feem to diftruft the evidence of our fenfes, when in reality we only doubt whether we have that evidence. I may appeal to any man, if he were thoroughly convinced that he had really when awake, feen and converfed with a ghoft, whether any reafoning would convince him that it was a delufion. Reafoning might lead him to fufpect that he had been
dreaming,

---

* See fect, 8. of this chapter.   † See part 2. chap. 1. fect 2.

dreaming, and therefore to doubt whether or
not he had the evidence of fenfe; but if he were
affured that he had that evidence, no arguments
would fhake his belief.

S E C T.   III.

Of the Evidence of Internal Senfe, or Confciouf-nefs.

B Y attending to what paffes in my mind, I
know, not only that it exifts, but that it exerts
certain powers of action and perception; which,
on account either of diverfity in their objects,
or of a difference in their manner of operating,
I confider as diftinct faculties; and which I
find it expedient to diftinguifh by different
names, that I may be able to fpeak of them fo
as to be underftood. Thus I am confcious
that at one time I exert memory, at another
time imagination: fometimes I believe, fometimes I doubt: the performance of certain actions, and the indulgence of certain affections,
is attended with an agreeable feeling of a peculiar kind, which I call *moral approbation*; different actions and affections excite the oppofite
feeling, of *moral difapprobation:* to relieve diftrefs, I feel to be meritorious and praife-wor-
thy; to pick a pocket, I know to be blameable,
and worthy of punifhment: I am confcious
that fome actions are in my power, and that
others are not; that when I neglect to do
what I ought to do, and can do, I
                                    deferve

deferve to be punifhed; and that when I act neceffarily, or upon unavoidable and irrefiftable compulfion, I deferve neither punifhment nor blame. Of all thefe fentiments I am as con‑ fcious, and as certain, as of my own exiftence. I cannot prove that I feel them, neither to my‑ felf, nor to others; but that I do really feel them, is as evident to me as demonftration could make it. I cannot prove, in regard to my moral feelings, that they are conformable to any extrinfic and eternal relations of things; but I know that my conftitution neceffarily de‑ termines me to believe them juft and genuine, even as it determines me to believe that I myfelf exift, and that things are as my external fenfes reprefent them. An expert logician might puzzle me with words, and propofe difficulties I could not folve: but he might as well attempt to convince me, that I do not exift, as that I do not feel what I am con‑ fcious I do feel. And if he could induce me to fufpect that I may be miftaken, what ftan‑ dard of truth could he propofe to me, more evident, and of higher authority in thefe mat‑ ters, than my own feelings? Shall I believe his teftimony, and difbelieve my own fenfations? Shall I admit his reafons, becaufe I cannot con‑ fute them, although common fenfe tells me they are falfe? Shall I fuffer the ambiguities of artificial language to prevail againft the clear, the intelligible, the irrefiftible voice of Nature?

We cannot difbelieve the evidence of inter‑ nal fenfe, without offering violence to our na‑ ture. And if we be led into fuch difbelief, or diftruft, by the fophiftry of pretended philofophers,

philofophers, we act juft as wifely as a mariner would do, who fhould fuffer himfelf to be per-fuaded, that the pole-ftar is continually changing its place, but that the wind always blows from the fame quarter. Common fenfe, or inftinct, which prompts men to truft to their own feelings, hath in all ages continued the fame: but the interefts, purfuits, and abilities of philofophers, are fufceptible of endlefs variety; and their theories vary accordingly.

Let it not be thought, that thefe objects and faculties of internal fenfation are things too evanefcent to be attended to, or that their evidence is too weak to produce a fteady and well-grounded conviction. They are more neceffary to our happinefs than even the powers and objects of external fenfe; yea, they are no lefs neceffary to our exiftence. What can be of greater confequence to man, than his moral fentiments, his reafon, his memory, his imagination? What more interefting, than to know, whether his notions of duty and of truth be the dictates of his nature, that is, the voice of God, or the pofitive inftitutions of men? What is it to which a wife man will pay more attention, than to his reafon and confcience, thofe divine monitors, whereby he is to judge even of religion itfelf? The generality of mankind, however ignorant of the received diftinctions and explications of their internal powers, do yet by their conduct declare, that they feel their influence, and acknowledge their authenticity. Every inftance of their being governed by a principle of moral obligation, is a proof of this. They believe an action to be lawful

in

in the fight of God, when they are confcious of
a fentiment of lawfulnefs attending the performance of it : they believe a certain mode of
conduct to be incumbent on them in certain
circumftances, becaufe a notion of duty arifes
in their mind, when they contemplate that
conduct in relation to thofe circumftances.—
" I ought to be grateful for a favour received.
" Why? Becaufe my confcience tells me fo.
" How do you know that you ought to do
" that of which your confcience enjoins the
" performance? I can give no further reafon
" for it; but I *feel* that fuch is my duty."
Here the inveftigation muft ftop; or, if carried
a little further, it muft return to this point:—
" I know that I ought to do what my confci-
" ence enjoins, becaufe God is the author of
" my conftitution; and I obey His will, when
" I act according to the principles of my con-
" ftitution. Why do you obey the will of
" God? Becaufe it is my duty. How know
" you that? Becaufe my confcience tells me
" fo," &c.

If a man were fceptical in this matter, it would
not be in the power of argument to cure him *.
Such

* All that is here meant, in regard to Moral Obligation, is
that Morality like other fciences, is founded on certain firft principles, and that the dictates of confcience are to every good man
the higheft authority in matters of duty. I fee no paradox in this
doctrine; which, if I miftake not, is admitted by the beft divines
and moralifts, and by mankind in general. How far this doctrine may be affected by what cafuifts have urged in regard to an
erroneous confcience, or by the opinions of fome philofophers
concerning the mutability of moral fentiment, and its liablenefs
to be perverted by education and habit, is an enquiry of very
great extent, which I have not here entered upon at all, (though
I have written many a page on the fubject), becaufe I intended
long ago, and do ftill intend, when I fhall have health and
leifure, to make it the argument of another book. See below,
part 2. ch. 1. fect. 3. § 4.

Such a man could not be faid to have any moral principle diftinƈt from the hope of reward, the fear of punifhment, or the force of cuftom. But that there is in human nature a moral principle diftinƈt from thofe motives, has been felt and acknowledged by men of all ages and nations; and indeed was never denied or doubted, except by a few metaphyficians, who, through want either of fenfe or of honefty, found themfelves difpofed to deny the exiftence, or queftion the authenticity, of our moral feelings. In the celebrated difpute concerning liberty and neceffity, fome of the advocates for the latter have either maintained, that we have no fenfe of moral liberty; or, granting that we have fuch a fenfe, have endeavoured to prove it deceitful. Now, if we be confcious, that we have a fenfe of moral liberty, it is certainly as abfurd to argue againft the exiftence of that fenfe, as againft the reality of any other matter of faƈt. And if the real exiftence of that fenfe be acknowledged, it cannot be proved to be deceitful by any arguments which may not be applied to prove other powers of our nature deceitful, and, confequently, to fhow, that man ought not to believe any thing that depends, for its evidence, on thefe internal fuggeftions.——But more of this afterwards.

We have no other direƈt evidence than this of confcioufnefs, or internal fenfation, for the exiftence and identity of our own foul *. I exift;—

I am

* I fay, *direƈt* evidence. But there are not wanting other irrefragable, though indireƈt, evidences of the exiftence of the human foul. Such is that which refults from a comparifon of the known qualities

1 am the fame being to-day I was yefterday,
and twenty years ago;—— this principle, or
being,

qualities of matter with the phenomena of animal motion and
thought. The further we carry our inquiries into matter, the
more we are convinced of its incapacity to begin motion. And as
to thought, and its feveral modes, if we think that they *might*
be produced by any poffible arrangement of the minute particles
of matter, we form a fuppofition as arbitrary, as little warranted
by experience or evidence of any kind, and as contrary to the rules
that determine us in all our rational conjectures, as if we were to
fuppofe, that diamonds *might* be produced from the fmoke of a candle, or that men *might* grow like mufhrooms out of the earth.
There muft then, in all animals, and efpecially in man, be a principle, not only diftinct and different from body, but in fome refpects of a quite contrary nature. To afk, whether the Deity,
without uniting body with fpirit, could create thinking matter,
is juft fuch a queftion, as, whether he could create a being effentially active and effentially inactive, capable of beginning motion,
and at the fame time incapable of beginning motion : queftions,
which, if we allow experience to be a rational ground of knowledge, we need not fcruple to anfwer in the negative. For thefe
queftions, according to the beft lights that our rational faculties
can afford, feem to us to refer to the production of an effect as
truly impoffible, as round fquarenefs, hot cold, black whitenefs,
or true falfehood.

Yet I am inclined to think, it is not by this argument that the
generality of mankind are led to acknowledge the exiftence of their
own minds. An evidence more direct, much more obvious, and
not lefs convincing, every man difcovers in the inftinctive fuggeftions of nature. We perceive the exiftence of our fouls by intuition ; and this I believe is the only way in which the vulgar
perceive it. But their conviction is not on that account the
weaker ; on the contrary, they would think the man mad who
fhould feem to entertain any doubts on this fubject.

One of the firft thoughts that occur to Milton's Adam, when
" new-waked from foundeft fleep," is to inquire after the caufe of
his exiftence :

  " Thou fun, faid I, fair light !
 " And thou, enlighten'd earth, fo frefh and gay !
 " Ye hills, and dales, ye rivers, woods, and plains,
 " And ye that live and move, fair creatures, tell,
 " Tell, if ye faw, how came I thus, how here :
 " Not of myfelf ; by fome great Maker then,
 " In goodnefs and in power pre-eminent.
 " Tell me, how I may know him, how adore,
 " From whom I have, that thus I move and live,
 " And feel that I am happier than I know."

       Paradife Loft, viii. 273.

being, within me, that thinks and acts, is one permanent and individual principle, distinct from all other principles, beings, or things ;—— these are dictates of internal sensation natural to man, and universally acknowledged : and they are of so great importance, that while we doubt of their truth, we can hardly be interested in any thing else whatsoever.   If I were to believe, with some authors, that my mind is perpetually changing, so as to become every different moment a different thing, the remembrance of past, or the anticipation of future good or evil, could give me neither pleasure nor pain ; yea, though I were to believe, that a cruel death would overtake me within an hour, I should be no more concerned, than if I were told, that a certain elephant, three thousand years hence, would be sacrificed on the top of Mount Atlas. To a man who doubts the individuality or i-dentity of his own mind, virtue, truth, religion, good and evil, hope and fear, are absolutely nothing.

Metaphysicians have taken some pains to confound our notions on the subject of identity; and, by establishing the currency of certain ambiguous

Of the reality of his own life, motion, and existence, it is observable that he makes no question ; and indeed it would have been strange if he had.——But Dryden, in his opera called *The state of Innocence*, would needs attempt an improvement on this passage ; and to make surer work, obliges Adam to prove his existence by argument, before he allows him to enter upon any other inquiry :

        " What am I ? or from whence ?— For that I am
        " I know, *because I think* : but whence I came,
        " Or how this frame of mine began to be,
        " What other being can disclose to me ?

                                        Act 2. scene 1.
Dryden, it seems, had read Des Cartes ; but Milton had studied nature : Accordingly Dryden speaks like a metaphysician, Milton like a poet and philosopher.

ambiguous phrafes, have fucceeded fo well, that it is now hardly poffible for us to explain thefe dictates of our nature, according to common fenfe and common experience, in fuch language as fhall be liable to no exception. The misfortune is, that many of the words we muft ufe, though extremely well underftood, are either too fimple or too complex in their meaning, to admit a logical definition; fo that the caviller is never at a lofs for an evafive reply to any thing we may advance. But I will take it upon me to affirm, that there are hardly any human notions more clearly, or more univerfally underftood, than thofe we entertain concerning the identity both of ourfelves and of other things, however difficult we may fometimes find it to exprefs thofe notions in proper words. And I will alfo venture to affirm, that the fentiments of the generality of mankind on this head are grounded on fuch evidence, that he who refufes to be convinced by it, acts irrationally, and cannot, confiftently with fuch refufal, believe any thing.

   1. The exiftence of our own mind, as fomething different and diftinct from the body, is univerfally acknowledged. I fay univerfally; having never heard of any nation of men upon earth, who did not, in their converfation and behaviour, fhow, by the plaineft figns, that they made this diftinction. Nay, fo ftrongly are mankind impreffed with it, that the rudeft barbarians, by their incantations, their funeral folemnities, their traditions concerning invifible beings, and their hopes of a future ftate, feem to declare, that to the exiftence of the foul the body is not, in their opinion, neceffary. All
                                      philofophers,

philofophers, a few Epicureans and Pyrrhonifts
excepted, have acknowledged the exiftence of
the foul, as one of the firft and moft unexceptionable principles of human fcience. Now
whence could a notion fo univerfal arife? Let us
examine our own minds, and we fhall find,
that it could arife from nothing but confcioufnefs, a certain irrefiftible perfuafion, that we
have a foul diftinct from the body. The evidence of this notion is intuitive; it is the evidence of internal fenfe. Reafoning can neither
prove nor difprove it. Des Cartes, and his
difciple Malebranche, acknowledge, that the
exiftence of the human foul muft be believed by
all men, even by thofe who can bring themfelves
to doubt of every thing elfe.

Mr. Simon Browne *, a learned and pious
clergyman of the laft age, is perhaps the only
perfon on record of whom there is reafon to
think, that he ferioufly difbelieved the exiftence
of his own foul. He imagined, that in confequence of an extraordinary interpofition of divine power, his rational foul was gradually annihilated, and that nothing was now left him,
but a principle of animal life, which he held in
common with the brutes. But where-ever the
ftory of this excellent perfon is known, his unhappy miftake will be imputed to madnefs, and
to a depravation of intellect, as real, and as extraordinary, as if he had difbelieved the exiftence of his body, or the axioms of mathematics.

2. That the thinking principle, which we
believe to be within us, continues the fame through
life, is equally felf-evident, and equally agreeable

* See his affecting ftory in the Adventurer, vol. 3. No. 88.

able to the univerſal conſent of mankind. If a man were to ſpeak and act in the evening, as if he believed himſelf to have become a different perſon ſince the morning, the whole world would pronounce him mad. Were we to attempt to diſbelieve our own identity, we ſhould labour in vain; we could as eaſily bring our-ſelves to believe, that it is poſſible for the ſame thing to be and not to be. But there is no rea-ſon to think, that this attempt was ever made by any man, not even by Mr. HUME himſelf; though that author, in his Treatiſe of Human Nature, has aſſerted, yea, and proved too, (according to his notions of proof), that the human ſoul is perpetually changing; being no-thing but " a bundle of perceptions, that ſuc-" ceed each other with inconceivable rapidity, " and are (as he chuſes to expreſs it) in a per-" petual flux *." He might as eaſily, in my opinion, and as deciſively, with equal credit to his own underſtanding, and with equal advan-tage to the reader, by a method of reaſoning no leſs philoſophical, and with the ſame degree of diſcretion in the uſe of words, have attacked the axioms of mathematics, or any other truths inſtructive or demonſtrable, and produced a formal and ſerious confutation of them. In ex-plaining the evidence on which we believe our own identity, it is not neceſſary that I ſhould here examine his arguments againſt that belief: firſt, becauſe the point in queſtion is ſelf-evident; and therefore all reaſoning on the other ſide unphi-loſophical and irrational: and, ſecondly, be-cauſe I ſhall afterwards prove, that ſome of Mr. HUME's firſt principles are inconceivable; and

that

* Treatiſe of Human Nature, vol. 1. p. 438. &c.

that this very notion of his, concerning identity, when fairly ftated, is palpably abfurd.

It has been afked, how we can pretend to have
full evidence of our identity, when of identity
itfelf we are fo far from having a diftinct notion,
that we cannot define it. It might, with as good reafon be afked, how we come to believe that two and
two are equal to four; or, that a circle is different
from a triangle, if we cannot define either equality
or diverfity:—why we believe in our own exiftence, fince we cannot define exiftence:—why,
in a word, the vulgar believe any thing at all,
fince they know nothing about the rules of definition, and hardly ever attempt it. In fact,
we have numberlefs ideas that admit not of
definition, and yet concerning which we may
argue, and believe, and know, with the utmoft
clearnefs and certainty. To define heat or cold,
identity or diverfity, red or white, an ox or an
afs, would puzzle all the logicians on earth;
yet nothing can be clearer, or more certain,
than many of our judgements concerning thofe
objects. The rudeft of the vulgar know moft
perfectly what they mean, when they fay, Three
months ago I was at fuch a town, and have ever
fince been at home: and the conviction they
have of the truth of this propofition is founded
on the beft of evidence, namely, on that of internal fenfe; in which all men, by the law of
their nature, do and muft implicitly believe.

It has been afked, whether this continued
confcioufnefs of our being always the fame, does
not conftitute our famenefs or identity. No
more, I fhould anfwer, than our perception of
truth, light or cold, is the efficient caufe of

truth, light, or cold. Our identity is perceived
by confcioufnefs; but confcioufnefs is as different from identity, as the underftanding is different from truth, as paft events are different from
memory, as colours from the power of feeing. Confcioufnefs of identity is fo far from conftituting
identity, that it prefuppofes it. An animal
might continue the fame being, and yet not be
confcious of its identity; which is probably the
cafe with many of the brute creation; nay,
which is often the cafe with man himfelf.
When we fleep without dreaming, or fall into
a fainting fit*, or rave in a fever, and often too
in our ordinary dreams, we lofe all fenfe of our
identity, and yet never conceive that our identity

---

* The following cafe, which M. Crozaz gave in to the Academy of Sciences, is the moft extraordinary inftance of interrupted
confcioufnefs I have ever heard of. A nobleman of Laufanne, as
he was giving orders to a fervant, fuddenly loft his fpeech and all
his fenfes. Different remedies were tried without effect for fix
months; during all which time he appeared to be in a deep fleep,
or deliquium, with various fymptoms at different periods, which
are particularly fpecified in the narration. At laft, after fome
chirurgical operations, at the end of fix months his fpeech and
fenfes were fuddenly reftored. When he recovered, the fervant
to whom he had been giving orders when he was firft feized with
the diftemper, happening to be in the room, he afked whether he
had executed his commiffion; not being fenfible, it feems, that
any interval of time, except perhaps a very fhort one, had elapfed
during his illnefs. He lived ten years after, and died of another
difeafe. See L'Hiftoire de l' Academie Royale des Sciences, pour l'
année 1719, p. 28. Van Swieten alfo relates this ftory in his Commentaries on Boerhaave's Aphorifms, under the head *Apoplexy*.
I mention it chiefly with a view to the reader's amufement: he
may confider the evidence, and believe or difbelieve as he pleafes.
But that confcioufnefs may be interrupted by a total deliquium,
without any change in our notions of our own identity, I know by
my own experience. I am therefore fully perfuaded, that the
identity of this fubftance which I call my foul, may continue even
when I am unconfcious of it: and if for a fhorter fpace, why not
for a longer?

ity has fuffered any interruption or change: the moment we awake or recover, we are confcious that we are the fame individual beings we were before.

Many doubts and difficulties have been ftarted about our manner of conceiving identity of perfon under a change of fubftance. Plutarch tells us, that in the time of Demetrius Phalereus, the Athenians ftill preferved the cuftom of fending every year to Delos the fame galley which, about a thoufand years before, had brought Thefeus and his company from Crete; and that it then ufed to be a queftion in the fchools, how this could be the fame veffel, when every part of its materials had been changed oftener than once* It is afked, how a tree can be accounted the fame, wben from a plant of an inch long, it has grown to the height of fifty feet; and how identity can be afcribed to the human body, fince its parts are continually changing, fo that not one particle of the body I now have, belonged to the body I had twenty years ago.

It were well if metaphyficians would think more and fpeak lefs on thefe fubjects: they would then find, that the difficulties fo much complained of are rather verbal than real. Was there a fingle Athenian, who did not know in what refpects the galley of Thefeus continued the fame, and in what refpects it was changed? It was the fame in refpect of its name, its deftination, its fhape perhaps, and fize, and fome other particulars; in refpect of fubftance it was altogether different. And when one party in the fchools maintained, that it was the fame,

F 2 and

* Plutarch, in Thefeo. Plato, in Phædone.

and the other, that it was not the fame, all the difference between them was this, that the one ufed the word *fame* in one fenfe, and the other in another.

The identity of vegetables is as eafily conceived. No man imagines, that the plant of an inch long is the fame in fubftance with the tree of fifty feet. The latter is by the vulgar fuppofed to retain all the fubftance of the former, but with the addition of an immenfe quantity of adventitious matter. Thus far, and no further, do they fuppofe the fubftance of the tree to continue the fame. They call it, however, the fame tree : and the fame it is, in many refpects, which to every perfon of common underftanding, are obvious enough, though not eafily expreffed in unexceptionable language.

Of the changes made in the human body by attrition, the vulgar have no notion. They believe the fubftance of a full-grown body to continue the fame, notwithftanding its being fometimes fatter, and fometimes leaner; even as they fuppofe the fubftance of a wall to be the fame before, and after it is plaiftered, or painted. They therefore do not afcribe to it identity of perfon, and diverfity of fubftance, but a real and proper identity both of fubftance and perfon. Of the identity of the body while encreafing in ftature, they conceive, nearly in the fame way, as of the identity of vegetables : they know in what refpect it continues the fame, and in what refpect it becomes different; there is no confufion in their notions ;

ons; they never fuppofe it to be different in thofe refpects in which they know it to be the fame.

When philofophers fpeak of the identity of the human body, they muft mean, not that its fubftance is the fame, for this they fay is perpetually changing; but that it is the fame, in refpect of its having been all along animated with the fame vital and thinking principle, diftinguifhed by the fame name, marked with the fame or fimilar features, placed in the fame relations of life, &c.——It muft be obvious to the intelligent reader, that the difficulties attending this fubject arife not from any ambiguity or intricacy in our notions or judgements, for thefe are extremely clear, but from our way of expreffing them : the particulars in which an object continues the fame, are often fo blended with thofe in which it has become different, that we cannot find proper words for marking the diftinction, and therefore muft have recourfe to obfcure circumlocutions.

But whatever judgements we form of the identity of corporeal objects, we cannot from them draw any inference concerning the identity of our mind. We cannot afcribe extenfion or folidity to the foul, far lefs any encreafe or diminution of folid or extended parts. Here, therefore, there is no ground for diftinguifhing diverfity of fubftance from identity of perfon. Our foul is the very fame being now it was yefterday, laft year, twenty years ago. This is a dictate of common fenfe, and intuitive truth, which all mankind, by the law of their nature, do and muft believe, and the contrary of which is inconceivable. We have perhaps changed many of our principles; we may have acquired many new ideas and notions, and loft many of thofe we once had; but that the fub-ftance, effence or perfonality, of the foul, has fuffered any change, increafe or diminution, we never have fuppofed, nor can fuppofe. New faculties have perhaps appeared, with which we were formerly unacquainted; but thefe we can-not conceive to have affected the identity of the foul, any more than learning to write, or to play on a mufical inftrument, is conceived to affect the identity of the hand; or than the perception of harmony the firft time one hears mufic, is conceived to affect the identity of the ear*.

But if we perceive our identity by confciouf-nefs, and if the acts of confcioufnefs by which we perceive it be interrupted, how can we know that our identity is not interrupted? I anfwer,

---

* I beg leave to quote a few lines from an excellent poem, written by an author whofe genius and virtue were an honour to his country, and to human nature:

"Am I but what I feem, mere flefh and blood,
" A branching channel, and a mazy flood?
" The purple ftream, that through my veffels glides,
" Dull and unconfcious flows like common tides.
" The pipes, through which the circling juices ftray,
" Are not that thinking I, no more than they.
" This frame compacted with tranfcendent fkill,
" Of moving joints obedient to my will,
" Nurfed from the fruitful glebe like yonder tree,
" Waxes and waftes: I call it MINE not ME.
" New matter ftill the mouldering mafs fuftains;
" The manfion changed, the tenant ftill remains,
" And, from the fleeting ftream repair'd by food,
" Diftinct, as is the fwimmer from the flood."

ARBUTHNOT. See Dodfley's Collection, vol. 1. p. 180.

I anſwer, the law of our nature determines us, whether we will or not, to believe that
we continue the ſame thinking beings. The
interruption of conſciouſneſs, whether more or
leſs frequent, makes no change in this belief.
My perception of the viſible creation is every
moment interrupted by the winking of my eyes.
Am I therefore to believe, that the viſible univerſe, which I this moment perceive, is not the
ſame with the viſible univerſe I perceived laſt
moment ? Then muſt I alſo believe, that the
exiſtence of the univerſe depends on the motion
of my eyelids; and that the muſcles which
move them have the power of creating and annihilating worlds.

To conclude : That our ſoul exiſts, and continues through life the ſame individual being, is a
dictate of common ſenſe; a truth which the
law of our nature renders it impoſſible for us
to diſbelieve; and in regard to which, we cannot ſuppoſe ourſelves in an error, without ſuppoſing our faculties fallacious, and conſequently diſclaiming all conviction, and all certainty,
and diſavowing the diſtinction between truth
and falſehood.

S E C T.   IV.

Of the Evidence of Memory.

THE evidence of memory commands our belief as effectually as that of fenfe. With regard to any of my tranfactions of yefterday which I now remember, I cannot doubt whether I performed them or not. That I dined to-day, and was in bed laft night, is as certain to me, as that I at prefent fee the colour of this paper. If we had no memory, knowledge and experience would be impoffible; and if we had any tendency to diftruft our memory, knowledge and experience would be of as little ufe in directing our conduct and fentiments, as our dreams now are. Sometimes we doubt, whether in a particular cafe we exert memory or imagination; and our belief is fufpended accordingly: but no fooner do we become confcious, that we *remember*, than conviction inftantly takes place; we fay, I am certain it was fo, for now I remember I was an eye-witnefs.

But who is it that teaches the child to believe, that yefterday he was punifhed, becaufe he remembers to have been punifhed yefterday? Or, by what argument will you convince him, that, notwithftanding his remembrance, he ought not to believe that he was punifhed yefterday, becaufe his memory is fallacious? The matter depends not upon education or reafoning. We truft to the evidence of memory, becaufe we cannot help trufting to it. The
fame

fame Providence that endued us with memory, without any care of ours, endued us alfo with an inftinctive propenfity to believe in it, previoufly to all reafoning and experience. Nay, all reafoning fuppofes the teftimony of memory to be authentic: for, without trufting implicitly to this teftimony, no train of reafoning could be profecuted; we could never be convinced, that the conclufion is fair, if we did not *remember* the feveral fteps of the argument, and if we were not certain that this remembrance is not fallacious.

The diverfities of memory in different men are very remarkable; and in the fame man the remembrance of fome things is more lafting, and more lively, than that of others. Some of the ideas of memory feem to decay gradually by length of time; fo that there may be fome things which I diftinctly remembered feven years ago, but which at prefent I remember very imperfectly, and which in feven years more (if I live fo long) I fhall have utterly forgotten. Hence fome have been led to think, that the evidence of memory decays gradually, from abfolute certainty, through all the degrees of probability, down to that fufpenfe of judgement which we call *doubt*. They feem to have imagined, that the vivacity of the idea is in fome fort neceffary to the eftablifhment of belief. Nay, one author * has gone fo far as to fay, that belief is nothing elfe but this vivacity of ideas; as if we never believed what we have no lively conception of, nor doubted of any thing

---

* Treatife of Human Nature, vol. 1. p. 172.

of which we have a lively conception. But
this doctrine is so absurd, that it hardly deserves confutation. I have a more lively idea
of Don Quixote than of the present King of
Pruffia; and yet I believe that the latter does
exist, and that the former never did. When I
was a schoolboy, I read an abridgement of the
History of Robinson Crusoe, and believed every
word of it; since I grew up, I have read that
ingenious work at large, and consequently
have a much livelier conception of it than before: yet I now believe the whole to be a fiction. Some months ago, I read the *Treatise of
Human Nature*, and have at present a pretty
clear remembrance of its contents; but I shall
probably forget the greater part in a short
time. When that happens, I ought not, according to this theory, to believe that I ever
read it. As long, however, as my faculties remain unimpaired, I fear I shall hardly be able
to bring myself to this pitch of scepticism. No,
no; I shall ever have good reason to remember
my having read that book; however imperfect
my remembrance may be, and however little
ground I may have to congratulate myself upon my acquaintance with it.

The vivacity of a perception does not seem
neceffary to our belief of the existence of the
thing perceived. I see a town afar off; its
vifible magnitude is not more than an inch
square, and therefore my perception of it is neither lively nor distinct; and yet I as certainly
believe that town to exist, as if I were in the
centre of it. I see an object in motion on the
top of yonder hill; I cannot discern whether

ther it be a man, or a horfe, or both; I therefore exert no belief in regard to the clafs or
fpecies of things to which it belongs: but I
believe with as much affurance that it exifts, as
if I faw it diftinctly in all its parts and dimen-
fions.   We have never any doubt of the exiftence of an object fo long as we are fure that we
perceive it by our fenfes, whether the perception be ftrong or weak, diftinct or confufed;
but whenever we begin to doubt, whether the
object be perceived by our fenfes, or whether
we only imagine that we perceive it, then we
likewife begin to doubt of its exiftence.

Thefe obfervations are applicable to memory.   I faw a certain object fome years ago;
my remembrance of it is lefs diftinct now than
it was the day after I faw it; but I believe the
evidence of my memory as much at prefent as
I did then, in regard to all the parts of it
which I now am confcious that I remember.
Let a paft event be ever fo remote in time, if I
am confcious that I remember it, I ftill believe,
with equal affurance, that this event did once
take place.   For what is memory, but a confcioufnefs of our having formerly done or perceived fomething? And if it be true, that
fomething is perceived or done at this prefent
moment, it will always be true that at this
moment that thing was perceived or done.
The evidence of memory does not decay in
proportion as the ideas of memory become lefs
lively; as long as we are confcious that we
remember, fo long will the evidence attending
that remembrance produce abfolute certainty;
and abfolute certainty admits not of degrees.

                                   Indeed,

Indeed as was already obferved, when remembrance becomes fo obfcure, that we are at a
lofs to determine whether we *remember* or only
imagine an event, — in this cafe belief will be
fufpended till we become certain whether we
remember or not; whenever we become certain
that we do remember, conviction inftantly
arifes.

Some have fuppofed that the evidence of memory is liable to become uncertain, becaufe we
are not well enough acquainted with the difference between memory and imagination, to be
able at all times to determine, whether the one
or the other be exerted in regard to the events
or facts we may have occafion to contemplate.
" You fay, that while you only imagine an e-
" vent, you neither believe nor difbelieve the
" exiftence or reality of it: but as foon as you
" become confcious that you remember it, you
" inftantly believe it to have been real. You muft
" then know with certainty the difference be-
" tween memory and imagination, and be able
" to tell by what marks you diftinguifh the
" operations of the former from thofe of the
" latter. If you cannot do this, you may mif-
" take the one for the other, and think that
" you *imagine* when you really *remember*, and
" that you *remember* when you only *imagine*.
" That belief, therefore, muft be very precari-
" ous, which is built upon the evidence of me-
" mory, fince this evidence is fo apt to be con-
" founded with the vifionary exhibitions of
" imagination, which, by your own acknow-
" ledgement, can never conftitute a foundation

" for

" for true rational belief *." This is an objection according to the metaphyfical mode;
which, without confulting experience, is fatisfied if a few plaufible words can be put together in the form of an argument: but this
objection will have no credit with thofe who
acknowledge ultimate inftinctive principles of
conviction, and who have more faith in their
own feelings than in the fubtleties of logic.

It is certain the vulgar are not able to give a
fatisfactory account of the difference between
memory and imagination; even philofophers
have not always fucceeded in their attempts to
illuftrate this point †. Mr. HUME tells us,
that ideas of memory are diftinguifhed from
thofe of imagination by the fuperior vivacity of
the former ‡. This may fometimes, but cannot
always

* I do not remember where I have met with this argument. Perhaps I may have heard it in converfation.

· † Addifon, in the Spectator, No. 411. feems to confider imagination as a faculty converfant among thofe ideas only which are
derived from the fenfe of feeing. But is not this acceptation of
the word too limited? I can invent, and confequently imagine,
a tune which I never heard. When I look at Hogarth's humour-
ous print of *The Enraged Mufician*, I can imagine the feveral dif-
cordant founds fuppofed to proceed from the perfons and inftruments there affembled. Men born blind, or who have loft all
remembrance of light and colours, are as capable of invention,
and dream as frequently, as thofe who fee; my learned ingenious,
and worthy friend Dr. Blacklock of Edinburgh, who loft his fight
at five months old, is an example of both.——Some authors have
defined imagination, The fimple apprehenfion of corporeal objects
when abfent. But cannot a good man imagine the remorfe of a
murderer, or the anxieties of a mifer? Cannot one invent new
theories in the abftract philofophy, or even an entire new fyftem
of it?— Imagination, in the modern philofophic language, feems
to denote two things: 1. That power of the mind which contemplates *ideas* (that is, *thoughts* or *notions*) without referring
them to real exiftence, or to our paft experience; 2. That power
which combines ideas into new forms or affemblages.

‡ Treatife of Human Nature, vol. 1. p. 153.

always be true: for ideas of imagination are
often miſtaken for objeƈts of ſenſe; ideas of memory never.   The former, therefore, muſt often be more lively than the latter; for, according to this author's own account, all ideas are
weaker than impreſſions, or informations of
ſenſe *.   Dreaming perſons, lunatics, ſtage-
players, enthuſiaſts, and all who are agitated
by fear, or other violent paſſions, are apt to
miſtake ideas of imagination for real things, and
the perception of thoſe ideas for real ſenſation.
And the ſame thing is often experienced by perſons of ſtrong fancy, and great ſenſibility of
temper, at a time when they are not troubled
with any fits of irrationality or violent paſſion.

But whatever difficulty we may find in de-
fining or deſcribing memory, ſo as to diſtinguiſh
it from imagination, we are never at any loſs
about our own meaning, when we ſpeak of remembering and of imagining. We all know what
it is to remember, and what it is to imagine :
a retroſpeƈt to former experience always attends
the exertions of memory; but thoſe of imagination are not attended with any ſuch retroſpeƈt.
" I remember to have ſeen a lion, and I can
" imagine an elephant or centaur, which I
" have never ſeen :" — Every body who uſes
theſe words knows very well what they mean,
whether he be able to explain his meaning by
other words or not.   The truth is, that when
we remember, we generally know that we
remember; when we imagine, we generally
                                    know

* Treatiſe of Human Nature, vol. 1. p. 41.

know that we imagine † : such is our constitution. We therefore do not suppose the evidence of memory uncertain, notwithstanding that we may be at a loss to explain the difference between that faculty and imagination : this difference is perfectly known to every man by experience, though perhaps no man can fully express it in words. There are many things very familiar to us, which we have no words to express. I cannot describe or define, either a red colour, which I know to be a simple object, or a white colour, which I know to be a composition of seven colours: but will any one hence infer, that I am ignorant of their difference, so as not to know, when I look on ermine, whether it be white or red? Let it not then be said, that because we cannot define memory and imagination, therefore we are ignorant of their difference: every person of a sound mind knows their difference, and can with certainty determine, when it is that he exerts the one, and when it is that he exerts the other.

S E C T. V.

Of Reasoning from the Effect to the Cause.

I Left my chamber an hour ago, and now at my return find a book on the table, the size,
and

---

† In dreams indeed this is not the case ; but the delusions of dreaming, for all our frequent experience of them, are never supposed to affect in the least degree either the veracity of our faculties, or the certainty of our knowledge. See below, Part 2. chap. 2. sect. 2.

and binding, and contents of which are fo remarkable, that I am certain it was not here
when I went out; and that I never faw it before.   I afk, who brought this book; and am
told, that nobody has entered my apartment
fince I left it.   That, fay I, is *impoffible*.   I
make a more particular inquiry; and a fervant,
in whofe veracity I can confide, affures me, that
he has had his eye on my chamber-door the
whole day, and that no perfon has entered it
but myfelf only.   Then, fay I, the perfon who
brought this book muft have come in by the
window or the chimney; for it is *impoffible* that
this book could have come hither of itfelf.   The
fervant bids me remember, that my chimney
is too narrow to admit any human creature,
and that the window is fecured on the infide
in fuch a manner that it cannot be opened from
without.   I examine the walls; it is evident no
breach has been made; and there is but one
door to the apartment.   What fhall I think?
If the fervant's report be true, and if the book
have not been brought by any vifible agent, it
muft have come in a miraculous manner, by the
interpofition of fome invifible caufe; for ftill I
muft repeat, that without fome caufe it *could
not poffibly* have come hither.

Let the reader confider the cafe, and deliberate with himfelf, whether I think irrationally
on this occafion, or exprefs myfelf too ftrongly,
when I fpeak of the *impoffibility* of a book appearing in my chamber without fome caufe of
its appearance, either vifible or invifible.   I
would not willingly refer fuch a phenomenon to
a miracle; but ftill a miracle is poffible; whereas

as it is abfolutely impoffible; that this could have happened without a caufe; at leaft it feems to me to be as real an impoffibility, as that a part fhould be greater than the whole, or that things equal to one and the fame thing fhould be unequal to one another. And I prefume the reader will be of my opinion; for in all my intercourfe with others, and after a careful examination of my own mind, I have never found any reafon to think, that it is poffible for a human, or for a rational creature, to conceive a thing beginning to exift, and proceeding from no caufe.

I pronounce it therefore to be an axiom, clear, certain, and undeniable, That " whatever be- " ginneth to exift, proceedeth from fome caufe." I cannot bring myfelf to think, that the reverfe of any geometrical axiom is more incredible than the reverfe of this; and therefore I am as certain of the truth of this, as I can be of the truth of the other; and cannot, without contradicting myfelf, and doing violence to my nature, even attempt to believe otherwife.

Whether this maxim be intuitive or demonftrable, may perhaps admit of fome difpute; but the determination of that point will not in the leaft affect the truth of the maxim. If it be demonftrable, we can then affign a reafon for our belief of it: if it be intuitive, it is on the fame footing with other intuitive axioms; that is, we believe it, becaufe the law of our nature renders it impoffible for us to difbelieve it.

In proof of this maxim it has been faid, that nothing can produce itfelf. But this truth is not more evident than the truth to be proved,

and therefore is no proof at all. Nay, this laſt
propoſition ſeems to be only a different, and
leſs proper, way of expreſſing the ſame thing :——
Nothing can produce itſelf ;—that is, every
thing produced muſt be produced by ſome other
thing ;—that is, every effect muſt proceed from
a cauſe ;—and that is, (for all effects being poſte-
rior to their cauſes, muſt neceſſarily have a beginning), " every thing beginning to exiſt pro-
" ceeds from ſome cauſe." Other arguments
have been offered in proof of this maxim, which
I think are ſufficiently confuted by Mr. HUME,
in his Treatiſe of Human nature *. This maxim therefore he affirms, and I allow, to be not
demonſtrably certain. But he further affirms,
that it is not intuitively certain ; in which I
cannot agree with him. " All certainty," ſays
he, " ariſes from the compariſon of ideas, and
" from the diſcovery of ſuch relations as are
" unalterable ſo long as the ideas continue
" the ſame ; but the only relations † of this
" kind are reſemblance, proportion in quantity
" and number, degrees of any quality and
" contrariety ; none of which is implied in the
" maxim, *Whatever begins to exiſt, proceeds from*
" *ſome cauſe* :—that maxim therefore is not in-
" tuitively certain."—This argument, if it prove
any

---

* Book 1. part 3. ſect. 3.

† There are, according to Mr. HUME, ſeven different kinds
of philoſophical relation, to wit, Reſemblance, Identity, Relations of time and place, Proportion in quantity or number, Degrees in any common quality, Contrariety, and Cauſation. And
by the word *Relation* he here means, that particular circumſtance
in which we may think proper to compare ideas. See *Treatiſe of
Human Nature, vol.* 1. *p.* 32. 142.

any thing at all, would prove, that the maxim
is not even certain; for we are here told, that
it has not that character or quality from which
all certainty arises.

But, if I mistake not, both the premises of
this syllogism are false. In the first place, I
cannot admit, that all certainty arises from a
comparison of ideas. I am certain of the existence of myself and of the other things that
affect my senses; I am certain, that " whatever
is, is ;" and yet I cannot conceive, that any
comparison of ideas is necessary to produce these
convictions in my mind. Perhaps I cannot
speak of them without using words expressive of
relation; but the simple act or perception of
the understanding by which I am conscious of
them, implies not any comparison that I can
discover. If it did, then the simplest intuitive
truth requires proof, or illustration at least,
before it can be acknowledged as truth by the
mind; which I presume will not be found warranted by experience. Whether others are conscious of making such a comparison, before
they yield assent to the simplest intuitive truth,
I know not; but this I know, that my mind is
often conscious of certainty where no such
comparison has been made by me. I acknowledge, indeed, that no certain truth can become an object of science, till it be expressed in
words; that, if expressed in words, it must as-
sume the form of a proposition; and that every
proposition, being either affirmative or negative,
must imply a comparison of the thing or subject,
with that quality or circumstance which is affirmed or denied to belong to or agree with it :

G 2   and

and therefore I acknowledge, that in science all certainty may be said to arise from a comparison of ideas. But the generality of mankind believe many things as certain, which they never thought of expressing in words. An ordinary man believes, that himself, his family, his house, and cattle, exist; but, in order to produce this belief in his mind, is it necessary, that he compare those objects with the general idea of existence or non-existence, so as to discern their agreement with the one, or disagreement with the other? I cannot think it: at least, if he has ever made such a comparison, it must have been without his knowledge; for I am convinced, that, if we were to ask him the question, he would not understand us.

Secondly, I apprehend, that our author has not enumerated all the relations which, when discovered, give rise to certainty. I am certain, that I am the same person to-day I was yesterday. This indeed our author denies *. I cannot help it; I am certain notwithstanding; and I flatter myself, there are not many persons in the world who would think this sentiment of mine a paradox. I say, then, I am certain, that I am the same person to-day I was yesterday. Now, the relation expressed in this proposition is not resemblance, nor proportion in quantity and number, nor degrees of any common quality, nor contrariety: it is a relation different from all these; it is identity or sameness.—That London is contiguous to the Thames, is a proposition which many of the most sensible people in Europe hold to be certainly true; and yet the relation expressed in

it

* See part 2. chap. 2. sect. 1. of this Essay.

it is none of thofe four which our author fuppofes to be the fole properties of certainty.
For it is not in refpect of refemblance, of proportion in quantity or number, of contrariety,
or of degrees in any common quality, that
London and the Thames are here compared,
but purely in refpect of place or fituation.

Again, that the foregoing maxim is neither
intuitively nor demonftrably certain, our author
attempts to prove from this confideration, that
we cannot demonftrate the impoffibility of the
contrary. Nay, the contrary, he fays, is not
inconceivable: "for we can conceive an ob-
"ject non-exiftent this moment, and exiftent
"the next, without joining it to the idea of a
"caufe, which is an idea altogether diftinct
"and different." But this, I prefume, is not
a fair ftate of the cafe. Can we conceive a
thing beginning to exift, and yet bring ourfelves to think that a caufe is not neceffary to
the production of fuch a thing? If we cannot,
(I am fure I cannot), then is the contrary of
this maxim, when fairly ftated, found to be
truly and properly inconceivable.

But whether the contrary of this maxim be
inconceivable or not, the maxim itfelf may be
intuitively certain. Of intuitive, as well as of
demonftrable truths, there are different kinds.
It is a character of fome, that their contraries
are inconceivable: fuch are the axioms of geometry. But of many other intuitive truths,
the contraries are conceivable. "I do feel a
"hard body,"—"I do not feel a hard body;"
—thefe propofitions are equally conceivable:
the firft is true, for I have a pen between my fin-

gers;

gers; but I cannot prove its truth by argument; therefore its truth is perceived intuitively.

Thus far we have argued for the fake of argument, and oppofed metaphyfic to metaphyfic*, in order to prove, that our author's reafoning on the prefent fubject is not conclufive. It is now time to enter into the merits of the caufe, and confider the matter philofophically, that is, according to fact and experience. And in this way we bring it to a very fhort iffue. The point in difpute is, Whether this maxim, " Whatever be-" gins to exift, proceeds from fome caufe," be intuitively certain? That the mind naturally and necessarily affents to it without any doubt, and confiders its contrary as impoffible, I have already fhewn; the maxim, therefore, is certainly true. That it cannot, by any argument or medium of proof, be rendered more evident than it is when firft apprehended by the mind, is alfo certain; for it is of itfelf as evident as any propofition that can be urged in proof of it. If, therefore, this maxim be true, (as every rational being feels, and acknowledges), it is a principle of common fenfe: we believe it, not becaufe we can give a reafon, but becaufe, by the law of our nature, we muft believe it.

Our opinion of the neceffity of a caufe to the production of every thing that has a beginning, is by our author fuppofed to arife from obfervation and experience. It is true, that in our experience we have never found any thing beginning to exift, and proceeding from no caufe; but

_____

* See part 3. chap. 2. of this Effay.

but I imagine it will not appear, that our belief of this axiom hath experience for its foundation.   For let it be remarked, that fome children, at a time when their experience is very
fcanty, feem to be as fenfible of the truth of
this axiom, as many perfons arrived at maturity.
I do not mean, that they ever repeat it in the
form of a propofition; or that, if they were to
hear it repeated in that form, they would inftantly declare their affent to it; for a propofition can never be rationally affented to, except
by thofe who underftand the words that compofe it: but I mean, that thefe children have a
natural propenfity to inquire after the caufe of
any effect or event that engages their attention; which they would not do, if the view of an
event or effect did not fuggeft to them, that a
caufe is neceffary to its production.   Their curiofity in afking the reafons and caufes of every
thing they fee and hear, is often very remarkable, and rifes even to impertinence; at leaft
it is called fo when one is not prepared to give
them an anfwer.   I have known a child break
open his drum, to fee if he could difcover the
caufe of its extraordinary found: and that at the
hazard of rendering the plaything unferviceable, and of being punifhed for his indifcretion.
If the ardor of this curiofity were always pro-
portioned to the extent of a child's experience,
or to the care his teachers have taken to make
him attentive to the dependance of effects on
caufes, we might then afcribe it to the power of
education, or to a habit contracted by experience.   But every one who has had an opportunity of converfing with children, knows that

this

this is not the cafe; and that their curiofity cannot otherwife be accounted for, than by fuppofing it inftinctive, and, like other inftincts, ftronger in fome minds, and weaker in others, independently on experience and education, and in confequence of the appointment of that Being who has been pleafed to make one man differ from another in his intellectual accomplifh-ments, as well as in his features, complexion, and fize. Nor let it be imagined, becaufe fome children are in this refpect more curious than others, that therefore the belief of this maxim is inftinctive in fome minds only: the maxim may be equally believed by all, not-withftanding this diverfity. For do we not find a fimilar diverfity in the genius of differ-ent *men*? Some men have a philofophical turn of mind, and love to inveftigate caufes, and to have a reafon ready on every occafion; others are indifferent as to thefe matters, being ingroffed by ftudies of ano-ther kind. And yet I prefume it will be found, that the truth of this maxim is felt by every man, though perhaps many men never thought of putting it in words in the form of a propo-fition.

We repeat therefore that this axiom is one of the principles of common fenfe, which every rational mind does and muft acknowledge to be true; not becaufe it can be proved, but be-caufe the law of nature determines us to believe it without proof, and to look upon its contrary as abfurd and impoffible.

The

The axiom now before us is the foundation of the moſt important argument that ever employed human reaſon; I mean that which, from the works that are created, evinces the eternal power and godhead of the Creator. That argument, as far as it reſolves itſelf into this axiom, is properly a demonſtration, being a clear deduction from a ſelf-evident principle; and therefore no man can pretend to underſtand it without feeling it to be concluſive. So that what the Pſalmiſt ſays of the Atheiſt is literally true, *He is a fool*; as really irrational as if he refuſed to be convinced by a mathematical demonſtration. Nay, he is more irrationonal; becauſe there is no truth demonſtrated in mathematics which ſo many powers of our nature conſpire to ratify, and with which all rational minds are ſo deeply impreſſed. The contemplation of the Divine Nature is the moſt uſeful and the moſt ennobling exerciſe in which our faculties can be engaged; and recommends itſelf to every man of ſound judgement and good taſte, as the moſt durable and moſt perfect enjoyment that can fall to the ſhare of any created being. Sceptics may wrangle, and mockers may blaſpheme; but the pious man knows by evidence too ſublime for their comprehenſion *, that his affections are not miſplaced, and that his hopes ſhall not be diſappointed; by evidence which, to the humble and tender hearted, is altogether overwhelming, irreſiſtible, and divine.

That

* My meaning is only this, that the faith of pious men will be ſtrengthened by ſuch ſupernatural aid as unbelievers or blaſphemers can have no reaſon to expect; a doctrine which, if I miſtake not, is warranted by the ſcripture; John vii. 17.

That many of the objects in nature have had
a beginning; is obvious to our own fenfes and
memory, or confirmed by unqueftionable teftimony: thefe, therefore, according to the axiom
we are here confidering, muft, be believed to
have proceeded from a caufe adequate at leaft
to the effects produced. That the whole fenfible univerfe hath to us the appearance of an
effect, of fomething which once was not, and
which exifts not by any neceffity of nature, but
by the appointment of fome powerful and intelligent caufe different from and independent
on it;—that the univerfe I fay, has this appearance, cannot be denied: and that it is
what it appears to be, an effect; that it had a
beginning, and was not from eternity, is proved
by every fort of evidence the fubject will admit.
And if fo, we offer violence to our underftanding, when we attempt to believe that the whole
univerfe does not proceed from fome caufe;
and we argue unphilofophically, when we endeavour to difprove this natural and univerfal
fuggeftion of the human mind.

It is true, the univerfe is, as one may fay, a
work *fui generis*, altogether fingular, and fuch
as we cannot properly compare to other works;
becaufe indeed all works are comprehended in
it. But that natural dictate of the mind by
which we believe the univerfe to have proceeded from a caufe, arifes from our confidering it
as an effect; a circumftance in which it is perfectly fimilar to all works whatfoever. The fin-
gularity of the effect rather confirms (if that
be poffible) than weakens our belief of the neceffity of a caufe; at leaft it makes us more
attentive

attentive to the cauſe, and intereſts us more
deeply in it.   What is the univerſe, but a vaſt
ſyſtem of works or effects, ſome of them great,
and others ſmall; ſome more, and ſome leſs
conſiderable? If each of theſe works, the leaſt
as well as the greateſt, require a cauſe for its production; is it not in the higheſt degree abſurd
to ſay, that the whole is not the effect of a cauſe?
---Each link of a great chain muſt be ſupported by ſomething, but the whole chain may be
ſupported by nothing:---Nothing leſs than an
ounce can be a counterpoiſe to an ounce, nothing leſs than a pound to a pound; but the
wing of a gnat, or nothing at all, may be a
ſufficient counterpoiſe to ten hundred thouſand
pounds:——Are not theſe aſſertions too abſurd
to deſerve an anſwer?

The reader, if he be acquainted with Mr.
HUME's *Eſſay on a particular providence and a
future ſtate*, will ſee, that theſe remarks are intended as an anſwer to a very ſtrange argument
there advanced againſt the belief of a Deity.
" The univerſe," we are told, " is an object
" quite ſingular and unparalleled; no other ob-
" ject that has fallen under our obſervation
" bears any ſimilarity to it; neither it nor its
" cauſe can be comprehended under any known
" ſpecies; and therefore concerning the cauſe of
" the univerſe we can form no rational conclu-
" ſion at all."—I appeal to any man of ſound
judgement, whether that ſuggeſtion of his underſtanding, which prompts him to infer a cauſe
from an effect, has any dependence upon a prior
operation of his mind, by which the effect in
queſtion is referred to its genus or ſpecies.
                                                    When

When he pronounces concerning any object which he conceives to have had a beginning, that it muſt have proceeded from ſome cauſe, does this judgement neceſſarily imply any compariſon of that object with others of a like kind? If the new object were in every reſpect unlike to other objects, would this have any influence on his judgement? Would he not acknowledge a cauſe to be as neceſſary for the production of the moſt uncommon, as of the moſt familiar object?---If therefore I believe, that I myſelf owe my exiſtence to ſome cauſe, becauſe there is ſomething in my mind which neceſſarily determines me to this belief, I muſt alſo, for the very ſame reaſon, believe, that the whole univerſe (ſuppoſed to have had a beginning) proceeds from ſome cauſe. The evidence of both is the ſame. If I believe the firſt and not the ſecond, I believe and diſbelieve the ſame evidence at the ſame time; I believe that the very ſame ſuggeſtion of my underſtanding is both true and falſe.

Though I were to grant, that, when an object is reducible to no known genus, no rational inference can be made concerning its cauſe; yet it will not follow, that our inferences concerning the cauſe of the univerſe are irrational, ſuppoſing it reaſonable to believe that the univerſe had a beginning. If there be in the univerſe any thing which is reducible to no known genus, let it be mentioned: if there be any preſumption for the exiſtence of ſuch a thing, let the foundation of that preſumption be explained. And, if you pleaſe, I ſhall, for argument's ſake, admit, that concerning the cauſe of that

particular

particular thing, no rational conclusion can be formed. But it has never been asserted, that the existence of such a thing is either real or probable. Mr. HUME only asserts, that the universe itself, not any particular thing in the universe, is reducible to no known genus. Well, then, let me ask, What is the universe? A word? No; it is a vast collection of things.—Are all these things reducible to genera? Mr. HUME does not deny it.---Each of these things, then, if it had a beginning, must also have had a cause? It must.—What thing in the universe exists uncaused? Nothing.—Is this a rational conclusion? So it seems.—It seems, then, that though it be rational to assign a cause to every thing in the universe, yet to assign a cause to the universe is not rational! It is shameful thus to trifle with words.—In fact, this argument, so highly admired by its author, is no argument at all. It is founded on a distinction that is perfectly inconceivable. Twenty shillings make a pound: though you lay twenty shillings on the table, you have not laid down a pound, you have only laid down twenty shillings. If the reader cannot enter into this distinction, he will never be able to conceive in what the force of Mr. HUME's argument consists.

If the universe had a beginning, it must have had a cause. This is a self-evident axiom, or at least an undeniable consequence of one. We necessarily assent to it; such is the law of our nature. If we deny it, we cannot, without absurdity, believe any thing else; because we at the same time deny the authenticity of those instinctive suggestions which are the foundati-

ons

ons of all truth. The Atheift will never 'be
able to elude the force of this argument, till he
can prove, that every thing in nature exifts neceffarily, independently, and from eternity.

If Mr. HUME's argument be found to turn
to fo little account, from the fimple confideration of the univerfe, as exifting, and as having
had a beginning, it will appear (if poffible)
ftill more irrational, when we take a view of the
univerfe, and its parts, as of works curioufly
adapted to certain ends. Their exiftence difplays the neceffity of a powerful caufe; their
frame proves the caufe to be intelligent, good,
and wife. The meaneft of the works of nature,
(if any of Nature's works may be called mean),
—the arrangement neceffary for the production
of the fmalleft plant, requires in the caufe a
degree of power and wifdom, which infinitely
tranfcends the fublimeft exertions of human ability. What then fhall we fay of the caufe that
produces an animal, a rational foul, a world, a
fyftem of worlds, an univerfe? Shall we fay,
that infinite power and wifdom are not neceffary attributes of that univerfal caufe, though
they be neceffary attributes of the caufe, that
produces a plant? Shall we fay, that the maker
of a plant may be acknowledged to be powerful,
intelligent, and wife; becaufe there are many
other things in nature that refemble a plant;
but that we cannot rationally acknowledge the
maker of the univerfe to be wife, powerful, or
intelligent, becaufe there is nothing which the
univerfe refembles, or to which it may be compared?

pared? Can the man who argues in this manner have any meaning to his words?

The other cavils thrown out againft the divine attributes, in this flimfy effay, I may perhaps have occafion to animadvert on hereafter. Meantime to thofe readers who may be in danger from them, I would recommend a careful perufal of Butler's Analogy of Natural and Revealed Religion.

S E C T.   VI.

Of Probable or Experimental Reafoning.

IN all our reafonings from the caufe to the effect, we proceed on a fuppofition, and a belief, that the courfe of nature will continue to be in time to come what we experience it to be at prefent, and remember it to have been in time paft. This prefumption of continuance is the foundation of all our judgements concerning future events; and this, in many cafes, determines our conviction as effectually as any proof or demonftration whatfoever; although the conviction arifing from it be different in kind from what is produced by ftrict demonftration, as well as from thofe kinds of conviction that attend the evidence of fenfe, memory, and abftract intuition. The higheft degree of conviction in reafoning from caufes to effects, is called *moral certainty*; and the inferior degrees refult from that fpecies of evidence which is called *probability* or *verifimilitude*. That all men
will

will die ; that the fun will rife to-morrow, and
the fea ebb and flow ; that fleep will continue
to refrefh, and food to nourifh us ; that the
fame articulate founds which to-day communicate the ideas of virtue and vice, meat and
drink, man and beaft, will to-morrow commu-
nicate the fame ideas to the fame perfons,—no
man can doubt, without being accounted a fool.
In thefe, and in all other inftances where our
experience of the paft has been equally extenfive and uniform, our judgement concerning
the future amounts to moral certainty : we believe, with full affurance, or at leaft without
doubt, that the fame laws of nature which have
hitherto operated, will continue to operate, as
long as we forefee no caufe to interrupt or
hinder their operation.

But no perfon who attends to his own mind
will fay, that, in thefe cafes, our belief, or conviction, is the effect of a proof, or any thing
like it. If reafoning be at all employed, it is
only in order to give us a clear view of our
paft experience with regard to the point in
queftion. When this view is obtained, reafoning is no longer neceffary ; the mind, by its
own innate force, and in confequence of an irrefiftible and inftinctive impulfe, infers the future from the paft, immediately, and without
the intervention of any argument. The fea
has ebbed and flowed twice every day in time
paft ; therefore the fea will continue to ebb and
flow twice every day in the time to come, — is
by

by no means a logical deduction of a conclusion from premises *.

When our experience of the past has not been uniform nor extensive, our opinion with regard to the future falls short of moral certainty; and amounts only to a greater or less degree of persuasion, according to the greater or smaller proportion of favourable instances:— we say, such an event will probably happen, such another is wholly improbable. If a medicine has proved salutary in one instance, and hurtful in five, a physician would not chuse to recommend it, except in a desperate case; and would then consider its success as a thing rather to be wished than expected. An equal number of favourable and unfavourable instances leave the mind in a state of suspense, without exciting the smallest degree of assurance on either side, except, perhaps, what may arise from our being more interested on the one side than on the other. A physician influenced by such evidence would say, " My patient may recover, and he " may die: I am sorry to say, that the former " event is not one whit more probable than the " latter." When the favourable instances exceed the unfavourable in number, we begin to think the future event in some degree probable; and more or less so, according to the surplus of favourable instances. A few favourable instances, without any mixture of unfavourable ones, render an event probable in a pretty high degree; but the favourable experience must be

VoL. I.   H   both

* This remark was first made by Mr. Hume. See it illustrated at great length in his Essays, part 2. sect. 4. See also Dr. Campbell's Dissertation on Miracles, p. 13. 14. edit. 2.

both extenfive and uniform, before it can produce moral certainty.

A man brought into being at maturity, and
placed in a defert ifland, would abandon himfelf
to defpair, when he firft faw the fun fet, and
the night come on; for he could have no expectation that ever the day would be renewed.
But he is tranfported with joy, when he again
beholds the glorious orb appearing in the eaft,
and the heavens and the carth illuminated as
before. He again views the declining fun with
apprehenfion, yet not without hope; the fecond
night is lefs difmal than the firft, but is ftill
uncomfortable, on account of the weaknefs of
the probability produced by one favourable inftance. As the inftances grow more numerous,
the probability becomes ftronger and ftronger:
yet it may be queftioned, whether a man in thefe
circumftances would ever arrive at fo high a
degree of moral certainty in this matter as we
experience; who know, not only that the fun
has rifen every day fince we began to exift, but
alfo that the fame phenomenon has happened
regularly for more than five thoufand years,
without failing in a fingle inftance. The
judgement of our great epic poet appears no
where to more advantage than in his eighth book;
where Adam relates to the angel what paffed in
his mind immediately after his awaking into life.
The following paffage is at once tranfcendently
beautiful, and philofophically juft.

" While thus I call'd, and ftray'd I knew not whither,
" From where I firft drew air, and firft beheld
" This happy light, when anfwer none return'd,
" On a green fhady bank, profufe of flowers,
"Penfive I fat me down ; there gentle fleep

" Firft

" *Firſt* found me, and with ſoft oppreſſion ſeiz'd
" My drouſed ſenſe ; *untroubled, though I thought*
" *I then was paſſing to my former ſtate*
" *Inſenſible, and forthwith to diſſolve* *."

Paradiſe Loſt, b. 8. l. 283.

Adam at this time had no experience of ſleep, and therefore could not, with any probability, expeĉt that he was to recover from it. Its approaches were attended with feelings ſimilar to thoſe he had experienced when awaking from non-exiſtence, and would naturally ſuggeſt that idea to his mind; and as he had no reaſon to expeĉt that his life was to continue, would intimate the probability that he was again upon the verge of an inſenſible ſtate †.

Now it is evident, from what has been already ſaid, that the degree of probability muſt be intuitively perceived, or the degree of aſſurance ſpontaneouſly and inſtinĉtively excited in the mind, upon the bare conſideration of the inſtances on either ſide; and that without any medium of argument to conneĉt the future event with the paſt experience. Reaſoning may be employed in bringing the inſtances into view; but when that is done, it is no longer neceſſary. And if you were to argue with a man, in order to convince him that a certain future event is not ſo improbable as he ſeems to think, you

H 2   would

---

* The beauty of theſe lines did not eſcape the elegant and judicious Addiſon ; but that author does not aſſign the reaſon of his approbation. Speĉt. No. 345.

† " Several things (ſays Butler) greatly affeĉt all our li-
" ving powers, and at length ſuſpend the exerciſe of them; as,
" for inſtance, drouſineſs, increaſing till it ends in ſound ſleep:
" and from hence we might have imagined it would deſtroy them
" till we found by experience the weakneſs of this way of judging."

Butler's Analogy, part 1. *ch.* 1.

would only make him take notice of fome favourable inftance which he had overlooked, or
endeavour to render him fufpicious of the reality
of fome of the unfavourable inftances; leaving
it to himfelf to eftimate the degree of probability. If he continue refractory, notwithftanding that his view of the fubject is the fame with
yours, he can be reafoned with in no other
way, than by your appealing to the common
fenfe of mankind.

To the fupreme intelligence all knowledge is
intuitive and certain. But it is not unreafonable to fuppofe, that probabilities of one fort
or other may fometimes employ the underftanding of all created beings. To man, probability (as an excellent author † obferves) is
the very guide of life.

S E C T.   VII.

Of Analogical Reafoning.

REafoning from analogy, when traced up to
its fource, will be found in like manner to terminate in a certain inftinctive propenfity, implanted in us by our Maker, which leads us to
expect, that fimilar caufes, in fimilar circumftances, do probably produce, or will probably
produce, fimilar effects. The probability which
this kind of evidence is fitted to illuftrate, does,
like the former, admit of a vaft variety of degrees,

---

† Butler's Analogy. Introduction.

grees, from abfolute doubting up to moral certainty. When the ancient philofopher, who
was fhipwrecked in a ftrange country, difcovered certain geometrical figures drawn upon the
fand by the fea-fhore, he was naturally led to
believe, with a degree of affurance not inferior
to moral certainty, that the country was inhabited by men, fome of whom were men of ftudy and fcience, like himfelf. Had thefe figures
been lefs regular, and liker chance-work, the
prefumption from analogy, of the country
being inhabited, would have been weaker; and
had they been of fuch a nature as left it altogether dubious, whether they were the work of
accident or of defign, the evidence would have
been too ambiguous to ferve as a foundation
for any opinion.

In reafoning from analogy, we argue *from*
a fact or thing experienced *to* fomething fimilar not experienced; and from our view of the
former arifes an opinion with regard to the latter; which opinion will be found to imply a
greater or lefs degree of affurance, according as
the inftance *from* which we argue is more or lefs
fimilar to the inftance *to* which we argue. Why
the degree of our affurance is determined by
the degree of likenefs, we cannot tell; but we
know by experience, that this is the cafe: and
by experience alfo we know, that our affurance,
fuch as it is, arifes immediately in the mind,
whenever we fix our attention on the circumftances in which the probable event is expected,
fo as to trace their refemblance to thofe circumftances in which we have known a fimilar event
to take place. A child who has been burnt

H 3   with

with a red-hot coal, is careful to avoid touching the flame of a candle; for as the vifible qualities of the latter are like to thofe of the former, he expeéts, with a very high degree of affurance, that the effeéts produced by the candle operating on his fingers, will be fimilar to thofe produced by the burning coal. And it deferves to be remarked, that the judgement a child forms on thefe occafions may arife, and often doth arife, previous to education and reafoning, and while experience is very limited. Knowing that a lighted candle is a dangerous objeét, he will be fhy of touching a glow-worm, or a piece of wet fifh fhining in the dark, becaufe of their refemblance to the flame of a candle: but as this refemblance is but imperfeét, his judgement, with regard to the confequences of touching thefe objeéts, will probably be more inclined to doubt, than in the former cafe, where the inftances were more fimilar.

Thofe who are acquainted with aftronomy, think it probable, that the planets are inhabited by living creatures, on account of their being in all other refpeéts fo like our earth. A man who thinks them not much bigger than they appear to the eye, never dreams of fuch a notion; for to him they feem in every refpeét unlike our earth: and there is no other way of bringing him over to the aftronomer's opinion, than by explaining to him thofe particulars in which the planets and our earth refemble one another. As foon as he comprehends thefe particulars, and this refemblance, his mind of its own accord admits the probability of the new opinion, without being led to it by any medium of proof.

proof, connecting the facts he hath experienced with other similar and probable facts lying beyond the reach of his experience. Such a proof indeed could not be given. If he were not convinced of the probability by the bare view of the facts, you would impute his perseverance in his old opinion, either to obstinacy, or to want of common sense ; two mental diforders for which logic provides no remedy.

<h2 style="text-align:center">S E C T. VIII.</h2>

Of Faith in Testimony.

THere are in the world many men, whose declaration concerning any fact which they have seen, and of which they are competent judges, would engage my belief as effectually as the evidence of my own senses. A metaphysician may tell me, that this implicit confidence in testimony is unworthy of a philofopher, and that my faith ought to be more rational. It may be so ; but I believe as before notwithstanding. And I find that all men have the same confidence in the testimony of certain persons ; and that if a man should refuse to think as other men do in this matter, he would be called obstinate, whimsical, narrow-minded, and a fool. If, after the experience of so many ages, men are still disposed to believe the word of an honest man, and find no inconvenience in doing so, I must conclude, that it is not only natural, but rational, expedient, and

manly,

manly, to credit fuch teftimony: and though I were to perufe volumes of metaphyfic written in proof of the fallibility of teftimony, I fhould ftill, like the reft of the world, believe credible teftimony without fear of inconvenience. I know very well, that teftimony is not admitted in proof of any doctrine in mathematics, becaufe the evidence of that fcience is of a different kind. But is truth to be found in mathematics only? is the geometrician the only perfon who exerts a rational belief? do we never find conviction arife in our minds, except when we contemplate an intuitive axiom, or run over a mathematical demonftration? In natural philofophy, a fcience not inferior to pure mathematics in the certainty of its conclufions, teftimony is admitted as a fufficient proof of many facts.   To believe teftimony, therefore, is agreeable to nature, to reafon, and to found philofophy.

When we believe the declaration of an honeft man, in regard to facts of which he has had experience, we fuppofe, that by the view or perception of thofe facts, his fenfes have been affected in the fame manner as ours would have been, if we had been in his place. So that faith in teftimony is in part refolvable into that conviction which is produced by the evidence of fenfe: at leaft if we did not believe our fenfes, we could not without abfurdity, believe teftimony; if we have any tendency to doubt the evidence of fenfe, we muft, in regard to teftimony, be equally fceptical. Thofe philofophers, therefore, who would perfuade us to reject the evidence of fenfe, among whom are to
be

be reckoned all who deny the exiſtence of matter, are not to be conſidered as mere theoriſts,
whoſe ſpeculations are of too abſtract a nature
to do any harm, but as men of very dangerous
principles. Not to mention the bad effects of
ſuch doctrine upon ſcience in general*, I
would only at preſent call upon the reader to
attend to its influence upon our religious opinions and hiſtorical knowledge. Teſtimony is
the grand external evidence of Chriſtianity.
All the miracles wrought by our Saviour, and
particularly that great deciſive miracle, his reſurrection from the dead, were ſo many appeals to
the ſenſes of men, in proof of his divine miſ-
ſion: and whatever ſome unthinking cavillers
may object, this we affirm to be not only the
moſt proper, but the only proper, kind of external evidence, that can be employed, conſiſt-
ently with man's free agency and moral probation, for eſtabliſhing a popular and univerſal religion among mankind. Now, if matter
has no exiſtence but in our mind, our ſenſes
are deceitful: and if ſo, St. Thomas muſt have
been deceived when he felt, and the reſt of the
apoſtles when they ſaw, the body of their Lord
after his reſurrection; and all the facts recorded in hiſtory, both ſacred and civil, were no better than dreams or deluſions, with which perhaps St. Mathew, St. John, and St. Luke, Thu-
cydides, Xenophon, and Cæſar, were affected,
but which they had no more ground of believing to be real, than I have of believing, in conſequence of my having dreamed it, that I was
                                          laſt

* See below, part 2. chap 2. ſect. 2.

laſt night in Conſtantinople. Nay, if I admit the non-exiſtence of matter, I muſt believe, that what my ſenſes declare to be true, is not only not truth, but contrary to it. For does not this philoſophy teach, that what ſeems to human ſenſe to exiſt does not exiſt; and that what ſeems corporeal is incorporeal? and are not exiſtence and non-exiſtence, materiality and immateriality, contraries? Now, if men ought to believe the contrary of what their ſenſes declare to be true, the evidence of all hiſtory, of all teſtimony, and indeed of all external perception, is no longer any evidence of the reality of the facts warranted by it; but becomes, rather a proof that thoſe facts did never happen. If it be urged, as an objection to this reaſoning, that BERKELEY was a Chriſtian, notwithſtanding his ſcepticiſm (or paradoxical belief) in other matters; I anſwer, that though he maintained the doctrine of the non-exiſtence of body, there is no evidence that he underſtood it: nay, there is poſitive evidence that he did not; as I ſhall have occaſion to ſhew afterwards *

Again, when we believe a man's word, becauſe we know him to be honeſt, or, in other words, have had experience of his veracity, all reaſoning on ſuch teſtimony is ſupported by the evidence of experience, and by our preſumption of the continuance of the laws of nature :—the firſt evidence reſolves itſelf into inſtinctive conviction, and the ſecond is itſelf an inſtinctive preſumption. The principles of common ſenſe, therefore, are the foundation of all true reaſoning concerning teſtimony of this kind.

It

* See part 2. chap. 2. ſect. 2. of this Eſſay.

It is faid by Mr. HUME, in his Effay on Miracles, that our belief of any fact from the report of eye-witneffes is derived from no other
principle than experience; that is, from our
obfervation of the veracity of human teftimony,
and of the ufual conformity of facts to the report of witneffes. This doctrine is confuted
with great elegance and precifion, and with
invincible force of argument, in Dr. Campbell's
Differtation on Miracles.   It is, indeed, like moft
of Mr. HUME's capital doctrines, repugnant to
matter of fact: for our credulity is greateft
when our experience is leaft; that is, when we
are children; and generally grows lefs and lefs,
in proportion as our experience becomes more
and more extenfive: the very contrary of which
muft happen, if Mr. HUME's doctrine were
true.

There is then in man a propenfity to believe
teftimony antecedent to that experience, which
Mr. HUME fuppofes, of the conformity of
facts to the report of witneffes.   But there is
another fort of experience, which may perhaps
have fome influence in determining children to
believe in teftimony.   Man is naturally difpofed
to fpeak as he thinks; and moft men do fo: for
the greateft liars fpeak truth much oftener than
they utter falfehood.   It is unnatural for human
creatures to falfify; and they never think of de-
parting from the truth, except they have fome
end to anfwer by it.   Accordingly children,
while their native fimplicity remains uncorrupt-
ed, while they have no vice to difguife, no punifhment to fear, and no artificial fcheme to promote, do always fpeak as they think: and fo
generally

generally is their veracity acknowledged, that it has paffed into a proverb, That children and fools tell truth. Now I am not certain, but this their innate propenfity to fpeak truth, may in part account for their readinefs to believe what others fpeak. They do not fufpect the veracity of others, becaufe they are confcious and confident of their own. However, there is nothing abfurd or unphilofophical in fuppofing, that they believe teftimony by one law of their nature, and fpeak truth by another. I feek not therefore to refolve the former principle into the latter; I mention them for the fake only of obferving, that whether they be allowed to be different principles, or different effects of the fame principle, our general doctrine remains equally clear, namely, That all reafoning concerning the evidence of teftimony does finally terminate in the principles of common fenfe. This is true, as far as our faith in teftimony is refolvable into experimental conviction; becaufe we have already fhown, that all reafoning from experience is refolvable into intuitive principles, either of certain or of probable evidence; and furely it is no lefs true, as far as our faith in teftimony is itfelf inftinctive, and fuch as cannot be refolved into any higher principle.

Our faith in teftimony does often, but not always, amount to abfolute certainty. That there is fuch a city as Conftantinople, fuch a country as Lapland, and fuch a mountain as the peak of Teneriffe; that there were fuch men as Hannibal and Julius Cæfar; that England was conquered by William the Norman; that Charles
                                        I. was

I. was beheaded;—of thefe, and fuch like truths, every perfon acquainted with hiftory and geography accounts himfelf abfolutely certain. When a number of perfons, not acting in concert, having no intereft to difguife the truth, and fufficient judges of that to which they bear teftimony, concur in making the fame report, it would be accounted madnefs not to believe them. Nay, when a number of witnef-fes, feparately examined, and having had no opportunity to concert a plan before hand, do all agree in their declarations, we make no fcruple of yielding full faith to their teftimony, even though we have no evidence of their honefty or fkill; nay though they be notorious both for knavery and folly: becaufe the fictions of the human mind being infinite, it is impof-fible that each of thefe witneffes fhould, by mere accident, devife the very fame circum-ftances; if therefore their declarations concur, this is a proof, that there is no fiction in the cafe, and that they all fpeak from real experience and knowledge. The inference we form on thefe occafions is fupported by arguments drawn from our experience; and all arguments of this fort are refolvable into the principles of common fenfe. In general, it will be found true of all our reafoning concerning teftimony, that they are founded, either mediately or immediately, upon inftinctive conviction or inftinctive affent; fo that he who has refolved to believe nothing but what he can give a reafon for, can never, confiftently with this refolution, believe any thing, either as certain or as probable, upon the teftimony of other men.

S E C T.

S E C T. IX.

Conclusion of this Chapter.

THE conclusion to which we are led by the above induction, would perhaps be admitted by some to be self-evident, or at least to stand in no great need of illustration; to others it might have been proved *a priori* in very few words; but to the greater part of readers, a detail of particulars may be necessary, in order to produce that *steady and well-grounded conviction* which it is my ambition to establish.

The argument *a priori* might be comprehended in the following words. If there be any creatures in human shape, who deny the distinction between truth and falsehood, or who are unconscious of that distinction, they are far beyond the reach, and below the notice, of philosophy, and therefore have no concern in this inquiry. Whoever is sensible of that distinction, and is willing to acknowledge it, must confess, that truth is something fixed and determinate, depending not upon man, but upon the Author of nature. The fundamental principles of truth must therefore rest upon their own evidence, perceived intuitively by the understanding. If they did not, if reasoning were necessary to enforce them, they must be exposed to perpetual vicissitude, and appear under a different form in every individual, according to the peculiar turn and character of his reasoning

ing powers. Were this the cafe, no man could know, of any propofition, whether it were true or falfe, till after he had heard all the arguments that had been urged for and againft it; and, even then, he could not know with certainty, whether he had heard all that could be urged: future difputants might overturn the former arguments, and produce new ones, to continue unanfwered for a while, and then fubmit, in their turn, to their fucceffors. Were this the cafe, there could be no fuch thing as an appeal to the common fenfe of mankind, even as in a ftate of nature there can be no appeal to the law; every man would be " a law " unto himfelf," not in morals only, but in fcience of every kind.

We fometimes repine at the narrow limits prefcribed to human capacity. *Hitherto fhalt thou come, and no further*, feems a hard prohibition, when applied to the operations of mind. But as in the material world, it is to this prohibition man owes his fecurity and exiftence; fo, in the immaterial fyftem, it is to this we owe our dignity, our virtue, and our happinefs. A beacon blazing from a well-known promontory is a welcome object to the bewildered mariner; who is fo far from repining that he has not the beneficial light in his own keeping, that he is fenfible its utility depends on its being placed on the firm land, and committed to the care of others.

We have now proved, that " except we " believe many things without proof, we never " can believe any thing at all; for that all " found reafoning muft ultimately reft on the " principles

" principles of common fenfe, that is, on prin-
" ciples intuitively certain, or intuitively pro-
" bable ; and, confequently, that com-
" mon fenfe, is the ultimate judge
" of truth, to which reafon muft con-
" tinually act in fubordination *." To common fenfe, therefore, all truth muft be conformable ; this is its fixed and invariable ftandard.
And whatever contradicts common fenfe, or is
inconfiftent with that ftandard, though fupported by arguments that are deemed unanfwerable, and by names that are celebrated by
all the critics, academies, and potentates on
earth, is not truth but falfehood. In a word,
the dictates of common fenfe are, in refpect to
human knowledge in general, what the axioms of geometry are in refpect to mathematics :
on the fuppofition that thofe axioms are falfe
or dubious, all mathematical reafoning falls to
the ground ; and on the fuppofition that the
dictates of common fenfe are erroneous or deceitful, all fcience, truth, and virtue, are
vain.

I know not but it may be urged as an objection to this doctrine, that, if we grant common fenfe to be the ultimate judge in all difputes, a greater part of ancient and modern
philofophy becomes ufelefs. I admit the objection with all my heart, in its full force, and
with all its confequences ; and yet I muft repeat, that if common fenfe be fuppofed fallacious, all knowledge is at an end; and that
even a demonftration of the fallacy would itfelf be fallacious and frivolous. For if the dic-

tates

---

* See part 1. chap. 1. fub. fin.

tates of my nature deceive me in one cafe, how fhall I know that they do not deceive me in another? When a philofopher demonftrates to me, that matter exifts not but in my mind, and, independent on me and my faculties, has no exiftence at all; before I admit his demonftration, I muft difbelieve all my fenfes, and diftruft every principle of belief within me: before I admit his demonftration, I muft be convinced, that I and all mankind are fools; that our Maker made us fuch, and from the beginning intended to impofe on us; and that it was not till about the fix thoufandth year of the world when this impofture was difcovered; and then difcovered, not by a divine revelation, not by any rational inveftigation of the laws of nature, not by any inference from previous truths of acknowledged authority, but by a pretty play of Englifh and French words, to which the learned have given the name of metaphyfical reafoning. Before I admit this pretended demonftration, I muft bring myfelf to believe what I find to be incredible; which feems to me not a whit lefs difficult than to perform what is impoffible. And when all this is done, if it were poffible that all this could be done, pray what is fcience, or truth, or falfehood? Shall I believe nothing? or fhall I believe every thing? Or am I capable either of belief, or of difbelief? Or do I exift? or is there fuch a thing as exiftence?

The end of all fcience, and indeed of every ufeful purfuit, is to make men happier, by improving them in wifdom and virtue. I beg leave to afk, whether the prefent race of men

owe any part of their virtue, wifdom, or happinefs, to what metaphyficians have written in
proof of the non-exiftence of matter, and the neceffity of human actions? If it be anfwered,
That our happinefs, wifdom, and virtue, are
not at all affected by fuch controverfies, then I
muft affirm, that all fuch controverfies are ufelefs.   And if it be true, that they have a tendency to promote wrangling, which of all kinds
of converfation is the moft unpleafant, and the
moft unprofitable; or vain polemical difquifition, which cannot be carried on without wafte
of time, and proftitution of talents; or fcepticifm,
which tends to make a man uncomfortable in
himfelf, and unferviceable to others: then I
muft affirm, that all fuch controverfies are both
ufelefs and mifchievous : and that the world would
be more wife, more virtuous, and more happy,
without them.—But it is faid, that they improve
the underftanding, and render it more capable
of difcovering truth, and detecting error.   Be
it fo : --- but though bars and locks render our
houfes fecure; and though acutenefs of hearing and feeling be a valuable endowment; it
will not follow, that thieves are a public bleffing; or that the man is intitled to my gratitude, who quickens my touch and hearing, by
putting out my eyes.

It is further faid, that fuch controverfies make
us fenfible of the weaknefs of human reafon,
and the imperfection of human knowledge; and
for the fanguinary principles of bigotry and enthufiafm, fubftitute the milky ones of fcepticifm and
moderation.   And this is conceived to be of
prodigious emolument to mankind; becaufe a
firm

firm attachment to religion, which a man may
call bigotry if he pleafes, doth often give rife to
a perfecuting fpirit ; whereas a perfect indifference about it, which fome men are good-natured enough to call moderation, is a principle of
great good-breeding, and gives no fort of dif-
turbance, either in private or public life.   This
is a plea on which our modern fceptics plume
themfelves not a little.   And who will venture
to arraign the virtue or the fagacity of thefe
projectors ? To accomplifh fo great effects by
means fo fimple ; to prevent fuch dreadful calamities by fo innocent an artifice,---does it
not difplay the perfection of benevolence and
wifdom ? Truly I can hardly imagine fuch a-
nother fcheme, except the following. Suppofe a phyfician of the Sangrado fchool, out
of zeal for the intereft of the faculty, and the
public good, to prepare a bill to be laid before
the parliament in thefe words: " That whereas
" good health, efpecially when of long ftanding,
" has a tendency to prepare the human frame
" for inflammatory diftempers, which have been
" known to give extreme pain to the unhappy
" patient, and fometimes even bring him to the
" grave ; and whereas the faid health, by ma-
" king us brifk, and hearty, and happy, is apt
" alfo, on fome occafions, to make us difor-
" derly and licentious, to the great detriment
" of glafs-windows, lanthorns, and watchmen :
" Be it therefore enacted, That all the inhabi-
" tants of thefe realms, for the peace of go-
" vernment, and the repofe of the fubject, be
" compelled, on pain of death, to bring their
" bodies down to a confumptive habit ; and that
" henceforth no perfon prefume to walk abroad
" with

" with a cane, on pain of having his head broke
" with it, and being set in the stocks for six
" months; nor to walk at all, except with
" crutches, to be delivered at the public charge
" to each person who makes affidavit, that he
" is no longer able to walk without them,"
&c. --- He who can eradicate conviction from
the human heart, may doublefs prevent all the
fatal effects of enthufiafm and bigotry; and if
all human bodies were thrown into a confumpti-
on, I believe there would be an end of riot, as well
as of inflammatory difeafes.   Whether the in-
conveniencies, or the remedies, be the greater
grievance, might perhaps bear a queftion.   Bigotry, enthufiafm, and a perfecuting fpirit, are
very dangerous and deftructive; univerfal fcep-
ticifin, would, I am fure, be equally fo, if it
were to infect the generality of mankind.   But
what has religion and rational conviction to
do with either ? Nothing more than good health
has to do with acute diftempers, and rebellious
infurrections; or than the peace of government, and tranquility of the fubject, have to do
with a gradual decay of our mufcular flefh.
True religion tends to make men great, and
good, and happy; and if fo, its doctrines can
never be too firmly believed, nor held in too
high veneration.   And if truth be at all attainable in philofophy, I cannot fee why we fhould
fcruple to receive it as fuch, when we have attained it; nor how it can promote candour,
good-breeding, and humanity, to pretend to
doubt what we do and muft believe, to
                                          profefs

profefs to maintain doctrines of which we are
confcious that they fhock our underftanding,
to differ in judgement from all the world except a few metaphyficians, and to queftion the
evidence of thofe principles which all other
men think unqueftionable and facred. Conviction, and fteadinefs of principle, is. that
which gives dignity, uniformity, and fpirit, to
human conduct, and without which our happinefs can neither be lafting nor fincere. It con-
ftitutes, as it were, the vital ftamina of a great
and manly character : whereas fcepticifm betrays
a fickly underftanding, and a levity of mind,
from which nothing can be expected but incon-
fiftence and folly. In conjunction with ill-
nature, bad tafte, and a hard heart, fteadinefs
and ftrong conviction will doubtlefs make a bad
man, and fcepticifm will make a worfe : but
good-nature, elegant tafte, and fenfibility of
heart, when united with firmnefs of mind, become doubly refpectable; whereas no man can
act on the principles of fcepticifm, without
incurring univerfal contempt.——But to return :

Mathematicians, and natural philofophers,
do in effect admit the diftinction between common fenfe and reafon, as illuftrated above; for
they are content to reft their fciences either on
felf-evident axioms, or on experiments warranted by the evidence of external fenfe. The philofophers who treat of the mind, do alfo fometimes profefs to found their doctrines on the
evidence of fenfe : but this profeffion is merely
verbal; for whenever experience contradicts
the fyftem, they queftion the authenticity of

that

that experience, and fhow you, by a moft elaborate inveftigation, that it is all a cheat. For
it is ea~'y to write plaufibly on any fubject, and
in vinu.cation of any doctrine, when either the
indolence of the reader, or the nature of the
compofition, gives the writer an opportunity
to avail himfelf of the ambiguity of language.
It is not often that men attend to the operations of the mind; and when they do, it is perhaps with fome metaphyfical book in their
hands, which they read with a refolution to
admire or defpife, according as the fafhion or
their humour directs them. In this fituation,
or even when they are difpofed to judge impartially of the writer, their attention to what
paffes in their own mind is but fuperficial, and
is very apt to be fwayed by a fecret bias in favour of fome theory. And then, it is fometimes
difficult to diftinguifh between a natural feeling
and a prejudice of education; and our deference
to the opinion of a favourite author, makes us
think it more difficult than it really is, and often leads us to miftake the one for the other.
Nay, the very act of ftudying difcompofes our
minds a little, and prevents that free play of the
faculties from which alone we can judge with
accuracy of their real nature.—Befides, language,
being originally intended to anfwer the obvious
exigencies of life, and exprefs the qualities of
matter, becomes metaphorical when applied to
the operations of mind. Thus we talk meta-
phorically, when we fpeak of a warm imagination, a found judgement, a tenacious memory,
an enlarged underftanding; thefe epithets being
originally and *properly* expreffive of material qualities.

lities. This circumftance, however obvious, is
not always attended to; and hence we are apt
to miftake verbal analogies for real ones, and
to apply the laws of matter to the operations of
mind; and thus, by the mere delufion of words,
are led into error before we are aware, and
while our premifes feem to be altogether unexceptionable. It is a favourite maxim with
LOCKE, as it was with fome ancient philofophers, that the human foul, previous to education, is like a piece of white paper, or *tabula
rafa*; and this fimile, harmlefs as it may appear,
betrays our great modern into feveral important
miftakes. It is indeed one of the moft unlucky
allufions that could have been chofen. The
human foul, when it begins to think, is not
extended, nor of a white colour, nor incapable
of energy, nor wholly unfurnifhed with ideas,
(for, if it think at all, it muft have fome ideas,
according to LOCKE's definition of the word *),
nor as fufceptible of any one impreffion or character as of any other.—Even when the terms
we ufe are not metaphorical, the natural ab-
ftrufenefs of the fubject makes them appear
fomewhat myfterious; and we are apt to confider them as of more fignificancy than they really are. Had Mr. HUME told the world in
plain terms, that virtue is a fpecies of vice,
darknefs a fort of light, and exiftence, a kind
of non-exiftence, I know not what metaphyficians might have thought of the difcovery; but

I 4   fure

---

* The word *idea* ferves beft to ftand for whatfoever is the object
of the underftanding when a man thinks.—I have ufed it to exprefs
whatever it is which the mind can be employed about in thinking.
Introduction to Effay on Human Underftanding, fect. 8.

fure I am, no reader of tolerable underſtanding would have paid him any compliments upon it*. But when he ſays, that contrariety is a mixture of cauſation and reſemblance; and, ſtill more, when he brings a formal proof of this moſt ſage remark, he impoſes on us by the ſolemnity of the expreſſion; we conclude, that " more is " meant than meets the ear;" and begin to fancy, not that the author is abſurd or unintelligible, but that we have not ſagacity enough to diſcover his meaning. It were tedious to reckon up one half of the improprieties and errors which have been introduced into the philoſophy of human nature, by the indefinite application of the words, *idea, impreſſion, perception, ſenſation,* &c. Nay, it is well known, that BERKELEY's pretended proof of the nonexiſtence of matter, at which common ſenſe ſtood aghaſt for many years, has no better foundation.

***

* Mr. HUME had ſaid, that the only principles of connection among ideas are three, to wit, reſemblance, contiguity in time or place, and cauſe or effect; *Inquiry concerning Human Underſtanding,* ſect. 3. It afterwards occurred to him, that contrary ideas have a tendency to introduce one another into the mind. But inſtead of adding contrariety to the liſt of connecting principles, which he ought to have done, and which would have been philoſophical, he aſſumes the metaphyſician, and endeavours to prove his enumeration right, by reſolving contrariety, as a ſpecies, into reſemblance and cauſation, as genera. " Contraſt, or contrariety," ſays he, " is a connection among ideas, which may perhaps be conſidered " as a mixture of cauſation and reſemblance. Where two ob" jects are contrary, the one deſtroys the other, *i. e.* is the cauſe " of its annihilation; and the idea of the annihilation of an ob" ject implies the idea of its former exiſtence." Is it poſſible to make any ſenſe of this? Darkneſs and light are contrary; the one deſtroys the other, or is the cauſe of its annihilation; and the idea of the annihilation of darkneſs implies the idea of its former exiſtence. This is given as a proof, that darkneſs partly reſembles light, and partly is the cauſe of light. Indeed! But, O *ſi ſic omnia dixiſſet!* This is a harmleſs abſurdity.

foundation, than the ambiguous ufe of a word. He who confiders thefe things, will not be much difpofed to overvalue metaphyfical truth, (as it is called), when it happens to contradict any of the natural fentiments of mankind.

In the laws of nature, when thoroughly underftood, there appear no contradictions: it is only in the fyftems of philofophers that reafon and common fenfe are at variance. No man of common fenfe ever did or could believe, that the horfe he faw coming toward him at full gallop, was an idea in his mind, and nothing elfe; no thief was ever fuch a fool as to plead in his own defence, that his crime was neceffary and unavoidable, for that man is born to pick pockets as the fparks fly upward. When Reafon invades the rights of Common Senfe, and prefumes to arraign that authority by which fhe herfelf acts, nonfenfe and confufion muft of neceffity enfue; fcience will foon come to have neither head nor tail, beginning nor end; philofophy will grow contemptible; and its adherents, far from being treated, as in former times, upon the footing of conjurers, will be thought by the vulgar, and by every man of fenfe, to be little better than downright fools.

PART

PART II.

ILLUSTRATIONS OF THE PRECEDING DOCTRINE, WITH INFERENCES.

B U T now a difficulty occurs, which it is not eafy to folve. Granting what is faid above to be true; that all legitimate reafoning, whether of certain or of probable evidence, does not finally refolve itfelf into principles of common fenfe, which we muft admit as certain, or as probable, upon their own authority; that therefore common fenfe is the foundation and the ftandard of all juft reafoning; and that the genuine fentiments of nature are never erroneous:—yet, by what criterion fhall we know a fentiment of nature from a prejudice of education, a dictate of common fenfe from the fallacy of an inveterate opinion? Muft every principle be admitted as true, which we believe without being able to affign a reafon? then where is our fecurity againft prejudice and implicit faith! Or muft every principle that feems intuitively certain, or intuitively probable, be reafoned upon, that we may know whether it be really what it feems? then where our fecurity againft the abufe fo much infifted on, of fubjecting common fenfe to the teft of reafoning!—At what point muft reafon ftop in its inveftigations, and the dictates of common fenfe be admitted as decifive and final?

It

It is much to be regretted, that this matter has been fo little attended to: for a full and fatisfactory difcuffion of it would do more real fervice to the philofophy of human nature, than all the fyftems of logic in the world; would at once exalt pneumatology to the dignity of fcience, by fettling it on a firm and unchangeable foundation; and would go a great way to banifh fophiftry from fcience, and rid the world of fcepticifm. This is indeed the grand defideratum in logic; of no lefs importance to the moral fciences, than the difcovery of the longitude to navigation. That I fhall fully folve this difficulty, I am not fo vain, nor fo ignorant, as to imagine. But I humbly hope I fhall be able to throw fome light on the fubject, and contribute a little to facilitate the progrefs of thofe who may hereafter engage in the fame purfuit. If I can accomplifh even this, I fhall do a fervice to truth, philofophy and mankind: if I fhould be thought to fail, there is yet fomething meritorious in the attempt. To have fet the example, may be of confequence.

I fhall endeavour to conduct the reader to the conclufion I have come to on this fubject, by the fame fteps that led me thither; a method which I prefume will be more perfpicuous, and more fatisfying, than if I were firft to lay down a theory, and then affign the reafons. By the way, I cannot help expreffing a wifh, that this method of inveftigation were lefs uncommon, and that philofophers would fometimes explain to us, not only their difcoveries, but alfo the procefs of thought and experiment,

whether

whether accidental or intentional, by which they were led to them.

If the boundary of Reafon and Common Senfe had never been fettled in any fcience, I would abandon my prefent fcheme as defperate. But when I reflect, that in fome of the fciences it has been long fettled, with the utmoft accuracy, and to univerfal fatisfaction, I conceive better hopes; and flatter myfelf, that it may perhaps be poffible to fix it even in the philofophy of the mind. The fciences in which this boundary has been long fettled and acknowledged, are, mathematics, and natural philofophy; and it is remarkable, that more truth has been difcovered in thofe fciences than in any other. Now, there is not a more effectual way of learning the rules of any art, than by attending to the practice of thofe who have performed in it moft fuccefsfully: a maxim which, I fuppofe, is no lefs applicable to the art of inveftigating truth, than to the mechanical and the fine arts. Let us fee then, whether, by attending to the practice of mathematicians and natural philofophers, as contrafted with the practice of thofe who have treated of the human mind, we can make any difcoveries preparatory to the folution of this difficulty.

C H A P.

C H A P.   I.

Confirmation of this theory from the practice of Mathematicians and Natural Philosophers.

S E C T.   I.

THAT the diftinction between Reafon and Common Senfe, as here explained, is acknowledged by mathematicians, we have already fhown *. They have been wife enough to truft to the dictates of common fenfe, and to take that for truth which they were under a neceffity of believing, even though it was not in their power to prove it by argument. When a mathematician arrives, in the courfe of his reafoning, at a principle which he muft believe, and which is of itfelf fo evident, that no arguments could either illuftrate or enforce it, he then knows, that his reafon can carry him no further, and he fits down contented; and if he can fatisfy himfelf, that the whole inveftigation is fairly conducted, and does indeed terminate in this felf-evident principle, he is perfuaded, that his conclufion is true, and cannot be falfe. Whereas the fceptics, from a ftrange conceit, that the dictates of their underftanding are fallacious, and that Nature has her roguifh emiffaries in every corner, commiffioned and fworn to play

tricks

* See part 1. chap. 2. fect. 1.

tricks with poor mortals, cannot find in their heart to admit any thing as truth, upon the bare authority of their common fenfe. It is doubt-lefs a great advantage to geometry, that its firſt principles are ſo few, its ideas ſo diſtinct, and its language ſo definite. Yet a captious and pa-radoxical wrangler might, by dint of ſophiſtry, involve the principles even of this ſcience in confuſion, provided he thought it worth his while *. But geometrical paradoxes would not rouſe the attention of the public; whereas moral paradoxes, when men begin to look about for arguments in vindication of impiety and immorality, become intereſting, and can hardly fail of a powerful and numerous pa-tronage. The corrupt judge; the proſtituted courtier; the ſtateſman who enriches himſelf by the plunder and blood of his country; the pettifogger, who fattens on the ſpoils of the fa-therleſs and the widow; the oppreſſor, who to pamper his own beaſtly appetite, adbandons the deſerving peaſant to beggary and deſpair; the hypocrite, the debauchee, the gameſter, the blaſphemer,—prick up their ears when they are told, that a celebrated author has written a book containing ſuch doctrines, or leading to ſuch conſequences, as the following :— " That " moral and intellectual virtues are nearly of " the ſame kind † :"—in other words, That to want honeſty, and to want underſtanding,

are

---

* The author of the *Treatiſe of Human Nature* has actually af-tempted this in his firſt volume ; but finding, no doubt, that the public would not take any concern in that part of his ſyſtem, he has not republiſhed it in his ESSAYS.

† Treatiſe of Human Nature, vol. 3. part 3. ſect. 4.

are equally the objects of moral difapprobation : —" That every human action is ne-
" ceffary, and could not have been different
" from what it is ✝ :"—" That when we fpeak
" of power as an attribute of any being, God
" himfelf not excepted, we ufe words without
" meaning : — That we can form no idea of
" power, nor of any being endued with any
" power, *much lefs* of one endued with infinite
" power ; and that we can never have reafon to
" believe, that any object, or quality of an
" object, exifts, of which we cannot form an
" idea ‡ : — That it is unreafonable to believe
" God to be infinitely wife and good, while
" there is any evil or diforder in the univerfe ;
" and that we have no good reafon to think,
" that the univerfe proceeds from a caufe ‖ : —
" That the external world does not exift, or at
" leaft that its exiftence may reafonably be
" doubted ** ;" and " that if the external
" world be once called in doubt, we fhall be
" at a lofs to find arguments, by which we
" may prove the exiftence of the Supreme Be-
" ing, or any of his attributes * : — That thofe
" who believe any thing certainly are fools ‖‖‖ :"
" — That adultery muft be practifed, ifmen
" would obtain all the advantages of life ; that,
" if generally practifed, it would in time ceafe to
" be fcandalous ; and that, if practifed fecretly
" and

✝ Hume's Effays, vol. 2. p. 91. edit. 1767.
‡ Treatife of Human Nature, vol. 1. p. 284. 302. 432. &c.
‖ Hume's Effay on a Particular Providence, and Future Stat.
** Berkeley and Hume, *paffim.*
* Hume's Effay on the Sceptical Philofophy, part 1.
‖‖‖ Treatife of Human Nature, vol. 1. p. 468.

" and frequently, it would by degrees come to be
" thought no crime at all * : --- " That the quef-
" tion concerning the fubftance of the foul is
" unintelligible † : --- That matter and motion
" may often be regarded as the caufe of thought
" ‡ : --- and, That the foul of man becomes
" every different moment a different being ‖ :"
from which doctrine it muft follow as a confequence, that the actions I performed laft year,
or this morning, whether virtuous or vicious,
are no more imputable to me, than the virtues
of Ariftides are imputable to Nero, or the crimes
of Nero to the MAN OF ROSS.

I know no geometrical axiom, more perfpicuous, more evident, more generally acknowledged, than this propofition, (which every man
believes of himfelf), " My body exifts ;" yet
this has been denied, and volumes written to
prove it falfe.   Who will pretend to fet bounds
to this fpirit of fcepticifm and fophiftry ? Where
are the principles that can ftop its progrefs,
when it has already attacked the exiftence, both
of the human body, and of the human foul ?
When it denies, and attempts to difprove this,
I cannot fee why it may not as well deny a
whole to be greater than a part, the radii of the
fame circle to be equal to one another ; and
affirm, that two right lines do contain a fpace,
and that it is poffible for the fame thing to be
and not to be.

Had

* Hume's Effays, vol. 2. p. 409. edit. 1767.
† Treatife of Human Nature, vol. 1. p. 434.
‡ Id. ibid.
‖ Id. vol. 1. p. 48.

Had our fceptics been confulted when the firft geometrical inftitutions were compiled, they would have given a ftrange turn to the face of affairs.   They would have demanded reafons for the belief of every axiom : and as none could have been given, would have fufpected a fallacy; and probably (for the art of metaphyfical book-making is not of difficult attainment) have made books to prove *a priori*, that an axiom, from its very nature, cannot be true; or at leaft that we cannot with certainty pronounce whether it is fo or not.   " Take heed " to yourfelves, gentlemen; you are going to " lay the foundations of a fcience; be careful " to lay them as deep as poffible.   Let the love " of doubt and difputation animate you to in- " vincible perfeverance.   You muft go deeper ; " truth (if there be any fuch thing) loves pro- " fundity and darknefs. · Hitherto I fee you " quite diftinctly; and, let me tell you, that " is a ftrong prefumption againft your method " of operation.   I would not give two pence " for that philofophy which is obvious and in- " telligible *.   Tear up that prejudice, that I " may fee what fupports it.   I fee you cannot " move it, and therefore am difpofed to quef- " tion its ftability ; you cannot pierce it, there- " fore who knows but it may be made of un- " found materials ?   There is no trufting to " appearances.   It is the glo.y of a philofo- " pher to doubt; yea, he muft doubt, both " when he is doubtful, and when he is not
VOL. I.   K   " doubt-

---

* See Treatife of Human Nature, Vol 1. p. 3. 4.

" doubtful †. Sometimes, indeed, we philoso-
" phers are abfolutely and neceffarily determin-
" ed to live, and talk, and act, like other peo-
" ple, and to believe the exiftence both of our-
" felves and of other things : but to this abfo-
" lute and neceffary determination, we ought
" not to fubmit, but in every incident of life
" ftill to preferve our fcepticifm. Yes, friend,
" I tell you, we ought ftill to do what is con-
" trary to that to which we are abfolutely and
" neceffarily determined *. I fee you prepar-
" ing to fpeak ; but I tell you once for all, that
" if you reafon or believe any thing *certainly*
" you are a fool †.--- Good Sir, how deep muft
" we dig ? Is not this a fure foundation ?---
" I have no reafon to think fo, as I cannot fee
" what is under it. Then we muft dig down-
" ward *in infinitum !* --- And why not ? You
" think you are arrived at certainty. This ve-
                                    " ry

† " A true fceptic will be diffident of his philofophical doubts,
" as well as of his philofophical conviction."

                    Treatife of Human Nature, vol. 1. *p.* 474.
    * I dine, I play a game at back-gammon, I converfe, and am
" merry with my friends ; and when, after three or four hours
" amufement, I would return to thefe fpeculations, they appear
" fo cold, fo ftrained, and fo ridiculous, that I cannot find in my
" heart to enter into them any further. Here then I find myfelf
" abfolutely and neceffarily determined to live, and talk, and
" act, like other people in the common affairs of life." *Treatife
of Human Nature, vol.* 1. *p.* 467.
    " In all the incidents of life we ought ftill to preferve our fcep-
" ticifm. If we believe that fire warms, or water refrefhes, 'tis
" only becaufe it cofts us too much pains to think otherwife. Nay,
" if we are philofophers, it ought only to be upon fceptical prin-
" ciples." *Id. p.* 469.
    † " If I muft be a fool, as all thofe who reafon or believe any
" thing *certainly* are, my follies fhall at leaft be natural and agree-
" able." *Id. p.* 468.

" ry conceit of yours is a proof that you have
" not gone deep enough : for you muſt know,
" that the underſtanding, when it acts alone,
" and according to its moſt general principles,
" entirely ſubverts itſelf, and leaves not the low-
" eſt degree of evidence in any propoſition,
" either in philoſophy or common life ‡.   This
" to the illiterate vulgar may ſeem as great a
" contradiction or paradox, as if we were to
" talk of a man's jumping down his own throat :
" but we whoſe brains are heated with meta-
" phyſic, are not ſtartled at paradoxes or con-
" tradictions, becauſe we are ready to reject all
" belief and reaſoning, and can look upon no
" opinion even as more probable or more likely
" than another *.   You are no true philoſo-
" pher if you either begin or end your inqui-
" ries with the belief of any thing.---Well,
" Sir, you may doubt and diſpute as long as
" you pleaſe ; but I believe that I am come to
" a ſure foundation : here therefore will I begin
" to build, for I am certain there can be no
" danger in truſting to the ſtability of that
" which is immoveable.---Certain ! Poor cre-
" dulous fool ! Hark ye, Sir, you may be what
" the vulgar call an honeſt man, and a good
" workman ; but I am certain (I mean I am
" in doubt whether I may not be certain) that
                    K 2   " you

‡ Verbatim from Treatiſe of Human Nature, vol. 1. p. 464.
465.
        * " The intenſe view of theſe manifold contradictions and im-
" perfections in human reaſon, has ſo wrought upon me, and
" heated my brain, that I am ready to reject all belief and
" reaſoning, and can look upon no opinion even as more proba-
" ble or likely than another."   Treatiſ. of Human Nature, vol. 1.
p. 466.

" you are no philosopher. Philosopher indeed!
" to take a thing of such consequence for
" granted, without proof, without examinati-
" on! I hold you four to one, that I shall
" demonstrate *a priori*, that this same edifice of
" yours will be good for nothing.   I am inclin-
" ed to think, that we live in too early a period
" to discover ANY PRINCIPLES that will bear
" the examination of the latest posterity; the
" world, Sir, is not yet arrived at the years of
" discretion: it will be time enough, two or
" three thousand years hence, for men to be-
" gin to dogmatise, and affirm, that two and
" two are four, that a triangle is not a square,
" that the radii of the same circle are equal,
" that a whole is greater than one of its parts ;
" that ingratitude and murder are crimes;
" that benevolence, justice, and fortitude, are
" virtues ; that fire burns, that the sun shines,
" that human creatures exist, or that there is
" such a thing as existence. These are points,
" which our posterity, if they be wise, will
" probably reject *. These are points, which
                                                " if

* " Perhaps we are still in too early an age of the world, to
" discover *any principles* which will bear the examination of the
" latest posterity."
                    Treatise of Human Nature, vol. 1. p. 473.
  Some perhaps may blame me for laying any stress on detached
sentences, and for understanding these strong expressions in a strict
signification.   But it is not my intention to take any unfair advantages.   I should willingly impute these absurd sentences and expressions to the author's inadvertency : but then I must impute the
whole system to the same cause ; for they imply nothing that is not
again and again inculcated, either directly or indirectly, in Mr.
HUME's writings.   It is true some of them are self-contradictory,
and all of them strongly display the futility of this pretended sci-
                                                        ence.

" if they do not reject, they will be arrant fools.
" This is my judgement, and I am certain it is
" right.　I maintain, indeed, that mankind
" are certain of nothing : but I maintain, not-
" withstanding, that my own opinions are
" true.　And if any body is ill-natured enough
" to call this a contradiction, I protest against
" his judgement, and once for all declare, that
" I mean not either to contradict myself, or to
" acknowledge myself guilty of self-contradic-
" tion."

I am well aware, that mathematical certainty is not to be expected in any science but mathematics.　But I suppose that in every science,
some kind of certainty is attainable, or something at least sufficient to command belief : and
whether this rest on self-evident axioms, or on
the evidence of sense, memory, or testimony,
it is still certain to me, if I feel that I must
believe it.　And in every science, as well as in
geometry, I presume it would be consistent both
with logic and with good sense, *to take that for
an ultimate principle, which forces our belief by its
own intrinsic evidence, and which cannot by any reasoning be rendered more evident.*

K 3　　　　　　S E C T.

ence.　But who is to blame for this ?—Again, if this science be so
useless, and if its inutility be sometimes acknowledged even by
Mr. HUME himself, why, it may be said, so much zeal in confuting it ? For this plain reason, Because it is immoral and pernicious,
as well as unprofitable and absurd ; and because, with all its absurdity, it has been approved and admired ; and been the occasion
of evil to individuals, and of detriment as well as danger to society.

S E C T.   II.

IN natural philofophy, the evidence of fenfe and mathematical evidence go hand in hand; and the one produces conviction as effectually as the other. A natural philofopher would make a poor figure, fhould he take it in his head to difbelieve or diftruft the evidence of his fenfes. The time was, indeed, when matters were on a different footing; when phyfical truths were made out, not by experiment and obfervation, but by dint of fyllogifm, or in the more compendious way of *ipfe dixit*. But natural philofophy was then, what the philofophy of the mind in the hands of our fceptics is now, a fyftem of fophifms, contrived for the vindication of falfe theories.

That natural philofophers never queftion the evidence of fenfe, nor feek either to difprove or to correct it by reafoning, is a pofition, which to many may at firft fight feem difputable. I forefee feveral objections, but fhall content myfelf with examining two of the moft important. And thefe I fhall fet in fuch a light, as will, I hope, fhow them to be inconclufive, and at the fame time preclude all other objections.

1. Do we not, (it will be faid), both in our phyfical obfervations, and in the common affairs of life, reject the evidence of fight, in regard to the magnitude, extenfion, figure, and diftance of vifible objects, and truft to that of touch, which we know to be lefs fallacious?

I fee

I fee two buildings on the top of yonder mountain ; they feem to my eyes to be only three or
four feet afunder, of a round fhape, and not
larger than my two thumbs : but I have been
at the place, and having afcertained their diftance, fize, and figure, by touch or menfura-
tion, I know, that they are fquare towers, forty yards afunder, and fifty feet high.   Do I not
in this cafe rejeĉt the evidence of my fight as
fallacious, and truft to that of touch ? And
what is it but reafon that induces me to do fo ?
How then can it be faid, that from the evidence
of fenfe there is no appeal to reafon ? — It will,
however, be eafy to fhow, that in this inftance
we diftruft neither fight nor touch, but believe
implicitly in both ; not becaufe we can confirm their evidence by reafoning, but becaufe
the law of our nature will not permit us to
difbelieve their evidence.

Do you perceive thefe two objeĉts when you
fhut your eyes ? No. — It is, then, by your fight
only that you perceive them ? It is. — Does your
fight perceive any thing in thefe two objeĉts,
but a certain vifible magnitude, extenfion and
figure ? No. — Do you believe that thefe towers
really appear to your eyes round, three feet
afunder, and of the fize of your thumbs ?
Yes, I believe they have that appearance to
my eyes. — And do you not alfo believe, that,
to the eyes of all men who fee as you do, and
look at thefe objeĉts from the place in which
you now ftand, they have the very fame appearance ? I have no reafon to think otherwife.
— You believe, then, that the vifible magnitude,
diftance, and fhape, of thefe towers, is what
it

it appears to be? or do you think that your
eyes fee wrong? Be fure, the vifible magnitude,
figure, and diftance, are not different from what
I perceive them to be.—But how do you know,
that what you perceive by fight either exifts, or
is what it appears to be? Not by reafoning, but
by inftinct.

Of the vifible magnitude, extenfion, and
figure, our eyes give us a true perception.   It
is a law of nature, That while vifible objects
retire from the eye, the vifible magnitude becomes lefs as the diftance becomes greater:
and the proportion between the increafing diftance and the decreafing vifible magnitude is
fo well known, that the vifible magnitude of
any given object placed at a given diftance, may
be afcertained with geometrical exactnefs.   The
true vifible magnitude of objects is therefore a
fixed and determinate thing; that is, the vifible
magnitude of the fame object, at the fame diftance, is always the fame: we believe, that it
is what our eyes perceive it to be; if we did not,
the art of perfpective would be impoffible; at
leaft we could not acknowledge, that there is
any truth in that art.

But the object (you reply) feems no bigger
than your thumb; and you believe it to be fifty feet high: how is that fenfation reconcileable
with this belief? You may eafily reconcile them,
by recollecting, (what is obvious enough),
that the object of your belief is the tangible
magnitude; that of your fenfation, the vifible.
The vifible magnitude is a perception of fenfe;
and we have feen already, that it is conceived
to be a true, and not a fallacious perception:
the

the tangible magnitude you do not at prefent perceive by fenfe; you only remember it; or perhaps you infer it from the vifible, in confequence of your knowledge of the laws of perfpective. When we fee a lump of falt at a little diftance, we may perhaps take it for fugar. Is this a falfe fenfation? is this a proof, either that our tafte, or that our fight is fallacious? No : this is only an erroneous opinion formed upon a true fenfation. A falfe fenfation we cannot fuppofe it to be, without fuppofing that taftes are perceived by the eyes. And you cannot believe your opinion of the magnitude of thefe towers to be a falfe fenfation, except you believe that tangible qualities are perceived by fight. When we fpeak of the magnitude of objects, we generally mean the tangible magnitude, which is no more an object of fight than of hearing. For it is demonftrated in optics, that a perfon endued with fight, but fo fettered from his birth as to have no opportunity of gaining experience by touch, could never form any diftinct notion of the diftance, extenfion, magnitude, or figure of any thing. Thefe are perceptions, not of fight, but of touch. We judge of them indeed from the vifible appearance; but it is only in confequence of our having found, that certain changes in the vifible appearance do always accompany, and intimate, certain changes in the tangible diftance, magnitude, and figure. Vifible magnitude, and tangible magnitude, are quite different things; the former changes with every change of diftance, the latter is always the fame; the one is per-

ceived

ceived by one fenfe, the other by another. So
that when you fay, I fee a tower two miles off,
which appears no bigger than my thumb, and
yet I believe it to be a thoufand times bigger
than my whole body;---your fenfation is perfectly confiftent with your belief: the contrariety is merely verbal; for the word *bigger*, in
the firft claufe, refers to vifible, in the fecond,
to tangible magnitude.   There is here no more
real inconfiftency than if you were to fay, I
fee a conical body of a white colour, and I believe it to have a fweet tafte.   If there be any
difficulty in conceiving this, it muft arife from
our being more apt to confound the objects of
fight and touch, than thofe of any other two
fenfes.   As the knowledge of tangible qualities
is of more confequence to our happinefs and prefervation, than the knowledge of vifible appearances, which in themfelves can do neither good
nor harm; we fix our principal attention on
the tangible magnitude, the vifible appearance
ferving only as a fign by which we judge of it:
the mind makes an inftantaneous tranfition
from the vifible appearance, which it overlooks,
to the tangible quality, on which it fixeth its
attention: and the fign is as little attended to,
in comparifon of the thing fignified, as the
fhape of written characters, or the found of articulate voices, in comparifon of the ideas
which the writer or fpeaker means to communicate.

    But all men (it may be faid) do not thus dif-
tinguifh between vifible and tangible magnitude.   Many philofophers have affirmed, and
the vulgar ftill believe, that magnitude is a fen-

                                            fation

fation both of fight and touch : thofe people, therefore, when fenfible of the diminifhed vifible appearance of the diftant object, muft fuppofe, that the perception they receive by fight of the magnitude of that object, is really a falfe perception; becaufe different from what they fhould receive by touch, or even by fight, if the object were within three yards of their eyes. At any rate, they muft fuppofe, that what their fight perceives concerning magnitudes is not always to be depended on; and therefore that their fight is a fallacious faculty.

Let this objection have as much weight as you pleafe; yet will it not prove, that the evidence of fenfe may be either confirmed or confuted by reafon. Suppofe then I perceive real magnitude, both by fight and touch. I obferve, that what my fight perceives of magnitude is not always confiftent, either with itfelf, or with the fenfations received by touch from the fame object. The fame man, within the fame hour, appears fix feet high, and not one foot high, according as I view him at the diftance of two yards or of two miles. What is to be done in this cafe? both fenfations I cannot believe; for that the man really changes his ftature, is altogether incredible. I believe his ftature to be always the fame; and I find, that to my touch it always appears the fame; and that, when I look at the man at the diftance of a few feet, my vifible perception of his magnitude coincides with my tangible perception. I muft therefore believe, that what my fight intimates concerning the magnitude of diftant objects is not to

be

be depended on.   But whence arifes this belief?
Can I prove, by argument, that the man does
not change his ftature? that the fenfe, whofe
perceptions are all confiftent, is a true, and not
a fallacious faculty? or that a fenfe is not
fallacious, when its perceptions coincide with
the perceptions of another fenfe? No; I can
prove none of thefe points.   It is inftinct, and
not reafon, that determines me to believe my
touch: it is inftinct and not reafon that determines me to believe, that vifible fenfations, when
confiftent with tangible, are not fallacious;
and it is either inftinct, or reafoning founded
on experience, (that is, on the evidence of
fenfe), that determines me to believe the man's
ftature a permanent, and not a changeable
thing.   The evidence of fenfe is therefore decifive; from it there is no appeal to reafon: and
if I were to become fceptical in regard to it, I
fhould believe neither the one fenfe nor the
other; and of all experience, and experimental
reafoning, I fhould become equally diftruftful.

As the experience of an undifcerning or
carelefs fpectator may be confirmed, or corrected, by that of one who is more attentive,
or more fagacious, fo the evidence of an imperfect fenfe may be corrected by that of another fenfe which we conceive to be more perfect.
But the evidence of fenfe can never be corrected by any reafoning, except by that which proceeds on a fuppofition, that our fenfes are not
fallacious.   And all our notions concerning the
perfection or imperfection of fenfe are either inftinctive, and therefore principles of common
fenfe;

senfe ; or founded in experience, and therefore ultimately refolvable into this maxim, That things are what our fenfes reprefent them.

Lucretius is much puzzled (as his mafter Epicurus had been before him) about the degree of credit due to our vifible perceptions of magnitude. He obferves, juftly enough, that no principle can be confuted, except by another more evident principle; and, therefore, that the teftimony of fenfe, than which nothing is more evident, cannot be confuted at all * : that the teftimony of the noftrils concerning odour cannot be corrected or refuted by that of the eye, nor the eye by the ear, nor the ear by the touch, nor the touch by the tafte ; becaufe each of thefe fenfes hath a fet of objects peculiar to itfelf, of which the other fenfes cannot judge, becaufe indeed they cannot perceive them. All this

* See Diogenes Laertius, book 10.—Lucretius de rerum natura, lib. 4. ver.480. This author had fagacity enough to perceive the abfurdity of Pyrrhonifm, and to make feveral judicious remarks on the nature of evidence. But in applying thefe to his own theory, every one knows that he is by no means confiftent. The poem of Lucretius is a melancholy fpectacle ; it is the picture of a great genius in the ftate of lunacy. Except when the whim of his fect comes acrofs his imagination, he argues with propriety, perfpicuity, and elegance. Pathos of fentiment, fweetnefs of ftyle, harmony of numbers, and a beauty, and fometimes a majefty, of defcription, not unworthy of Virgil, renders his poem highly amufing, in fpite of its abfurd philofophy. A talent for extenfive obfervation he feems to have poffeffed in an extraordinary degree ; but wherever the peculiar tenets of Epicureanifm are concerned, he fees every thing through a falfe medium. So fatal is the admiffion of wrong principles. Perfons of the moft exalted underftanding have as much need to guard againft them, as thofe of the meaneft capacity. If they are fo imprudent, or fo unfortunate, as to adopt them, their fuperior genius, like the ftrength of a madman, will ferve no other purpofe than to involve them in greater difficulties, and give them the power of doing more mifchief.

this is very well; but there is one thing wanting, which I fhould think obvious enough,
even to one of Epicurean principles. Of taftes
we judge by the palate only; of fmell, by the
noftrils only; of found, by the ears only; of
colours, by the fight only; of hardnefs, foftnefs, heat, cold, &c. by the touch only; but of
magnitude we judge both by fight and touch.
In regard to magnitude, we muft therefore believe either our fight, or our touch, or both,
or neither. To believe neither is impoffible:
if we believe both, we fhall contradict ourfelves:
if we truft our fight, and not our touch, our
belief at one time will be inconfiftent with our
belief at another; we fhall think the fame man
fix feet high, and not one foot high: we muft
therefore believe our touch, if we would exert
any confiftent belief in regard to magnitude.

2. But do we not, in phyfical experiments,
acknowledge the deceitfulnefs of fenfe, when we
have recourfe to the telefcope and microfcope;
and when, in order to analyfe light, which, to
our unaffifted fight, appears one uniform uncompounded thing, we tranfmit the rays of it
through a prifm? I anfwer, this implies the
imperfection, not the *deceitfulnefs*, of fenfe. For
I fuppofe my fight deceitful, I can no more
truft it, when affifted by a telefcope or microfcope, than when unaffifted. I cannot prove
that things are as they appear to my unaffifted
fight; and I can as little prove, that things are
as they appear to my fight affifted by glaffes.

But is it not agreeable to common fenfe to
believe, that light is one uniform uncompounded thing? and if fo, is not common fenfe in an
                                        error?

error? and what can rectify this error but reafoning?—I anfwer, it is undeniable, that light
to the unaffifted eye appears uncompounded and
uniform.   If from this I infer, that light is
precifely what it appears to be, I form a wrong
judgement, which I may afterwards rectify, upon the evidence of fenfe, when I fee a ray of
light tranfmitted through a prifm.   Here an
error of judgement, or a falfe inference of reafon, is rectified by my trufting to the evidence
of fenfe; to which evidence inftinct or common
fenfe determines me to truft.

But is it not common fenfe that leads me to
form this wrong judgement? Do not all mankind naturally, and previoufly to all influence
from education, judge in the fame manner?
Did not all philofophers before Newton, and
do not all the unlearned to this day, believe that
light is a fimple fluid?—I anfwer, common fenfe
teacheth me, and all mankind, to truft to experience.   Experience tells us, that our unaffifted fight, though fufficiently acute for the ordinary purpofes of life, is not acute enough to
difcern the minute texture of vifible objects.
If, notwithftanding, this experience, we believe,
that the minute texture of light, or of any
other vifible fubftance, is nothing different from
that appearance which we perceive by the naked
eye; then our belief contradicts our experience,
and confequently is inconfiftent with common
fenfe.

But what if you have had no experience fufficient to convince you, that your fenfes are not
acute enough to difcern the texture of the minute

nute parts of bodies?—Then it is certain, that
I can never attain this conviction by mere reasoning. If a man were to reason *a priori* about
the nature of light, he might chop logic till
doomsday, before he convinced me, that light
is compounded of rays of seven different colours. But if he tell me of experiments which
he has made, or which he knows to have been
made, this is quite another matter. I believe
his testimony, and it makes up for my own
want of experience. When I confide in his veracity, I conceive, and believe, that his senses
communicated a true perception; and that, if
I had been in his place, I should also have been
convinced, by the evidence of my sense, that
light is truly compounded of rays of seven different colours. But I must repeat, that a supposition of my senses being fallacious, would
render me wholly inaccessible to conviction,
both on the one side and on the other.

Suppose a man, on seeing the coloured rays
thrown off from the prism, should think the
whole a delusion, and owing to the nature of
the medium through which the light is transmitted, not to the nature of the light itself;
and should tell me, that he could as easily believe my face to be of a green colour, because
it has that appearance when viewed through a
pair of green spectacles, as that every ray of
light consists of seven distinct colours, because
it has that appearance when transmitted through
a prism:—would it be possible to get the better
of this prejudice, without reasoning? I answer, it would not: but the reasoning used
                                        must

muſt all depend upon experiments; every one of which muſt be rejected, if the teſtimony of ſenſe be not admitted as deciſive. I could think of ſeveral expedients, in the way of appeals to ſenſe, by which it might be poſſible to reconcile him to the Newtonian theory of light; but, in the way of argument, I cannot deviſe a ſingle one.

On an imperfect view of nature, falſe opinions may be formed : but theſe may be rectified by a more perfect view ; or, which in many caſes will amount to the ſame thing, by the teſtimony of thoſe who have obtained a more perfect view. The powers of man operate only within a certain ſphere ; and till an object be brought within that ſphere, it is impoſſible for them to perceive it. I ſee a ſmall object, which I know to be a man, at the diſtance of half a mile : but cannot diſcern his complexion, whether it be black or fair ; nor the colour of his cloaths, whether it be brown, or black, or blue ; nor his noſe, whether it be long or ſhort : I cannot even diſcern, whether he have any noſe at all : and his whole body ſeems to be of one uniform black colour. Perhaps I am ſo fooliſh as to infer, that therefore the man has no noſe : that his cloaths are black, and his face of the colour of his cloaths. On going up to him, I diſcover that he is a handſome man, of a fair complexion, dreſſed in blue, Surely it is not reaſoning that ſets me right in this inſtance ; but it is a perfect view of an object that rectifies a wrong opinion formed upon an imperfect view.

Vol. I. · L I hear

I hear the found of a mufical inftrument at a diftance; but hear it fo faintly, that I cannot determine whether it be that of a trumpet, a hautboy, a German flute, a French horn, or a common flute. I want to know from what in-ftrument the found proceeds; and I have no opportunity of knowing from the information of others. Shall I ftand ftill where I am, and reafon about it? No: that would make me no wifer. I go forward to the place from whence the found feems to come: and by and by I can perceive, that the found is different from that of a French horn and of a trumpet: but as yet I cannot determine whether it be the found of a hautboy or of a flute. I go on a little fur-ther, and now I plainly diftinguifh the found of a flute; but perhaps I fhall not be able to know whether it be a German or a common flute, except by means of my other fenfes, that is, by handling or looking at it.

It is needlefs to multiply inftances for illuf-trating the difference between a perfect and an imperfect view of an object, and for fhowing, that the mind trufts to the former, but diftrufts the latter. For obtaining a perfect view, (or perfect conception), we fometimes employ the fame fenfe in a nearer fituation; fometimes we make ufe of inftruments, as ear-trumpets, fpec-tacles, microfcopes, telefcopes; fometimes we have recourfe to the teftimony of our other fenfes, or of the fenfes of other men: in a word, we rectify or afcertain the evidence of fenfe by the evidence of fenfe: but we never fubject the evidence of fenfe to the cognifance of reafon; for in fenfations that are imperfect

or

or indiftin&t, reafoning could never fupply what
is deficient, nor afcertain what is indefinite.

Our internal, as well as external fenfes, may
be, and often are, impofed upon, by inaccurate
views of their objects. We may in fincerity
of heart applaud, and afterwards condemn,
the fame perfon, for the fame action, according to the different lights in which that action
is prefented to our moral faculty.   Juft now I
hear a report, that a human body is found dead
in the neighbouring fields, with marks of violence upon it.   Here a confufed fufpicion arifes
in my mind of murder committed; but my
confcience fufpends its judgement till the true
ftate of the cafe be better known: I am not as
yet in a condition to perceive thofe qualities of
this event which afcertain the morality of the
action; no more than I can perceive the beauty
or deformity of a face while it is veiled, or at
too great a diftance.   A paffenger informs me,
that a perfon has been apprehended who con-
feffes himfelf the murderer: my moral faculty inftantly fuggefts, that this perfon has committed a crime worthy of a moft fevere and exemplary punifhment.   By and by I learn, from
what I think good authority, that my former
information is falfe, for that the man now dead
had made an unprovoked affault on the other,
who was thus driven to the neceffity of killing
him in felf-defence: my confcience immediately acquits the manflayer.   I fend a meffenger to
make particular inquiry into this affair; who
brings word, that the man was accidentally
killed by a fowler fhooting at a bird, who, before he fired, had been at all poffible pains to

difcover

difcover whether any human creature was in the
way; but that the deceafed was in fuch a fituation that he could not be difcovered.   I regret the accident; but I blame neither party.
Afterwards I learn, that this fowler was a carelefs fellow, and though he had no bad intention, was not at due pains to obferve whether
any human creature would be hurt by his fir-
ing.   I blame his negligence with great feverity;
but I cannot charge him with guilt fo enormous as that of murder.   Here my moral faculty paffes feveral different judgements on *the
fame aftion*; and each of them is right, and
will be in its turn believed to be right, and
trufted to accordingly, as long as the information which gave rife to it is believed to be true.
I fay, *the fame aftion*, not *the fame intention*; a
different intention appears in the manflayer from
each information; and it is only the intention
and affeftions that the moral faculty condemns
or approves.   To difcover the intention where-
with aftions are performed, reafoning is often
neceffary: but the defign of fuch reafoning,
is not to fway or inform the confcience, but
only to afcertain thofe circumftances or qualities of the aftion from which the intention of
the agent may appear.   When this becomes
manifeft, the confcience of mankind immediately and intuitively declares it to be virtuous,
or vicious, or innocent.—Thefe different judgements of the moral faculty are fo far from
proving it fallacious, that they prove the contrary: at leaft this faculty would be extremely
fallacious, and abfolutely ufelefs, if, in the cafe
now fuppofed, it did not form different judgements.

ments.——While the intention of the agent is wholly unknown, an action is upon the same footing with regard to its morality, as a human face in regard to its beauty, while it is veiled, or at too great a distance. By removing the veil, or walking up to the object, we perceive its beauty and features; and by reasoning, or by information concerning the circumstances of the action, we are enabled to discover or infer the intention of the agent. The act of removing the veil, or of walking up to the object, has no effect on the eye; nor has the reasoning any effect on the conscience.——While we view an object through an impure or unequal medium, through a pair of green spectacles, or an uneven pane of glass, we see it discoloured or distorted: just so, when misrepresented, a good action may seem evil, and an evil action good. If we be suspicious of the representation, if we be aware of the improper medium, we distrust the appearance accordingly; if not, we do and must believe it genuine. It is by reasoning from our experience of human actions and their causes, or by the testimony of credible witnesses, that we detect misrepresentations concerning moral conduct; and it is also by the experience of our own senses, or by our belief in those who have had such experience, that we become sensible of inequalities or obscurities in the medium through which we contemplate visible objects. In either case the evidence of sense is admitted as finally decisive. A distempered sense, as well as an impure or unequal medium, may doubtless communicate false sensations; but we are never imposed upon by

them

them in any thing material. A perſon in a fever may think honey bitter, and the ſmell of a roſe offenſive; but the deluſion is of ſo ſhort continuance, and of ſo ſingular a kind, that it can do no harm, either to him, or to the cauſe of truth. To a jaundiced eye, the whole creation may ſeem tinctured with yellow; but the patient's former experience, and his belief in the teſtimony of others, who aſſure him, that they perceive no alteration in the colour of bodies, and that the alteration he perceives is a common attendant on his diſeaſe, will ſufficiently guard him againſt miſtakes. If he were to diſtruſt the evidence of ſenſe, he could believe neither his own experience nor their teſtimony. He corrects, or at leaſt becomes ſenſible of, the falſe ſenſation, by means of ſenſations formerly received when he was in health; that is, he corrects the evidence of an ill-informed ſenſe by that of a well-informed ſenſe, or by the declaration of thoſe whoſe ſenſes he believes to be better informed than his own. Still it is plain, that from the evidence of ſenſe there can be no appeal to reaſon.

We conclude, therefore, that in natural philoſophy, our ſenſations are not ſuppoſed deceitful, and that reaſoning is not carried beyond the principles of common ſenſe. And yet in this ſcience full ſcope is given to impartial inveſtigation. If, after the firſt experimental proceſs, you ſuſpect that the object may be ſet in a ſtill fairer light, I know no law in logic, or in good ſenſe, that can or ought to hinder you from making a new trial: but if this new

trial

trial turn to no account, if the object still appear the fame, or if it appear lefs diftinct than before, it were folly not to remain fatisfied with the firft trial.   Newton tranfmitted one of the refracted primitive colours through a fecond prifm, thinking it not impoffible that this colour might refolve itfelf into others ftill more fimple ; but finding it remain unaltered, he was fatisfied that the primitive colours are not compounded, but fimple, and that the experimental procefs had been carried far enough.—— I take in my hand a perfpective glafs, whofe tube may be lengthened and fhortened at pleafure; and I am to find out, by my own induftry, that precife length at which the maker defigned it fhould be ufed in looking at diftant objects.   I make feveral trials to no purpofe: the diftant object appears not at all, or but very confufedly.   I hold one end of the perfpective at my eye with one hand, and with the other I gradually fhorten the tube, having firft drawn it out to its greateft length.   At firft all is confufion ; now I can difcern the inequalities of the mountains in the horifon ; now the object I am in queft of begins to appear ; it becomes lefs and lefs confufed ; I fee it diftinctly.   I continue to fhorten the tube ; the object lofes its diftinct appearance, and begins to relapfe into its former obfcurity.   After many trials, I find, that my perfpective exhibits no diftinct appearance, except when it is of one particular length.   Here then I fix; I have adgufted the glaffes according to the intention of the maker : and I believe, that the diftinct appearance is an accurate reprefentation of the

diftant

diſtant objeɛt, or at leaſt more accurate than any of the confuſed appearances ; of which I believe, that they come the nearer to truth the more they approach to diſtinɛtneſs, and that the moſt confuſed repreſentations are the moſt falſe,

It was not by reaſoning about the fallacy of the ſenſes, and proſecuting a train of argument beyond the principles of common ſenſe, that men diſcovered the true ſyſtem of the world. In the earlier ages, when they imagined the ſun to be little bigger than the mountain beyond which he diſappeared, it was abſurd to think of the earth revolving round him. But in pro- ceſs of time, ingenious men, who applied them- ſelves to the obſervation of the heavenly bodies, not with a view to confute popular errors, for they could not as yet even ſuſpeɛt the vulgar opinion to be erroneous, but merely to gratify their own laudable curioſity, began to conceive more exalted notions of the mundane ſyſtem. They ſoon diſtinguiſhed the planets from the fixed ſtars, by obſerving the former to be more variable in their appearances. After a long ſucceſſion of years, they came at laſt to under- ſtand the motions of the ſun and moon ſo well, that, to the utter aſtoniſhment of the vulgar, they began to calculate eclipſes, : a degree of knowledge they could not attain, without being convinced, that the ſun and moon are very large bodies, placed at very great diſtances from the earth, the former much larger, and more re- mote, than the latter. Thus far it is impoſſible to ſhow, that any reaſoning had been employed

by

by thofe ancient aftronomers, either to prove, or to difprove, the evidence of the fenfes.   On the contrary, they muft all along have taken it for granted, that the fenfes are not fallacious; fuppofing only, (what is certainly agreeable to common fenfe to fuppofe), that the experience of a diligent obferver is more to be depended on than that of the inattentive multitude. As men grew more and more acquainted with the motions and appearances of the heavenly bodies, they became more and more fenfible, that the fun, earth, and planets, bear fome very peculiar relation to one another: and having learned from the phenomena of eclipfes, and fome other natural appearances, that the fun is bigger than the earth *, they might, without abfurdity, begin to fufpect, that poffibly the fun might be the centre round which the earth and other planets revolve; efpecially confidering the magnificence of that glorious luminary, and the wonderful and delightful effects produced by the influence of his beams, while at the fame time he feems not to derive any advantage from the earth, or other planets.   But if the matter had been carried no further, no reafoning from thefe circumftances could ever have amounted to a proof of the point in queftion,

---

* Heraclitus maintained, that the fun is but a foot broad; Anaxagoras, that he is much larger than the country Peloponnefus; and Epicurus, that he is no bigger than he appears to the eye. But the aftronomers of antiquity maintained, that he is bigger than the earth; eight times, according to the Egyptians; eighteen times, according to Eratofthenes; three hundred times, according to Cleomedes; one thoufand and fifty times, according to Hipparchus; and fifty-nine thoufand three hundred and nineteen times, according to Poffidonius.

tion, though it might breed a faint prefumption in its favour. For ftill the evidence of fenfe
feemed to contradict it; an evidence that nothing can difprove, but the evidence of fenfe
placed in circumftances more favourable to accurate obfervation; and thus the point was
brought to the teft of common fenfe. And
now, we not only know, that the Copernican
theory is true, for every perfon who underftands it is convinced of its truth; but we alfo know to what caufes the univerfal belief of
the contrary doctrine is to be afcribed. We
know that men, confidering the remote fituation of our earth, and the imperfection of our
fenfes, could not have judged otherwife than
they did, till that imperfection was remedied,
either by accuracy of obfervation, or by the
invention of optical inftruments. We fpeak
not of revelation; which has indeed been
vouchfafed to man for the regulation of his
moral conduct; but which it would be prefumption to expect, or defire, merely for the gratification of curiofity.

It is evident, from what has been faid, that
in natural philofophy, as well as in mathematics, no argumentation is profecuted beyond felf-
evident principles; that as in the latter all reafoning terminates in intuition, fo in the former
all reafoning terminates in the evidence of fenfe.
And as, in mathematics, that is accounted an
intuitive axiom, which is of itfelf fo clear and
evident, that it cannot be illuftrated or enforced by any medium of proof, and which muft
be believed, and is in fact believed, by all, on
its own authority; fo, in natural philofophy,
that

that is accounted an ultimate principle, undeniable and unqueſtionable, which is ſupported by the evidence of a well-informed ſenſe,
placed ſo as to perceive its object. In mathematics, that is accounted falſe doctrine which
is inconfiſtent with any ſelf-evident principle;
in natural philoſophy, that is rejected which
contradicts matter of fact, or, in other words,
which is repugnant to the appearances of things
as perceived by external ſenſe.

Regulated by this criterion of truth, mathematics and natural philoſophy have become of
all ſciences the moſt reſpectable in point of certainty. Hence I am encouraged to hope, that
if the ſame criterion were univerſally adopted in
the philoſophy of the mind, the ſcience of human nature, inſtead of being, as at preſent,
a chaos of uncertainty and contradiction, would
acquire a conſiderable degree of certainty, per-
ſpicuity, and order. If truth be at all attainable in this ſcience, (and if it is not attainable,
why ſhould we trouble our heads about it?),
ſurely it muſt be attained by the ſame means
as in thoſe other ſciences.

I therefore would propoſe, " That in the
" philoſophy of human nature, as well as in
" phyſics and mathematics, principles be ex-
" amined according to the ſtandard of common
" ſenſe, and be admitted or rejected as they are
" found to agree or diſagree with it;" more explicitly, " That thoſe doctrines be rejected
" which contradict matter of fact, that is, which
" are repugnant to the appearance of things,
" as perceived by external and internal ſenſe;
" and that thoſe principles be accounted ulti-
" mate,

" mate, undeniable, and unqueftionable, which
" are warranted by the evidence of a well-
" informed fenfe, placed in circumftances fa-
" vourable to a diftinct perception of its ob-
" ject."

But what do you mean by a *well-informed
fenfe*? How fhall I know, that any particular
faculty of mine is not defective, depraved, or
fallacious?—Perhaps it is not eafy, at leaft it
would furnifh matter for too long a digreffion,
to give a full anfwer to this queftion. Nor is
it at prefent neceffary; becaufe it will appear
in the fequel, that, however difficult it may
be in fome cafes, to diftinguifh a firft principle, yet there are certain marks, by which thofe
reafonings that tend to the fubverfion of a firft
principle, may be detected, at leaft in all cafes
of importance. However, we fhall offer a remark or two in anfwer to the queftion; which,
though they fhould not appear perfectly unexceptionable, may yet throw light on the fubject, and ferve to prepare the mind of the reader for fome things that are to follow.

Firft, then, if I wanted to certify myfelf
concerning any particular fenfe or percipient
faculty, that it is neither depraved nor defective, I fhould attend to the feelings or fenfations communicated by it; and obferve, whether
they be clear and definite, and fuch as I am,
of my own accord, difpofed to confide in without hefitation, as true, genuine, and natural.
If they are fuch, I fhould certainly act upon
them till I had fome pofitive reafon to think
them fallacious. --- Secondly, I confider whether

ther the sensations received by this faculty be uniformly similar in similar circumstances. If they are not, I should suspect, either it is now depraved, or was formerly so; and if I had no other criterion to direct me, should be much at a loss to know whether I ought to trust the former or the latter experience; perhaps I should distrust both. If they are uniform, if my present and my past experience do exactly coincide, I shall then be disposed to think them both right.---Thirdly, I consider, whether, in acting upon the supposition that the faculty in question is well-informed, I have ever been misled to my hurt or inconvenience; if not, then have I good reason to think, that I was not mistaken when I formed that supposition, and that this faculty is really what I supposed it to be.---Fourthly, If the sensations communicated by this faculty be incompatible with one another, or irreconcileable to the perceptions of my other faculties, I should suspect a depravation of the former: for the laws of nature, as far as my experience goes, are consistent; and I am apt to believe that they are universally so. It is therefore a presumption, that my faculties are well informed, when the perceptions of one are quite consistent with those of the rest, and with one another.--- In a state of solitude I must satisfy myself with these *criteria*; but in society I have access to another criterion, which, in many cases, will be reckoned more decisive than any of these, and which, in concurrence with these, will be sufficient to banish doubt from every rational mind. I compare my sensations and

and notions with thofe of other men; and if I find a perfect coincidence, I fhall then be fatif-fied that my fenfations are according to the law of human nature, and therefore right.—To illuf-trate all this by an example :

I want to know whether my fenfe of feeing be a well-informed faculty.—Firft, I have rea-fon to think that it is; becaufe my eyes commu-nicate to me fuch fenfations as I, of my own accord, am difpofed to confide in. There is fomething in my perceptions of fight fo diftinct, and fo definite, that I do not find myfelf in the leaft difpofed to doubt whether things be what my eyes reprefent them. Even the obfcurer in-formations of this faculty carry along with them their own evidence, and my belief. I am confi-dent, that the fun and moon are round, as they appear to be, that the rainbow is arched, that grafs is green, fnow white, and the heavens a-zure; and this I fhould have believed, though I had paffed all my days in folitude, and never known any thing of other animals, or their fenfes.——Secondly, I find that my notions of the vifible qualities of bodies are the fame now they have always been. If this were not the cafe; if where I faw greennefs yefterday I were to fee yellow to day, I fhould be apt to fuppofe, that my fight had fuffered fome depravation, un-lefs I had reafon to think, that the object had really changed colour. But indeed we have fo ftrong a tendency to believe our fenfes, that I doubt not but in fuch a cafe I fhould be more difpofed to fufpect a change in the object than in my eye-fight: much would depend on the cir-cumftances of the cafe. We rub our eyes when

we

we want to look at any thing with accuracy; for
we know by experience, that motes, and clou-
dy ſpecks, that may be removed by rubbing, do
ſometimes float in the eye, and hurt the ſight.
But if the alteration of the viſible qualities in the
external object be ſuch as we have never experienced from a depravation of the organ, we ſhould
be inclined to truſt our eye-ſight, rather than to
ſuppoſe, that the external object has remained
unaltered.---Thirdly, No evil conſequence has
ever happened to me when acting upon the ſuppoſition, that my faculty of ſeeing is a well-informed ſenſe: whereas, if I were to act on the
contrary ſuppoſition, I ſhould ſoon have cauſe
to regret my ſcepticiſm.   I ſee a poſt in my way;
by turning a little aſide, I paſs it unhurt: but if I
had ſuppoſed my ſight fallacious, and gone
ſtraight forward, a bloody noſe, or ſomething
worſe, might have been the conſequence.   If,
when I bend my courſe obliquely, in order to a-
void the poſt that ſeems to ſtand directly before
me, I were to run my head full againſt it, I ſhould
inſtantly ſuſpect a depravation in my eye-ſight:
but as I never experience any misfortune of this
kind, I believe that my ſenſe of ſeeing is a well-
informed faculty.---Fourthly, The perceptions
received by this ſenſe are perfectly conſiſtent with
one another, and with the perceptions received
by my other faculties.   When I ſee the appearance of a ſolid body in my way, my touch always
confirms the teſtimony of my ſight; if it did not,
I ſhould ſuſpect a fallacy in one or other of thoſe
ſenſes, perhaps in both.   When I look on a line
of ſoldiers, they all ſeem ſtanding perpendicular,
as I myſelf ſtand; but if the men at the extremi-
ties

ties of the line, without leaning againſt any thing, were to appear as if they formed an angle of forty-five degrees with the earth's ſurface, I ſhould ſuſpeĉt ſome unaccountable obliquity in my viſion.---Laſtly, After the experience of many years, after all the knowledge I have been able to gather, concerning the ſenſations of other men, from reading, diſcourſe, and obſervation, I have no reaſon to think their ſenſations of ſight different from mine. Every body who uſes the Engliſh language, calls ſnow white, and graſs green; and it would be in the higheſt degree abſurd to ſuppoſe, that what they call the ſenſation of whiteneſs, is not the ſame ſenſation which I cal by that name. Some few, perhaps, ſee differently from me. A man in the jaundice ſees that roſe yellow which I ſee red; a ſhort-ſighted man ſees that piĉture confuſedly at the diſtance of three yards, which I ſee diſtinĉtly. But far the greater part of mankind ſee as I do, and differently from thoſe few individuals; whoſe ſenſe of ſeeing I therefore conſider as leſs perfeĉt than mine. Nay, tho' the generality of mankind were ſhort-ſighted, ſtill it would be true, that we, who are not ſo, have the moſt perfeĉt ſight; for our ſight is more accurate in its perceptions, qualifies us better for the buſineſs of life, and coincides more exaĉtly, or more immediately, with the ſenſations received by the other ſenſes. Yet the ſhort-ſighted, as well as they who have the acuteſt ſight, truſt to this ſenſe, as ſoon as they are placed in a ſituation favourable to accurate obſervation : all the difference is, that it is more difficult, and often more inconvenient, for ſhort-ſighted perſons to place

themſelves

themselves in such a situation. Still it should be remembered that a *perfect sense* and a *well-informed sense* are not synonymous terms. We call a sense *well-informed*, in opposition to one that is *depraved* or *fallacious*. *Perfection* and *imperfection* of sense are relative terms; implying a comparison, either between different men, in respect of the acuteness of their senses and faculties; or between any sense, as it appears in a particular man, and the degree of acuteness which is found to belong to that sense as it appears in the generality of mankind. There are two telescopes, one of which gives a distinct view of an object at two, and the other at four miles distance: both are equally *well-informed*, (if I may so speak); that is, equally true in their representations; but the one is much more *imperfect* than the other.

I do not, at present, offer any further illustrations of these *criteria* of a well-informed sense. The reader who examines them by the rules of common prudence, will perhaps be satisfied with them: at least I am apt to think, that few will suspect the veracity of their faculties when they stand this test. But let it not be supposed, that I mean to insinuate, that a man never trusts his faculties till he first examine them after this manner: we believe our senses previously to all reflection or examination; and we never disbelieve them, but upon the authority of our senses placed in circumstances more favourable to accurate observation.

If the reader is not satisfied with these *criteria*, it is no great matter. The question concerning a well-informed sense it is not perhaps easy to an-

fwer. I offer thefe remarks rather as hints
to be attended to by other adventurers in
this part of fcience, than as a complete folution
of the difficulty. If it were not that I prefume
fome advantage may be derived from them in
this way, I fhould have omitted them altogether; for on them does not depend the doctrine I
mean to eftablifh.

S E C T. III.

The fubject continued.   Intuitive truths diftinguifh-
able into claffes.

OF the notions attending the perception of
certain truth, we formerly mentioned this as one,
" That in regard to fuch truth, we fuppofe we
" fhould entertain the fame fentiments and be-
" lief if we were perfectly acquainted with all
" nature*." Left it fhould be thought that we
mean to extend this notion too far, it feems proper to introduce here the following remarks.

1. The axioms and demonftrated conclufions
of geometry are certainly true, and certainly a-
greeable to the nature of things. Thus we
judge of them at prefent; and thus we neceffarily believe, that we fhould judge of them, even
if we were endued with omnifcience and infal-
libility. It is a natural dictate of human underftanding, that the contrary of thefe truths
muft for ever remain abfurd and impoffible;
and that omnipotence itfelf cannot change
                                                    their

---

* See part 1. chap. 1.

their nature; though it might fo deprave our judgement, as to make us difbelieve, or not perceive them†.

2. That my body exifts, and is endued with a thinking, active, and permanent principle, which I call my foul;——That the material world hath fuch an exiftence as the vulgar afcribe to it, that is, a real feparate exiftence, to which its being perceived is in no wife neceffary;——That the men, beafts, houfes, and mountains, we fee and feel around us, are not imaginary, but real and material beings, and fuch, in refpect of fhape and tangible magnitude, as they appear to our fenfes; I am not only confcious that I believe, but alfo certain, that fuch is the nature of thefe things; and that, thus far at leaft, in regard to

M 2 the

† Some authors are of opinion, that all mathematical truth is refolvable into identical propofitions. The following remark to this purpofe is taken from a Differtation on Evidence, printed at Berlin in the year 1764. " Omnes mathematicorum propofitiones " funt identicæ, et repræfentantur hac formula, $a=a$. Sunt veri- " tates identicæ, fub varia forma expreffæ, imo ipfum, quod dici-' " tur, contradictionis principium, vario modo enunciatum et in- " volutum; fiquidem omnes hujus generis propofitiones revera in " eo contineantur. Secundum noftram autem intelligendi facul- " tatem ea eft propofitionum differentia, quod quædam longa ra- " tiociniorum ferie, alia autem breviori via, ad primum omnium " principium reducantur, et in illud refolvantur. Sic. v. g. propo- " fitio $2+2=4$, ftatim huc cedit $1+1+1+1=1+1+1+1$, i. e. " idem eft idem; et, proprie loquendo, hoc modo enunciari debet: " ——Si contingat, adeffe vel exiftere quatuor entia, tum exiftunt " quatuor entia; nam de exiftentia non agunt geometræ, fed ea hy- " pothetice tautum fubintelligitur. Inde fumma oritur certitudo " ratiocinia perfpicienti; obfervat nempe idearum identitatem; et " hæc eft evidentia, affenfum immediate cogens, quam mathema- " ticam aut geometricam vocamus. Mathefi tamen fua natura " priva non eft et propria; oritur etenim ex identitatis perceptione, " quæ locum habere poteft, etiamfi ideæ non repræfentent exten- " fum."——Of the connection of geometrical axioms with identical propofitions, fee Dr. Campbell's Philofophy of Rhetorick, book 1, chap. 5. fect. 1.

the nature of thefe things; an omnifcient and infallible being cannot think me miftaken. Of thefe truths I am fo certain, that I fcruple not to pronounce every being in an error who is of a contrary fentiment concerning them. For fuppofe an intelligent creature, an angel for inftance, to believe that there are not in the univerfe any fuch things as this folar fyftem, this earth, thefe mountains, houfes, animals, this being whom I call myfelf; could I, by any effort, bring myfelf to believe, that his opinion is a true one, and implies a propofition expreffive of fomething agreeable to the nature of things? It is impoffible and inconceivable. My underftanding intimates, that fuch an opinion would as certainly be falfe, as it is falfe that two and two are equal to ten, or that things equal to one and the fame thing are unequal to one another. Yet this is an opinion which omnipotence could render true, by annihilating the whole of this folar fyftem; or make me admit as true, by depriving me of underftanding. But fo long as this folar fyftem remains unannihilated, and my intellect undepraved, there is not a geometrical axiom more true, or more evident to me, than that this folar fyftem, and all the objects above-mentioned, do exift; there is not a geometrical axiom that has any better title to be accounted a principle of human knowledge; there is not a geometrical axiom againft which it is more abfurd, more unreafonable, more unphilofophical, to argue.

3. That fnow is white, fire hot, gold yellow, and fugar fweet, we believe to be certainly true. Thefe bodies affect our eyes, touch, and palate, in
                                                        a peculiar

a peculiar manner; and we have no reason to think, that they affect the organs of different men in a different manner. The peculiar sensation we receive from them depends on three things; on the nature of the object perceived, on the nature of the organ of perception, and on the nature of the percipient being. Of each of these things the Deity could change the nature; and make sugar bitter, fire cold, snow black, and gold green. But till this be done, in other words, while things continue as they are, it is as certainly true, that snow is white, fire hot, &c. as that two and two are equal to four, or a whole greater than a part. If we suppose, that snow, notwithstanding its appearance, is black, or not white, we must also suppose, that our senses and intellect are fallacious faculties; and therefore cannot admit any thing as true which has no better evidence than that of sense and intellect. If a creature of a different nature from man were to say, that snow is black, and hot, I should reply, (supposing him to use these words in the same sense in which I use them), it may possibly have that appearance to your senses, but it has not that appearance to mine: it may therefore, in regard to your faculties, be true; and if so, it ought to constitute a part of your philosophy: but of my philosophy it cannot constitute a part, because, in respect of my faculties, it is false, being contrary to my experience*. If the same

M 3   being

* This does not imply, that the same thing may be both true and false; true in respect of one, and false in respect of another: and consequently, that truth is not something absolute and immutable, but variable and relative. I had remarked, that our sensations depend

being were to affirm, that a part is equal to a
whole, I fhould anfwer, it is impoffible; none
can think fo but thofe who are deftitute of underftanding.   If he were to fay, The folar fyftem explained by Newton does not exift, I fhould
anfwer, You are miftaken; if your knowledge
were not imperfect, you would think otherwife; I am certain that it does exift. —We fee,
by thus ftating the cafe, what is the difference
between thefe three forts of certainty.   But ftill,
in refpect to man, thefe three forts are all equally evident, equally certain, and equally unfuf-
ceptible of confutation: and none of them can
be difbelieved or doubted by us, except we difa-
vow the diftinction between truth and falfehood,
by fuppofing our faculties fallacious.

   4. Of moral truth, we cannot bring ourfelves
to think that the Deity's notions (pardon the expreffion) are contrary to ours.   If we believe
Him omnifcient and infallible, can we alfo believe, that, in his fight, cruelty, injuftice, and
ingratitude, are worthy of reward and praife,
and

depend on three things, the nature of the object perceived,
the nature of the organ of perception, and the nature of
the percipient.   Confequently, an alteration in any one of
thefe, though the other two remain unaltered, alters the fenfation.
The quality of the fnow, therefore, the thing perceived, remaining
the fame, it may affect one kind of percipient being with one fort of
fenfation, and another kind with a fenfation entirely different.—A
difference of fenfation will alfo arife from the different ftates of the
organ.   A man who has one hand wrapt up in his bofom, and the
other expofed to frofty air, will feel the fame water cold with one
hand, and warm with the other.   Yet he does not believe that there
is any change in the water; but he believes that the fame temperature
in it occafions both feelings.   In like manner, we do not conceive any change to be made on the cloth, or even on the colour confidered as a quality in the body; though in day-light it appear to us
green, and in candle-light blue, and in every light to a perfon in the
jaundice yellow.

and the oppofite virtues of blame and punifhment? It is abfolutely impoffible.   The one belief deftroys the other.   Common fenfe declares,
that a being poffeffed of perfect knowledge can
no more entertain fuch a fentiment, than I with
my eyes open can juft now avoid feeing the
light.   If a created being were to think that virtue which we think vice, and that vice which
we think virtue, what would be our notions of
his intelligence? Should we not, without hefitation, pronounce him irrational, and his opinion an abfurdity ? The abfurdity indeed is conceivable, and may be expreffed in words that
imply no contradiction : but that any being
fhould think in this manner, and yet not
think wrong, is to us as perfectly inconceivable, as that the fame thing fhould be both true
and falfe*.

We fpeak here of the great and leading principles of moral duty.   Many fubordinate duties
there are, which refult from the form of particular governments, and from particular modes of
education; and there are fome, which, though
admirably adapted to the improvement of our
nature, are yet fo fublime, that the natural confcience

* Locke fays, that Moral Truth is fufceptible of demonftration.
If by this he means, that it admits of evidence fufficient to fatisfy
every rational mind, he is certainly in the right.   But if by the
word *demonftration* be meant, what Geometricians mean by it, a
proof that may be refolved into one or more felf-evident axioms
whofe contraries are inconceivable, we confefs that neither moral nor
hiftorical truth is fufceptible of demonftration, nor many other
truths of the moft unqueftionable certainty.   However, it is not to
be fuppofed, that Locke intended to ufe this word in any ftricter
fenfe than what is fixed by general practice ; according to which, e-
very proof that brings indubitable evidence to the reafon or fenfes
may properly be called a demonftration.

ſcience of mankind, unaſſiſted by revelation, can
hardly be ſuppoſed capable of diſcovering them:
but in regard to juſtice, gratitude, and thoſe o-
ther virtues, of which no rational beings (ſo
far as we know) are or can be ignorant, it
is impoſſible for us to believe that our ſentiments are wrong. I ſay, there are duties of
which no rational beings can be ignorant:
for if moral ſentiments be the reſult of a bias,
or *vis inſita*, communicated to the rational
ſoul by its Creator, then muſt they be as univerſal as rational nature, and as permanent
as the effects of any other natural law; and
it is as abſurd to argue againſt their truth or
authenticity, as againſt the reality of any o-
ther matter of fact.   But ſeveral authors of note
have denied this inference, as well as the principle whence it proceeds; or at leaſt, by calling
the one in queſtion, have endeavoured to make
us ſceptical in regard to the other.   They have
endeavoured to prove, that moral ſentiment is
different in different countries, and under different forms of religion, government, and manners; that therefore, in reſpect of it, there is no
vis inſita in the mind; for that, previous to e-
ducation, we are in a ſtate of perfect indifference
as to virtue and vice; and that an oppoſite courſe
of education would have made us think that virtue which we now think vice, and that vice
which we now think virtue: in a word, that
moral ſentiments are as much the effect of cuſ-
tom and human artifice, as our taſte in dreſs,
furniture, and the modes of converſation.   In
proof of this doctrine, a multitude of facts
have been brought together, to ſhow the prodigious

gious diverſity, and even contrariety, that takes
place in the moral opinions of different ages, nations, and climates.   Of all our modern ſceptical notions, this ſeemed to me one of the moſt
dangerous.   For my own ſatisfaction, and for
the ſake of thoſe whom it is my duty to inſtruct,
I have been at great pains to examine it; and
the examination has turned out to my entire ſatisfaction.   But the materials I have collected
on this ſubject are far too bulky to be inſerted
here.   The ſceptical arguments are founded, not
only on miſtakes concerning the nature of virtue, but alſo on ſome hiſtorical facts miſrepreſented, and on others ſo equivocal, and bare of
circumſtances, that they really have no meaning.
From the number of hiſtorical, as well as philoſophical, diſquiſitions, which I found it necef-
ſary to introduce, the *inquiry concerning the uni-
verſality and immutability of moral truth*, which I
thought to have compriſed in a few pages,
ſoon ſwelled into a treatiſe.   I meant to have fi-
niſhed it ſome years ago; but have been prevented by a number of unforeſeen accidents.

5. Of probable truth, a ſuperior being may
think differently from us, and yet be in the
right.   For every propoſition is either true or
falſe; and every probable paſt event has either
happened, or not happened; as every probable
future event will either happen or not happen.
From the imperfection of our faculties, and from
the narrowneſs of our experience, we may judge
wrong, when we think that a certain event has
happened, or will happen: and a being of more
extenſive experience, and more perfect underſtanding, may ſee that we judge wrong; for that
the

the event in queftion never did happen, nor e-
ver will. Yet it does not follow, that a man
may either prudently or rationally diftruft his
probable notions as fallacious. That which
man, by the conftitution of his nature, is determined to admit as probable, he ought to
admit as probable; for, in regard to man,
that is probable truth. Not to admit it probable, when at the fame time he muft believe
it to be fo, is mere obftinacy: and not to believe
that probable, which all other men who have
the fame view of all the circumftances, believe
probable, would be afcribed to caprice, or want
of underftanding. If one in fuch a cafe were
refractory, we fhould naturally afk, How comes
it that you think differently from us in this matter? have you any reafon to think us in a miftake? is your knowledge of the circumftances
from which we infer the probability of this e-
vent, different from ours? do you know any
thing about it of which we are ignorant? If he
reply in the negative, and yet perfift in contradicting our opinion, we fhould certainly think
him an unreafonable man. Every thing, therefore, which to human creatures feems intuitively probable, is to be accounted one of the firft
principles of probable human knowledge. A
human creature acts an irrational part when he
argues againft it; and if he refufe to acknowledge it probable, he cannot, without contradicting himfelf, acquiefce in any other human
probability whatfoever.

It appears from what has been faid, that there
are various kinds of intuitive certainty; and that
thofe who will not allow any truth to be felf-evident,

vident, except what has all the characteristics of a geometrical axiom, are much mistaken. From the view we have given of this subject, it would be easy to reduce these intuitive certainties into classes; but this is not necessary on the present occasion.   We are here treating of the nature and immutability of truth as perceived by human faculties.   Whatever intuitive proposition man, by the law of his nature, must believe as certain, or as probable, is, in regard to him, certain or probable truth; and must constitute a part of human knowledge, and remain unalterably the same, as long as the human constitution remains unaltered.   And we must often repeat, that he who attempts to disprove such intuitive truth, or to make men sceptical in regard to it, acts a part as inconsistent with sound reasoning, and as affectually subversive of human knowledge, as if he attempted to disprove truths which he knew to be agreeable to the eternal and necessary relations of things.   Whether the Deity can or cannot change these truths into falsehoods, we need not seek to determine, because it is of no consequence to us to know.   It becomes us better to inquire, with humility and reverence, into what he has done, than vainly, and perhaps presumptuously, into what he can do.   Whatever he has been pleased to establish in the universe, is as certainly established, as if it were in itself unchangeable and from eternity; and, while he wills it to remain what he made it, is as permanent as his own nature.

C H A P.

C H A P. II.

The preceding theory rejected by Sceptical Writers.

WE have feen, that mathematicians and natural philofophers do, in effect, acknowledge the diftinction between common fenfe and reafon, as above explained; admitting the dictates of the former as ultimate principles, and never attempting either to prove or difprove them by reafoning. If we inquire a little into the genius of modern fcepticifm, we fhall fee, that, there, a very different plan of inveftigation has been adopted. This will beft appear by inftances taken from that pretended philofophy. But firft let us offer a few general remarks.

S E C T. I.

General Obfervations. Rife and Progrefs of Modern Scepticifm.

1. THE Cartefian philofophy is to be confidered as the ground-work of modern fcepticifm. The fource of LOCKE's reafoning againft the feparate exiftence of the fecondary qualities of matter, of BERKELEY's reafoning againft the exiftence of a material world, and of HUME's reafoning againft the exiftence both of foul and body, may be found in the firft part of the *Principia*

cipia of DES CARTES. Yet nothing feems to
have been further from the intention of this worthy and moft ingenious philofopher, than to give
countenance to irreligion or licentioufnefs. He
begins with doubting; but it is with a view to arrive at conviction: his fucceffors (fome of them at
leaft) the further they advance in their fyftems,
become more and more fceptical; and at length
the reader is told, to his infinite pleafure and e-
molument, that the underftanding, acting alone,
does entirely fubvert itfelf, and leaves not the
loweft degree of evidence in any propofition*.

The firft thing a philofopher ought to do, according to DES CARTES, is to diveft himfelf of
all prejudices, and all his former opinions; to
reject the evidence of fenfe, of intuition, and of
mathematical demonftration; to fuppofe that
there is no God, nor heaven, nor earth; and
that man has neither hands, nor feet, nor body;—in a word, he is to doubt of every thing
of which it is poffible to doubt, and to be perfuaded, that every thing is falfe which can poffibly be conceived to be doubtful. Now there
is only one point of which it is impoffible to
doubt, namely, That I, the perfon who doubts,
am thinking. This propofition, therefore *I
think*, and this only, may be taken for granted;
and nothing elfe whatfoever is to be believed
without proof.

What is to be expected from this ftrange introduction? One or other of thefe two things
muft neceffarily follow. This author will either believe nothing at all; or if he believe any
thing,

---

* Treatife of Human Nature, vol. 1. p. 464.

thing, it muſt be upon the recommendation of ſophiſtical reaſoning*. But Des Cartes is no ſceptic in his moral reaſonings: therefore, in his moral reaſonings, he muſt be a ſophiſter. Let us ſee, whether we can make good this charge againſt him by facts.

Taking it for granted that he thinks, he thence infers, that he exiſts : *Ego cogito, ergo ſum :* I think; therefore I exiſt. Now there cannot be thought where there is no exiſtence; before he take it for granted that he thinks, he muſt alſo take it for granted that he exiſts. This argument, therefore, proceeds on a ſuppoſition, that the thing to be proved is true; in other words, it is a ſophiſm, a *petitio principii.* Even ſuppoſing it poſſible to conceive thinking, without at the ſame time conceiving exiſtence, ſtill this is no concluſive argument, except it could be ſhown, that it is more evident to a man that he thinks, than that he exiſts; for in every true proof a leſs evident propoſition is inferred from one that is more evident. But, *I think*, and, *I exiſt*, are equally evident. Therefore this is no true proof.—To ſet an example of falſe reaſoning in the very foundation of a ſyſtem, can hardly fail to have bad conſequences.

Having in this manner eſtabliſhed his own exiſtence, our author next proceeds to prove the veracity of his faculties ; that is, to ſhow by reaſoning, that what he thinks falſe is really falſe. He would have done better to have taken this alſo for granted: the argument by which he attempts

tempts

---

* See the firſt part of this Eſſay.

tempts to prove it, does more honour to his
heart than to his underftanding. It is indeed
a fophifm of the fame kind with the former,
in which he takes that for granted which he
meant to prove. It runs thus. We are confcious, that we have in our minds the idea of a
being infinitely perfeᴄt, intelligent, and powerful, neceffarily exiftent and eternal. This idea
differs from all our other ideas in two refpeᴄts:
—It implies the notions of eternal. and neceffary exiftence, and of infinite perfeᴄtion ;—it
neither is, nor can be, a fiᴄtion of the fancy;
and therefore exhibits no chimera or imaginary
being, but a true and immutable nature, which
muft of neceffity exift, becaufe neceffary exiftence is comprehended in the idea of it. Therefore there is a God, neceffarily exiftent, infinitely wife, powerful, and true, and poffeffed
of all perfeᴄtion. This Being is the maker of
us and of all our faculties; he cannot deceive,
becaufe he is infinitely perfeᴄt; therefore our
faculties are true, and not fallacious *.—The
fame argument has been adopted by others, particularly by Dr. Barrow. " Cartefius, fays
that pious and learned author, " hath well
" obferved, that, to make us abfolutely certain
" of our having attained the truth, it is re-
" quired to be known, whether our faculties of
" apprehending and judging the truth, be true;
" which can only be known from the power,
" goodnefs, and truth of our Creator †."
I ob-

* Cartefii Princip. Philof. part 1. § 14. 15. 18.
† Leᴄt. Geomet. 7.

I object not to this argument for the divine existence, drawn from the idea of an all-perfect being, of which the human mind is conscious: though perhaps this is not the moft unexceptionable method of evincing that great truth. I allow, that when a man believes a God, he cannot, without abfurdity and impiety, deny or question the veracity of the human faculties; and that to acknowledge a diftinction between truth and falfehood, implies a perfuafion, that certain laws are eftablifhed in the univerfe, on which the natures of all created things depend, which (to me at leaft) is incomprehenfible, except on the fuppofition of a fupreme, intelligent, directing caufe. But I acquiefce in thefe principles, becaufe I take the veracity of my faculties for granted; and this I feel myfelf neceffitated to do, becaufe I feel it to be the law of my nature, which I cannot poffibly counteract. Proceeding then upon this innate and irrefiftible notion, that my faculties are true, I infer, by the jufteft reafoning, that God exifts; and the evidence of this great truth is fo clear and convincing, that I cannot withftand its force, if I believe any thing elfe whatever.

DES CARTES argues in a different manner. Becaufe God exifts, (fays he), and is perfect, therefore my faculties are true. Right.—But how do you know that God exifts? I infer it from the fecond principle of my philofophy, already eftablifhed, *Cogito ergo fum.*—How do you know that your inference is juft? It fatisfies my reafon.—Your argument proceeds on a fuppofition, that what fatisfies your reafon is true?

It

It does.---Do you not then take it for granted, that your reafon is not a fallacious, but a true faculty? This muft be taken for granted, otherwife the argument is good for nothing. And if fo, your argument proceeds on a fuppofition, that the point to be proved is true. In a word, you pretend to prove the truth of our faculties, by an argument which evidently and neceffarily fuppofes their truth. Your philofophy is built on fophifms; how then can it be according to common fenfe?

As this philofopher doubted where he ought to have been confident, fo he is often confident where he ought to doubt. He admits not his own exiftence, till he thinks he has proved it; yet his fyftem is replete with hypothefes taken for granted, without proof, almoft without examination. He fets out with the profeffion of univerfal fcepticifm; but many of his theories are founded in the moft unphilofophical credulity. Had he taken a little more for granted, he would have proved a great deal more: he takes almoft nothing for granted, (I fpeak of what he profeffes, not of what he performs); and therefore he proves nothing. In geometry, however, he is rational and ingenious; there are fome curious remarks in his difcourfe on the paffions; his phyfics are fanciful and plaufible; his treatife on mufic perfpicuous, though fuperficial: a lively imagination feems to have been his chief talent; want of knowledge in the grounds of evidence his principal defeat.

We are informed by Father MALEBRANCHE, that the fenfes were at firft as honeft faculties

as one could defire to be endued with, till after
they were debauched by original fin; an adven-
ture, from which they contracted fuch an invincible propenfity to cheating, that they are
now continually lying in wait to deceive us.
But there is in man, it feems, a certain clear-
fighted, ftout, old faculty, called *Reafon*, which,
without being deceived by appearances, keeps
an eye upon the rogues, and often proves too
cunning for them. MALEBRANCHE therefore
advifeth us to doubt with all our might. " If
" a man has only learned to doubt," fays he,
" let him not imagine that he has made an
" inconfiderable progrefs *." Progrefs! in what?
—in fcience? Is it not a contradiction, or at
leaft an inconfiftency, in terms, to fay that a
man makes progrefs in fcience by doubting † ?
If one were to afk the way to Dublin, and to
receive for anfwer, that he ought firft of all to
fit down; for that if he had only learned to fit
ftill, he might be affured, that he had made no
inconfiderable progrefs in his journey; I fuppofe he would hardly trouble his informer with
a fecond queftion.

It is true, this author makes a diftinction between the doubts of paffion, brutality, and
blindnefs, and thofe of prudence, diftruft, and
penetration: the former, fays he, are the doubts
of Academics and Atheifts; the latter are the
doubts of the true philofopher ‡. It is true alfo,

---

* Qu'on ne s'imagine on pas, que l'on ait peu avancé, fi on a
feulement appris à douter.
                La Recherche de la Verite, liv. 1. *ch.* 20.
† Eft contrarietas inter verba *fcivi,* et *dubia funt.*
                Des Cartes, Objeû. et Refponf. feptimæ.
‡ Recherche de la Verité, liv. 1. ch. 20. feû. 3.

fo, that he allows us to give an entire confent to the things that appear entirely evident *. But he adopts, notwithftanding, the principles of DES CARTES' firft philofophy, That we ought to begin our inquiries with univerfal doubt, taking only our own confcioufnefs for granted, and thence inferring our exiftence, and the exiftence of God, and proving, from the divine veracity, that our faculties are not fallacious. Where-ever it is poffible that a deluding fpirit may deceive us, there, fays MALEBRANCHE, we ought to doubt † : but a deluding fpirit may deceive us where-ever our memory is employed in reafoning; therefore, in all fuch reafonings, there may be error. And if fo, there may be error in reafoning of every kind; for without memory there can be no reafoning : but in the truths difcovered by a fingle glance, (connoiffances de fimple vuë), fuch as this, That two and two make four, it is not poffible, he fays, for a deluding god, (dieu trompeur), however powerful, to deceive him. —It is eafy to fee, that fuch doctrines muft lead to fophiftry, or to univerfal fcepticifm, or rather to both. For if a demonftrated conclufion may be falfe for any thing I know to the contrary, an axiom may be fo too: my belief of the firft is not lefs neceffary, than my belief of the laft. Intuition is, of all evidence, the cleareft, and moft immediately convinc-

N 2   ing ?

---

* Qu'on ne doit jamais donner un confentement entier, qu' à des chofes qui paroiffent entierement evidentes. *Recherche de la Verite, liv.* 1. *ch.* 20. *fect.* 3.—This is indeed a rational fcepticifm, fuch as Ariftotle recommends, and every friend to truth muft approve

† Id. liv. 6. ch. 6.

ing ; but demonſtration produces abſolute certainty, and full conviction, in the mind of
him who underſtands it *.—MALEBRANCHE,
indeed, acknowledges, that we may reaſon
when once we know that God is no deceiver :
but this, he ſays, muſt be known at one glance,
(that is, I ſuppoſe, intuitively,) or it cannot be
known at all ; for all reaſoning on this ſubject
may be fallacious †.

· But I do not pretend to unfold all the falſe
and ſceptical principles of this author's philoſophy. To confeſs the truth, I do not well underſtand it. He is generally myſtical ; often,
if I miſtake not, ſelf-contradictory ; and his
genius is ſtrangely warped by a veneration for
the abſurdities of Popery. He rejects the evidence of ſenſe, becauſe it ſeems repugnant to
his reaſon ; he admits tranſubſtantiation, though
certainly repugnant both to reaſon and ſenſe.
Of Ariſtotle and Seneca, and the other ancient
philoſophers, he ſays, that their lights are nothing but thick darkneſs, and their moſt illuſ-
trious virtues, nothing but intolerable pride ‡.
Fy, M. MALEBRANCHE! Popery, with all its
abſurdities, requires not from its adherents ſo
illiberal a declaration. An Ariſtotelian, of
your own religion and country, and nearly
of your own age, delivers a very different doctrine : " Ariſtotle, ſupported by philoſophy,
" hath

---

* See the ſecond chapter of the firſt book of the latter Analytics
of Ariſtotle. The great philoſopher holds, that intuition and demonſtration are equally productive of knowledge ; though the former be the firſt, the cleareſt, and moſt immediate evidence.
† Recherche de la Verité, liv. 6. ch. 6.
‡ Recherche de la Verité, liv. 6. ch. 6.

" hath afcended by the fteps of motion even
" to the knowledge of one firft mover, who is
" God.   In order to arrive at the knowledge
" of divine things, we muft learn science,
" otherwife we fhall fall into error.   Philo-
" fophy and theology bear teftimony to, and
" mutually confirm, each other, and produce
" a more perfect knowledge of the truth : the
" latter teaches what we ought to believe, and
" reafon makes us believe it more eafily, and
" with greater fteadinefs.   They are two lights,
" which, by their union, yield a more brilliant
" luftre than either of them could yield fing-
" ly, or both if feparated.   Mofes learned
" the philofophy of the Egyptians, and Da-
" niel in Babylon that of the Chaldeans *."
This learned Peripatetic goes on to fhow, that
Jerome, Auguftine, Gregory of Nice, and
Clemens Alexandrinus, entertained the fame honourable opinion of the ancient philofophers.
—If Des Cartes, and his difciple Malebranche, had ftudied the ancients more, and
indulged their own imagination lefs, they would
have made a better figure in philofophy, and
done much more fervice to mankind.   But it
was their aim to decry the ancients as much
as poffible : and ever fince their time, it has
been too much the fafhion, to overlook the
difcoveries of former ages, as unneceffary to
the improvement of the prefent.   Malebranche often inveighs againft Ariftotle in
particular, with the moft virulent bitternefs;

N 3   and

* Bonju.   Introduction à la Philofophie, chap. 9.   Paris 1614.
folio.

and affects, on all occasions, to treat him with supreme contempt *. Had this great ancient employed his genius in the subversion of virtue, or in establishing tenets incompatible with the principles of natural religion, he would have deserved the severest censure. But MALE-BRANCHE lays nothing of this kind to his charge; he only finds him guilty of some speculative errors in natural philosophy. Aristotle was not exempted from that fallibility which is incident to human nature; yet it would not be amiss, if our modern wits would study him a little, before they venture to decide so positively on his abilities and character. It is observable, that he is most admired by those who best understand him. Now, the contrary is true of our modern sceptics: they are most admired by those who read them least, and who take their characters upon trust, as they find them delivered in coffee-houses and drawing-rooms, and other places of fashionable conversation, whose doctrines do so much honour to the virtue and good sense of this enlightened age.

I have sometimes heard the principles of the Socratic school urged as a precedent to justify our modern sceptics. Modern scepticism is of two kinds, unlike in their nature, though the one be the foundation of the other. DES CARTES begins with universal doubt, that in the end he may arrive at conviction: HUME begins with hypothesis, and ends with universal doubt. Now, does not Aristotle propose, that all investigation should begin with doubt?
And

* See Recherche de la Verité, liv. 6. ch. 5.

And does not Socrates affirm, that he knows nothing certainly, except his own ignorance?

All this is true. Ariftotle propofes, that inveftigation fhould begin with doubt *. He compares doubting to a knot, which it is the end of inveftigation to difintangle; and there can be no folution where there is no knot or difficulty to be folved. But Ariftotle's doubt is quite of a different nature from that of Des Cartes. The former admits as true whatever is felf-evident, without feeking to prove it : nay, he affirms, that thofe men who attempt to prove felf-evident principles, or who think that fuch principles may be proved, are ignorant of the nature of proof †. It differs alfo moft effentially from the fcepticifm of Mr. Hume. The reafonings of this author terminate in doubt; whereas Ariftotle's conftant aim is, to difcover truth, and eftablifh conviction. He defines philofophy *the fcience of Truth*; divides it into fpeculative and practical; and exprefsly declares, that truth is the end of the former, and action of the latter ‡.

Cicero, in order to compliment a fect, of which, however, he was not a confiftent difciple, afcribes to Socrates a very high degree of fcepticifm ‖; making his principles nearly the fame with thofe of the New Academy, who profeffed to believe, that all things are fo involved in
darknefs,

* Ariftot. Metaphyf. lib. 3. cap. 1.Λύειν δ' ὐκ ἴσιν ἀγνοὖντα τὸν δισμον, &c.
† Ariftot. Metaphyf. lib. 4. cap. 4.
‡ O'ρθῶς δ' ἔχει καὶ τὸ καλἰσαί τὴν φιλοσοφίαν ἰπιςτ́μην τῆς ἀληθίιας. Θιωρητικησ μὶν γὰρ τέλος Ἀ'λτθίια. πεαχτικῆς, δ' ἔργόν.
Metaphyf. lib. 2. cap. 1.
‖ Cic. Academ. lib. 1. cap. 12.

darknefs, that nothing can be known with certainty. The only difference between them, according to Cicero in this place, is, that Socrates affirmed, that he knew nothing but his
own ignorance: whereas Arcefilas, and the reft
of the New Academy, held, that man could
know nothing, not even his own ignorance,
with certainty; and therefore, that affirmati-
on of every kind is abfurd and unphilofophical.
But we need not take this on the authority of
Cicero; as we have accefs to the fame original
authors from whom he received his information. And if we confult them, particularly Xenophon, the moft unexceptionable of them all
in point of veracity, we fhall find, that the reafonings, the fentiments, and the conduct of
Socrates, are altogether incompatible with fcepticifm. The firft fcience that engaged his attention was natural philofophy; which, as it
was taught in thofe days by Zeno, Anaxagoras,
and Xenophanes, had little to recommend it to
a man of fenfe and candour. Socrates foon
relinquifhed it, from a perfuafion that it was
at once unprofitable, and founded in uncertainty: and employed the reft of his life in the
cultivation of moral philofophy, a fcience
which to him feemed more fatisfactory in its
evidence, and more ufeful in its application *.
So far was he from being fceptical in regard to
the principles of moral duty, that he inculcated them with earneftnefs where-ever he found
opportunity, and thought it incumbent on every man to make himfelf acquainted with them.

In

* Xenoph. Memorab. lib. 1. cap. 1. et lib. 4. cap. 7.

In his reasonings, indeed, he did not formally lay down any principle, because it was his method to deduce his conclusions from what was acknowledged by his antagonist: but is this any proof, that he himself did not believe his own conclusions? Read the story of his life; his conduct never belied his principles: observe the manners of our sceptics; their conduct and principles do mutually and invariably belie one another. Do you seek still more convincing evidence, that Socrates felt, believed, and avowed the truth? Read the defence he made before his judges. See you there any signs of doubt, hesitation, or fear? any suspicion of the possibility of his being in the wrong? any dissimulation, sophistry, or art? See you not, on the contrary, the utmost plainness and simplicity, the calmest and most deliberate fortitude, and that noble assurance which so well becomes the cause of truth and virtue? Few men have shown so firm an attachment to truth, as to lay down their life for its sake: yet this did Socrates. He made no external profession of any philosophical creed; but in his death, and through the whole of his life, he showed the steadiest adherence to principle; and his principles were all consistent. Xenophon has recorded many of these; and tells us in regard to some of them, that Socrates scrupled not to call those men fools who differed from his opinion *—The sophists of his age were not solicitous to discover truth, but only to confute an adversary, and reason plausibly in behalf of their theories.

That

* Xenoph. Memorab. lib. 1. cap. 1. passim.

That they might have the ampler field for this
fort of fpeculation, they confined themfelves,
like our modern metaphyficians, to general
topics, fuch as the nature of good, of beauty,
and the like; on which one may fay a great
many things with little meaning, and offer a
variety of arguments without one word of
truth. Socrates did much to difcredit this abufe
of fcience. In his converfations he did not
trouble himfelf with the niceties of artificial logic. His aim was, not to confute an adverfary, nor to guard againft that verbal confutation which the fophifts were perpetually attempting; but to do good to thofe with whom he
converfed, by laying their duty before them in
a ftriking and perfuafive manner †. He was
not fond of reafoning on abftract fubjects, efpecially when he had to do with a fophift; well
knowing, that this could anfwer no other purpofe than to furnifh matter for endlefs and unprofitable logomachy. When, therefore, Arif-
tippus afked him concerning the nature of
good ‡, with a view to confute, or at leaft to
teafe him, with quibbling evafions, Socrates de-
clined to anfwer in general terms; and defired
the fophift to limit his queftion, by confining
the word *good* to fome particular thing. Do
you afk me, fays he, what is good for a fever,
for fore eyes, or for hunger? No, fays the fophift.

---

† Ἀρίσιππε δὲ ἐπιχειροῦντος ἐλέγχειν τὸν Σωκράτη,—βαλόμενος τὰς
συνόντας ὠφελεῖν ὁ Σωκρατης ἀπεκρίνατο, ἠχ ὥσπερ οἱ φυλαττόμενοι, μη
τι ὁ λογος ἐπαλλαχθῆ, ἀλλ' ὡς ἂν πεπεισμένοι μάλιςα πράτlοιεν τα
δέοντα.   *Xenoph. Memorab. lib. 3. cap.* 8.

‡ Id. ibid.

phift.   If, replies he, you afk me concerning
the nature of a good which is good for no particular purpofe, I tell you once for all, that I
know of none fuch, and have no defires after
it.   In like manner, he anfwers to the general
queftion concerning beauty, by defiring his adverfary to confine himfelf to fome particular
kind of beauty.   What would the great moralift have thought of thofe modern treatifes,
which feem to have nothing elfe in view, but
to contrive vain definitions of general ideas!
Simple, certain, and ufeful truth, was the
conftant, and the only, object of this philofopher's inquiry.

True it is, he fometimes faid, that he knew
nothing but his own ignorance.   And furely
the higheft attainments in human knowledge
are imperfect and unfatisfying.   Yet man
knows fomething : Socrates was confcious that
he knew fomething; otherwife Xenophon would
not have afferted, that his opinions concerning God, and Providence, and Religion, and
Moral Duty, were well known to all the Athenians *.   But Socrates was humble, and made
no pretenfions to any thing extraordinary, either in virtue or in knowlege.   He profeffed
no fcience; he inftructed others, without pedantry, and without parade; exemplifying the
beauty and the practicability of virtue, by the
integrity of his life, and by the charms of an
inftructive, though moft infinuating, converfation †.   His addrefs, in conducting an argument

---

* Xenoph. Memorab. lib. 1. cap. 1.
† Ibid. cap. 2.

ment or inquiry, was very remarkable. He put on the appearance of an ignorant perfon, and feemed to be only afking queftions for his information, when he was leading his difciple or antagonift to the acknowledgement of fome ufeful truth. It is pity that this mode of inftruction is not more generally practifed. No other method conveys fo clear conviction to the mind of the young ftudent, or fo effectually cultivates his underftanding : for, by thus co-operating with the teacher in the inveftigation of truth, his attention is fixed, his fancy directed, and his judgement exercifed, no lefs than if the difcovery were altogether his own.

Cicero feems to have been an Academic rather in name than in reality. And I am apt to think, from feveral paffages in his works *, that he made choice of this denomination, in order to have a pretence for reafoning on either fide of every queftion, and confequently an ampler field for a difplay of his rhetorical talents †. To Pyrrho, Herillus, Arifto, and other fceptics, who, by afferting that all things are indifferent, deftroy the diftinction of virtue and vice, he will not allow even the name of philofopher : nay, he infinuates that it is impudence in fuch perfons to pretend to it ‡. " I " wifh," fays he in another place, " that they " who fuppofe me a fceptic were fufficiently " acquainted

---

* See particularly *De Officiis*, *lib. 3. cap. 4. De Fato, cap. 2. De Oratore, lib. 3. cap. 21,*

† See this point illuftrated in REMARKS UPON A DISCOURSE OF FREETHINKING, &c. *By Phileleutherus Lipfienfis (Dr. Bentley)* Edit. 7. p. 262.

‡ De officiis, lib. 1. cap. 2.

" acquainted with my sentiments. For I am
" not one of those whose mind wanders in er-
" ror, without any fixed principle. For what
" sort of understanding must that man pos-
" sess, what sort of life must that man lead,
" who, by divesting himself of principle, di-
" vests himself of the means, both of reason-
" ing and of living * !" Let it be observed also, that when the subject of his inquiry is of
high importance, as in his books on moral duties, and on the nature of the gods, he follows
the doctrine of the Dogmatists, particularly the
Stoics; and asserts his moral and religious principles with a warmth and energy which prove
him to have been in earnest.

2. Nothing was further from the intention
of LOCKE, than to encourage verbal controver-
sy, or advance doctrines favourable to scepticism. To do good to mankind, by inforcing
virtue, illustrating truth, and vindicating liberty, was his sincere purpose: and he did not
labour in vain. His writings are to be reckoned among the few books that have been productive of real utility to mankind. But candour
obliges me to remark, that some of his tenets
seem to be too rashly admitted, for the sake of
a favourite hypothesis. That some of them
have promoted scepticism, is undeniable. He
seems indeed to have been sensible, that there
were inaccuracies in his work; and candidly
owns, that " some hasty and indigested thoughts
" on

---

* Quibus vellem satis cognita esset nostra sententia. Non enim
sumus ii, quorum vagetur animus errore, nec habeat unquam quid
sequatur. Quæ enim esset ista mens, vel quæ vita, potius, non
modo disputandi, sed videndi ratione sublata! *Cic. de Officiis, lib.*
2. *cap.* 2.

" on a subject never before confidered, gave
" the first entrance to his Effay; which, being
" begun by chance, was continued by intreaty,
" written by incoherent parcels, and after long
" intervals of neglect refumed again, as humour
" or occafion permitted*."

The firft book of his Effay, which, with fub-
miffion, I think the worft, tends to eftablifh this
dangerous doctrine, That the human mind,
previous to education and habit, is as fufceptible of any one impreffion as of any other: a
doctrine which, if true, would go near to prove,
that truth and virtue are no better than human
contrivances; or, at leaft, that they have nothing permanent in their nature, but may be as
changeable as the inclinations and capacities of
men; and that, as we underftand the term,
there is no fuch thing as common fenfe in the
world.   Surely this is not the doctrine that
LOCKE meant to eftablifh; but his zeal againft
innate ideas, and innate principles, put him off
his guard, and made him allow too little to inftinct, for fear of allowing too much.   This
controverfy, as far as it regards moral fentiment, I propofe to examine in another place.
At prefent I would only obferve, that if truth be
any thing permanent, which it muft be if it be
any thing at all, thofe perceptions or impulfes
of underftanding, by which we become confcious of it, muft be equally permanent; which
they could not be, if they depended on education, and if there were not a law of nature, independent on man, which determines the underftanding

---

* Preface to the Effay on Human Underftanding.

derftanding in fome cafes to believe, in others
to difbelieve. Is it poffible to imagine, that any
courfe of education could ever bring a rational
creature to believe, that two and two are equal
to three, that he is not the fame perfon to-day
he was yefterday, that the ground he ftands on
does not exift? could make him difbelieve the
teftimony of his own fenfes, or that of other
men? could make him expect unlike events in
like circumftances? or that the courfe of nature, of which he has hitherto had experience,
will be changed, even when he forefees no caufe
to hinder its continuance? I can no more believe, that education could produce fuch a depra-
vity of judgement, than that education could
make me fee all human bodies in an inverted pofition, or hear with my noftrils, or take pleafure
in burning or cutting my flefh. Why fhould
not our judgements concerning truth be acknowledged to refult from a bias impreffed upon
the mind by its Creator, as well as our defire of
felf-prefervation, our love of fociety, our refentment of injury, our joy in the poffeffion of
good? If thofe judgements be not inftinctive, I
fhould be glad to know how they come to be
univerfal: the modes of fentiment and behaviour produced by education are uniform only
where education is uniform; but there are many truths which have obtained univerfal acknowledgement in all ages and nations. If thofe
judgements be not inftinctive, I fhould be glad
to know how men find it fo difficult, or rather
impoffible, to lay them afide: the falfe opinions
we imbibe from habit and education, may be, and
often are, relinquifhed by thofe who make a pro-
                                                    per

per ufe of their reafon; and he who thus re-
nounces former prejudices, upon conviction of
their falfity, is applauded by all as a man of
candour, fenfe, and fpirit; but if one were
to fuffer himfelf to be argued out of his common fenfe, the whole world would pronounce
him a fool.

The fubftance, or at leaft the foundation, of
BERKELEY's argument againft the exiftence of
matter, may be found in LOCKE's Effay, and in
the *Principia* of DES CARTES. And if this argument be conclufive, it proves that to be falfe
which every man muft neceffarily believe every
moment of his life to be true, and that to be
true which no man fince the foundation of the
world was ever capable of believing for a fingle
moment. BERKELEY's doctrine attacks the
moft inconteftable dictates of common fenfe;
and pretends to demonftrate, that the cleareft
principles of human conviction, and thofe
which have determined the judgement of all men
in all ages, and by which the judgement of all
rational men muft be determined, are certainly
fallacious.

Mr. HUME, more fubtle, and lefs referved,
than any of his predeceffors, hath gone ftill
greater lengths in the demolition of common
fenfe; and reared in its place a moft tremendous
fabric of doctrine; upon which, if it were not
for the flimfinefs of its materials, engines might
eafily be erected, fufficient to overturn all belief,
fcience, religion, virtue, and fociety, from the
very foundation. He calls this work, " A
" Treatife of Human Nature; being an attempt
" to introduce the experimental method of rea-
                                    " foning

" foning into moral fubjects."   This is, in the
ftyle of Edmund Curl, a *taking title page*; but,
alas! " Fronti nulla fides!"   The whole of
this author's fyftem is founded on a falfe hypothefis taken for granted ; and whenever a
fact contradictory to that falfe hypothefis
occurs to his obfervation, he either denies it,
or labours hard to explain it away.   This, it
feems, in his judgement, is experimental reafoning!

He begins his book with affirming, That all
the perceptions of the human mind refolve
themfelves into two claffes, impreffions, and i-
deas; that the latter are all copied from the former; and that an idea differs from its corref-
pondent impreffion only in being a weaker perception.   Thus, when I fit by the fire I have an
impreffion of heat, and I can form an idea of
heat when I am fhivering with cold; in the one
cafe I have a ftronger perception of heat, in the
other a weaker.   Is there any warmth in this
idea of heat? There muft, according to this
doctrine; only the warmth of the idea is not
quite fo ftrong as that of the impreffion.   For
this author repeats it again and again, that " an
" idea is by its nature weaker and fainter than
" an impreffion, but is in every other refpect"
" (not only fimilar, but) the fame*."   Nay, he
goes further, and fays, that " whatever is true
" of the one muft be acknowledged concerning
" the other†;" and he is fo confident of the

---

* Treatife of Human Nature, vol. 1. p. 131.
† Ibid. p. 41.

truth of this maxim, that he makes it one of the
pillars of his philofophy. To thofe who may
be inclined to admit this maxim on his authority, I would propofe a few plain queftions. Do
you feel any, even the leaft warmth, in the idea
of a bonfire, a burning mountain, or the general conflagration? Do you feel more real cold in
Virgil's Scythian winter, than in Milton's defcription of the flames of hell? Do you acknowledge that to be true of the idea of eating,
which is certainly true of the impreffion of it,
that it alleviates hunger, fills the belly, and con-
tributes to the fupport of human life? If you
anfwer thefe queftions in the negative, you deny one of the fundamental principles of this
philofophy. We have, it is true, a livelier perception of a friend when we fee him, than when
we think of him in his abfence.   But this is not
all: every perfon of a found mind knows, that
in the one cafe we believe, and are certain, that
the object exifts, and is prefent with us; in the
other we believe, and are certain, that the object
is not prefent: which, however, they muft deny, who maintain, that an idea differs from an
impreffion only in being weaker, and in no other
refpect whatfoever.

   That every idea fhould be a copy and refemblance of the impreffion whence it is derived;—
that, for example, the idea of red fhould be a
red idea; the idea of a roaring lion a roaring
idea; the idea of an afs, a hairy, long-eared,
fluggifh idea, patient of labour and much addicted to thiftles; that the idea of extenfion
fhould be extended, and that of folidity folid; •
---that a thought of the mind fhould be endued
                                                   with

with all, or any, of the qualities of matter,---is,
in my judgement, inconceivable and impoſſible.
Yet our author takes it for granted; and it is
another of his fundamental maxims.   Such is
the credulity of Scepticiſm !

If every idea be an exaɛt reſemblance of its
correſpondent impreſſion, (or objeɛt, for theſe
terms, according to this author, ſeem to amount
to the ſame thing*);---if the idea of extenſion
be extended, as the ſame author allows†; ———
then the idea of a line, the ſhorteſt that ſenſe
can perceive, muſt be equal in length to the
line itſelf; for if ſhorter it would be imperceptible; and it will not be ſaid, either that an imperceptible idea can be perceived, or that the
idea of an imperceptible objeɛt can be formed :---conſequently the idea of a line a hundred
times as long, muſt be a hundred times as long as
the former idea; for if ſhorter, it would be the idea,
not of this, but of ſome other ſhorter line.
And ſo it clearly follows, nay it admits of demonſtration, that the idea of an inch is really
an inch long; and that of a mile, a mile long.
In a word, every idea of any particular extenſion
is equal in length to the extended objeɛt.   The
ſame reaſoning holds good in regard to the other
dimenſions of breadth and thickneſs.   All ideas,
therefore, of ſolid objeɛts, muſt be (according
to this philoſophy) equal in magnitude and ſolidity to the objeɛts themſelves.   Now mark the
conſequence.   I am juſt now in an apartment
containing a thouſand cubic feet, being ten feet

---

* Treatiſe of Human Nature, vol. 1. p. 12. 13. 362.
† Ibid. p. 416. 417.

square, and ten high; the door and windows
are shut, as well as my eyes and ears. Mr.
Hume will allow, that in this situation, I may
form ideas, not only of the visible appearance,
but also of the real tangible magnitude of the
whole house, of a first-rate man of war, of St.
Paul's cathedral, or even of a much larger object.
But the solid magnitude of these ideas is equal
to the solid magnitude of the objects from which
they are copied: therefore I have now present
with me an idea, that is, a solid extended thing,
whose dimensions extend to a million of cubic
feet at least. The question now, is, Where is
this thing placed? for a place it must have, and
a pretty large one too. I should answer, In my
mind; for I know not where else the ideas of my
mind can be so conveniently deposited. Now my
mind is lodged in a body of no great dimensions, and my body is contained in a room ten
feet square, and ten feet high. It seems then,
that, into this room, I have it in my power at
pleasure to introduce a solid object a thousand,
or ten thousand, times larger than the room itself. I contemplate it a while, and then by another volition send it a-packing, to make way
for another object of equal or superior magnitude. Nay, in no larger vehicle than a common
postchaise, I can transport from one place to a-
nother, a building equal to the largest Egyptian
pyramid. and a mountain as big as the peak of
Teneriff.—Take care, ye disciples of Hume, and
be very well advised before ye reject this mystery
as impossible and incomprehensible. It seems
to be geometrically deduced from the principles,
nay from the first principles of your master.

Say,

Say, ye candid and intelligent, what are we to expect from a logical and fyftematic treatife founded on a fuppofition that leads into fuch abfurdity ? Shall we expect truth ? then muft it not be inferred by falfe reafoning ?—Shall we expect found reafoning ? then muft not the inferences be falfe ?—Indeed, though I cannot much admire this author's fagacity on the prefent occafion, I muft confefs myfelf not a little aftonifhed at his courage.   A witch going to fea in an egg-fhell, or preparing to take a trip through the air on a broom-ftick, would be a furprifing phenomenon; but it is nothing to Mr. HUME, on fuch a bottom, " launching out " into the immenfe depths of philofophy."

To multiply examples for the confutation of fo glaring an abfurdity, is ridiculous.   I therefore leave it to the reader to determine, whether, if this doctrine of folid and extended ideas be true, it will not follow, that the idea of a roaring lion muft emit audible found, almoft as loud and as terrible, as the royal beaft in perfon could exhibit;—that two ideal bottles of brandy will intoxicate as far at leaft as two genuine bottles of wine;—and that I muft be greatly hurt, if not dafhed to pieces, if I am fo imprudent as to form only the idea of a bomb burfting under my feet.   For has not our author faid, that " impreffions and ideas com-" prehend all the perceptions (or objects) of " the human mind; that whatfoever is true of " the one muft be acknowledged concerning " the other; nay, that they are in every ref-" pect the fame, except that the former ftrike " with more force than the latter ?"

The

The abfurdity and inconceivablenefs of the diftinction between objects and perceptions, is another of our author's doctrines. " How-
" ever philofophers may diftinguifh (fays he)
" betwixt the objects and perceptions of the
" fenfes;—this is a diftinction which is not
" comprehended by the generality ' of man-
" kind*." Now how are we to know, whether this diftinction be conceived and acknowledged by the generality ? If we put the queftion to any of them, we fhall find it no eafy
matter to make ourfelves underftood, and, after all, perhaps be laughed at for our pains.
Shall we reafon *a priori* about their fentiments and comprehenfions ? this is neither philofophical nor fair. Will you allow me to
reckon myfelf one of the generality ? Then I
declare, for my own part, that I do comprehend and acknowledge this diftinction, and
                                              have

---

* See Treatife o Human Nature, vol. 1. p. 353. 365. The word *perception*, (and the fame is true of the words *fenfation, fmell, tafte,* and many others) has, in common language, two, and fome-times three, diftinct fignifications. It means, 1. The thing per-ceived. Thus we fpeak of the *tafte* of a fig, the *fmell* of a rofe. 2. The power or faculty perceiving ; as when we fay, " I have " loft my *fmell* by a fevere cold, and therefore my *tafte* is not fo " quick as ufual." 3. It fometimes denotes that impulfe or im-preffion which is communicated to the mind by the external ob-ject operating upon it through the organ of fenfation. Thus we fpeak of a *fweet* or *bitter tafte,* a *diftinct* or *confufed,* a *clear* or *ob-fcure, fenfation* or *perception.* Moft of our fceptical philofophers have either been ignorant of, or inattentive to, this diftinction. MALEBRANCHE, indeed, (liv. 1. ch. 10.) feems to have had fome notion of it ; but either I do not underftand this author, or there is a ftrange obfcurity and want of precifion in almoft every thing he fays. Hr. HUME's philofophy does not allow this to be a ra-tional diftinction ; fo that it is impoffible to know precifely what he means by the word *perception* in this and many other places. But I have difproved his affertion, whatever fenfe (confiftent with common ufe) we affix to the word.

have done fo ever fince I was capable of reflection.

Suppofe me to addrefs the common people in
thefe words : " I fee a ftrange fight a little way
" off; but my fight is weak, fo that I fee it
" imperfectly; let me go nearer, that I may
" have a more diftinct fight of it."——If the
generality of mankind be at all incapable of
diftinguifhing between the object and the perception, this incapacity will doubtlefs difcover
itfelf moft, when ambiguous words are ufed on
purpofe to confound their ideas; but if their
ideas on this fubject are not confounded even
by ambiguous language, there is reafon to
think, that they are extremely clear, diftinct,
and accurate. Now I have here propofed a
fentence, in which there is a ftudied ambiguity
of language; and yet I maintain, that every
perfon, who underftands Englifh, will inftantly, on hearing thefe words, perceive, that by
the word *fight* I mean, in the firft claufe, the
thing feen; in the fecond, the power, or perhaps the organ, of feeing; in the third, the
perception itfelf, as diftinguifhed both from the
percipient faculty, and from the vifible object *.

If

* To every perfon of common underftanding this diftinction is
in reality and practice quite familiar. But as the words we ufe
in expreffing it are of ambiguous fignification, it is not eafy to
write about it fo as to be immediately underftood by every reader.
—The thing feen or perceived is fomething permanent and external, and is believed to exift, whether perceived or not; the
faculty of feeing or perceiving is alfo fomething permanent in the
mind, and is believed to exift, whether exerted or not; but
what I here call *the perception itfelf* is temporary, and is conceived to have no exiftence but in the mind that perceives it, and
to exift no longer than while it is perceived; for in being perceived, its very effence does confift; fo that *to be*, and *to be perceived,*

If one of the multitude, on hearing me pronounce this sentence, were to reply as follows:
" The sight is not at all strange : it is a man
" on horseback : but your sight must needs be
" weak, as you are lately recovered from sick-
" nefs : however, if you wait a little, till the
" man and horse, which are now in the shade,
" come into the sunshine, you will then have a
" much more distinct sight of them :"—I
would ask, Is the study of any part of philosophy necessary to make a man comprehend the
meaning of these two sentences ? Is there any
thing absurd or unintelligible, either in the
former or in the latter ? Is there any
thing in the reply, that seems to exceed the
capacity of the vulgar, and supposes them to be
more acute than they really are ? If there be
not, and I am certain there is not, here is an un-
questionable proof, that the vulgar, and indeed
all men whom metaphysic has not deprived

ed, when predicated of it, do mean precisely the same thing.
Thus, I just now see this paper, which I call the external object:
I turn away, or shut my eyes, and then I see it no longer, but
I still believe it to exist ; though buried an hundred fathom deep
in the earth, or left in an uninhabitable island, its existence would
be as real as if it were gazed at by ten thousand men.   Again,
when I shut my eyes, or tie a bandage over them, or go into a
dark place, I see no longer ; that is, my faculty of seeing acts,
or is acted upon, no longer; but I still believe it to remain in
my mind, ready to act, or to be acted upon, whenever it is again
placed in the proper circumstances ; for nobody supposes, that
by shutting our eyes, or going into a dark place, we annihilate
our faculty of seeing.   But, thirdly, my *perception* of this paper
is no permanent thing ; nor has it any existence, but while it is perceived ; nor does it at all exist, but in the mind that perceives it ;
I can put an end to, or annihilate it ; whenever I please, by shutting my eyes ; and I can at pleasure renew it again, by opening
them.—It is really astonishing, that so many of our modern philosophers should have overlooked a distinction, which is of so great
importance, that if we were unacquainted with it, a great part of
human language would seem to be perfect nonsense.

ed of their senses, do distinguish between the object perceived, the faculty perceiving, and the perception or impulse communicated by the external object to the mind through the organ of sensation. What though all the three are sometimes expressed by the same name? This only shows, that accuracy of language is not always necessary for answering the common purposes of life. If the ideas of the vulgar are sufficiently distinct, notwithstanding, what shall we say of that philosopher, whose ideas are really confounded by this inaccuracy, and who, because there is no difference in the signs, imagines that there is none in the things signified! That the understanding of such a philosopher is not a vulgar one, will be readily allowed; whether it exceeds, or falls short, let the reader determine*.

This author's method of investigation is no less extraordinary than his fundamental principles. There are many notions in the human mind, of which it is not easy perhaps to explain the origin. If you can describe in words what were the circumstances in which you received an impression of any particular notion, it is well; he will allow that you may form an idea of it. But if you cannot do this, then, says he, there is no such notion in your mind; for all perceptions are either impressions or ideas; and it is not possible for us so much as to conceive any
thing

---

* Mr. HUME does not seem to me to be always consistent with himself in affirming, that the vulgar do not comprehend the distinction between perceptions and objects. But, upon the whole, he seems to hold this distinction to be unreasonable, unphilosophical, and unsupported by the evidence of sense. See Treatise of Human Nature, p. 330—338.

thing fpecifically different from ideas and impreffions*: now all ideas are copied from impreffions: therefore you can have no idea nor
conception of any thing of which you have not
received an impreffion.---All mankind have a
notion of power or energy. No, fays he; an
impreffion of power or energy was never received by any man; and therefore an idea of it can
never be formed in the human mind. If you
infift on your experience and confcioufnefs of
power, it is all a miftake: his hypothefis admits
not the idea of power; and therefore there is no
fuch idea†.---All mankind have an idea of felf.
That I deny, fays our author; I maintain, that
no man ever had, or can have, an impreffion of felf; and therefore no man can form any
idea of it‡. If you perfift, and fay, that certainly you have fome notion or idea of yourfelf:
My dear Sir, he would fay, you do not confider, that this affertion contradicts my hypothefis
of impreffions and ideas; how then is it poffible it fhould be true!

But though the author deny, that I have any
notion of *felf*, furely he does not mean to affirm,
that I do not exift, or that I have no notion of
myfelf as an exiftent being. In truth, it is not eafy
to fay what he means on this fubject. Moft philofophical fubjects become obfcure in the hands of
this author; for he has a notable talent at puzzling
his readers and himfelf: but when he treats of
confcioufnefs, of perfonal identity, and of the
nature of the foul, he expreffes himfelf fo
　　　　　　　　　　　　　　　　　ftrangely,

* Treatife of Human Nature, vol. 1. p. 123.
† Ibid. p. 282.
‡ Ibid. p. 437. 438.

ftrangely, that his words either have no meaning, or imply very great abfurdity. " The
" queftion," fays he, " concerning the fub-
" ftance of the foul is unintelligible‡."——
Well, Sir, if you think fo, you may let it a-
lone.—No; that muft not be neither. " What
" we call a *mind*, is nothing but a heap or col-
" lection of different perceptions (or objects)
" united together by certain relations, and fup-
" pofed, though falfely, to be endowed with per-
" fect fimplicity and identity*.---If any one,
" upon ferious and ' unprejudiced reflection,
" thinks he has a different notion of himfelf, I
" muft confefs I can reafon with him no longer.
" All I can allow him is, that he may be in the
" right as well as I, and that we are effentially
" different in this particular.   He may perhaps
" perceive fomething fimple and continued,
" which he calls *himfelf*; though I am certain
" there is no fuch principle in me.   But fetting
" afide fome metaphyficians of this kind,"---
that is, who feel and believe that they have a
foul,---" I may venture to affirm of the reft of
" mankind, that they are nothing but a bundle
" or collection of different perceptions, which
" fucceed each other with inconceivable rapidi-
" ty, and are in a perpetual flux and move-
" ment.——There is properly no fimplicity in
" the mind at one time, nor identity in different
" (times), whatever natural propenfion we may
" have to imagine that fimplicity and identity.
            " —They

‡ Treatife of Human Nature, vol. 1. p. 434. 435.
* Ibid. p. 361. 362.

" —They are the fucceffive perceptions only that
" conftitute the mind†."

If thefe words have any meaning, it is this;
My foul (or rather that which I call my foul) is
not one fimple thing, nor is it the fame thing to-
day it was yefterday; nay, it is not the fame
this moment it was the laft; it is nothing but a
mafs, collection, heap, or bundle, of different
perceptions, or objects, that fleet away in fuccef-
fion, with inconceivable rapidity, perpetually
changing, and perpetually in motion.   There
may be fome metaphyficians, to whofe fouls this
defcription cannot be applied; but I am certain,
that this is a true and complete defcription of
my foul, and of the foul of every other individual of the human race, thofe few metaphyficians
excepted.

That body has no exiftence, but as a bundle of
perceptions, whofe exiftence confifts in their being perceived, our author all along maintains.
He now affirms, that the foul, in like manner,
is a bundle of perceptions, and nothing elfe.   It
follows, then, that there is nothing in the univerfe but impreffions and ideas; all poffible perceptions being by our author comprehended in
thofe two claffes.   This philofophy admits of no
other exiftence whatfoever, not even of a percipient being, to perceive thefe perceptions.   So
that we are now arrived at the height of human
wifdom; at that intellectual eminence, from
whence there is a full profpect of all that we can
reafonably believe to exift, and of all that can
poffibly become the object of our knowledge.
Alas!

† Treatife of Human Nature, vol. 1. p. 438. 439. 440.

Alas! what is become of the magnificence of external nature, and the wonders of intellectual energy, the immortal beauties of truth and virtue, and the triumphs of a good conscience! Where now the warmth of benevolence, the fire of generosity, the exultations of hope, the tranquil ecstasy of devotion, and the pang of sympathetic delight! All, around, above, and beneath, is one vast vacuity, or rather an enormous chaos, encompassed with darkness universally and eternally impenetrable. Body and spirit are annihilated; and there remains nothing (for we must again descend into metaphysic) but a vast collection, bundle, mass, or heap, of impressions and ideas.

Such, in regard to existence, seems to be the result of this theory of the understanding. And what is this result? If the author can prove, that there is a possibility of expressing it in words which do not imply a contradiction, I will not call it nonsense. If he can prove, that it is compatible with any one acknowledged truth in philosophy, in morality, in religion natural or revealed, I will not call it impious. If he can prove, that it does not arise *from common facts misrepresented,* and *common words misunderstood,* I shall admit that it may have arisen from accurate observation, candid and liberal enquiry, perfect knowledge of human nature, and the enlarged views of true philosophic genius.

S E C T.   II.

Of the Non-exiſtence of Matter.

IN the preceding ſection I have taken a ſlight ſurvey of the principles, and method of inveſtigation, adopted by the moſt celebrated promoters of modern ſcepticiſm. And it appears that they have not attended to the diſtinction of reaſon and common ſenſe, as explained in the firſt part of this Eſſay, and as acknowledged by mathematicians and natural philoſophers. Erroneous, abſurd, and ſelf-contradictory notions, have been the conſequence. And now, by entering into a more particular detail, we might eaſily ſhew, that many of thoſe abſurdities that diſgrace the philoſophy of human nature, would never have exiſted, if men had acknowledged and attended to this diſtinction ; regulating their inquiries by the criterion above-mentioned, and never proſecuting any chain of argument beyond ſelf-evident principles. I ſhall confine myſelf to two inſtances; one of which is connected with the evidence of external ſenſe, and the other with that of internal.

That matter or body has a real, ſeparate, independent exiſtence* ; that there is a real ſun above us, a real air around us, and a real earth
under

---

* By *independent exiſtence*, we mean an exiſtence that does not depend on us, nor, ſo far as we know, on any being except the Creator. BERKELEY, and others, ſay, that matter exiſts not but in the minds that perceive it; and conſequently depends, in reſpect of its exiſtence, upon thoſe minds.

under our feet,—has been the belief of all men who were not mad, ever fince the creation. This is believed, not becaufe it is or can be proved by argument, but becaufe the conftitution of our nature is fuch that we muft believe it. It is abfurd, nay it is impoffible to believe the contrary. I could as eafily believe, that I do not exift, that two and two are equal to ten, that whatever is, is not; as that I have neither hands, nor feet, nor head, nor cloaths, nor houfe, nor country, nor acquaintance; that the fun, moon, and ftars, and ocean, and tempeft, thunder, and lightning, mountains, rivers, and cities, have no exiftence but as ideas or thoughts in my mind, and, independent on me and my faculties, do not exift at all, and could not exift if I were to be annihilated; that fire, and burning, and pain, which I feel, and the recollection of pain that is paft, and the idea of pain which I never felt, are all in the fame fenfe ideas or perceptions in my mind, and nothing elfe; that the qualities of matter are not qualities of matter, but affections of fpirit; and that I have no evidence that any being exifts in nature but myfelf. Philofophers may fay what they pleafe; and the world, who are apt enough to admire what is monftrous, may give them credit; but I affirm, that it is not in the power, either of wit or of madnefs, to contrive any conceit more abfurd, or more nonfenfical, than this, That the material world has no exiftence but in my mind.

DES CARTES admits, that every perfon muft be perfuaded of the exiftence of a material world: but he does not allow this point to be
felf-evident,

felf-evident, or fo certain as not to admit of
doubt; becaufe, fays he, we find in experience,
that our fenfes are fometimes in an error, and
becaufe, in dreams we often miftake ideas for external things really exifting. He therefore begins his philofophy of bodies with a formal proof
of the exiftence of body*.

But however imperfect, and however fallacious, we acknowledge our fenfes to be in other
matters, it is certain, that no man ever thought
them fallacious in regard to the exiftence of body;
nay, every man of a found mind, is, by the law
of his nature, convinced, that, in this refpect at
leaft, they are not, and cannot be miftaken.
Men have fometimes been deceived by fophiftical
argument, becaufe the human underftanding is
in fome and indeed in many, refpects, fallible;
but does it follow, that we cannot, without
proof, be certain of any thing, not even of our
own exiftence, nor of the truth of a geometrical axiom? Some difeafes are fo fatal to the mind,
as to confound mens notions even of their own
identity; but does it follow, that I cannot be
certain of my being the fame perfon to-day I was
yefterday, and twenty years ago, till I have firft
proved this point by argument? And becaufe we
are fometimes deceived by our fenfes, does it therefore follow, that we never are certain of our not
being deceived by them, till we have firft convinced
ourfelves by reafoning, that they are not deceitful?—If a Cartefian can prove, that there have
been a few perfons of found underftanding, who,
from a conviction of the deceitfulnefs of their
fenfes,

* Cartefii Principia, part 1. § 4. part 2. § 1.

senses, have really disbelieved, or seriously doubted, the existence of a material world, I shall allow a conviction of this deceitfulness to be a
sufficient ground for such doubt or disbelief, in
one or a few instances : and if he can prove
that such doubt, or disbelief has at any time been
general among mankind, I shall allow that it
may be so again :——but if it be certain, as I
think it is, that no man of a sound mind, however suspicious of the veracity of his senses, ever
did or could really disbelieve, or seriously doubt,
the existence of a material world, then is this
point self-evident, and a principle of common
sense, even on a supposition that our senses are
as deceitful as Des Cartes and Malebranche
chuse to represent them.   But we have formerly proved that our senses are never supposed to
be deceitful, except when we are conscious, that
our experience is partial, or our observation inaccurate ; and that even then, the fallacy is detected, and rectified, only by the evidence of sense
placed in circumstances more favourable to accurate observation.   In regard to the *existence*
of matter there cannot be a suspicion, that our
observation is inaccurate, or our experience
partial ; and therefore it is not possible, that
ever we should distrust our senses in this particular.   If it were possible, our distrust could
never be removed either by reasoning or by experience.

As to the suspicion against the existence of
matter that is supposed to arise from our experience of the delusions of dreaming ; we observe, in the first place, that if this be allowed a sufficient ground for suspecting, that our

waking perceptions are equally delusive, there is at once an end of all truth, reasoning, and common sense. That I am at present awake, and not asleep, I certainly know; but I cannot prove it: for there is no criterion for distinguishing dreaming fancies from waking perceptions, more evident than that I am now awake, which is the point in question; and, as we have often remarked, it is essential to every proof, to be more evident than that which is to be proved. That I am now awake, must therefore carry its own evidence along with it; if it be evident at all, it must be self-evident. And so it is: we may mistake dreams for realities, but no rational being ever mistook a reality for a dream. Had we the command of our understanding and memory in sleep, we should probably be sensible, that the appearances of our dreams are all delusive: which, in fact, is sometimes the case; at least I have sometimes been conscious, that my dream was a dream: and when it was disagreeable, have actually made efforts to awake myself, which have succeeded. But sleep has a wonderful power over all our faculties. Sometimes we seem to have lost our moral faculty; as when we dream of doing that, without scruple or remorse, which when awake we could not bear to think of. Sometimes memory is extinguished; as when we dream of conversing with our departed friends, without remembering any thing of their death, though it was, perhaps, one of the most striking incidents we had ever experienced, and is seldom or never out of our thoughts when we are awake. Sometimes our understanding

seems

feems to have quite forfaken us ; as when we dream of talking with a dead friend, remembering at the fame time that he is dead, but without being confcious of any thing abfurd or unufual in the circumftance of converfing with a dead man. Confidering thefe and the other effects of fleep upon the mind, we need not be furprifed, that it fhould caufe us to miftake our own ideas for real things, and be affected with thofe in the fame manner as with thefe. But the moment we awake, and recover the ufe of our faculties, we are fenfible, that the dream was a delufion, and that the objects which now folicit our notice are real. To demand a reafon for the implicit confidence we repofe in our waking perceptions ; or to defire us to prove, that things are as they appear to our waking fenfes, and not as they appear to us in fleep, is as unreafonable as to demand a reafon for our belief in our own exiftence : in both cafes our belief is neceffary and unavoidable, the refult of a law of nature, and what we cannot in practice contradict, but to our fhame and perdition.

Further : If Des Cartes thought an argument neceffary to convince him, that his perception of the external world was not imaginary, but real, I would afk, how he could know that his argument was real, and not imaginary. How could he know that he was awake, and not afleep, when he wrote his Principles of Philofophy, if his waking thoughts did not, previous to all reafoning, carry along with them undeniable evidence of their reality ? *I am awake,* is a principle which he muft have taken for

·granted, even before he could fatisfy himfelf of the truth of what he thought the firft of all principles, *Cogito, ergo fum.*—To which we may add, that if there be any perfons in the world who never dream at all *, (and fome fuch I think there are), and whofe belief in the exiftence of a material world is not a whit ftronger than that of thofe whofe fleep is alway attended with dreaming; this is a proof from experience, that the delufions of fleep do not in the leaft affect our conviction of the authenticity of the perceptions we receive, and of the faculties we exert, when we awake.

The firft part of DES CARTES' argument for the exiftence of bodies, would prove the reality of the vifionary ideas we perceive in dreams; for they, as well as bodies, prefent themfelves to us, independent on our will. But the principal part of his argument is founded on the veracity of God, which he had before inferred from our confcioufnefs of the idea of an infinitely perfect, independent, and neceffarily-exiftent being : Our fenfes inform us of the exiftence of body; they give us this information in confequence of a law eftablifhed by the divine will : but God is no deceiver; therefore is their information true. I have formerly given my opinion

---

* " I once knew a man," fays Mr. LOCKE, " who was bred a " fcholar, and had no bad memory, who told me, that he had " never dreamed in his life, till he had that fever he was then " newly recovered of, which was about the five or fix and twenti- " eth year of his age. I fuppofe the world affords more fuch in- " ftances."

Effay on Human Underftanding, Book 2. cb 1.

A young gentleman of my acquaintance never dreams at all, except when his health is difordered.

opinion of this argument, and fhown that it is a fophifm, as the author ftates it. We muft believe our faculties to be true, before we can be convinced, either by proof, or by intuitive evidence. If we refufe to believe in our faculties, till their veracity be firft afcertained by reafoning, we fhall never believe in them at all *.

MALEBRANCHE † fays, that men are more certain of the exiftence of God, than of the exiftence of body. He allows, that DES CARTES has proved the exiftence of body, by the ftrongeft arguments that reafon alone could furnifh ; nay, he feems to acknowledge thofe arguments to be unexceptionable ‡ : yet he does not admit, that they amount to a full demonftration of the exiftence of matter. In philofophy, fays he, we ought to maintain our liberty as long as we can, and to believe nothing but what evidence compels us to believe. To

P 3   be

---

* See the preceding fection.

† Recherche de la Verité, tom. 3. p. 30.   A Paris, chez Pralard, 1679.

‡ Mais quoique M. DES CARTES ait donné les preuves les plus fortes que la raifon toute feule puiffe fournir pour l'exiftence des corps ; quiqu' il foit evident, que Dieu n'eft point trompeur, et qu'on puiffe dire qu'il nous tromperoit effectivement, fi nous nous trompions nous-mêmes en faifant l'ufage que nous devons faire de nôtre efprit, et des autres facultez dont il eft l'auteur ; cependant on peut dire que l'exiftence de la matiere n'eft point encore parfaitement demontrée.   Car, enfin, en matiere de philofophie, nous ne devons croire quoique ce foit *que lorfque l'evidence nous y oblige.*   Nous devons faire ufage de nôtre liberté autant que nous le pouvons.—Pour être plainement convaincus qu'il y a des corps, il faut qu'on nous demontre, non feulement qu'il y a un Dieu, et que Dieu n'eft point trompeur, mais encore que Dieu nous a affuré qu'il en a effectivement cree : ce que je ne trouve point prouvé dans les ouvrages de M. DES CARTES.

Tom. 3. *p.* 37. 38. 39.

be fully convinced of the exiſtence of bodies, it is neceſſary that we have it demonſtrated to us, not only that there is a God, and that he is no deceiver, but alſo that God hath aſſured us, that he has actually created ſuch bodies; and this, he ſays, I do not find proved in the works of M. Des Cartes.

There are, according to Malebranche, but two ways in which God ſpeaks to the mind, and compels (or obliges) it to believe; to wit, by evidence, and by the faith. " The faith " obliges us to believe that bodies exiſt; but " as to the evidence of this truth, it certainly " is not complete : and it is alſo certain, that " we are not invincibly determined to believe, " that any thing exiſts, but God, and our own " mind. It is true, that we have an extreme " propenſity to believe, that we are ſurrounded " with corporeal beings; ſo far I agree with " M. Des Cartes : but this propenſity, natu- " ral as it is, doth not force our belief by evi- " dence: it only inclines us to believe by im- " preſſion. Now we ought not to be deter- " mined, in our free judgements, by any thing " but light and evidence; if we ſuffer ourſelves " to be guided by the ſenſible impreſſion, we " ſhall be almoſt always miſtaken *."—Our author

* Dieu ne parle à l'eſprit, et ne l' oblige à croire qu'en deux manieres ; par l'evidence, et par la foi. Je demeure d'accord, que *la foi oblige a croire* qu'il y a des corps : mais pour l'evidence, il eſt certain, qu'elle n'eſt point entiere, et que nous ne ſommes point invinciblement portez à croire qu'il y ait quelqu' autre choſe que Dieu et nôtre eſprit. Il eſt vray, que nous avons un penchant extréme à croire qu'il y a des corps qui nous environnent. Je l'accorde à M. Des Cartes : mais ce penchant, tout naturel qu'il eſt, *ne nous y force* point par evidence ; il nous y incline ſeulement

author then propofes in brief, the fubftance of that
argument againft the exiftence of body, which
BERKELEY afterwards took fuch pains to illuftrate ; and difcovers, upon the whole, that, as a
point of philofophy, the exiftence of matter is a
probability, to which we have it in our power either to affent, or not to affent, as we pleafe. In a
word, it is by the faith, and not by evidence,
that we become certain of this truth.

This is not a proper place for analyfing the
paffage above quoted, otherwife it would be eafy to fhow, that the doctrine (fuch as it is)
which the author here delivers, is not reconcileable with other parts of his fyftem. But I
only mean to obferve, that what is here afferted, of our belief in the exiftence of body being
not neceffary, but fuch as we may with-hold if
we pleafe, is contrary to my experience. That
my body, and this pen and paper, and the
other corporeal objects around me, do really
exift, is to me as evident, as that my foul exifts ; it is indeed fo evident, that nothing is or
can be more fo ; and though my life depended
upon the confequence, I could not bring myfelf to entertain a doubt of it, even for a fingle
moment.

I muft therefore affirm, that the exiftence of
matter can no more be difproved by argument,
than the exiftence of myfelf, or than the truth
of

---

ment par impreffion. Or nous ne devons fuivre dans nos jugemens
libres que la lumiere et l'evidence ; et fi nous nous laiffons conduire
à l'impreffion fenfible, nous nous tromperons prefque toujours.
Tom. 3. *p.* 39.—*La foi* I tranflate *The faith*, becaufe I fuppofe the
author to mean the *Chriftian* or *Catholic faith.* If we take it to denote *faith* or *belief in general* I know not how we fhall make any
fenfe of the paffage.

of a felf-evident axiom in geometry. To argue againſt it, is to fet reaſon in oppoſition to
common fenſe ; which is indirectly to ſubvert
the foundation of all juſt reaſoning, and to call
in queſtion the diſtinction between truth and
falſehood. We are told, however, that a great
philoſopher has actually demonſtrated, *that matter does not exiſt.* Demonſtrated! truly this is
a piece of ſtrange information. At this rate,
any falſehood may be proved to be true, and
any truth to be falſe. For it is impoſſible,
that any truth ſhould be more evident to me
than this, *that matter does exiſt.* Let us ſce, however, what BERKELEY has to ſay in behalf of this
extraordinary doctrine. It is natural for demonſtration, and for all found reaſoning, to
produce conviction, or at leaſt ſome degree of
aſſent, in the perſon who attends to it, and
underſtands it. I read *The Principles of Human
Knowledge,* together with *The Dialogues between
Hylas and Phylonous.* The arguments, I confeſs,
are ſubtle, and well adapted to the purpoſe of
puzzling and confounding. Perhaps I will not
undertake to confute them. Perhaps I am bu-
ſy, or indolent, or unacquainted with the principles of this philoſophy, or little verſed in your
metaphyſical logic. But am I convinced, from
this pretended demonſtration, that matter has
no exiſtence but as an idea in the mind ? Not in
the leaſt ; my belief now is preciſely the ſame
as before.——Is it unphiloſophical, not to be convinced by arguments which I am not able to
confute ? Perhaps it may, but I cannot help
it : you may, if you pleaſe, ſtrike me off the
liſt of philoſophers, as a nonconformiſt ; you
                                            may

may call me unpliant, unreaſonable, unfaſhion-
able, and a man with whom it is not worth
while to argue : but till the frame of my nature
be unhinged, and a new ſet of faculties given
me, I cannot believe this ſtrange doɛtrine, becauſe it is perfeɛtly incredible.   But if I were
permitted to propoſe one clowniſh queſtion, I
would fain aſk, Where is the harm of my con-
tinuing in my old opinion, and believing, with
the reſt of the world, that I am not the only
created being in the univerſe, but that there
are many others, whoſe exiſtence is as independent on me, as mine is on them? Where is
the harm of my believing, that if I were to fall
down yonder precipice, and break my neck, I
ſhould be no more a man of this world? My
neck, Sir, may be an idea to you, but to me
it is a reality, and an important one too.   Where
is the harm of my believing, that if in this ſe ·
vere weather, I were to negleɛt to throw (what
you call) the idea of a coat over the ideas of my
ſhoulders, the idea of cold would produce the
idea of ſuch pain and diſorder as might poſſibly
terminate in my real death? What great offence
ſhall I commit againſt God or man, church or
ſtate, philoſophy or common ſenſe, if I continue to believe, that material food will nouriſh
me, though the idea of it will not: that the
real ſun will warm and enlighten me, though
the livelieſt idea of him will do neither; and
that, if I would obtain true peace of mind and
ſelf-approbation, I muſt not only form ideas of
compaſſion, juſtice, and generoſity, but alſo
really exert thoſe virtues in external performance? What harm is there in all this?—O ! no
harm

harm at all, Sir;—but—the truth,—the truth,
—will you ſhut your eyes againſt the truth ?
—No honeſt man ever will : convince me that
your doctrine is true, and I will inſtantly em-
brace it.—Have I not convinced thee, thou ob-
ſtinate, unaccountable, inexorable———; Anſwer my arguments, if thou canſt.—Alas, Sir,
you have given me arguments in abundance,
but you have not given me conviction; and if
your arguments produce no conviction, they
are worth nothing to me.   They are like coun-
terfeit bank-bills; ſome of which are ſo dexterouſly forged, that neither your eye nor mine
can detect them; yet a thouſand of them would
go for nothing at the bank; and even the pa-
per-maker would allow me more handſomely for
old rags.   You need not give yourſelf the trouble to tell me, that I ought to be convinced : I
ought to be convinced only when I feel conviction : when I feel no conviction I ought not to
be convinced.—It has been obſerved of ſome
doctrines and reaſonings, that their extreme
abſurdity prevents their admitting a rational
confutation.   What! am I to believe ſuch a
doctrine? am I to be convinced by ſuch reaſoning? Now, I never heard of any doctrine more
ſcandalouſly abſurd, than this of the non-exiſtence of matter.   There is not a fiction in the
Perſian Tales that I could not as eaſily believe;
the ſillieſt conceit of the moſt contemptible ſu-
perſtition that ever diſgraced human nature, is
not more ſhocking to common ſenſe, nor more
repugnant to every principle of human belief.
And muſt I admit this jargon for truth, becauſe
I cannot confute the arguments of a man who
is

is a more fubtle difputant than I? Does philofophy require this of me? Then it muft fuppofe,
that truth is as variable as the fancies, the characters, and the intellectual abilities of men, and
that there is no fuch thing in nature as common
fenfe.

But all this, I fhall perhaps be told, is but
cavil and declamation.   What if, after all, this
very doctrine be believed, and the fophiftry (as
you call it) of BERKELEY be admitted as found
reafoning, and legitimate proof? What then
becomes of your common fenfe, and your inftinctive convictions?—What then, do you afk?
Then indeed I acknowledge the fact to be very
extraordinary; and I cannot help being in fome
pain about the confequences, which muft be important and fatal.   If a man, out of vanity, or
from a defire of being in the fafhion; or in order to pafs for wonderfully wife, fhall fay, that
BERKELEY's doctrine is true, while, at the fame
time his belief is precifely the fame with mine, it is
well; I leave him to enjoy the fruits of his hypocrify, which will no doubt contribute mightily to his
improvement in candour, happinefs, and wifdom.
If a man profeffing this doctrine, act like other men
in common affairs of life, I will not believe his profeffion to be fincere.   For this doctrine, by removing body out of the univerfe, makes a total change
in the circumftances of men; and therefore, if it is
not merely verbal, muft produce a total change in
their conduct.   When a man is only turned out of
his houfe, or ftripped of his cloaths, or robbed of
his money, he muft change his behaviour, and act
differently from other men, who enjoy thofe advantages.   Perfuade a man that he is a beggar and a
                                        vagabond

vagabond, and you ſhall inſtantly ſee him change his manners. If your arguments againſt the exiſtence of matter have ever carried conviction along with them, they muſt at the ſame time have produced a much more extraordinary change of conduct; but if they have produced no change of conduct, I inſiſt on it, they have never carried conviction along with them, whatever vehemence of proteſtation men may have uſed in avowing ſuch conviction. If you ſay, that though a man's underſtanding be convinced, there are certain inſtincts in his nature that will not permit him to alter his conduct; or, if he did, the reſt of the world would account him a mad-man; by the firſt apology, you allow the belief of the non-exiſtence of body to be inconſiſtent with the laws of nature; by the ſecond, to be inconſiſtent with common ſenſe.

But if a man be convinced, that matter has no exiſtence, and believe this ſtrange tenet as ſteadily, and with as little diſtruſt, as I believe the contrary; he will, I am afraid, have but little reaſon to applaud himſelf on this new acquiſition in ſcience; he will ſoon find, it had been better for him to have reaſoned, and believed, and acted, like the reſt of the world. If he fall down a precipice, or be trampled under foot by horſes, it will avail him little, that he once had the honour to be a diſciple of Berkeley, and to believe that thoſe dangerous objects are nothing but ideas in the mind. And yet, if ſuch a man be ſeen to avoid a precipice, or to get out of the way of a coach and ſix horſes at full ſpeed, he acts as inconſiſtently with his belief, as if he ran away from the picture of an angry man, even while he believed it to be a picture. Suppoſing

his

his life preſerved by the care of friends, or by
the ſtrength of natural inſtinct urging him to
act contrary to his belief; yet will this belief
coſt him dear, For if the plaineſt evidence,
and fulleſt conviction, be certainly fallacious, I
beg to be informed, what kind of evidence,
and what degree of conviction, may reaſonably
be depended on. If nature be a juggler by
trade, is it for us, poor purblind reptiles to attempt to penetrate the myſteries of her art, and
take upon us to decide, when it is ſhe preſents a
true, and when a falſe appearance! I will not ſay,
however, that this man runs a greater riſk of univerſal ſcepticiſm, than of univerſal credulity.
Either the one or the other, or both, muſt be his
portion ; and either the one or the other would
be ſufficient to imbitter my whole life, and to
diſqualify me for every duty of a rational creature. He who can believe againſt common
ſenſe, and againſt the cleareſt evidence, and a-
gainſt the fulleſt conviction, in any one caſe,
may do the ſame in any other; conſequently he
may become the dupe of every wrangler who is
more acute than he ; and then, if he is entirely ſe-
cluded from mankind, his liberty, and happineſs,
are gone for ever. Indeed a chearful temper, ſtrong
habits of virtue, and the company of the wiſe
and good, may ſtill ſave him from perdition, if he
have no temptations nor difficulties to encounter.
But it is the end of every uſeful art, to teach us to
ſurmount difficulties, not to diſqualify us for attempting them. Men have been known to live many years in a warm chamber, after they were become too delicate to bear the open air; but who will
ſay, that ſuch a habit of body is deſireable ? what
                                    phyſician

phyfician will recommend to the healthy fuch a regimen as would produce it.

But, that I may no longer fuppofe, what I maintain to be impoffible, that mankind in general, or even one rational being, could, by force of argument, be convinced, that this doctrine is true;— what if all men were in one inftant deprived of their underftanding by almighty power, and made to believe, that matter has no exiftence but as an idea in the mind, all other earthly things remaining as they are?---Doubtlefs this cataftrophe would, according to our metaphyficians, throw a wonderful light on all the parts of knowledge. I pretend not even to guefs at the number, extent, or quality, of aftonifhing difcoveries that would then ftart forth into view. But of this I am certain, that, in lefs than a month after, there could not, without another miracle, be one human creature alive on the face of the earth*.

BERKELEY forefaw, and has done what he could to obviate *fome* of thefe objections. There are two points which he has taken great pains to prove. The firft is, That his fyftem differs not from the belief of the reft of mankind; the fecond, That our conduct cannot be in the leaft affected by our difbelief of the exiftence of a material world.

1. As

---

* This, I think, muft follow, if we allow that our external fenfes are neceffary to our prefervation. And I do not fee how that can be denied. A blind or deaf man may live not uncomfortably in the fociety of thofe who fee or hear; but if all mankind were blind and deaf, or deprived of their reafon fo as to difbelieve their eyes and ears, and other percipient faculties, I know not how human life could be preferved without a miracle.

1. As to the firft, it is certainly falfe.   Mr.
HUME himfelf feems willing to give it up.   I
have known many who could not anfwer BERKE-
LEY's arguments; I never knew one who believed his doctrine.   I have mentioned it to fome
who were unacquainted with philofophy, and
therefore could not be fuppofed to have any
bias in favour of either fyftem; they all treated
it as moft contemptible jargon, and what no
man in his fenfes ever did or could believe.   I
have carefully attended to the effects produced
by it upon my own mind; and it appears to me
at this moment, as when I firft heard it, incredible and incomprehenfible: for though, by
reading it over and over, I have got a fet of
phrafes and arguments by heart, which would
enable me, if I were fo difpofed, to talk, and argue, and write, " about it and about it;" yet,
when I lay fyftems and fyllogifms afide, when I
enter on any part of the bufinefs of life, or when
I refer the matter to the unbiaffed decifion of
my own mind, I plainly fee, that I had no diftinct meaning to my words when I faid, that the
material world has no exiftence but in the mind
that perceives it.   In a word, if this author had
afferted, that I and all mankind acknowledge
and believe the *Arabian Nights Entertain-*
ment to be a true hiftory, I could not have had
any better reafon for contradicting that affertion,
than I have for contradicting this, " That
" BERKELEY's principles in regard to the exift-
" ence of matter, differ not from the belief of
" the reft of mankind."

2. In behalf of the fecond point he argues,
" That nothing gives us an intereft in the ma-
" terial

" terial world, except the feelings pleasant or
" painful which accompany our perceptions;
" that these perceptions are the same, whether
" we believe the material world to exist or not
" to exist; consequently, that our pleasant or
" painful feelings are also the same; and there-
" fore, that our conduct, which depends on our
" feelings and perceptions, must be the same
" whether we believe or disbelieve the existence
" of matter."

But if it be certain, that by the law of our nature we are unavoidably determined to believe
that matter exists, and to act upon this belief,
(and nothing, I think, is more certain), how can
it be imagined, that a contrary belief would produce no alteration in our conduct and sentiments? Surely the laws of nature are not such
trifles, as that it should be a matter of perfect
indifference, whether we act and think agreeably
to them or not? I believe that matter exists;---
I must believe that matter exists;---I must continually act upon this belief; such is the law of
my constitution. Suppose my constitution changed in this respect, all other things remaining as
they are;---would there then be no change in
my sentiments and conduct? If there would
not, then is this law of nature, in the first place,
useless, because men could do as well without
it; secondly, inconvenient, because its end is to
keep us ignorant of the truth; and, thirdly, absurd, because insufficient for answering its end,
the Bishop of Cloyne, and others, having, it
seems, discovered the truth in spite of it. Is this
according to the usual economy of Nature?
Does this language become her servants and
                                   interpreters?

interpreters? Is it poffible to devife any fentiments or maxims more fubverfive of truth,
and more repugnant to the fpirit of true philofophy?

Further: All external objects have fome qualities in common; but between an external object and an idea, or thought of the mind, there
is not, there cannot poffibly be, any refemblance. A grain of fand, and the globe of the
earth; a burning coal, and a lump of ice; a
drop of ink, and a fheet of white paper refemble each other, in being extended, folid, figured,
coloured, and divifible; but a thought or idea
has no extenfion, folidity, figure, colour, nor
divifibility: fo that no two external objects can
be fo unlike, as an external object and (what
philofophers call) the idea of it. Now we are
taught by BERKELEY, that external objects
(that is, the things we take for external objects) are nothing but ideas in our minds; in
other words, that they are in every refpect different from what they appear to be. This candle, it feems, hath not one of thofe qualities it
appears to have: it is not white, nor luminous,
nor round, nor divifible, nor extended; for to
an idea of the mind, not one of thefe qualities
can poffibly belong. How then fhall I know
what it really is? From what it feems to be, I
can conclude nothing; no more than a blind
man, by handling a bit of black wax, can judge
of the colour of fnow, or the vifible appearance of the ftarry heavens. The candle may be
an Egyptian pyramid, the King of Pruffia, a
mad dog, or nothing at all: it may be the
ifland of Madagafcar, Saturn's ring, or one of

the Pleiades, for any thing I know, or can e-
ver know, to the contrary, except you allow me
to judge of its nature from its appearance;
which, however, I cannot reasonably do, if its
appearance and nature are in every respect so
different and unlike as not to have one single
quality in common.   I must therefore believe it
to be, what it appears to be, a real, corporeal,
external object, and so reject BERKELEY's system; or I never can, with any shadow of reason, believe any thing whatsoever concerning it.
—Will it yet be said, that the belief of this system cannot in the least affect our sentiments
and conduct?   With equal truth may it be
said, that Newton's conduct and sentiments
would not have been in the least affected by
his being metamorphosed into an ideot, or a
pillar of salt.

Some readers may perhaps be dissatisfied with
this reasoning on account of the ambiguity of
the words *external object* and *idea*, which, however, the assertors of the non-existence of matter have not as yet fully explained.   Others
may think that I must have misunderstood the
author; for that he was too acute a logician
to leave his system exposed to objections so decisive, and so obvious.   To gratify such readers, I will not insist on these objections.——
That I may have misunderstood the author's doctrine, is not only possible, but highly probable; nay, I have reason to think, that it was
not perfectly understood even by himself.   For
did not BERKELEY write his *Principles of human
Knowledge*, with this express view, (which does
him great honour), to banish scepticism both
from

from fcience and from religion ? Was he not fanguine in the hope of fuccefs ? And has not the event proved, that he was egregiously mif-taken ? For is it not evident, from the ufe to which other authors have applied it, that his fyftem leads to Atheifm and univerfal fcepti-cifm ? And if a machine difappoint its inventor fo far as to produce effects contrary to thofe he wifhed, intended, and expected; may we not, without breach of charity, conclude, that he did not perfectly underftand his plan ? At any rate, it appears from this fact, that our author did not forefee all the objections to which his theory is liable. He did not forefee, that it might be made the foundation of a fceptical fyftem: if he had, we know he would have re-nounced it with abhorrence.

This one objection, therefore (in which I think I cannot be miftaken), will fully anfwer my prefent purpofe: Our author's doctrine is contrary to common belief, and leads to uni-verfal fcepticifm. Suppofe it, then, univerfally and ferioufly adopted ; fuppofe all men divefted of all belief, and confequently of all prin-ciple: would not the diffolution of fociety, and the deftruction of mankind, neceffarily enfue ?

Still I fhall be told that BERKELEY was a good man, and that his principles did him no hurt. I allow it; he was indeed a moft excellent per-fon ; none can revere his memory more than I. But does it appear, that he ever acted according to his principles, or that he thoroughly under-ftood them ? Does it appear, that if he had put them in practice, no hurt would have enfued to

Q 2   himfelf,

himſelf*, or to ſociety? Does it appear, that he was a ſceptic, or a friend to ſcepticiſm? Does it appear, that men may adopt his principles without danger of becoming ſceptics? The contrary of all this appears with uncontrovertible evidence.

Surely pride was not made for man. The moſt exalted genius may find in himſelf many affecting memorials of human frailty, and ſuch as often render him an object of compaſſion to thoſe who in virtue and underſtanding are far inferior. I pity BERKELEY's weakneſs in patroniſing an abſurd and dangerous theory; I doubt not but it may have overcaſt many of his days with a gloom, which neither the approbation of his conſcience, nor the natural ſerenity of his temper, could entirely diſſipate. And though I were to believe, that he was intoxicated with this theory, and rejoiced in it; yet ſtill I ſhould pity the intoxication as a weakneſs: for candour will not permit me to give it a harſher name; as I ſee in his other writings, and know by the teſtimony of his contemporaries, particularly

* Let it not be pretended, that a man may diſbelieve his ſenſes without danger of inconvenience. Pyrrho (as we read in Diogenes Laertius) profeſſed to diſbelieve his ſenſes, and to be in no apprehenſion from any of the objects that affected them. The appearance of a precipice or wild beaſt was nothing to Pyrrho; at leaſt he ſaid ſo: he would not avoid them; he knew they were nothing at all, or at leaſt they were not what they ſeemed to be. Suppoſe him to have been in earneſt; and ſuppoſe his keepers to have in earneſt adopted the ſame principles: would not their limbs and lives have been in as great danger, as the limbs and life of a blind and deaf man wandering by himſelf in a ſolitary place, with his hands tied behind his back? I would as ſoon ſay, that our ſenſes are uſeleſs faculties, as that we might diſbelieve them without danger of inconvenience.

larly Pope and Swift, that he was a friend to virtue, and to human nature.

We muſt not ſuppoſe a falſe doctrine harm-leſs, merely becauſe it has not been able to corrupt the heart of a good man. Nor, becauſe a few ſceptics have not authority to render ſci-ence contemptible, nor power to overturn ſoci-ety, muſt we ſuppoſe, that therefore ſcepticiſm is not dangerous to ſcience or mankind. The effects of a general ſcepticiſm would be dreadful and fatal. We muſt therefore, notwithſtanding our reverence for the character of BERKELEY, be permitted to affirm, that we have ſufficient-ly proved, that his doctrine is ſubverſive of man's moſt important intereſts, as a moral, intelligent, and percipient being.

After all, though I were to grant, that the diſbelief of the exiſtence of matter could not pro-duce any conſiderable change in our principles of action and reaſoning, the reader will find in the ſequel *, that the point I have chiefly in view would not be much affected even by that conceſſion. 1 ſay not this, as being diffident or ſceptical in regard to what I have advanced on the preſent ſubject. Doctrines which I do not believe, I will never recommend to others. I am abſolutely certain, that to me the belief of BERKELEY's ſyſtem would be attended with the moſt fatal conſequences ; and that it would be equally dangerous to the reſt of mankind, I can-not doubt, ſo long as I believe their nature and mine to be the ſame.

Q 3

Though

* Part 2. chap. 3.

Though it be abfurd to attempt a proof of what is felf-evident, it is manly and meritorious to confute the objections that fophiftry may urge againft it.   This, with refpect to the fubject in queftion, has been done, in a decifive and maf-terly manner, by the learned and fagacious Dr. Reid *; who proves, that the reafonings of BERKELEY, and others, concerning primary and fecondary qualities +, owe all their ftrength to the ambiguity of words.   I have proved, that, though this fundamental error had never been detected, the philofophy of BERKELEY is in its own nature abfurd, becaufe it fuppofes the original principles of common fenfe controvert-ible and fallacious: a fuppofition repugnant to the genius of true philofophy; and which leads to univerfal credulity, or univerfal fcepticifm; and, confequently, to the fubverfion of all know-ledge and virtue.

It is proper, before we proceed to the next inftance, to make a remark or two on what has been faid.

1. Here we have an inftance of a doctrine advanced by fome philofophers, in direct con-tradiction

_____

* Inquiry into the Human Mind on the Principles of Com-mon Senfe,

+ DES CARTES, LOCKE, and BERKELEY, fuppofe, that what we call *a body* is nothing but a collection of qualities; and thefe they divide into *primary* and *fecondary*.   Of the former kind are magnitude, extenfion, folidity, &c. which LOCKE and the CAR-TESIANS allow to belong to bodies at all times, whether perceived or not.   Of the latter kind are the *heat* of fire, the *fmell* and *tafte* of a rofe, &c. and thefe, by the fame authors, and by BERKELEY, are faid to exift, not in the bodies themfelves, but only in the mind that perceives them: an error they are led into by fuppofing, that the words *heat*, *tafte*, *fmell*, &c. fignify nothing but *a percep-*
tion;

tradiction to the general belief of all men in all ages.

2. The reasoning by which it is supported, though long accounted unanswerable, did never produce a serious and steady conviction. Common sense still declared the doctrine to be false ; we were sorry to find the powers of human reason so limited, as not to afford a logical confutation of it ; we were convinced it merited confutation, and flattered ourselves, that one time or other it would be confuted.

3. The real and general belief of this doctrine would be attended with fatal consequences to science, and to human nature ; for this is a doctrine according to which a man could not act nor reason in the common affairs of life, without incurring the charge of insanity or folly, and involving himself in distress and perdition.

2. An ingenious man, from a sense of the bad tendency of this doctrine, applies himself to examine the principles on which it is founded ; discovers them to be erroneous ; and proves, to the full conviction of competent judges, that from beginning to end it is all a mystery of falsehood, arising from the use of ambiguous words, and from the gratuitous admission of

principles

---

tion ; whereas we have formerly shown, that they also signify *an external thing*. BERKELEY, following the hints which he found in DES CARTES, MALEBRANCHE and LOCKE, has applied the same mode of reasoning to prove, that primary, as well as secondary qualities, have no external existence ; and consequently, that body (which consists of these two classes of qualities, and nothing else)exists only as an idea in the mind that perceives it, and exists no longer than while it is perceived.

principles which never could have been admitted if they had been thoroughly underftood.

S E C T. III.

Of Liberty and Neceffity.

THE fecond inftance to which I purpofe to apply the principles of this difcourfe, by fhowing the danger of carrying any inveftigation beyond the dictates of common fenfe, is no other than the celebrated queftion concerning liberty and neceffity ; a queftion on which many things have been faid, and fome things, I prefume, to little purpofe. To enter into all the particulars of this controverfy, is foreign to my prefent defign ; and I would not wifh to add to a difpute already too bulky. My intention is, to treat the doctrine of neceffity as I treated that of the non-exiftence of matter ; by enquiring, whether the one be not, as well as the other, contrary to common fenfe, and therefore abfurd,

1. That certain intentions and actions are in themfelves, and previous to all confideration of their confequences, good, laudable, and meritorious ; and that other actions and intentions are bad, blameable, and worthy of punifhment, —has been felt and acknowledged by all reafonable creatures in all ages and nations. We need not wonder at the univerfality of this fentiment : it is as natural to the human conftitution, as
the

the faculties of hearing, feeing, and memory; it is as clear, unequivocal, and affecting, as any intimation from any fenfe external or internal.

2. That we cannot do fome things, but have it in our power to do others, is what no man in his fenfes will hefitate to affirm. I can take up my ftaff from the ground, but I cannot lift a ftone of a thoufand weight. On a common, I may walk fouthward or northward, eaftward, or weftward; but I cannot afcend to the clouds, nor fink downward to the centre of the earth. Juft now I have power to think of an abfent friend, of the Peak of Teneriffe, of a paffage in Homer, or of the death of Charles I. When a man afks me a queftion, I have it in my power to anfwer or be filent, to anfwer foftly or roughly, in terms of refpect or in terms of contempt. Frequent temptations to vice fall in my way; I may yield, or I may refift: if I refift, I applaud myfelf, becaufe I am confcious it was in my power to do otherwife; if I yield, I am filled with fhame and remorfe, for having neglected to do what I might have done, and ought to have done. My liberty in thefe inftances I cannot prove by argument; but there is not a truth in geometry of which I am more certain.

Is not this doctrine fufficiently obvious? Muft I quote Epictetus, or any other ancient author, to prove that men were of the fame opinion in former times? No idea occurs more frequently in my reading and converfation, than that of *power* or *agency*; and I think I underftand my own meaning as well when I fpeak of it as
when

when I fpeak of any thing elfe. But this idea
has had the misfortune to come under the examination of a certain author, who, according
to cuftom, has found means fo to darken and
disfigure it, that, till we have cleared it of his
mifreprefentations, we cannot proceed any further in the prefent fubject. And we are the
more inclined to digrefs on this occafion, becaufe he has made his theory of power the
ground of fome Atheiftical inferences, which
we fhould not fcruple at any time to ftep out of
our way to overturn.—Perhaps thefe frequent
digreffions are offenfive to the reader : they are
equally fo to the writer. To remove rubbifh
is neither an elegant nor a pleafant work, but
it is often neceffary. It is peculiarly neceffary
in the philofophy of human nature. The road
to moral truth has been left in fuch a plight by
fome modern projectors, that a man of honefty and plain fenfe muft either, with great labour and lofs of time, delve his way through,
or be fwallowed up in a quagmire. The metaphyfician advances more eafily. His levity, perhaps, enables him, like Camilla in Virgil, to
fkim along the furface without finking ; or perhaps, the extreme fubtlety of his genius can,
like Satan in Paradife Loft, penetrate this chaos,
without being much incumbered or retarded in
his progrefs. But men of ordinary talents have
not thofe advantages, and muft therefore be allowed to flounce along, though with no very
graceful motion, the beft way they can.

  All ideas, according to Mr. HUME's fundamental hypothefis, are derived from and reprefent impreffions : But we have never any impreffion

preffion that contains any power or efficacy:
We never, therefore, have any idea of power *.
In proof of the minor propofition of this fyllogifm, he remarks, That " when we think we
" perceive our mind acting on matter, or one
" piece of matter acting upon another, we do
" in fact, perceive only two objects or events
" contiguous and fucceffive, the fecond of
" which is always found in experience to fol-
" low the firft; but that we never perceive, ei-
" ther by external fenfe, or by confcioufnefs,
" that power, energy, or efficacy, which con-
" nects the one event with the other. By ob-
" ferving that the two events do always accom-
" pany each other, the imagination acquires a
" habit of going readily from the firft to the
" fecond, and from the fecond to the firft;
" and hence we are led to conceive a kind of
" neceffary connection between them. But in
" fact there is neither neceffity nor power in
" the objects we confider, but only in the mind
" that confiders them; and even in the mind,
" this power of neceffity is nothing but a de-
" termination of the fancy, acquired by habit,
" to pafs from the idea of an object to that of
" its ufual attendant †."——So that what we
call the efficacy of a caufe to produce an effect,
is neither in the caufe nor in the effect, but
only in the imagination, which has contracted
a habit of paffing from the object called the
caufe, to the object called the effect, and thus
affociating them together.   Has the fire a power

* Treatife of Human Nature, vol. 1. p. 282.
† Ibid. p. 272.---300.

er to melt lead? No; but the fancy is determined by habit to pafs from the idea of fire to
that of melted lead, on account of our having
always perceived them contiguous and fucceffive;---and this is the whole matter.   Have I
a power to move my arm ? No; the volition
that precedes the motion of my arm has no connection with that motion ; but the motion having been always obferved to follow the volition,
comes to be affociated with it in the fancy;
and what we call the power, or neceffary connection, has nothing to do, either with the volition, or with the motion, but is merely a determination of my fancy, or your fancy, or any
body's fancy, to affociate the idea or impreffion
of my volition with the impreffion or idea of
the motion of my arm.---I am forry I cannot
exprefs myfelf more clearly; but I fhould not
do juftice to my author, if I did not imitate his
language on the prefent occafion: plain words
will never do, when one has an unintelligible
doctrine to fupport.

    What fhall we fay to this collection of ftrange
phrafes ? or what name fhall we give it ? Shall
we call it a moft ingenious difcovery, illuftrated by a moft ingenious argument? This would
be complimenting the author at a very great expence ; for this would imply, not only that he
is the wifeft of mortal men, but alfo that he is
the only individual of that fpecies of animals who
is not a fool.   Certain it is, that all men have
in all ages talked, and argued, and acted, from
a perfuafion that they had a very diftinct notion of power. If our author can prove, that
they had no fuch notion, he can alfo prove,
                                    that

that all human difcourfe is nonfenfe, all human
actions abfurdity, and all human compofitions
(his own not excepted) words without meaning.
The boldnefs of his theory will, however, pafs
with many, for a proof of its being ingenious.
Be it fo, Gentlemen, I difpute not about epithets; if you will have it, that genius confifteth
in the art of putting words together fo as to
form abfurd propofitions, I have nothing more
to fay. Others will admire this doctrine, becaufe the words by which the author means to
illuftrate and prove it, if printed on a good paper and with an elegant type, would of themfelves make a pretty fizeable volume. It were
pity to deprive thefe people of the pleafure of
admiring; otherwife I might tell them, that nothing is more eafy than this method of compofition; for that I would undertake, at a very
fhort warning, (if it could be done innocently,
and without prejudice to my health), to write as
many pages, with equal appearance of reafon
and argument, and with equal advantage to
philofophy and mankind, in vindication of any
given abfurdity; provided only, that (like the
abfurdity in queftion) it were expreffed in words
of which one at leaft is ambiguous.

In truth, I am fo little difpofed to admire
this extraordinary paradox, that nothing could
make me believe its author to have been in
earneft, if I had not found him drawing inferences from it too ferious to be jefted with by
any perfon who is not abfolutely diftracted. It
is one of Mr. Hume's maxims, " That we can
" never have reafon to believe, that any object,
" or quality of an object, exifts, of which we
                          " cannot

" cannot form an idea *." But, according to
this aftonifhing theory of power, and caufation, " we have *no idea* of power, nor of a be-
" ing endowed with any power, MUCH LESS of
" one endowed with infinite power †." The
inference is but too glaring; and though our author does not plainly and avowedly exprefs it,
he once and again puts his reader in mind, that
this inference, or fomething very like it, is deducible from his theory ‡ :—for which, no
doubt, every friend to truth, virtue, and human nature, is infinitely obliged to him!

But what do you fay in oppofition to my theory? You affect to treat it with a contempt
which hardly becomes you, and which my philofophy has not met with from your betters!
pray let us hear your arguments.—And do you,
Sir, really think it incumbent on me to prove
by argument, that I, and all other men, have
a notion of power; and that the efficacy of a
caufe (of fire, for inftance, to melt lead) is in
the caufe, and not in my mind? Would you
think it incumbent on me to confute you with
arguments, if you were pleafed to affirm, that
all men have tails and cloven feet; and that it
was I who produced the earthquake that def-
troyed Lifbon, the plague that depopulates
Conftantinople, the heat that fcorches the wilds
of Africa, and the cold that freezes the Hyper-
borean ocean? Truly, Sir, I have not the face
to undertake a direct confutation of what I do

not

---

* Treatife of Human Nature, vol. 1. p. 302.
† Ibid. p. 432.
‡ Ibid. p. 284. 291. &c.

not underftand; and I am fo far from compre-
hending this part of your fyftem, that I will
venture to pronounce it perfectly unintelligible.
I know there are fome who fay they underftand it; but I alfo know, that there are fome
who fpeak, and read, and write too, with very
little expence of thought.

Thefe are all but evafions, you exclaim; and
infift on my coming to the point.   Never fear,
Sir; I am too deeply interefted in fome of the
confequences of this theory of yours, to put
you off with evafions.   To come therefore to the
point, I fhall firft ftate your doctrine in your
own words, that there may be no rifk of mifreprefentation; and then, if I fhould not be able
directly to prove it falfe, (for the reafon already
given), I fhall demonftrate, *indirectly* at leaft,
or by the apagogical method, that it is not, and
cannot be true.

" As the neceffity," fays our author " which
" makes two times two equal to four, or three
" angles of a triangle equal to two right ones,
" lies only in the act of the underftanding, by
" which we confider and compare thefe ideas*;
" in like manner, the neceffity or power which
" unites caufes and effects, lies in the determi-
" nation of the mind to pafs from the one to
" the other.   The efficacy, or energy, of caufes,
" is neither placed in the caufes themfelves, nor
                                              " in

---

* What! is it an act of my underftanding that makes two and
two equal to four! Was it not fo before I was born, and would
it not be fo though all intelligence were to ceafe throughout the
univerfe!---But it is idle to fpend time in confuting what every
child who has learned the very firft elements of fcience, knows to
be abfurd.

" in the Deity, nor in the concurrence of thefe
" two principles; but belongs entirely to the
" foul, which confiders the union of two or more
" objects in all paft inftances.　It is here that
" the real power of caufes is placed, along with
" their connection and neceffity*."

To find that his principles lead to Atheifm,
would ftagger an ordinary philofopher, and
make him fufpect his fundamental hypothefis,
and all his fubfequent reafonings.　But the author now quoted is not apt to be ftaggered by
confiderations of this kind.　On the contrary,
he is fo intoxicated with his difcovery, that,
however fceptical in other points, he feems
willing to admit this as one certain conclu-
fion†.

If a man can reconcile himfelf to Atheifm,
which is the greateft of all abfurdities, I fear I
fhall hardly put him out of conceit with his
doctrine,

---

* Treatife of Human Nature, vol. 1. p. 291.

† Speaking of it in another place, he fays, " A conclufion
" which is fomewhat extraordinary, but which feems founded on
" fufficient evidence.　Nor will its evidence be weakened by any
" general diffidence of the underftanding, or fceptical fufpicion,
" concerning every conclufion which is new and extraordinary.
" No conclufions can be more agreeable to fcepticifm than fuch
" as make difcoveries concerning the weaknefs and narrow limits
" of human reafon and capacity."

Hume's Effays, vol. 2. p. 87. edit. 1767.

I know not what difcoveries this conclufion may lead others to
make concerning our author's reafon and capacity; but I have
fome ground to think, that in him it has not wrought any extraordinary felf-abafement; otherwife he would not have afferted,
with fo much confidence, what he acknowledges to be a *moft violent paradox*, and what is indeed contrary to the experience and conviction of every perfon of common fenfe.　See *Treatife of Human
Nature, vol. 1. p. 291. 299.*

doctrine, when I show him, that other lefs e-
normous abfurdities are implied in it.   We may
make the trial however.   Gentlemen are fometimes pleafed to entertain unaccountable prejudices againft their Maker; who yet, in other matters, where neither fafhion nor hypothefis interfere, condefcend to acknowledge, that the good
old diftinction between truth and falfehood is not
altogether without foundation.

On the fuppofition that we have no idea of
power or energy, and that the preceding theory of caufation is juft, our author gives the following definition of a caufe; which feems to be
fairly deduced from his theory, and which he
fays is the beft that he can give.   " A caufe is
" an object precedent and contiguous to ano-
" ther, and fo united with it, that the idea of
" the one determines the mind to form the idea
" of the other, and the impreffion of the one to
" form   a   more   lively   idea   of   the   other*."
There are now in my view two contiguous hou-

Vol. I.   R   fes,

---

* Treatife of Human Nature, vol 1. p. 298.   This is not the
only definition of a caufe which Mr. Hume has given.   But his
other definitions are all, in my opinion, inadequate; being all founded on the fame abfurd theory.   My bufinefs, however, at prefent
is, not to criticife Mr. Hume's definitions, but to confute (if I
can) his licentious doctrines.   Thefe will be allowed to be abfurd,
if they be found to lead to abfurd confequences.   So Mr. Hume
himfelf, in another place, very juftly determines: " When any
" opinion leads into abfurdities, it is certainly falfe."   *Effay on
Liberty and Neceffity, part 2.*---The definition of a caufe, here
quoted, is a confequence drawn by Mr. Hume himfelf (and in my
opinion fairly drawn) from his theory of power and caufation.   By
proving that confequence to be abfurd, I prove (according to Mr.
Hume's own rules of logic) the abfurdity of the opinion that leads
to it.   This is all that I mean by quoting it; and this I prefume is
enough.   A doctrine is fufficiently confuted, if it be fhown to lead
into *one abfurdity.*

fes, one of which was built laft fummer, and the other two years ago, By feeing them conftantly together for feveral months, I find, that the idea of the one determines my mind to form the idea of the other, and the impreffion of the one to form a more lively idea of the other. So that, according to our author's definition, the one houfe is the caufe, and the other the effect!—Again, day and night have always been contiguous and fucceffive; the imagination naturally runs from the idea or impreffion of the one to the idea of the other: confequently, according to the fame profound theory and definition, either day is the caufe of night, or night the caufe of day, juft as we confider the one or the other to have been originally prior in time; that is, in other words, light is either the caufe or the effect of darknefs; and its being the one or the other depends entirely on my imagination! Let thofe admire this difcovery who underftand it.

Caufation * implies more than priority and contiguity of the caufe to the effect. This relation cannot be conceived at all, without a fuppofition of power or energy in the caufe†. Let the reader recollect two things that ftand related as caufe and effect; let him contemplate them with a view to this relation; then let him conceive the caufe divefted of all power; and he muft at the fame inftant conceive, that it is a caufe no longer : for a caufe divefted of power, is divefted of that by which it is a caufe.   If a man,

---

* *Caufation* denotes *the relation of caufe and effect*.

† Non fic caufa intelligi debet, ut quod cuique antecedat id ei caufa fit, fed quod cuique *efficienter* antecedat.

Cicero De Fato, cap. 15.

man, after examining his notion of caufation in this manner, is confcious that he has an idea of power, then I fay he has that idea. If all men, in all ages, have ufed the word *power*, or fomething fynonimous to it, and if all men know what they mean when they fpeak of power, I maintain, that all men have a notion, conception, or idea of power, in whatever way they came by it : and I alfo maintain, that no true philofopher ever denied the exiftence or reality of any thing, merely becaufe he could not give an account of its origin, or becaufe the opinion commonly received concerning its origin did not happen to quadrate with its fyftem.

When, therefore, our author fays, that the efficacy or energy of caufes is not placed in the caufes themfelves, he fays neither lefs nor more than this, that what is effential to a caufe is not in a caufe ; or, in other words,---that a caufe is not a caufe.---Are there any perfons who, upon the authority of this theorift, have rafhly adopted Atheiftical principles ? I believe there are fuch. Ye dupes of unmeaning words and incomprehenfible arguments, behold on what a champion ye have placed your confidence ! All the comfort I can give you is, that if it be poffible for the fame thing at the fame time to be and not to be, you may poffibly be in the right.

It follows from what has been faid, that we cannot admit this theory of power and caufation, without admitting, at the fame time, the groffeft and moft impious abfurdities. Is this a fufficient confutation of it ? I think it is. If

any

any perfon think otherwife, I take a fhorter method, and utterly deny all the premiffes from which this ftrange conclufion is fuppofed to refult. I deny the doctrine of impreffions and ideas, as the author has explained it; nay, I have already affirmed, and proved, it to be not only falfe, but unintelligible. And I maintain, that though it could be fhown, that all fimple ideas are derived from impreffions, or intimations of fenfe, it is true, notwithftanding, that all men have an idea of power. They get it by experience, that is, by intimations of fenfe, both external and internal. Their mind acting upon their body gives them this notion or idea; their body acting on other bodies, and acted on by other bodies, gives them the fame idea; which is alfo fuggefted by all the effects and changes they fee produced in the univerfe. So thoroughly are we acquainted with it, that we can, in cafes innumerable, determine, with the utmoft accuracy and certainty, the degree of power neceffary to produce a given effect.

I repeat therefore, that fome things are in our power, and others are not; and that we perfectly underftand our own meaning when we fay fo.—That the reader may not lofe any chain in our reafoning, he will pleafe to look back to the fecond and third paragraphs of this fection.

3. By attending to my own internal feelings, and to the evidence given by other men of theirs, I am fenfible, that I deferve reward or punifhment for thofe actions only which are in my own power. I am no more accountable for the evil which I can neither prevent nor remedy,

dy, than for the deſtruction of Troy, or the plagues of Egypt; and for the good which happens by my means, but againſt my will, I no more deſerve reward or praiſe, than if I were a piece of inanimate matter.

This is the doctrine of common ſenſe; and this doctrine has in all ages been ſupported by ſome of the moſt powerful principles of our nature; by principles which, in the common affairs of life, no man dares ſuppoſe to be equivocal or fallacious. A man may as well tell me that I am blind, or deaf, or that I feel no heat when I approach the fire, as that I have not a natural ſentiment diſpoſing me to blame intentional injury, and to praiſe intentional beneficence; and which makes me feel and be conſcious, that the evil I am compelled to do is not criminal, and that the good I perform againſt my will is not meritorious. That other men are conſcious of the ſame ſentiment, I know with as much certainty as I can know any thing of what paſſes in the minds of other men; for I have daily and hourly opportunities of making obſervations in regard to this very point. The greateſt part of converſation turns upon the morality of human actions; and I never yet heard any perſon ſeriouſly blamed or applauded, by a reaſonable creature, for an action in the performance of which he was not conſidered as a free agent *. The moſt rigid Predeſtinarians

R 3　　　　　　　ſuppoſe

---

* Si omnia fato fiunt, omnia fiunt cauſa antecedente; et, ſi appetitus, illa etiam quæ appetitum ſequuntur: ergo, etiam aſſenſiones. At ſi cauſa appetitus non eſt ſita in nobis, ne ipſe quidem appetitus eſt in noſtra poteſtate. Quod ſi ita eſt, ne illa quidem quæ appetitu efficiuntur ſunt ſita in nobis. Non ſunt igitur, neque aſſenſiones neque actiones, in noſtra poteſtate: *ex quo efficitur,*

suppose freedom of will to be in one way or other confistent with eternal and unconditional decrees : if they cannot explain in what way, —they call it a myftery; it furpaffes their underftanding;—but it muft be fo; for other-wife the morality of actions is altogether inconceivable +. Do the interefts of fcience, or of virtue, fuffer by this reprefentation of the matter? I think not.

But fome philofophers, not fatisfied with this view of it, are for bringing the fentiment of moral liberty to the teft of reafon. They want
to

---

tur, ut nec laudationes juftæ fint, nec vituperationes, nec honores, nec fupplicia. Quod cum vitiofum fit, probabiliter concludi putant, non omnia fato fieri quæcunque fiant.

Cicero, de Fato, cap. 17.

+ The reader, I hope, does not think me fuch a novice in reafoning, as to urge the judgement of the council of Trent in behalf of any doctrine, philofophical or religious. Yet every fact in logic and morality is worth our notice, if we would eftablifh thofe fciences on their only firm foundation, the univerfal confent and practice of mankind. It deferves, therefore, to be remarked, that, at the Reformation, this confcioufnefs of free will was acknowledged, both by the Lutherans, and by the church of Rome, to be a principle of common fenfe, which was to be afcertained, not by reafoning, but by experimental proof. So fays a moft judicious and elegant hiftorian, whofe words are remarkably appofite to the prefent fubject, and to the manner in which we treat it. Speaking of fome articles faid to be maintained by the Lutherans, in oppofition to free-will, the hiftorian informs us, that, in the judgement of many of that celebrated council, the opinion implied in thefe articles, " E empia, e biasfema contra Dio. --- Ch'era una pazzia *contra il* " *fenfo comune, efperimentando ogni buomo la propria libert*ἀ, *che non* " *merita conteftatione, ma, comme Ariftotele dice, o caftigo, o prova* " *efperimentale.* Che i medifimi difcepoli di Luthero s'erano ac-" corti della pazzia; e, moderando l'affordità, differo poi, ef-" fervi libertà nell'huomo in quello, che tocca le attioni le attioni " efterne politiche ed economiche, e quanto ad ogni giuftitia ci-" vile; *le quali e fciocco chi non conofce venir dal confeglio ed ellettio-* " *ne*; reftringendofi a negar la liberta quanto alla fola giuftitia " divina."

Iftoria del Concili Trid. di P. Serpi, lib. 2. *p.* 214. *edit.* 4.

to prove by argument, either that I have, or that I have not, such a feeling : or, if I shall be found to have it, they want to know whether it be fallacious or not. In other words, they want to prove, or to disprove, what I know by inftinct to be unqueftionably certain : or they want to inquire, whether it be reafonable for me to act and think according to a principle, which, by the law of my nature, I cannot contradict, either in thought or in action. Would not the fame fpirit of inquiry lead a geometrician to attempt a proof or confutation of his axioms; a natural philofopher to doubt whether things be what his fenfes reprefent them; an ordinary man to argue concerning the propriety of perceiving colours by the eyes, and odours by the noftrils? Would not the fame fpirit of doubt and difputation, applied to more familiar inftances, transform a philofopher into a madman, and a perfon of plain fenfe into an idiot ?

But let us not be too rigid. If a philofopher muft needs have his rattles and playthings, let him have them : only, for his own fake, and for the fake of the neighbours, I would advife, that edge-tools, and other dangerous inftruments of amufement, be kept out of his reach, If a Cartefian will not, on any account, believe his own exiftence, except I grant him his *Cogito, ergo fum*, far be it from me to deprive the poor man of that confolation. The reafoning indeed is bad, but the principle is good ; and a good principle is fo good a thing, that rather than oblige a man to renounce it, I would difpenfe with the ftrict obfervance of a logical precept.

cept. If a ſtar-gazer cannot ſee the inhabitants
of the moon with one perſpective, let him tie a
ſcore of them together, with all my heart. If
a virtuoſo is inclined to look at the ſun through
a microſcope, and at rotten cheeſe through a te-
leſcope, to apply ear-trumpets to his eyes, and
equip his two ears with as many pair of ſpecta-
cles, he has my full permiſſion; and much good
may it do him. Theſe amuſements are idle, but
they are innocent. The Carteſian, if the truth
were known, would be found neither the better
nor the worſe for his enthymeme. The ſtar-
gazer has not atchieved a ſingle glimpſe of his
lunar friends, but ſees more confuſedly than before: however, he may conſole himſelf with this
reflection, that one may paſs through life, with
the character of a very honeſt and tolerably happy man, though he ſhould never have it in his
power to extend the ſphere of his acquaintance
beyond this ſublunary globe. The virtuoſo
takes a wrong, and indeed a prepoſterous method, for improving his ſight and hearing; but
if he is careful to confine theſe frolics to his private apartment, and never boaſt in public of his
auditory, or optical apparatus, he may live com-
fortably and reſpectably enough, though he
ſhould never ſee the ſpots in the ſun, nor the
briſtles on a mite's back.

I would, however, earneſtly exhort my friend
the metaphyſician, to believe himſelf a free agent
upon the bare authority of his feelings, and not
to imagine that Nature is ſuch a bungler in her
trade, as firſt to intend to impoſe upon him,
and then inadvertently give him ſagacity to ſee
through the impoſture. Indeed, if it were a
matter

matter of indifference, whether we believe our moral feelings or difbelieve them, I fhould not object to the ufe of a little unbelief now and then, by way of experiment or cordial, provided it were a thing that a reafonable man could take any pleafure in.   But I am convinced, that habitual dram-drinking is not more pernicious to our animal nature, than habitual fcepticifm to our rational.   And when once this fcepticifm comes to affect our moral fentiments, or active principles, all is over with us: we are in the condition of a man intoxicated; fit only for raving, dozing, and doing mifchief.

But alas! the metaphyfician is too headftrong to follow my advice.   It would be a fine thing, indeed, fays he, if gentlemen were to yield to the dictates of nature.   Is there a fingle dictate of nature to which people of fafhion now-a-days pay any regard? No, no; the world is grown wifer.   As to this fentiment of moral liberty, I very much queftion its title to be ranked with the dictates of nature.   It feems to be a piece of vile fophiftication, a paltry prejudice, hatched by the nurfe, and foftered by the prieft.   I am determined to take it roundly to tafk, and examine its pretenfions with the eye of a philofopher and free-thinker.---Very well, Sir, you may take your own way; it requires no fkill in magic to be able to foretell the confequence. A traveller no fooner quits the right road, on fuppofition of its being wrong, than he gets into one that is really fo. If you fet out in your inquiry, with fufpecting the principles of common fenfe to be erroneous, you have little chance of falling in with any other principles that are not erroneous.

The

The refult of the metaphyfical inquiry is as
follows. " Every human action muft proceed
" from fome motive as its caufe. The motive
" or caufe muft be fufficient to produce the ac-
" tion or effect; otherwife it is no motive:
" and, if fufficient to produce it, muft necelfa-
" rily produce it; for every effect proceeds ne-
" ceffarily from its caufe, as heat neceffarily
" proceeds from fire. Now, the immediate
" caufes of action are volitions, or energies of
" the will: thefe arife neceffarily from paf-
" fions or appetites; which proceed neceffarily
" from judgements or opinions; which are the
" neceffary effect of external things, or of ideas,
" operating, according to the neceffary laws of na-
" ture, upon our fenfes, intellect, or fancy: and
" thefe ideas, or things, prefent themfelves to our
" powers of perception, as neceffarily as light pre-
" fents itfelf when we turn our open eyes to the
" fun. In a word, every human action is the effect
" of a feries of caufes, each of which does neceffa-
" rily produce its own proper effect: fo that if the
" firft operate, all the reft muft follow.   It is
" confeffed, that an action may proceed imme-
" diately from volition, and may therefore pro-
" perly be called voluntary: but the *primum*
" *mobile* or firft caufe, even of a voluntary ac-
" tion, is fomething as independent on our will,
" as the production of the great-grandfather is
" independent on the grandfon.   Between phy-
" fical and moral neceffity there is no diffe-
" rence; the phenomena of the moral world
" being no lefs neceffary than thofe of the ma-
" terial. And, to conclude, if we are con-
" fcious of a feeling or fentiment of moral
                                   " liberty,

" liberty, it muft be a deceitful one; for no
" paft action of our lives could have been
" prevented, and no future action can be con-
" tingent. Therefore man is not a free, but a
" neceffary agent."

This is juft fuch a conclufion as I fhould
have expected; for thus it always has been, and
will be, when the dictates of common fenfe are
queftioned and difputed. The exiftence of body, the exiftence of the foul, the reality of our
idea of power, the difference between moral and
intellectual virtue, the certainty of the inference
from an effect to the caufe, and many other
fuch truths, dictates of common fenfe, have
been called in queftion, and argued upon.——
And what is the refult? Why truly it has been
found, that there is no body, that there is no
foul, that we have no idea of power, that moral
and intellectual virtue are not different, and that
a caufe is not neceffary to the production of that
which hath a beginning. And now the liberty
of human actions is queftioned and debated,
what could we expect, but that it would fhare
the fame fate! But paffing this for the prefent*,
which, however, feems to merit attention, we
fhall here only inquire, whether this doctrine of neceffity be not in fome important
points extremely fimilar to that of the non-exiftence of matter,   I. Of

* Some readers may poffibly, on this occafion, call to mind a
faying of an old Greek author, who, though now obfolete, was in
his day, and for feveral ages after, accounted a man of confiderable
penetration. I neither mention his name, nor tranflate his words,
for fear of offending (pardon a fond author's vanity) *my polite readers*.
ΑΝΘ 'ΩΝ ΤΗΝ ΑΓΑΠΗΝ ΤΗΣ ΑΛΗΘΕΙΑΣ ΟΥΚ ΕΔΕΞΑΝΤΟ—
ΔΙΑ ΤΟΥΤΟ ΠΕΜΨΕΙ ΑΥΤΟΙΣ 'Ο ΘΕΟΣ ΕΝΕΡΓΕΙΑΝ ΠΛΑΝΗΣ
ΕΙΣ ΤΟ ΠΙΣΤΕΥΣΑΙ ΑΥΤΟΥΣ ΤΩ ΨΕΥΔΕΙ.

1. Of this doctrine we obferve, in the firft place, that, if any regard is to be had to the meaning of words, and if human actions may reafonably be taken for the figns of human fentiments, all mankind have, in all ages, been of a different opinion. The number of profeffed philofophers who have maintained that all things happen through unavoidable neceffity, is but fmall; nor are we to imagine that all the ancient Fatalifts were of this number. The Stoics were Fatalifts by profeffion; but they ftill endeavoured, as well as they could, to reconcile fate with moral freedom†; and the firft fentence of the *Enchiridion* of Epictetus contains a declaration, that " opinion, purfuit, " defire, and averfion, and, in one word, what- " ever are our own actions, are in our own " power." We fee in Cicero's fragment *De Fato*, and in the beginning of the fixth book of Aulus Gellius, by what fubterfuges and quibbling diftinctions the Stoic Chryfippus reconciled the feemingly oppofite principles of fate and free-will. I am not furprifed, that what he fays on this fubject is unfatisfactory: for many Chriftians have puzzled themfelves to no purpofe in the fame argument. But though the manner in which the divine prefcience is exerted be myfterious and inexplicable, it does not follow, that the freedom of our will is equally

---

† " By Fate the Stoics feem to have underftood a feries of e- " vents appointed by the immutable counfels of God; or, that " law of his providence by which he governs the world. It is evi- " dent by their writings, that they meant it in no fenfe which in- " terferes with the liberty of human actions." See Mrs. Carter's admirable introduction to her very elegant tranflation of the works of Epictetus, § 17.

qually fo. Of this we may be, and we are, competent judges. It is fufficiently intimated to every man by his own experience; and every man is fatisfied with this intimation, and by his conduct declares, that he trufts to it as certain and authentic.   Nothing can be a clearer proof, that the fentiment of moral liberty is one of the moft powerful in human nature, than its having been fo long able to maintain its ground, and often in oppofition to other popular opinions apparently repugnant.   The notion of fate has prevailed much in the world, and yet could never fubvert this fentiment even in the vulgar.— If it be afked, where the vulgar opinions of ancient times are to be found? I anfwer, that in the writings of the moft popular poets we have a chance to find them more genuine than in fyftems of philofophy.——To advance paradoxes, and confequently to difguife facts, is often the moft effectual recommendation of a philofopher: but a poet muft conform himfelf to the general principles and manners of mankind; otherwife he can never become a general favourite.

Now the fyftem of Homer and Virgil concerning fate and free-will, is perfectly explicit. " Homer affigns three caufes," I quote the words of Pope, " of all the good and evil that " happens in this world, which he takes a par- " ticular care to diftinguifh. Firft, the will of " God, fuperior to all. Secondly, deftiny, or " fate, meaning the laws and order of nature, " affecting the conftitutions of men, and dif- " pofing them to good or evil, profperity or " misfortune; which the Supreme Being, if it

" be

" be his pleafure, may over-rule, (as Jupiter is
" inclined to do in the cafe of Sarpedon*); but
" which he generally fuffers to take effect.—
" Thirdly, our own free will, which either by
" prudence overcomes thofe natural influences
" and paffions, or by folly fuffers us to fall un-
" der them†." In regard to fome of the decrees of fate, Homer informs us, that they were
conditional, or fuch as could not take effect,
except certain actions were performed by men.
Thus Achilles had it in his power to continue
at Troy, or to return home before the end of the
war. If he chofe to ftay, his life would be
fhort and glorious; if to return, he was to enjoy peace and leifure to a good old age‡. He
prefers

---

* Iliad, xvi. 433.

† Iliad, i. 5. xix. 90. Odyff. i. 7. 39. See Pope's notes on
thefe paffages.

‡ Μήτηρ γαρ τί μι φησὶ θιά Θέτις ἀργυρόπιζα
   Διχθαδίας κῆρας φιρίμιν θανατοιο τίλοσδι—&c.   Iliad ix. 415.

My fates long fince by Thetis were difclos'd,
And each alternate, life or fame, propos'd.
Here if I ftay before the Trojan town,
Short is my date, but deathlefs my renown;
If I return, I quit immortal praife
For years on years, and long extended days.   *Pope.*

On voit (fays M. Dacier, in her note on this paffage) partout
dans Homere des marques qu'il avoit connu cette double deftinée
des hommes, fi neceffaire pour accorder le libre arbitre avec la pre-
deftination. En voicy un tefmoignage bien formel et bien exprès.
Il y a deux chemins pour tous les hommes: s'ils prennent celuy-la,
il leur arrivera telle chofe; s'ils prennent celuy-cy, leur fort fera
different.

Sophocles, in like manner, reprefents the decree of Deftiny concerning Ajax, as conditional. The anger of Minerva againft that
hero

prefers the former, though he well knew what was to follow: and I know not whether there be any other circumſtance in the character of this hero, except his love to his friend and to his father, which ſo powerfully recommends him to our regard. This gloomy reſolution inveſts him with a mournful dignity, the effects of which the reader often feels at his heart, in a ſentiment made up of admiration, pity, and horror. But this by the by.——According to Virgil, the completion, even of the abſolute decrees of fate, may be retarded by the agency of beings inferior to Jupiter*: a certain term is fixed to every man beyond which his life cannot laſt; but before this period arrives, he may die, by accidental misfortune, or deſerved puniſhment†: to virtue and vice neceſſity reaches not at all ‡.

In

hero was to laſt only one day : if his friends kept him within doors during that ſpace all would be well; if they ſuffered him to go abroad unattended, his death was inevitable. *Ajax Maſtig.* 772. 794. 818. Εἰ μὲν ἴνδον μίνη (ſays the ſcholiaſt), σωθήσεται ἢ δὲ μὴ, ἀπόλλυται· διὰ τουτο δὲ τὸ δίτλον τῦ μοιριδίου δηλοῖ ὡς και Ὁμηρος, Διχθαδίας κῆρας φιρέμεν θανατοίο τιλοσδι.
                                   Sophocles, apud H. Steph. 1588. *p.* 48.

* Non dabitur regnis (eſto) prohibere Latinis,
   Atque immota manet fatis Lavinia conjux;
   At trahere, atque moras tantis licet addere rebus.
                                   Æneid. vii. 313.

† Nam quia nec fato, merita nec morte peribat,
   Sed miſera ante diem, ſubitoque accenſa furore,
   Nondum illi flavum Proſerpina vertice crinem
   Abſtulerat.——————   *Æneid.* iv. 696.

‡ Stat ſua cuique dies; breve et irreparabile tempus
   Omnibus eſt vitæ; ſed famam extendere factis,
   Hoc virtutis opus.——————   *Æneid* x. 467.
                                   I agree

In all the histories I have read of ancient or modern, savage or civilized nations, I find the conduct of mankind has ever been such as I should expect from creatures possessed of moral freedom, and conscious of it. Several forms of false religion, and some erroneous commentaries on the true, have imposed tenets inconsistent with this freedom; but men have still acted, notwithstanding, as if they believed themselves to be free. Creeds, expressed in general terms may easily be imposed on the ignorant, and the selfish; by the former they are misunderstood, by the latter disregarded: but to overpower a natural instinct is a difficult task; and a doctrine which is easily swallowed when proposed in general terms, may prove disgustful when applied to a particular case.

" The

I agree with Servius (not in Æneid. x.) that the philosophical maxims to be found in poets are not always consistent. The reason is plain: Poets imitate the sentiments of people of different characters, placed in different circumstances, and actuated by different passions; and no body expects, that the language or thoughts suitable to a certain character, placed in certain circumstances, and actuated by certain passions, should be consistent with those of a different character whose circumstances and passions are different. But I cannot agree with that annotator, in supposing the passage quoted from the fourth book, inconsistent with what is quoted from the 10th; and that the former is according to the Epicurean, and the latter according to the Stoical, philosophy. In the latter passage, it is said, that a certain day or time is appointed by fate for the utmost limit of every man's life: in the former the very same thing is implied; only it is said further, that Dido died before her time; and there is nothing in the tenth book that insinuates the impossibility of this. The sentiments contained in these three quotations are conformable to Homer's theology, and to one another; and it deserves our notice, that the first comes from the mouth of Juno, the second from the poet or his muse, and the third from Jupiter himself; whence I infer, that they were agreeable to the poet's creed, or at least to the popular creed of his age.

" The belief of a deftiny," fays Mr. Macau-
lay in his hiftory of St. Kilda*, " is one of the
" ftrongeft articles of this people's creed; and
" it will poffibly be found upon examination,
" that the common people in all ages, and in
" moft countries, give into the fame notion.—
" At St. Kilda, fate and providence are much
" the fame thing.   After having explained thefe
" terms, I afked fome of the people there, Whe-
" ther it was in their power to do good and evil?
" The anfwer made by thofe who were unac-
" quainted with the fyftematical doctrines of
" divinity was, That the queftion was a very
" childifh one; as every man alive muft be con-
" fcious, that he himfelf is a free agent."—If
it be true, as I believe it is, that the common
people in moft countries are inclined to acknowledge a deftiny or fate; and if it be alfo
true, that they are confcious of their own free
agency notwithftanding; this alone would convince me, though I had never confulted my own
experience, that the fentiment of moral liberty
is one of the ftrongeft in human nature.   For
how many of their vices might they not excufe,
if they could perfuade themfelves, or others,
that thefe proceed from caufes as independent
on their will, as thofe from which ftorms, earth-
quakes, and eclipfes, arife, and the temperature of foils and feafons, and the found and un-
found conftitutions of the human body! Such a
perfuafion however, we find not that they have
at any time entertained or attempted; from

V O L. I.   S   which

* p. 243.

which I think there is good reafon to conclude,
that it is not in their power.

There is no principle in man, religion excepted, that has produced fo great revolutions,
and makes fuch a figure in the hiftory óf the
world, as the love of political liberty : of which
indeed all men do not form the fame notion;
fome placing it in the power of doing what
they pleafe, others in the power of doing what
is lawful; fome in being governed by laws of
their own making, and others in being governed by equitable laws, and tried by equitable
judges --- but of which it is univerfally agreed,
that it leaves in our power many of our moft
important actions.   And yet, fay fome authors,
all things happen through irrefiftible neceffity,
and there is not in the human mind any idea of
any power.   Strange ! that fo many, efpecially
among the beft, the braveft, and the wifeft of
men, fhould have been fo paffionately enamour-
ed of an inconceivable nonentity, as to abandon,
for its fake, their eafe, their health, their fortunes, and their lives! At this rate we are wonderfully miftaken, when we fpeak of Don
Quixote as a madman, and of Leonidas, Bru-
tus, Wallace, Hampden, Paoli, as wife, and
good, and great ! The cafe it feems is juft the
reverfe : thefe heroes deferve no other name
than that of raving bedlamites ; and the illuf-
trious knight of La Mancha, to whom the
object of his valour was at leaft *a conceivable
phantcm*, was a perfon of excellent underftanding, and moft perfect knowledge of the
world !

Do

Do not all mankind diftinguifh between mere harm and injury? Is there one rational being unacquainted with this diftinction? If a man were to act as if he did not comprehend it, would not the world pronounce him a fool? And yet this diftinction is incomprehenfible, except we fuppofe fome beings to act neceffarily, and others from free choice. A man gives me a blow, and inftantly I feel refentment: but a byftander informs me, that the man is afflicted with the epilepfy, which deprives him of the power of managing his limbs; that the blow was not only without defign, but contrary to his intention: and that he could not have prevented it. My refentment is gone, tho' I ftill feel pain from the blow. Can there be any miftake in this experience? Can I think that I feel refentment, when in reality I do not feel it? that I feel no refentment, when I am confcious of the contrary? And if I feel refentment in the one cafe, and not in the other, it is certain there feems to me to be fome diffimilitude between them. But it is only in refpect of the intention of him who gave the blow that there can be any diffimilitude: for all that I learn from the information by which my refentment was extinguifhed is, that what I fuppofed to proceed from an evil intention, did really proceed from no evil intention, but from the neceffary effect of a material caufe, in which the will had no concern. What fhall we fay then? that the diftinction between injury and mere harm, acknowledged by all mankind, does imply, that all mankind fuppofe the actions of moral beings to be free? or fhall we

S 2   fay,

fay, that refentment, though it arifes uniformly in all men on certain occafions, does yet proceed from no caufe; the actions which do give
rife to it being in every refpect the fame with
thofe which do not give rife to it?

Further, all men expect, with full affurance,
that fire will burn to-morrow; but all men
do not with full affurance expect, that a thief
will fteal to-morrow, or a mifer refufe an alms
to a beggar, or a debauchee commit an act of
intemperance, even tho' opportunities offer. If
I had found, on blowing up my fire this morning, that the flame was cold, and converted
water into ice, I fhould have been much more
aftonifhed, than if I had detected a man reputed honeft in the commiffion of an act of theft.
The former I would call a prodigy, a contradiction to the known laws of Nature: of the latter I fhould fay, that I am forry for it, and
could never have expected it; but I fhould not
fuppofe any prodigy in the cafe. All general
rules, that regard the influence of human characters on human actions, admit of exceptions;
but the general laws of matter admit of none.
Ice was cold, and fire hot, ever fince the creation; hot ice, and cold fire, are, according to
the prefent conftitution of the world, impoffible: but that a man fhould fteal to-day, who
never ftole before, is no impoffibility at all.
The coldnefs of the flame I fhould doubtlefs
think owing to fome caufe, and the difhonefty
of the man to fome ftrange revolution in his
fentiments and principles; but I never could
bring myfelf to think the man as paffive, in regard to this revolution, as the fire muft be fuppofed

pofed to be, in regard to the caufe by which its nature is changed. The man has done what he ought not to have done, what he might have prevented, and what he deferves punifhment for not preventing ;—this is the language of all rational beings :—but the fire is wholly unconfcious and inert. Who will fay that there is the fame necefity in both cafes!

Fatalifts are fond of inferring moral neceffity from phyfical, in the way of analogy. But fome of their arguments on this topic are moft ridiculoufly abfurd. " There is," fays Voltaire's *Ignorant Philofopher*, " nothing with-
" out a caufe. An effect without a caufe, are
" words without meaning. Every time I have
" a will, this can only be in confequence of my
" judgement good or bad ; this judgement is
" neceffary ; therefore fo is my will."—All this hath been faid by others: but what follows is, I believe, peculiar to this *Ignorant Philofopher*.
" In effect," continues he, " it would be ve-
" ry fingular, that all nature, all the planets,
" fhould obey eternal laws, and that there
" fhould be a little animal, five feet high, who,
" in contempt of thefe laws, could act as he
" pleafed, folely according to his caprice."
Singular ! aye, fingular indeed. So very fingular, that yours, Sir, if I miftake not, is the firft human brain that ever conceived fuch a notion. If man be free, no body ever dreamed that he made himfelf fo, in contempt of the laws of Nature ; it is in confequence of a law of Nature that he is a free agent. But paf-

fing

fing this, let us attend to the reafoning. The
planets are not free agents;—therefore it would
be very fingular, that man fhould be one.
Not a whit more fingular, than that this fame
animal of five feet fhould perceive, and think,
and read, and write, and fpeak; attributes
which no aftronomer has ever fuppofed to belong
to the planets, notwithftanding their brilliant
appearance, and ftupendous magnitude *. We
do too much honour to fuch reafoning, when ·
we reply to it in the bold, but fublime words
of the poet:

Know'ft thou th' importance of a foul immortal ?
Behold this midnight glory, worlds on worlds !   ·
Amazing pomp ! redouble this amaze ;
Ten thoufand add ; and twice ten thoufand more ;
Then weigh the whole ; ONE SOUL outweighs them all,
And calls the aftonifhing magnificence
Of unintelligent creation poor.

Complaint, Night 7.

Or in the fimpler language of another great
genius : " If we confider the dignity of an in-̣ ·
                                 " telligent

---

* Mr. Voltaire has often laboured, with more zeal than fuccefs,
to prove, among other ftrange doctrines, that Shakefpeare and
Milton were no great poets. What if I fhould here help him to
an argument as decifive on that point as any he has yet invented,
and framed exactly according to the rules of his own logic, as
exemplified in the paffage now before us ? " The Englifh fay,
" that Shakefpeare and Milton were great poets. Now it is
" well known, that neither Plinlimmon in Wales, nor Meal-
" fourvouny in Scotland, neither Lebanon in Syria, nor Atlas in
" Mauritania, ever wrote one good verfe in their days ; and yet
" each of thefe mountains exceeds in corporeal magnitude ten
" thoufand Miltons, and as many Shakefpeares. But it would
" be very fingular, that maffes of fo great diftinction fhould ne-
" ver have been able to put pen to paper with any fuccefs, and
" yet that no fewer than two pieces of Englifh flefh and blood,
" fcarce fix feet long, fhould, in contempt of Nature and all her
" laws, have penned poems that are intitled to general admirati-
" on"

" telligent being, and put that in the fcale
" againſt brute and inanimate matter, we may
" affirm, without overvaluing human nature,
" that the foul of one virtuous and religious
" man is of greater worth and excellency,
" than the fun and his planets, and all the
" ſtars in the world *."

Mr. HUME, in an eſſay on this ſubjeɗt,
maintains, that the appearances in the moral
and material world are equally uniform, and
equally neceſſary; nay, and acknowledged to
be ſo, both by philoſophers and by the vulgar. In proof of this, he confines himſelf to
general topics, on which he declaims with ſome
plauſibility. Human nature has been nearly
the ſame in all ages. True. For all men
poſſeſs nearly the ſame faculties, which are
employed about nearly the ſame objeɗts, and
deſtined to operate within the ſame narrow
ſphere. And if a man have power to chuſe
one of two things, to aɗt or not to aɗt, he has
all the liberty we contend for. How is it poſſible, then, that human nature, taken in the
groſs, ſhould not be found nearly the ſame in
all ages! But if we come to particulars, we
ſhall not perhaps find two human minds exaɗt-
ly alike. In two of the moſt congenial characters on earth, the ſame cauſes will not produce
the ſame effeɗts; nay, the ſame cauſes will not
always produce the ſame effeɗts even in the ſame
charaɗter.

Some Fataliſts deny, that our internal feelings are in favour of moral liberty. " It is
                                      " true"

* Bentley's Sermons, at Boyle's Leɗtures, Serm. VIII.

" true," fays a worthy and ingenious, though
fanciful, author, " that a man by internal feel-
" ing may prove his own free-will, if by free-
" will be meant the power of doing what a
" man wills or defires ; or of refifting the mo -
" tives of fenfuality, ambition, &c. that is free-
" will in the popular and practical fenfe.   Eve-
" ry perfon may eafily recollect inftances, where
" he has done thefe feveral things.   But thefe
" are entirely foreign to the prefent queftion.
" To prove that a man has free will in the
" fenfe oppofite to mechanifm, he ought to
" feel, that he can do different things while
" the motives remain precifely the fame.   And
" here I apprehend the internal feelings are
" entirely againft free-will, where the motives
" are of a fufficient magnitude to be evident ;
" where they are not, nothing can be proved *".
" —Queftions of this kind would be more eafily
folved, if authors would explain their doctrine
by examples   When this is not done, we cannot always be fure that we underftand their
meaning, efpecially in abftract fubjects, where
language, after all our care, is often equivocal
and inadequate.   If I rightly underftand this
author, and am allowed to examine his principles by my own experience, I muft conclude,
that he very much miftakes the fact.   Let us
take an example.   A man is tempted to the
commiffion of a crime : his motive to commit,
is the love of money, or the gratification of
appetite : his motive to abftain, is a regard to
duty, or to reputation.   Suppofe him to weigh
thefe

---

* Hartley's Obfervations on man, vol. 1. p. 507.

thefe motives in his mind, for an hour, a day, or a week; and, fuppofe, that, during this fpace, no additional confideration occurs to him on either fide : which, I think, may be fuppofed, becaufe I know it is poffible, and I believe often happens. While his mind is in this ftate, the motives remain precifely the fame : and yet it is to me inconceivable, that he fhould at any time, during this fpace, feel himfelf under a neceffity of committing, or under a neceffity of not committing, the crime. He is indeed under a neceffity either to do, or not to do: but every man, in fuch a cafe, feels that he has it in his power to chufe the one or the other. At leaft, in all my experience, I have never been confcious, nor had any reafon to believe that other men were confcious, of any fuch neceffity as the author here fpeaks of.

Again : Suppofe two men, in the circumftances above-mentioned, to yield to the temptation, and to be differently affected by a review of their conduct; the one repining at fortune, or fate, or providence, for having placed him in too tempting a fituation, and folicited him by motives too powerful to be refifted ; the other blaming and upbraiding himfelf for yielding to the bad motive, and refifting the good:—I would afk, which of thefe two kinds of remorfe or regret is the moft rational ? The firft, according to the doctrine of the Fatalifts ; the laft, according to the opinion of mankind. No divine, no moralift, no man of fenfe, ever fuppofes true penitence to begin, till the criminal become confcious, that he has done, or neglected, fomething which he ought not to
have

have done or neglected : a sentiment which would be not only abfurd, but impoſſible, if all criminals and guilty perſons believed, from internal feeling, that what is done could not have been prevented.   Whenever you can ſatisfy a man of this, he may continue to bewail himſelf, or repine at fortune ; but his repentance is at an end.   It is always a part, and too often the whole, of the language of remorfe : " I wiſh the deed had never been done; wretch " that I was, not to refift the temptation!"— Does this imply, that the penitent fuppoſes himfelf to have been under a neceſſity of committing the action, and that his conduct could not have been different from what it is? To me it feems to imply juſt the contrary.   And am not I a competent judge of this matter ? Have not I been in thefe circumſtances ? Has not this been often the language of my foul? And will any man fay, that I do not know my own thoughts, or that he knows them better than I?---All men, indeed, have but too frequent experience of at leaſt this part of repentance: then why multiply words, when by facts it is fo eafy to determine the controverſy?

Other Fatalifts acknowledge, that the free agency of man is univerfally felt and believed : That though man in truth is a neceſſary agent, having all his actions determined by fixed and immutable laws ; yet, this being concealed from him, he acts with the conviction of being a free agent*.—Concealed from him ! Who conceals it ?

* In the former editions of this Eſſay, a particular book was here fpecified and quoted. But I have lately heard, that in a fecond

it? Does the author of nature conceal it,—and do thefe writers difcover it! What deference is not due to the judgement of a metaphyfician, whofe fagacity is fo irrefiftibly (I had almoft faid omnipotently) penetrating! But, Gentlemen, as ye.are powerful, ye fhould have been merciful. It was not kind to rob poor mortals of this crumb of comfort which had been provided for them in their ignorance; nor generous to pub-lifh fo openly the fecrets of Heaven, and thus baffle the defigns of Providence by a few ftrokes of your pen!—In truth, metaphyfic is a per-plexing affair to the paffions, as well as to the judgement. Sometimes it is fo abfurd, that not to be merry is impoffible; and fometimes fo im-pious, that not to be angry were unpardonable: but often it partakes fo much of both qualities, that one knows not with what temper of mind to confider it:

" To laugh were want of goodnefs, and of grace;
" And to be grave, exceeds all power of face;

But why infift fo long on the univerfal ac-knowledgement of man's free agency? To me it is as evident, that all men believe themfelves free, as that all men think. I cannot fee the heart; I judge of the fentiments of others from their outward behaviour; from the higheft to the loweft, as far as hiftory and experience can carry me, I find the conduct of human beings .fimilar in this refpect to my own: and of my own free agency I have never yet been able to entertain

cond edition of that book, which, however, I have not yet feen, the author has made fome alterations, by which he gets clear of the abfurdity expofed in this paffage.

entertain the leaft doubt. " Here then we have
" an inftance of a doctrine advanced by fome
" philofophers, in direct contradiction to the
" general belief of all men in all ages." This is
a repetition of the firft remark formerly made on
the non-exiftence of matter.

2. The fecond was to this purpofe: " The
" reafoning by which this doctrine is fupport-
" ed, though long accounted unanfwerable, did
" never produce a ferious and fteady convicti-
" on; common fenfe ftill declared it to be falfe; we
" were forry to find the powers of human reafon
" fo limited as not to afford a logical confutation
" of it; we were convinced it merited confutation,
" and flattered ourfelves, that one time or other
" it would be confuted."

I fhall here take it for granted, that the fcheme
of neceffity has not as yet been fully confuted;
and on this fuppofition (which the Fatalifts can
hardly fail to acknowledge a fair one) I would
afk, whether the remark juft now quoted be applicable to the reafonings urged in behalf of that
fcheme? My experience tells me, it is. After
giving the advocates for neceffity a fair hearing,
my belief is exactly the fame as before. I am
'puzzled perhaps, but not convinced, no not
in the leaft degree. In reading fome late effays
on this fubject, I find many things allowed to
pafs without fcruple, which I cannot admit;
and when I have got to the end, and afk myfelf,
whether I am a free or a neceffary agent, nature.
recurs to me fo irrefiftibly, that the inveftigation
I have juft finifhed feems (as Shakefpeare fays)
" like the fierce vexation of a dream," which,
while it lafted, had fome refemblance of reality,
but

but now, when it is gone, appears to have been altogether a delufion. This is prejudice, you fay; be it fo.   Before the confutation of BERKE-LEY's fyftem, would it have been called prejudice not to be convinced by his arguments? I know not but it might; but I am fure, that of fuch prejudice no honeft man, nor lover of truth, needs be afhamed.   I confefs, that when I enter upon the controverfy in queftion, I am not wholly indifferent; I am a little biaffed in favour of common fenfe, and I cannot help it: yet if the reafoning were conclufive, I am confident it would breed in my mind fome fufpicion, that my fentiment of moral liberty is ambiguous.— As I experience nothing of this kind, my conviction remaining the fame as before, what muft I infer? Surely I muft infer, and I fin againft my own underftanding if I do not infer, that though the reafoning be fubtle, the doctrine is abfurd.

But what if a man be really convinced by that reafoning, that he is a neceffary agent?— Then I expect he will think and act according to his conviction. If he continue to act and think as he did before, and as I and the reft of the world do now, he muft pardon me if I fhould fufpect his conviction to be infincere. For let it be obferved that the Fatalifts are not fatisfied with calling their doctrine probable; they affirm that it is certain, and refts on evidence not inferior to demonftration. If, therefore, it convince at all, it muft convince thoroughly. Between rejecting it as utterly falfe, and receiving it as undeniably true, there is no medium to a confiderate perfon. And let it be obferved further,

further, that the changes which the real belief of
fatality muft produce in the conduct and fentiments of men, are not flight and imperceptible,
but, as will appear afterwards, important and
ftriking. If you fay that the inftincts of your
nature, the cuftoms of the world, and the force
of human laws, oblige you to act like free
agents, you acknowledge fatality to be contrary to common fenfe ; which is the point I want
to prove.

Clay is not more obfequious to the potter,
than words to the fkilful difputant. They may
be made to affume almoft any form, to enforce
almoft any doctrine. So true it is, that much
may be faid on either fide of moft queftions,
that we have known dealers in controverfy, who
were always of the fame mind with the author
whom they read laft. We have feen theories of
morality deduced from pride, from fympathy,
from felf-love, from benevolence; and all fo
plaufible, as would furprife one who is unacquainted with the ambiguities of language. Of
thefe the advocates for fimple truth are lefs careful to avail themfelves, than their paradoxical
antagonifts. The arguments of the former, being more obvious, ftand lefs in need of illuftration; thofe of the latter require all the embel-
lifhments of eloquence and refinement to recommend them. Robbers feldom go abroad
without arms; they examine every corner and
countenance with a penetrating eye, which habitual diftruft and circumfpection have rendered intenfely fagacious : the honeft man walks
careleffly about his bufinefs, intending no harm,
and fufpecting none. It cannot be denied, that

philofophers

philofophers do often in the ufe of words, impofe on themfelves as well as on others; an ambiguous word flipping in by accident will often
perplex a whole fubject, to the equal furprife of
both parties; and perhaps, in a long courfe of
years, the caufe of this perplexity fhall not be
difcovered. This was never more remarkably
the cafe, than in the controverfy about the exiftence of matter; and this no doubt is one great
hinderance to the utter confutation of the doctrine of neceffity. Fatalifts, indeed, make a
ftir, and feem much in earneft, about fettling the
fignification of words: but " words beget words,"
as Bacon well obferveth ; and it cannot be expected, that they who are interefted in fupporting a fyftem will be fcrupuloufly impartial in
their definitions.

With a few of thefe a theorift commonly begins his fyftem. This has the appearance of
fairnefs and perfpicuity. We hold it for a maxim, that a man may ufe words in any fenfe he
pleafes, provided he explain the fenfe in which
he ufes them; and we think it captious to find
fault with words. We therefore are eafily prevailed on to admit his definitions, which are generally plaufible, and not apparently repugnant
to the analogy of language. But the underftanding of the author when he writes, and that
of the ftudent when he reads them, are in very
different circumftances. The former knows
his fyftem already, and adapts his definitions to
it : the latter is ignorant of the fyftem, and
therefore can have no notion of the tendency of
the definitions. Befides, every fyftem is in fome
degree obfcure to one who is but beginning to

ftudy

study it; and this obscurity serves to disguise whatever in the preliminary illustrations is forced or inexplicit. Thus the mind of the most candid and most attentive reader is prepared for the reception of error, long before he has any suspicion of the author's real design. And then, the more he is accustomed to use words in a certain signification, the more he is disposed to think it natural; so that, the further he advances in the system, he is still more and more reconciled to it. Need we wonder then at the variety of moral systems? need we wonder to see a man's judgement so easily, and often so egregiously, misled, by abstract reasoning? need we wonder at the success of any theorist, who has a tolerable command of language, and a moderate share of cunning, provided his system be adapted to the manners and principles of his age? Neither need we wonder to see the grossest and most detestable absurdities recommended by singular plausibility of argument, and such as may for a time impose even on the intelligent and sagacious; till at last, when the author's design becomes manifest, common sense begins to operate, and men have recourse on their instinctive and intuitive sentiments, as the most effectual security against the assaults of the logician.

Further, previous to all influence from habit and education, the intellectual abilities of different men are very different in respect of reasoning, as well as of common sense. Some men, sagacious enough in perceiving truth, are but ill qualified to reason about it; while others, not superior in common sense, or intuitive sagacity, are much more dextrous in devising and
                                              confuting

confuting arguments. If you propofe a fophifm to the latter, you are at once contradicted and confuted: the former, though they cannot confute you, are perhaps equally fenfible of your falfe doctrine, and unfair reafoning; they know, that what you fay is not true, though they cannot tell in what refpect it is falfe. Perhaps all that is wanting to enable them to confute as well as contradict, is only a little practice in fpeaking and wrangling: but furely this affects not the truth or falfehood of propofitions. What is falfe is as really fo to the perfon who perceives its falfity, without being able to prove it, as to him who both perceives and proves; and it is equally falfe, before I learn logic, and after.—Is it not therefore highly unreafonable to expect conviction from every antagonift who cannot confute you, and to afcribe to prejudice what is owing to the irrefiftible impulfe of unerring nature?

I have converfed with many people of fenfe on the fubject of this controverfy concerning liberty and neceffity. To the greater part, the arguments of Clarke and others, in vindication of liberty, feemed quite fatisfying; others owned themfelves puzzled with the fubtleties of thofe who took the oppofite fide of the queftion ; fome repofed with full affurance on that confcioufnefs of liberty which every man feels in his own breaft; in a word, as far as my experience goes, I have found the greater part of mankind, enemies to fatality in their hearts; willing to confider the arguments for it as rather fpecious than folid; and difpofed to receive, with joy and thankfulnefs, a thorough vindication of human liberty, and a logical confutation of the oppofite doctrine.

3. It has been faid, That philofophers are anfwerable, not for the confequences, but only for the truth, of their tenets; and that, if a doctrine be true, its being attended with difagreeable confequences will not render it falfe. We readily acquiefce in this remark; but we imagine it cannot be meant of any truth but what is certain and incontrovertible. No genuine truth did ever of itfelf produce effects inconfiftent with real utility*. But many principles pafs for truth, which are far from deferving that honourable appellation. Some give it to all doctrines which have been defended with fubtlety, and which, whether ferioufly believed or not, have never been logically confuted. But to affirm, that all fuch doctrines are cerᵗainly true, would argue great ignorance of human language, and human nature. It is therefore abfurd to fay, that the bad confequences of admitting fuch doctrines ought not to be urged as arguments againft them.——Now, there are many perfons in the world, of moft refpectable underftanding, who would be extremely averfe to acknowledge, that the doctrine of neceffity has ever been demonftrated beyond all doubt. I may therefore be permitted to confider it as a controvertible tenet, and to expofe the abfurdities and dangerous confequences with which the general belief of it may be attended.

Mr. Hume endeavours to raife a prejudice against

gainft

* Ζητῶ την αληθειαν ὑφ' ἧς ὀδὴς πώπολε ἰβλάβη.
Marc. Antonin.

gainſt this method of refutation.   He probably
foreſaw, that the tendency of his principles
would be urged as an argument againſt them;
and being ſomewhat apprehenſive of the conſequences, as well he might, he inſinuates, that
all ſuch reaſoning is no better than perſonal invective.   " There is no method of reaſoning,"
ſays he, " more common, and yet none more
" blameable, than in philoſophical debates to
" endeavour the refutation of any hypotheſis,
" by a pretence of its dangerous conſequences to
" religion and morality.   When any opinion
" leads into abſurdities, it is certainly falſe; but
" it is not certain that an opinion is falſe, be-
" cauſe it is of dangerous conſequence.   Such
" topics therefore ought entirely to be forborn;
" as ſerving nothing to the diſcovery of truth,
" but only to make the perſon of an antagoniſt
" odious*."   If your philoſophy be ſuch, that
its conſequences cannot be unfolded without
rendering your perſon odious, pray, Sir, who is
to blame? you, who contrive and publiſh it; or
I, who criticiſe it?   There is a kind of philoſophy ſo ſalutary in its effects, as to endear the
perſon of the author to every good man : why
is not yours of this kind? If it is not, as you
yourſelf ſeem to apprehend, do you think that I
ought to applaud your principles, or ſuffer
them to paſs unexamined, even though I am certain of their pernicious tendency? or that, out
of reſpect to your perſon, I ought not to put
others on their guard againſt them? Surely you
cannot be ſo blinded by ſelf-admiration, as to

T 2
think

* Eſſay on Liberty and Neceſſity, part 2.

think ' it the duty of any man to facrifice the intereft of mankind to your intereft, or rather to your reputation as a metaphyfical writer. If you do think fo, I muft take the liberty to differ from your judgement in this, as in many other matters.

Nor can I agree to what our author fays of this method of reafoning, that it tends nothing to the difcovery of truth. Does not every thing tend to the difcovery of truth, that difpofes men to think for themfelves, and to confider opinions with attention, before they adopt them? And have not many well-meaning perfons rafhly adopted a plaufible opinion on the fuppofition of its being harmlefs, who, if they had been aware of its bad tendency, would have proceeded with more caution, and made a better ufe of their underftanding?

This is truly a notable expedient for determining controverfy in favour of licentious theories.. An author publifhes a book, in which are many doctrines fatal to human happinefs, and fubverfive of human fociety,. If, from a regard to truth, and to mankind, we endeavour to expofe them in their proper colours, and, by difplaying their dangerous and abfurd confequences, to deter men from rafhly adopting them without examination; our adverfary immediately exclaims, " This is not fair reafon-" ing; this is perfonal invective." Were the fentiments of the public to be regulated by this exclamation, licentious writers might do what mifchief they pleafed, and no man durft appear in oppofition, without being hooted at for his want of breeding. --- It is happy for us all, that

the

the law is not to be brow-beaten by infinuations
of this kind; otherwife we fhould hear fome
folks exclaim againft it every day, as one of the
moft ungenteel things in the world. And truly they would have reafon: for it cannot be denied, that an indictment at the Old Bailey has
much the air of a perfonal invective; and ba-
nifhment, or burning in the hand, amounts
nearly to a perfonal affault; nay, both have often this exprefs end, to make the perfon of the
criminal odious; and yet, in his judgement,
perhaps, there was no great harm in picking a
pocket of a handkerchief, value thirteen pence,
provided it was done with a good grace. Let
not the majefty of fcience be offended by this al-
lufion; I mean not to argue from it, for it is
not quite fimilar to the cafe in hand. That
thofe men act the part of good citizens, who
endeavour to overturn the plaineft principles
of human knowledge, and to fubvert the foundations of all religion, I am far from thinking;
but I fhould be extremely forry to fee any
other weapons employed againft them than thofe
of reafon and ridicule chaftifed by decency and
truth. Other weapons this caufe requires not;
nay, in this caufe, all other weapons would do
more harm than good. And let it ftill be remembered, that the object of our ftrictures is
not men, but books; and that thefe incur our
cenfure, not becaufe they bear certain names,
but becaufe they contain certain principles.

The remarks relate rather to the doctrines
of fcepticifm in general, than to this of neceffity in particular; which I am not ignorant

T 3   that

that many men, refpectable both for their talents and principles, have afferted. I prefume,
however, they would have been more cautious,
if they had attended to the confequences that
may be drawn from it.—To which I now return.

Some of the Fatalifts are willing to reconcile their fyftem with our natural notions
of moral good and evil; but all they have
been able to do is, to remove the difficulty a
ftep or two further off. But others of that
party are not folicitous to render thefe points
confiftent. If they can only eftablifh neceffity,
they leave natural religion to fhift for itfelf.
Mr. HUME allows, that, on the principles of
thofe who deny liberty and contingence, it is
impoffible for natural reafon to vindicate the
divine character:—for that, on the fuppofition
that God is the ultimate caufe of every one of
our volitions and actions, either none of thefe
can be criminal; or, if they be criminal (which
Mr. HUME feems to admit), " we muft retract
" the attribute of perfection which we afcribe
" to the Deity, and acknowledge him to be
" the ultimate author of guilt and moral tur-
" pitude in all his creatures."—Were authors
poffeffed of that modefty, which Mr. HUME recommends in the conclufion of this effay, I
fhould think they would fhudder at the thought
of inculcating a doctrine, which *they know* to
be irreconcileable with the very firft principles
of religion; and of which, therefore, they muft
know that it tends to fubvert the only durable
foundation of human fociety and human happinefs.

The

The advocates for liberty, on the other hand, have zealoufly afferted the infinite wifdom and purity of the divine nature. Now, I confefs, that this very confideration is, according to my notion of things, a ftrong argument in favour of the laft-mentioned doctrine. Here are two opinions; the one inconfiftent with the firft principles of natural religion, as fome of thofe who maintain it acknowledge, as well as with the experience, the belief, and the practice, of the generality of rational beings; the other per-fectly confiftent with religion, confcience, and common fenfe. If the reader believe, with me, that the Deity is infinitely good and wife, he cannot balance a moment between them; nor hefitate to affirm, that the univerfal belief of the former would produce much mifchief and mifery to mankind. If he be prepoffeffed in favour of Mr. Hume's neceffity, he ought, however, before he acquiefce in it as true, to be well-affur-ed, that the evidences of natural religion, par-ticularly of the divine exiftence and attributes, are weaker than the proofs that have been urged in behalf of this neceffity. But will any one fay, that this doctrine admits of a proof, as un-exceptionable as that by which we evince the be-ing and attributes of God ? I appeal to his own heart, I appeal to the experience and confciouf-nefs of mankind :—are you as thoroughly con-vinced, that no paft action of your life could poffibly have been prevented, and that no future action can poffibly be contingent, as that God is infinitely wife, powerful, and good ?——Ex-amine the evidence of both propofitions, exa-mine with candour the inftinctive fuggeftions
of

of your own mind;—and then tell me, whether you find Atheifm or man's moral liberty hardeft to be believed.

Perhaps I fhall be told, that the belief of moral liberty is attended with equal difficulties; for that, to reconcile the contingency of human actions with the prefcience of God, is as impoffible as to reconcile neceffity with his goodnefs and wifdom. Others have anfwered this objection at length; I make therefore only two brief remarks upon it.   1. As it implies not any reflection on the divine power, to fay that it cannot perform impoffibilities; fo neither, I prefume, does it imply any reflection on his knowledge, to fay that he cannot forefee, *as certain*, that which he himfelf has determined to be *not certain*, but only *contingent*. Yet he fees all poffible effects of all poffible caufes; and our freedom to chufe good or evil can no more be conceived to interfere with the final purpofes of his providence, than our power of moving our limbs is inconfiftent with our inability to remove mountains.   2. No man will take it upon him to fay, that he diftinctly underftands the manner in which the Deity acts, perceives, and knows: but the incomprehenfiblenefs of his nature will never induce men to doubt his exiftence and attributes, unlefs there be men who fancy themfelves infallible, and of infinite capacity. Shall I then conclude, becaufe I cannot fully comprehend the manner in which the divine prefcience operates, that therefore the Deity is not infinitely perfect? or that therefore I cannot be certain of the truth of a fentiment which is warranted by my conftant experience,

and

and by that of all mankind? Shall I fay, that becaufe my knowledge is not infinite, therefore I have no knowledge? Becaufe I know not when I fhall die, does it follow, that I cannot be certain of my being now alive? Becaufe God has not told me every thing, fhall I refufe to believe what he has told me? To draw fuch a conclufion from fuch premifes, is, in my judgement, as contrary to reafon, as to fay, that, becaufe I am ignorant of the caufe of magnetical attraction, therefore I ought not to believe that the needle points to the north.---That I am a free agent, I know and believe; that God forefees whatever can be forefeen, as he can do whatever can be done, I alfo know and believe; nor have the Fatalifts ever proved, nor can they ever prove, that the one belief is inconfiftent with the other.

The afferters of human liberty have always maintained, that to believe all actions and intentions neceffary, is the fame thing as to believe, that man is not an accountable being, or, in other words, no moral agent. And indeed this notion is natural to every perfon who has the courage to truft his own experience, without feeking to puzzle plain matter of fact with verbal diftinctions and metaphyfical refinement. But, it is faid, the fenfe of moral beauty and turpitude ftill remains with us, even after we are convinced, that all actions and intentions are neceffary; that this fenfe maketh us moral agents; and therefore that our moral agency is perfectly confiftent with our neceffary agency. But this is nothing to the purpofe; it is putting

us

290 ANESSAY Part II.

us 'off with mere words. For what is moral
agency, and what is implied in it? This at leaſt
muſt be implied in it, that we ought to do ſome
things, and not to do others. But if every intention and action of my life is fixed by eternal
laws, which I can neither elude nor alter, it is
as abſurd to ſay to me, You ought to be honeſt
to-morrow, as to ſay, You ought to ſtop the
motion of the planets to-morrow. Unleſs ſome
events depend upon my determination *ought* and
ought not, have no meaning when applied to me.
Moral agency further implies, that we are accountable for our conduct; and that if we do
what we ought not to do, we deſerve blame and
puniſhment. My conſcience tells me, that I
am accountable for thoſe actions only that are
in my own power; and neither blames nor
approves, in myſelf or in others, that conduct
which is the effect, not of choice, but of neceſſity. Convince me, that all my actions are
equally neceſſary, and you ſilence my conſcience for ever, or at leaſt prove it to be a fallacious and impertinent monitor: you will then
convince me, that all circumſpection is unne-
ceſſary, and all remorſe abſurd. And is it a
matter of little moment, whether I believe my
moral feelings authentic and true, or equivocal
and fallacious? Can any principle be of more
fatal conſequence to me, or to ſociety, than to
believe, that the dictates of conſcience are falſe,
unreaſonable, or inſignificant? Yet this is one
certain effect of my becoming a Fataliſt, or
even ſceptical in regard to moral liberty.

I obſerve, that when a man's underſtanding
begins to be ſo far perverted by debauchery, as
to

to make him imagine his crimes unavoidable, from that moment he begins to think them innocent, and deems it a fufficient apology, that in refpect of them he is no longer a free, but a neceffary agent. The drunkard pleads his conftitution, the blafphemer urges the invincible force of habit, and the fenfualift would have us believe, that his appetites are too ftrong to be refifted. Suppofe all men fo far perverted as to argue in the fame manner with regard to crimes of every kind;—then it is certain, that all men would be equally difpofed to think all crimes innocent. And what would be the confequence? Licentioufnefs, mifery, and defolation, irremediable and univerfal. If God intended that men fhould be happy, and that the human race fhould continue for many generations, he certainly intended alfo that men fhould believe themfelves free, moral, and accountable creatures.

Suppofing it poffible for a man to act upon the belief of his being a neceffary agent, let us fee how he would behave in fome of the common affairs of life. He does me an injury. I go to him and remonftrate. You will excufe me, fays he; I was put upon it by one on whom I am dependent, and who threatened me with beggary and perdition if I refufed to comply. I acknowledge this to be a confiderable alleviation of the poor man's guilt. Next day he repeats the injury; and, on my renewing my remonftrances, Truly, fays he, I was offered fix-pence to do it; or I did it to pleafe my humour: but I know you will pardon me, when I tell you, that as all motives are the neceffary caufes of the actions

tions

tions that proceed from them, it follows, that all motives productive of the fame action are ir-refiftible, and therefore, in refpect of the agent, equally ftrong : I am therefore as innocent now as I was formerly ; for the event has proved, that the motive arifing from the offer of fix-pence, or from the impulfe of whim, was as effectual in producing the action which you call an injury, as the motive arifing from the fear of ruin. Notwithftanding this fine fpeech, I fhould be afraid, that thefe principles, if perfift-ed in, and acted upon, would foon bring the poor Fatalift to Tyburn or Bedlam.

Will you promife to affift me to-morrow with your labour, advice, or intereft ? No, fays the practical Fatalift ; I can promife nothing : for my conduct to-morrow will certainly be deter-mined by the motive that then happens to pre-dominate. Let your promife, fay I, be your motive. How can you be fo ignorant, he re-plies, as to imagine that our motives to action are in our own power ! O fad, O fad ! you muft ftudy metaphyfic, indeed you muft. Why, Sir, our motives to action are obtruded upon us by irrefiftible neceffity. Perhaps they arife, imme-diately, from fome paffion, judgement, fancy, or (if you pleafe) volition ; but this volition, fancy, judgement, or paffion ——what is it ? an effect without a caufe ? No, no ; it is necef-farily excited by fome idea, object, or notion, which prefents itfelf independently on me, and in confequence of fome extrinfic caufe, the ope-ration of which I can neither forefee nor pre-vent.—Where is the man who would chufe this Fatalift for his friend, companion, or fellow-citizen ?

citizen ? who will fay, that fociety could at all fubfift, if the generality of mankind were to think, and fpeak, and act, on fuch principles * ?

But, fays the Fatalift, is it not eafy to imagine cafes in which the men who believe themfelves free, would act the part of fools or knaves ? Nothing indeed is more eafy. But let it be obferved, that the folly or knavery of fuch men arifes, not from their perfuafion of their own free agency ; for many millions of this perfuafion have paffed through life with a fair character ; but from other caufes. I cannot conceive any greater difcouragement from knavery and folly, than the confideration, that man is an accountable being ; and I know not how we can fuppofe him *accountable*, in the common acceptation of that word, unlefs we fuppofe him free.

The reader, if difpofed to purfue thefe hints, and attend, in imagination, to the behaviour of the confiftent and practical Fatalift, in the more interefting fcenes of private and public life, may entertain himfelf with a feries of very ftrange and comical adventures. I prefume I have faid enough to fhow, that it is not without reafon I affirm, " That the real and general " belief

---

* This, it may be faid, would fuppofe a partial neceffity. It may be fo : but in this manner I apprehend that mankind will always argue, as long as they are confcious of a power of felf-determination. And while they are confcious of that power, and argue in this manner, they muft confider the doctrine of neceffity as repugnant to our moft familiar and moft permanent notions in regard to morality and human agency.

" belief of neceffity would be attended with fa-
" tal confequences to fcience, and to human
" nature;"---which is a repetition of the third
remark we formerly made on the doctrine of
the non-exiftence of body *.

And now we have proved, that if there was
any reafon for rejecting BERKELEY's doctrine as
abfurd, and contrary to common fenfe, before
his arguments were fhown to arife from the abufe
of words, there is at prefent the fame reafon for
rejecting the doctrine of neceffity, even on the
fuppofition that it hath not as yet been logically
confuted. Both doctrines are repugnant to the
general belief of mankind : both, notwithftanding all the efforts of the fubtleft fophiftry, are
ftill incredible: both are fo contrary to
nature, and to the condition of human beings,
that they cannot be carried into practice;
and fo contrary to true philofophy, that they
cannot be admitted into fcience, without
bringing fcepticifm along with them, and rendering queftionable the plaineft principles of
moral truth. In a word, we have proved, that
common fenfe, as it teacheth us to believe and
be affured of the exiftence of matter, doth alfo
teach us to believe and be affured, that man is a
free agent.

It would lead us too far from our prefent
purpofe, to enter upon a logical examination of
the argument for neceffity. Our defign is only
to explain, by what marks one may diftinguifh
the principles of common fenfe, that is, intuitive

---

* See the end of the preceding fection.

tive or felf-evident notions, from thofe deceitful
and inveterate opinions that have fometimes affumed the fame appearance.   If I have fatisfied
the reader, that the free agency of men is a felf-
evident fact, I have alfo fatisfied him, that all
reafoning on the fide of neceffity, though accounted unanfwerable, is, in its very nature, and
previoufly to all confutation, abfurd and irrational, and contrary to the practice and principles
of true philofophy.

Let not the friends of liberty be difcouraged
by the perplexing arguments of the Fatalift*.
Arguments in oppofition to felf-evident truth,
muft, if plaufible, be perplexing.   Think what
method of argumentation a man muft purfue,
who fets himfelf to confute any axiom in geometry, or to argue againft the exiftence of a fentiment, acknowledged and felt by all mankind.
Indeed I cannot fee how fuch a perfon fhould
ever impofe upon people of fenfe, except by
availing himfelf of expreffions, which either are
in themfelves ambiguous, or become fo by his
manner of applying them.   If the ambiguity be
difcernible, the argument can have no force; if
there be no fufpicion of ambiguity, the difpute
may

* There is no fubject on which doubts and difficulties may not
be ftarted by ingenious and difputatious men: and therefore, from
the number of their objections, and the length of the controverfy
to which they give occafion, we cannot, in any cafe, conclude,
that the original evidence is weak, or even that it is not obvious and
ftriking.   Were we to prefume, that every principle is dubious
againft which fpecious objections may be contrived, we fhould be
quickly led into univerfal fcepticifm.   The two ways in which the
ingenuity of fpeculative men has been moft commonly employed,
are dogmatical affertions of doubtful opinions, and fubtle cavils
againft certain truths.
                              Gerard's Differtations, ii. 4.

may be continued from generation to generation, without working any change in the fentiments of either party.   When fact is difregard-
ed, when intuition goes for nothing, when no
ftandard of truth is acknowledged, and every unanfwered argument is deemed unanfwerable,
true reafoning is at an end; and the difputant,
having long ago loft fight of common fenfe, is fo
far from regaining the path of truth, that like
Thomfon's peafant bewildered in the fnow, he
continues " to wander on, ftill more and more
" aftray." If any perfon will give himfelf the
trouble to examine the whole controverfy concerning liberty and neceffity, he will find, that
the arguments on both fides come at laft to appear unanfwerable :—there is no common principle acknowledged by both parties, to which
an appeal can be made, and each party charges
the other with begging the queftion.   Is it not
then better to reft fatisfied with the fimple feeling of the underftanding ? I feel that it is in
my power to will or not to will: all you can
fay about the influence of motives will never
convince me of the contrary; or if I fhould fay,
that I am convinced by your arguments, my
conduct muft continually belie my profeffion.
One thing is undeniable: your words are obfcure, my feeling is not;—this is univerfally attended to, acknowledged, and acted upon; thofe
to the majority of mankind would be unintelligible, nay, perhaps they are in a great meafure
fo even to yourfelves*.

C H A P.

---

* " It is evident (fays a great philofopher) that as it is from in-
" ternal confcioufnefs I know any thing of liberty, fo no affertion
" contrary

C H A P.   III.

Recapitulation, and Inference.

T H E substance of the preceding illustrations, when applied to the principal purpose of this discourse, is as follows.

Although it be certain, that all just reasoning does ultimately terminate in the principles of common sense; that is, in principles which must be admitted as certain, or as probable, upon their own authority, without evidence, or at least without proof; even as all mathematical reasoning does ultimately terminate in self-evident axioms: yet philosophers, especially those who have applied themselves to the investigation of the laws of human nature, have not always been careful to confine the reasoning faculty within its proper sphere, but have vainly imagined,

VOL. I.   U   that

" contrary to what I am conscious of concerning it can be ad-
" mitted: and it were better perhaps to treat of this abstruse sub-
" ject after the manner of experimental philosophy, than to fill
" a thousand pages with metaphysical discussions concerning it."
    Maclaurin's account of Newton's discoveries, book 1. *chap.* 4.

    " The constitution of the present world, (says Bishop Butler),
" and the condition in which we are actually placed, is as if we
" were free.   And it may perhaps be justly concluded, that since
" the whole process of action through every step of it is as if we
" were free, therefore we are so."
                            Analogy, part 1. *chap.* 6. § 6.

    One who is a Fatalist, and---one who keeps to his *natural sense* of things, and believes himself a free agent,---these two are con- trasted by the same excellent author, part 1. ch. 6. § 3.

that even the principles of common fenfe are
fubject to the cognifance of reafon, and may be
either confirmed or confuted by argument.——
They have accordingly, in many inftances, carried their inveftigations higher than the ultimate and felf-fupported principles of common
fenfe; and by fo doing, have introduced many
errors, and much falfe reafoning, into the moral
fciences.   To remedy this, it was propofed, as
a matter deferving ferious attention, to afcertain
the feparate provinces of reafon and common
fenfe.   And becaufe, in many cafes, it may be
difficult to diftinguifh a principle of common
fenfe from an acquired prejudice; and confequently, to know at what point reafoning ought
to ftop, and the authority of common fenfe to
be admitted as decifive; it was therefore judged
expedient to inquire, " Whether fuch reafon-
" ings as have been profecuted beyond ultimate
" principles, be not marked with fome peculiar
" characters, by which they may be diftinguifh-
" ed from legitimate inveftigation."   To illuftrate this point, the doctrines of *the non-exiftence of matter*, and *the neceffity of human actions*,
were given as examples; in which, at leaft in
the former of which, common fenfe, in the o-
pinion of all competent judges, is confeffedly
violated;——the natural effects produced upon
the mind by the reafonings that have been urged in favour of thefe doctrines, were confidered; and the confequences, refulting from the
admiffion of fuch reafonings, were taken notice
of, and explained.   And it was found, that the
reafonings that have been urged in favour of
thefe doctrines are really marked with fome peculiar

culiar characters, which, it is prefumed, can belong to no legitimate argumentation. Of thefe reafonings it was obferved, and proved, " That the doctrines they are intended to efta-
" blifh are contradictory to the general belief
" of all men in all ages ;——That, though
" enforced and fupported with fingular fubtle-
" ty, and though admitted by fome profeffed
" philofophers, they do not produce that con-
" viction which found reafoning never fails to
" produce in the intelligent mind ;—and, laft-
" ly, That really to believe, and to act from a
" real belief of, fuch doctrines and reafonings,
" muft be attended with fatal confequences to
" fcience, to virtue, and to human fociety."

I do not fuppofe, that all the errors which have arifen from not attending to the founda-tion of truth, and effential rules of reafoning, as here explained, are equally dangerous. Some of them perhaps may be innocent; to fuch the laft of thefe characters cannot belong. If whol-ly innocent, it is of little confequence, whe-ther we know them to be errors or not. When a new tenet is advanced in moral fci-ence, there will be a ftrong prefumption againft it, if contrary to univerfal opinion : for as eve-ry man may find the evidence of moral fcience in his own breaft, it is not to be fuppofed, that the generality of mankind would, for any length of time, perfift in an error, which their own daily experience, if attended to without pre-judice, could not fail to rectify. Let, there-fore, the evidence of the new tenet be carefully examined, and attended to. If it produce a full and clear conviction in the intelligent mind,

and

and at the fame time ferve to explain the caufes of the univerfality and long continuance of the old erroneous opinion, the new one ought certainly to be received as true. But if the affent produced by the new doctrine be vague, indefinite, and unfatisfying; if nature and common fenfe reclaim againft it; if it recommend modes of thought that are inconceivable, or modes of action that are impracticable;---it is not, it cannot be true, however plaufible its evidence may appear.

Some will think, perhaps, that a ftraighter and fhorter courfe might have brought me fooner, and with equal fecurity, to this conclufion. I acknowledge I have taken a pretty wide circuit. This was owing in part to my love of perfpicuity, which in thefe fubjects hath not always been ftudied fo much as it ought to have been; and partly, and chiefly, to my defire of confuting, on this occafion, as many of the moft pernicious tenets of modern fcepticifm as could be brought within my prefent plan. But the reader will perceive, that I have endeavoured to conduct all my digreffions in fuch a manner, as that they might ferve for illuftrations of the principal fubject.

To teach men to diftinguifh by intuition a dictate of common fenfe from an acquired prejudice, is a work which nature only can accomplifh. We fhall ever be more or lefs fagacious in this refpect, according as Heaven has endowed us with greater or lefs ftrength of mind, vivacity of perception, and folidity of judgement. The method here recommended is more laborious, and much lefs expeditious. Yet this method,

method, if I am not greatly miftaken, may be
of confiderable ufe, to enable us to form a proper eftimate of thofe reafonings, which, by vio-
lating common fenfe, tend to fubvert every principle of rational belief, to fap the foundations
of truth and fcience, and to leave the mind expofed to all the horrors of fcepticifm. To be
puzzled by fuch reafonings, is neither a crime
nor a difhonour; though in many cafes it may
be both difhonourable and criminal to fuffer
ourfelves to be deluded by them. For is not
this to prefer the equivocal voice of an enfnar-
ing wrangler, to the clear, the benevolent, the
infallible dictates of nature? Is not this to belie our fentiments, and to violate our conftitution? Is not this " to forfake the fountains of
" living water, and to hew out unto our-
" felves broken cifterns that can hold no wa-
" ter?"

P A R T   III.

Objections answered.

THEY who confider virtue as a fubject of
mere curiofity, and think that the principles of
morals and properties of conic fections ought
to be explained with the fame degree of apathy
and indifference, will find abundant matter for
cenfure in the preceding obfervations. As the
author is not very ambitious of the good opinion of fuch theorifts, he will not give himfelf
much trouble in multiplying apologies for what,

U 3   to

to them, may have the appearance of keenneſs or ſeverity in the animadverſions he has hither-to made, or may hereafter make, on the princi-ples of certain noted philoſophers. He conſi-ders happineſs as the end and aim of our be-ing; and he thinks philoſophy valuable only ſo far as it may be conducive to this end. Human happineſs ſeemeth to him wholly unat-tainable, except by the means that virtue and religion provide. He is therefore perſuaded, that while employed in pleading the cauſe of virtue, and of true ſcience, its beſt auxiliary, he ſupports, in ſome meaſure, the character of a friend to human-kind; and he would think his right to that glorious appellation extremely queſtionable, if the warmth of his zeal did not bear ſome proportion to the importance of his cauſe. However ſuſpicious he may be of his ability to vindicate the rights of his fellow-creatures, he is not ſuſpicious of his inclinati-tion. He feels, that, on ſuch a ſubject, he muſt ſpeak from the heart, or not ſpeak at all.— For the genius and manner of his diſcourſe he has no other apology to offer: and by every perſon of ſpirit, candour, and benevolence, he is ſure that this apology will be deemed ſuffici-ent.

As to the principles and matter of it, he is leſs confident. Theſe, though neither viſionary nor unimportant, may poſſibly be miſunder-ſtood. He therefore begs leave to urge a few things, for the further vindication and illuſ-tration of them. To his own mind they are fully ſatisfactory; he hopes to render them equally ſo to every candid reader. Happy! if

he

he fhould be as fuccefsful in eftablifhing conviction, as others have been in fubverting it.

C H A P.   I.

Further remarks on the confiftency of thefe
   principles with the interefts of Science and
   the Rights of Mankind.

IT may poffibly be objected to this difcourfe,
That " it tends to difcourage freedom of in-
" quiry, and to promote implicit faith."

But nothing is more contrary to my defign;
as thofe who attend, without prejudice, to the
full import of what I have advanced on the fubject of evidence, will undoubtedly perceive.
Let me be permitted to repeat, that the truths
in which man is moft concerned do not lie exceedingly deep; nor are we to eftimate either
their importance, or their certainty, by the
length of the line of our inveftigation, The
evidences of the philofophy of human nature,
are found in our own breaft; we need not roam
abroad in queft of them; the unlearned are
judges of them as well as the learned. Ambiguities have arifen, when the feelings of the
heart and underftanding were expreffed in words;
but the feelings themfelves were not ambiguous. Let a man attentively examine himfelf,
with a fincere purpofe of difcovering the truth,
and without any bias in favour of particular
theories, and he will feldom be at a lofs in regard to thofe truths, at leaft, that are moft effential to his happinefs and duty. If men muft
                                        needs

needs amuſe themſelves with metaphyſical inveſtigation, let them apply it, where it can do
no harm, to the diſtinctions and logomachies
of ontology.   In the ſcience of human nature
it cannot do good, but muſt of neceſſity do
great harm.   What avail the obſcure deductions
of verbal argument, in illuſtrating what we ſufficiently know by experience? or in ſhowing that
to be fictitious and falſe, whoſe energy we muſt feel
and acknowledge every moment? When therefore I find a pretended principle of human nature evinced by a dark and intricate inveſtigation, I am tempted to ſuſpect, not without reaſon, that its evidence is no where to be found
but in the arguments of the theoriſt; and theſe,
when diſguiſed by quaint diſtinctions, and ambiguous language, it is ſometimes hard to confute, even when the heart recoils from the doctrine with contempt or deteſtation.   If the doctrine be true, it muſt alſo be agreeable to experience : to experience, therefore, let the appeal
be made; let the circumſtances be pointed out,
in which the controverted ſentiment ariſes, or is
ſuppoſed to ariſe.   This is to act the philoſopher, not the metaphyſician? the interpreter of
nature, not the builder of ſyſtems.   But let us
conſider the objection more particularly.

What then do you mean by that implicit
faith, to which you ſuppoſe theſe principles too
favourable? Do you mean an acquieſcence in the
dictates of our own underſtanding, or in thoſe
of others? If the former, I muſt tell you, that
ſuch implicit faith is the only kind of belief
which true philoſophy recommends.   I have already remarked, that, while man continues in
his

his prefent ftate, our own intellectual feelings are, and muft be, the ftandard of truth to us. All evidence productive of belief, is refolvable into the evidence of confcioufnefs; and comes at laft to this point, I believe becaufe I believe, or becaufe the law of rational nature determines me to believe. This belief may be called implicit; but it is the only rational belief of which we are capable: and to fay, that our minds ought not to fubmit to it, is as abfurd as to fay, that our bodies ought not to be nourifhed with food. Revelation itfelf muft be attended with evidence to fatisfy confcioufnefs or common fenfe; otherwife it can never be rationally believed. By the evidence of the gofpel, the rational Chriftian is perfuaded that it comes from God. He acquiefces in it as truth, not becaufe it is recommended by others, but becaufe it fatisfies his own underftanding.

But if, by implicit faith, you mean, what I think is commonly meant by that term, an unwarrantable or unqueftioned acquiefcence in the fentiments of other men, I deny that any part of this difcourfe hath a tendency to promote it. I never faid, that doctrines are to be taken for granted without examination; though I affirmed, that, in regard to moral doctrines, a long and intricate examination is neither neceffary nor expedient. With moral truth, it is the bufinefs of every man to be acquainted; and therefore the Deity has made it level to every capacity.

Far be it from a lover of truth to difcourage freedom of inquiry! Man is poffeffed of reafoning powers; by means of which he may bring

that

that within the fphere of common fenfe, which
was originally beyond it.   Of thefe powers he
·may, and ought to avail himfelf; for many important truths are not felf-evident, and our faculties were not defigned for a ftate of inactivity.
But neither were they defigned to be employed
in fruitlefs or dangerous inveftigation.   Our
knowledge and capacity are limited; it is fit and
neceffary they fhould be fo: we need not wander into forbidden paths, or attempt to penetrate inacceffible regions, in queft of employment; the cultivation of ufeful and practical
fcience, the improvement of arts, and the indif-
penfable duties of life, will furnifh ample fcope
to all the exertions of human genius.   Surely
that man is my friend, who diffuades me from
attempting what I cannot perform, nor even attempt without danger.   And is not he a friend
to fcience and mankind, who endeavours to difcourage fallacious and unprofitable fpeculation,
and to propofe a criterion by which it may be
known and avoided?

But if reafoning ought not to be carried beyond a certain boundary, and if it is the authority of common fenfe that fixeth this boundary,
and if it be poffible to miftake a prejudice for a
principle of common fenfe, how (it may be
faid) are prejudices to be detected?   At this
rate a man has nothing to do, but to call his
prejudice a dictate of common fenfe, and then
it is eftablifhed in perfect fecurity, beyond the
reach of argument.   Does not this furnifh a
pretence for limiting the freedom of inquiry?
—Having already faid a great deal in anfwer to
the firft part of this queftion, I need not now
fay

fay much in anfwer to the laft. I fhall only
afk, on the other hand, what method of reafoning is the propereft for overcoming the prejudices of an obftinate man? Are we to wrangle
with him *in infinitum*, without ever arriving at
any fixed principle? That furely is not the way
to illuftrate truth, or rectify error. Do we
mean to afcertain the importance of our arguments by their number, and to pronounce
that the better caufe whofe champion gives the
laft word? This, I fear, would not mend the
matter.   Suppofe our antagonift fhould deny a
felf-evident truth, or refufe his affent to an intuitive probability; muft we not refer him to
the common fenfe of mankind? If we do not,
we muft either hold our peace, or have recourfe to fophiftry : for when a principle comes
to be intuitively true or falfe, all legitimate
reafoning is at an end, and all further reafoning impertinent.   To the common fenfe of
mankind we muft therefore refer him fooner
or later; and if he continue obftinate, we muft
leave him. Is it not then of confequence to
truth, and may it not ferve to prevent many a
fophiftical argument, and unprofitable logomachy, that we have it continually in view, that
common fenfe is the ftandard of truth? a maxim,
which men are not always difpofed to admit in its
full latitude, and which, in the heat and hurry of
difpute, they are apt to overlook altogether. Some
men will always be found who think the moft abfurd prejudices founded in common fenfe.   Reafonable men never fcruple to fubmit their prejudices or principles to examination : but if that
examination turn to no account, or if it turn to a
                                                    bad

bad account; if it only puzzle where it ought to
convince, and darken what it ought to illuſtrate;
if it recommend impracticable modes of action,
or inconceivable modes of thought;—I muſt
confeſs I cannot perceive the uſe of it. This
is the only kind of reaſoning that I mean to diſ-
courage. It is this kind of reaſoning that has
proved ſo fatal to the abſtract ſciences. In it all
our ſceptical ſyſtems are founded; of it they con-
ſiſt; and by it they are ſupported. Till the abſtract
ſciences be cleared of this kind of reaſoning, they
deſerve not the name of philoſophy: they may
amuſe a weak and turbulent mind, and render
it ſtill weaker and more turbulent; but they cannot convey any real inſtruction : they may undermine the foundations of virtue and ſcience; but
they cannot illuſtrate a ſingle truth, nor eſtabliſh
one principle of importance, nor improve the
mind of man in any reſpect whatſoever.

  By ſome it may be thought an objection to
the principles of this eſſay, " That they ſeem
" to recommend a method of confutation which
" is not ſtrictly according to logic, and do ac-
" tually contradict ſome of the eſtabliſhed laws
" of that ſcience."

  It will readily be acknowledged, that many of the
maxims of the ſchool-logic are founded in truth
and nature, and have ſo long obtained univerſal
approbation, that they are now become prover-
bial in philoſophy. Many of its rules and diſtinctions are extremely uſeful, not ſo much for
ſtrengthening the judgment, as for enabling the
diſputant quickly to comprehend, and perſpicu-
ouſly to expreſs, in what the force or fallacy of
an argument conſiſts. The ground-work of
                                                this

this fcience, the Logic of Ariftotle, if we may judge of the whole by the part now extant, is one of the moft fucceisful and moft extraordinary efforts of philofophic genius that ever appeared in the world. And yet, if we confider this fcience, with regard to its defign and confequences, we fhall perhaps fee reafon to think, that a ftrict obfervance of its laws is not always neceffary to the difcovery of truth.

It was originally intended as a help to difcourfe among a talkative and fprightly people. The conftitution of Athens made public fpeaking of great importance, and almoft a certain road to preferment or diftinction. This was alfo in fome meafure the cafe at Rome; but the Romans were more referved, and did not, till about the time of Cicero, think of reducing converfation or public fpeaking to rule. The vivacity of the Athenians, encouraged by their democratical fpirit, made them fond of difputes and declamations, which were often carried on without any view to difcover truth, but merely to gratify humour, give employment to the tongue, and amufe a vacant hour. Some of the dialogues of Plato are to be confidered in this light, rather as exercifes in declamation, than ferious difquifitions in philofophy. It is true, this is not the only merit even of fuch of them as feem the leaft confiderable. If we are often diffatisfied with his doctrine; if we have little curiofity to learn the characters and manners of that age, whereof he has given fo natural a reprefentation; we muft yet acknowledge, that as models for elegance and fimplicity of compofition, the moft inconfiderable of

Plato's

Plato's dialogues are very ufeful and ingenious. His fpeakers often compliment each o-
ther on the beauty of their ftyle, even when
there is nothing very ftriking in the fentiment*. If, therefore, we would form a juft
eftimate of Plato, we muft regard him not
only as a philofopher, but alfo as a rhetorici-
an; for it is evident he was ambitious to excel
in both characters. But it appears not to have
been his opinion, that the practice of extempo-
rary fpeaking and difputing, fo frequent in his
time, had any direct tendency to promote the
inveftigation of truth, or the acquifition of
wifdom. The Lacedemonians, the moft referved and moft filent people in Greece, and
who made the leaft pretenfions to a literary
character, were, in his judgement, a nation,
not only of the wifeft men, but of the greateft
philofophers. Their words were few, their addrefs not without rufticity; but the meaneft of
them was able, by a fingle expreffion, dexte-
roufly aimed, and feafonably introduced, to
make the ftranger with whom he converfed appear no wifer than a child†.

The Athenians, accuftomed to reduce every
thing to art, and among whom the fpirit of
fcience was more prevalent than in any other
nation,

---

* See the Sympofium. Platonis opera, vol. 3. p. 198. Edit.
Serran.

† Εἰ τίς ἐθέλοι Λακεδαιμονίων τῷ φαυλοτάτῳ συγγενέσθαι. τὰ μὲν
πολλὰ ἐν τοῖς λόγοις εὑρήσει αὐτὸν φαῦλόν τινα φαινόμενον, ἔπειτα ὅπου
ἂν τύχοι τῶν λεγομένων, ἐνέβαλε ῥῆμα ἄξιον λόγου βραχὺ καὶ συνε-
ϛραμμένον, ὥσπερ δεινὸς ἀκοντιϛής· ὥϛε φαίνεσθαι τὸν προσδιαλεγόμε-
νον παιδὸς μηδὲν βελτίω.

Socrates in Plat. Protagora, vol. 1. p. 342.

nation, had contrived a kind of technical logic
long before the days of Ariftotle. Their fophifts taught it in conjunction with rhetoric
and philofophy. But Ariftotle brought it to
perfection, and feems to have been the firft who
profeffedly disjoined it from the other arts and
fciences. On his logic was founded that of the
fchoolmen. But they, like other commentators,
often mifunderftood the text, and often perverted it to the purpofe of a favourite fyftem.
They differed from one another in their notions
of Ariftotle's doctrine, ranged themfelves into
fects and parties; and inftead of explaining the
principles of their mafter, made it their fole
bufinefs to comment upon one another. Now
and then men of learning arofe, who endeavoured to revive the true Peripatetic philofophy; but their efforts, inftead of proving fuccefsful, ferved only to provoke perfecution; and
at length the fcholaftic fyftem grew fo corrupt,
and at the fame time fo enormous in magnitude,
that it became an infuperable incumbrance to
the underftanding, and contributed not a little
to perpetuate the ignorance and barbarifm of
thofe times. The chief aim of the old logic,
even in its pureft form, (fo far at leaft as it was
a practical fcience), was to render men, expert
in arguing readily on either fide of any queftion. But it is one thing to employ our faculties
in fearching after truth, and a very different
thing to employ them equally in defence of truth
and of error: and the fame modification of intellect that fits a man for the one, will by no
means qualify him for the other. Nay, if I
miftake not, the talents that fit us for difcovering

ing truth are rather hurt than improved by the practice of fophiftry. To argue againft one's own conviction, muft always have a bad effect on the heart, and render one more indifferent about the truth, and perhaps more incapable of perceiving it *.

To difpute readily on either fide of any queftion, is admired by fome as a very high accomplifhment: but it is what any perfon of moderate abilities may eafily acquire by a little practice. Perhaps moderate abilities are the moft favourable to the acquifition of this talent. Senfibility and penetration, the infeparable attendants, or rather the moft effential parts, of true genius, qualify a man for difcovering truth with little labour of inveftigation; and at the fame time intereft him fo deeply in it, that he cannot bear to turn his view to the other fide of the queftion. Thus he never employs himfelf in devifing arguments; and, therefore, feldom arrives at any proficiency in that exercife. But the man of flow intellect and dull imagination advances ftep by ftep in his inquiries, without any keennefs of fentiment, or ardor of fancy, to diftract his attention; and without that inftantaneous anticipation of confequences, that leads the man of genius to the conclufion, even before he has examined all the intermediate relations. Hence he naturally acquires a talent for minute obfervation, and for a patient examination of circumftances; at the fame time that

* See the ftory of Pertinax in the Rambler, No. 95.; where the effects of habitual difputation, in perverting the judgement, and vitiating the heart, are illuftrated with the utmoft energy and elegance.

that his infenfibility prevents his interefting himfelf warmly on either fide, and leaves him leifure to attend equally to his own arguments, and to thofe of the antagonift. This gives him eminent fuperiority in a difpute, and fits him, not indeed for difcovering truth, but for baffling an adverfary, and fupporting a fyftem.

I have been told, that Newton, the firft time he read Euclid's Elements, perceived inftantly, and almoft intuitively, the truth of the feveral propofitions, before he confulted the proof. Such vivacity and ftrength of judgement are extraordinary : and indeed, in the cafe of mathematical and phyfical truths, we are feldom to expect this inftantaneous anticipation of confequences, even from men of more than moderate talents. But in moral fubjects, and in moft of the matters that are debated in converfation, there is rarely any need of comparing a great number of intermediate relations : every perfon of found judgement fees the truth at once : or, if he does not, it is owing to his ignorance of fome facts or circumftances, which may be foon learned from a plain narrative, but which are difguifed and confounded more and more by wrangling and contradiction. If there be no means of clearing the difputed facts and difficulties, it would not, I prefume, be imprudent to drop the fubject, and talk of fomething elfe.

It is pleafant enough to hear the habitual wrangler endeavouring to juftify his conduct by a pretence of zeal for the truth. It is not the love of truth, but of victory, that engages him in difputation. I have

witneffed many contefts of this kind; but
have feldom feen them lead, or even tend, to
any ufeful difcovery. Where oftentation, felf-
conceit, or love of paradox, are not concerned, they commonly arife from fome verbal ambiguity, or from the mifconception of fome
fact, which both parties taking it for granted
that they perfectly underftand, are at no pains
to afcertain: and, when once begun, are, by
the vanity or obftinacy of the fpeakers, or perhaps by their mere love of fpeaking, continued,
till accident put an end to them, by filencing
the parties, rather than reconciling their opinions. I once faw a number of perfons, neither
unlearned nor ill-bred, meet together to pafs
a focial evening. As ill-luck would have it, a
difpute arofe about the propriety of a certain
manoeuvre at *quadrille*, in which fome of the
company had been interefted the night before.
Two parties of difputants were immediately
formed; and the matter was warmly argued
from fix o'clock till midnight, when the company broke up. Being no adept in cards, I
could not enter into the merits of the caufe,
nor take any part in the controverfy; but I obferved, that each of the fpeakers perfifted to the
laft in the opinion he took up at the beginning,
in which he feemed to be rather confirmed than
ftaggered by the arguments that had been urged
in oppofition.—With fuch enormous wafte of
time, with fuch vile proftitution of reafon and
fpeech, with fuch wanton indifference to the
pleafures of friendfhip, all difputes are not attended; but moft of them, if I miftake not,
will be found to be equally unprofitable.

I grant,

I grant, that much of our knowledge is gathered from our intercourſe with one another ;
but I cannot think, that we are greatly indebted to the argumentative part of converſation ;
and nobody will ſay, that the moſt diſputati-
ous companions are the moſt agreeable. For
my own part, I have always found thoſe to be
the moſt delightful and moſt improving converſations, in which there was the leaſt contradiction ; every perſon entertaining the utmoſt
poſſible reſpect both for the judgement and for
the veracity of his aſſociate ; and none aſſum-
ing any of thoſe dictatorial airs, which are ſo
offenſive to the lovers of liberty, modeſty, and
friendſhip. --- If a catalogue were to be made of
all the truths that have been diſcovered by
wrangling in company, or by ſolemn diſputa-
tion in the ſchools, I believe it would appear,
that the contending parties might have been
employed as advantageouſly to mankind, and
much more ſo to themſelves, in whipping a
top, or brandiſhing a rattle.

The extravagant fondneſs of the Stoics for
logical quibbles is one of the moſt diſagreeable
peculiarities in the writings of that ſect. Every body muſt have been diſguſted with it in
reading ſome paſſages of the converſations of
Epictetus preſerved by Arrian ; and muſt be ſatisfied, that it tended rather to weaken and bewilder, than to improve the underſtanding.
One could hardly believe to what ridiculous exceſs they carried it. There was a famous problem among them called the *Pſeudomenos*, which
was to this purpoſe. " When a man ſays, *I lie*,
" does he lie, or does he not ? If he lies, he

" ſpeaks

" fpeaks truth : if he fpeaks truth, he lies." Many were the books that their philofophers wrote, in order to folve this wonderful problem. Chryfippus favoured the world with no fewer than fix : and Philetas ftudied himfelf to death in his attempts to folve it. Epictetus, whofe good fenfe often triumphs over the extravagance of Stoicifm, juftly ridicules this logical phrenzy*.

Socrates made little account of the fubtleties of logic; being more folicitous to inftruct others, than to diftinguifh himfelf +. He inferred his doctrine from the conceffions of thofe with whom he converfed; fo that he left no room for difpute, as the adverfary could not contradict him, without contradicting himfelf. And yet, to Socrates philofophy is perhaps more indebted, than to any other perfon whatever ‡.

We

---

* Arrian, lib. 2. cap. 17. Cicero Lucull. cap. 30.

† Supra, part 2. chap. 2. fect. 1.

‡ Cicero in one place (de Finib. lib. 2.) calls him *Parens Philofophiæ*, and in another (de Orat. lib. 3.) affirms, that, in the judgement of all Greece, and according to the teftimony of all the learned, Socrates, on every fubject to which he applied himfelf, excelled all men, in wifdom, politenefs, and penetration, as well as in copioufnefs and variety of eloquence; and that fucceeding philofophers, though they differed widely in their principles, were however ambitious to be thought to belong to the Socratic fchool, and willing to believe that they derived their doctrines from that great feminary of knowledge. --- Socrates was the firft Grecian philofopher who made experience the ground-work of all his reafonings, who applied philofophy to the regulation of human conduct; and who taught, that thofe theories only were valuable, which could be applied to practical and ufeful purpofes. The more we confider the ftate of learning at the time of his appearance, and the pride and infignificancy of thofe fophifts, whom Greece then regarded as the oracles of wifdom, and to whofe char·cter and profeffion

We have therefore no reason to think, that truth is discoverable by those means only which the technical logic prescribes. Aristotle knew the theory both of sophisms and syllogisms, better than any other man; yet Aristotle himself is sometimes imposed on by sophisms of his own invention *. And it is remarkable, that his moral, rhetorical, and political writings, in which his own excellent judgement is little warped by logical subtleties, are far the most useful, and, in point of sound reasoning, the most unexceptionable, part of his philosophy.

The apparent tendency of the school-logic is, to render men disputatious and sceptical, adepts in the knowledge of words, but inattentive to fact and experience. It makes them fonder of speaking than thinking, and therefore strangers to themselves; solicitous chiefly about rules, names and distinctions, and therefore leaves them neither leisure nor inclination for the study of life and manners. In a word, it makes them more ambitious to distinguish themselves

X 3   as

---

fession his conduct as a public teacher formed so striking a contrast, the more we shall be sensible of our obligations to this great and excellent man, who was said to have brought philosophy down from heaven; and who may truly be said to have

——————— turn'd the *reasoning* art
From words to things, from fancy to the heart.

* Thus he is said to have proved the earth to be the centre of the universe by the following sophism.---" Heavy bodies naturally " tend to the centre of the universe; we know by experience, " that heavy bodies tend to the centre of the earth; therefore the " centre of the earth is the same with that of the universe."—— Which is what the Logicians call *petitio principii*, or *begging the question*.

as the partifans of a dogmatift, than as inquirers after truth.   It is eafy to fee how far a man
of this temper is qualified to make difcoveries
in knowledge.   To fuch a man, indeed, the
name of truth is only a pretence: he neither
is, nor can be, much interefted in the folidity
or importance of his tenets; it is enough if he
can render them plaufible nay, it is e-
nough if he can filence his adverfary by any
means.   The captious turn of an habitual
wrangler deadens the underftanding, fours the
temper, and hardens the heart: by rendering
the mind fufpicious, and attentive to trifles, it
weakens the fagacity of inftinct, and extinguifh-
es the fire of imagination; it transforms converfation into a ftate of warfare; and reftrains
thofe lively fallies of fancy, fo effectual in promoting good-humour and good-will, which,
though often erroneous, are a thoufand times
more valuable than the dull correctnefs of a
mood-and-figure difciplinarian.

    One of the firft maxims of the fchool-logic
is, That nothing is to be believed, but what we
can give a reafon for believing; a maxim deftructive of all truth and fcience, as hath been
fully fhown in the former part of this difcourfe.
We muft not, however, lay this maxim to the
charge of the ancient logic.   DES CARTES,
and the modern fceptics, got it from the fchoolmen, who forged it out of fome paffages of Ariftotle mifunderftood.   The philofopher faid indeed, that all inveftigation fhould begin with
doubt; but this doubt is to remain only till the
underftanding be convinced; which, in Arif-
                                            totle's

totle's judgement, may be effected by intuitive evidence as well as by argumentative. The doctrine we have been endeavouring to illuſtrate, tends not to encourage any prejudices, or any opinions, unfriendly to truth or virtue : its only aim is, to eſtabliſh the authority of thoſe inſtinctive principles of conviction and aſſent, which the rational part of mankind have acknowledged in all ages, and which the condition of man, in reſpect both of action and intelligence, renders it abſurd not to acknowledge.—We cannot ſuppoſe, that the human mind, unlike to all other natural ſyſtems, is made up of incompatible principles; in it, as in all the reſt, there muſt be unity of deſign; and therefore the principles of human belief, and of human action, muſt have one and the ſame tendency. But many of our modern philoſophers teach a different doctrine; endeavouring to perſuade themſelves, and others, that they ought not to believe what they cannot poſſibly diſbelieve; and that thoſe actions may be abſurd, and contrary to truth, the performance of which is neceſſary to our very exiſtence. If they will have it, that this is philoſophy, I ſhall not diſpute about the word; but I inſiſt on it, that all ſuch philoſophy is no better than pedantic nonſenſe; and that, if a man were to write a book, to prove, that fire is the element in which we ought to live, he would not act more abſurdly, than ſome metaphyſicians of theſe times would be thought to have acted, if their works were underſtood, and rated according to their intrinſic merit.

That

That every thing may be made matter of difpute, is another favourite maxim of the school-
logic; and it would not be eafy to devife one
more detrimental to true fcience. What a
ftrange propenfity thefe doctors have had to difputation! One would think, that, in their
judgement, " the chief end of man is, to con-
" tradict his neighbour, and wrangle with him
" for ever." To attempt a proof of what I
know to be falfe, and a confutation of what
I know to be true, is an exercife from which I
can never expect advantage fo long as I deem
rationality a blefling. I never heard it prefcribed as a recipe for ftrengthening the fight,
to keep conftantly blindfolded in the day-time,
and put on fpectacles when we go to fleep; nor
can I imagine how the ear of a mufician
could be improved, by his playing frequently
on an ill-tuned fiddle. And yet the fchoolmen feem to have thought, that the more we
fhut our eyes againft the truth, we fhall the
more diftinctly perceive it; and that the oftener we practife falfehood, we fhall be the more
fagacious in detecting, and the more hearty in
abhorring it. To fuppofe, that we may make
every thing matter of difpute, is to fuppofe,
that we can account for every t.ing. Alas!
in moft cafes, to feel and believe, is all we have
to do, or can do. Deftined for action, rather
than for knowledge, and governed more by inftinct than by reafon, we can extend our inveftigations, efpecially with regard to ourfelves, but
a very little way. And, after all, when we acquiefce with implicit confidence in the dictates
of our nature, where is the harm or the danger

ger of fuch a conduct? Is our life fhortened, or health injured by it? No. Are our judgements perverted, or our hearts corrupted? No. Is our happinefs impaired, or the fphere of our gratification contracted? Quite the contrary. Have we lefs leifure for attending to the duties of life, and for adorning our minds with ufeful and elegant literature? We have evidently more time left for thofe purpofes. Why then fo much logic, fo many difputes, and fo many theories, about the firft philofophy? Rather than in difguifing falfehood, and labouring to fubvert the foundations of truth, why do we not, with humility and candour, employ our faculties in the attainment of plain, practical, and ufeful knowledge?*

The

---

* It is far from my intention to fay, that a talent for arguing on either fide of a controvertible queftion is of no ufe. When exerted with good-nature, and modefty, it may fometimes help to enliven converfation, and give play to the intellectual faculties. And it may alfo be applied with good effect to purpofes ftill more important.

It would feem that Cicero thought, that the end of public fpeaking was not to elucidate or inveftigate truth, but only to make one opinion appear more probable than another; and that when an orator had done his beft, it could only be faid, "Illum pruden- "tibus diferte, ftultis etiam vere dicere videri." *De Oratore, lib.* I. & 3. For fuch an employment, difputation was a very proper preparatory exercife, as the fame author often declares. But it does not follow, that a habit of difputation is of benefit to the philofopher, or to thofe public fpeakers, whofe aim, far more noble than that of the Ciceronian orator, is to inform the judgement, and improve the heart.

In a fenate or council, met for the purpofe of preparing or making laws, it is highly expedient, that the reafons for and againft every public meafure be urged with freedom. This tends not only to preferve the laws and conftitution, but alfo to quiet mens minds, by removing thofe jealoufies which are generally entertained againft perfons in high office. Befides, political truth depends

The consequences of submitting every sentiment and principle to the test of reasoning,
have been considered already. This practice
has, in every age, tended much to confound
science, to prevent the detection of error, and
(may we not add?) to debase the human understanding.   For have we not seen real genius,
under the influence of a disputatious spirit, derived from nature, fashion, or education, eva-
porate

pends often on principles so exceedingly complicated, that a ma-
giftrate or senator will hardly truft his own judgement, till he finds
it warranted by that of others, and has heard the moft material
reasons that can be urged in oppofition.   But to argue againft conviction, and for the fake of argument, or in order to gratify private pique, or to fupport a faction, is furely unworthy of senators
met in folemn affembly, and deliberating upon affairs of the utmoft importance, both to the prefent and to future generations.

Moreover: As it is better that a criminal efcape, than an innocent man fuffer punifhment; and as the law fhould not only determine the differences, but as much as poffible fatisfy the minds of
men; it will be readily allowed, that in a court of juftice every
prifoner fhould be prefumed to be innocent, till the proofs of his
guilt appear, and every caufe thoroughly difcuffed on both fides,
that the grounds upon which the fentence proceeds may be evident
to all concerned.   It is therefore right, that each party fhould be
permitted to exert itfelf, as far as truth and decency will permit,
in its own vindication.   So that a habit of devifing arguments on
either fide of controverted queftions feems to be a neceffary qualifi-
cation to every perfon who wifhes to make a figure at the bar.   For
the more fully thofe queftions are difcuffed before the judges, the
greater honour redounds, not to the pleader only, but to the law
alfo, and confequently the greater emolument to the community.
Yet even thefe judicial difputations may be carried too far.   And
the more a pleader indulges himfelf in deviating from truth, in
perplexing the caufe with arguments that he knows to be frivolous,
in confounding the judgement of his hearers by unreafonable appeals to their paffions, or in wearing out their attention with ftudied
prolixity, the lefs refpectable will he be in his private character,
and the lefs ufeful as a member of fociety.   I never heard a lawyer
blamed for declining a caufe notorioufly bad: but to engage
for hire in all caufes, good and bad, with equal zeal, and equal
alacrity, is furely not commendable.

To

porate in fubtlety, fophiftry, and vain refinement? Lucretius, Cicero, and Des Cartes,
might be mentioned as examples. And it will
be matter of lafting regret in the republic of
letters, that one, greater in fome refpects than
the greateft of thefe, I mean John Milton, had
the misfortune to be born in an age when the
ftudy of fcholaftic theology was deemed an effential part of intellectual difcipline.

It is either affectation, or falfe modefty, that
makes him fay they know nothing with certainty. Man's knowledge, indeed, compared with
that of fuperior beings, may be very inconfiderable : and compared with that of The Supreme,
is " as nothing, and vanity:" and it is true,
that we are daily puzzled in attempting to account for the moft familiar appearances. But
it is true, notwithftanding, that we do know,
and cannot doubt of our knowing, fome things
with certainty. And

> " Let fchool-taught pride diffemble all it can,
> " Thefe little things are great to little man. *"

To

To be able to fpeak readily and plaufibly in vindication of any
opinion, is no doubt an ornamental, and may be an ufeful accomplifhment, But to teach it, belongs rather to the rhetorici-
an, than to the philofopher. And it is to be feared, that, in their
ardour to acquire it, young men have fometimes become more en-
amoured of victory than of truth, and more intent upon words
than upon argument ; and that they may have alfo been too eager
to difplay it in private company, where, unlefs feafoned with wit
and modefty, with fweetnefs of temper, and foftnefs of voice, it
foon becomes a moft intolerable nuifance. --- To philofophy, that
is, to the right obfervation and interpretation of nature, habits
of wrangling, and theories of fyllogifm, feem to me to be juft as
neceffary a prelude, as the art of rope-dancing is to the ftudy of
agriculture.

* Goldfmith's Traveller.

To be vain of any attainment, is prefumption
and folly : but to think every thing difputable,
is a proof of a weak mind and captious
temper. And however fceptics may boaft of
their modefty, in difclaiming all pretenfions to
certain knowledge, I would appeal to the man
of candour, whether they or we feem to poffefs
leaft of that virtue ;—they, who fuppofe, that
they can raife infurmountable objections in every fubject ; or we, who believe, that our Maker has permitted us to know with certainty
fome few things ?

In oppofition to this practice of making every thing matter of difpute, we have endeavoured to fhow, that the inftinctive fuggeftions of
common fenfe are the ultimate ftandard of truth
to man; that whatever contradicts them is contrary to fact, and therefore falfe ; that to fuppofe them cognifable by reafon, is to fuppofe
truth as variable as the intellectual, or as the
argumentative, abilities of men ; and that it is
an abufe of reafon, and tends to the fubverfion
of fcience, to call in queftion the authenticity
of our natural feelings, and of the natural fuggeftions of the human underftanding.

That fcience never profpered while the old
logic continued in fafhion, is undeniable. Lord
Verulam was one of the firft who brought it
into difrepute ; and propofed a different method
of inveftigating truth, namely, that the appearances of nature fhould be carefully obferved ; and, inftead of facts being wrefted to
make them fall in with theory, that theory
fhould be cautioufly inferred from facts, and
from them only. The event has fully proved,
that

that our great philofopher was in the right:
for fcience has made more progrefs fince his
time, and by his method, than for a thoufand
years before. The court of Rome well knew
the importance of the fchool-logic in fupporting
their authority; they knew it could be employed more fuccefsfully in difguifing error, than
in vindicating truth : and Puffendorff fcruples
not to infinuate, that they patronifed it for this
very reafon *. Let it not then be urged, as an
objection to this difcourfe, that it recommends
a method of confutation which is not ftrictly
logical. It is enough for me, that the method
here recommended is agreeable to good fenfe
and found philofophy, and to the general notions and practices of men.

C H A P.   II.

The fubject continued. Eftimate of Meta-
    phyfic. Caufes of the Degeneracy of Mo-
    ral Science.

THE reader has no doubt obferved, that I
have frequently ufed the term *Metaphyfic*, as if
it implied fomething worthy of contempt or
cenfure. That no lover of fcience may be offended, I fhall now account for this, by explaining the nature of that metaphyfic which I
                                        conceive

* De Monarchia Pontificis Romani.

conceive to be repugnant to true philofophy, though it has often affumed the name; and which, therefore, in my judgement, the friends of truth ought folicitoufly to guard againft. This explanation will lead to fome remarks that may perhaps throw additional light on the pre-fent fubject.

Ariftotle bequeathed by legacy his writings to Theophraftus; who left them, together with his own, to Neleus of Scepfis. The pofterity of Neleus, being illiterate men, kept them for fome time locked up; but afterwards hearing, that the king of the country was making a ge-neral fearch for books to furnifh his library at Pergamus, they hid them in a hole under ground; where they lay for many years, and fuffered much from worms and dampnefs. At laft, however, they were fold to one Apellicon; who caufed them to be copied out; and, having, (according to Strabo) a greater paffion for books than for knowledge, ordered the tranfcribers to fupply the chafms from their own invention. When Sylla took Athens, he feized on Apelli-con's library, and carried it to Rome. Here the books of Ariftotle were revifed, by Tyrannio the grammarian, and afterwards by Androni-cus of Rhodes, a Peripatetic philofopher, who publifhed the firft complete edition of them *. To fourteen of thefe books, which it feems had no general title, Andronicus prefixed the words, *Ta meta ta phyfica* †; that is, *The books pofterior to the phyfics*; either becaufe, in the order of the

former

---

* Strabo, p. 609. Paris edit. 1620. Plut. Sylla,
† Τὰ μιτὰ τα φισικα.

former arrangement, they happened to be placed, or becaufe the editor meant that they fhould be ftudied, next after the phyfics.   This is faid to be the origin of the word *Metaphyfic*.

The fubject of thefe fourteen books is mif-cellaneous : yet the Peripatetics feem to have confidered them as conftituting but one branch of fcience; the place of which in their fyftem may be thus conceived.   All philofophy is ei-ther fpeculative or practical.   The practical regulates the moral and intellectual operations of men, and therefore comprehends ethics and logic.   The fpeculative refts in the knowledge of truth; and is divided into three parts, to wit, Phyfics, which inquire into the nature of mate-rial fubftances, and the human foul; Mathe-matics which confider certain properties of bo-dy as abftracted from body,; and this Metaphy-fic, (which Ariftotle is faid to have called *Theo-logy*, and the *Firft Philofophy)*, which, befides, fome remarks on truth in general, the method of difcovering it, and the errors of former philofophers, explains, firft, the general pro-perties of being; and fecondly, the nature of things feparate from matter, namely, of God the one firft caufe, and of the forty-feven in-ferior deities.

Following the notion, that thefe fourteen books comprehend only one part of philofo-phy, the Chriftian Peripatetics divided meta-phyfics into univerfal and particular.   In the firft, they treated of being, and its properties and parts confidered as it is being*; in the fecond, of God and angels.   The

---

* Metaphyfique univerfelle—à laquelle il eft traité de l'etant,

 et

The fchoolmen disjoined the philofophy of the human mind from phyfics where Ariftotle had placed it; and added it to metaphyfics, becaufe its objeſt is an immaterial fubftance. So that their metaphyfics confifted of three parts; Ontology, in which they pretended to explain the general properties of being; Pneumatics, which treated of the human mind; and Natural Theology, which treated of the Supreme Being, and of thofe fpirits which have either no body at all, or one fo very fine as to be imperceptible to human fenfe.

From the account we have given of the manner in which Ariftotle's works' were firft publifhed, the reader will admit, that fome of the errors to be found in them may reafonably enough be imputed to the firft tranfcribers and editors. It was a grofs error in diftribution, to reduce God, and the inferior deities, who were conceived to be a particular fpecies of beings, to the fame clafs with thofe qualities or attributes that are common to all being, and to treat of both in the fame part of philofophy. It was no lefs improper than if a phyfiologift fhould compofe a treatife, " Of men, horfes, and identity." This inaccuracy could not have efcaped Ariftotle: it is to be charged on his editors, who probably miftook a feries of treatifes on various fubjeſts for one treatife on one particular fubjeſt. To many this may feem a trifling miftake; but it has produced important confequences. It led the earlier Peripatetics into

to

---

et des fes proprietés, et des parties ou membres de l'etant, felon qu'il eft etant, &c. *Bouju.*

.to the impropriety of explaining the divine exiftence, and the general properties of being, by
the fame method of reafoning; and it induced
the fchoolmen to confound the important
fciences of pnumatics and natural theology
with the idle diftinctions and logomachies of
ontology. Natural theology ought to confift
of legitimate inferences from the effect to the
caufe; pneumatics, or the philofophy of the human mind, are nothing but a detail of facts me-
thodized, and applied to practice, by obvious
and convincing reafonings: both fciences are
founded in experience; but ontology pretends
to afcertain its principles by demonftrations *a
priori*. In fact, though ontology were, what it
profeffes to be an explication of the general
properties of being, it could not throw any
light on natural theology and pneumatics; for
in them the ontological method of reafoning
would be as improper as the mathematical.—
But the fyftems of ontology that have come into my hands are little better than vocabularies
of thofe hard words which the fchoolmen had
contrived, in order to give an air of myftery
and importance to their doctrine. While,
therefore, the fciences of Natural Theology and
Pneumatics were, by this prepofterous divifion,
referred to the fame part of philofophy with ontology, how was it poffible they could profper,
or be explained by their own proper evidence!
In fact, they did not profper: experience, their
proper evidence, was laid afide; and fictitious
theory, difguifed by ontological terms and diftinctions, and fupported by ontological reafoning, was fubftituted in its ftead.

LOCKE was one of the firſt who reſcued the philoſophy of human nature out of the hands of the ſchoolmen, cleared it of the enormous incumbrance of ſtrange words which they had heaped upon it, and ſet the example of aſcertaining our internal operations, not by theory but by experience. His ſucceſs was wonderful: for though he has ſometimes fallen into the ſcholaſtic way of arguing, as in his firſt book, and ſometimes ſuffered himſelf to be impoſed on by words, as in his account of ſecondary qualities, too raſhly adopted from the Carteſians; yet has he done more to eſtabliſh the abſtract ſciences on a proper foundation, than could have been expected from one man, who derived almoſt all his lights from himſelf. His ſucceſſors, BUTLER and HUTCHESON excepted, have not been very fortunate. BERKELEY's book, though written with a good deſign, did more harm than good, by recommending and exemplifying a method of argumentation ſubverſive of all knowledge, and leading directly to univerſal ſcepticiſm. Mr. HUME's *Treatiſe* and *Eſſays* are ſtill more exceptionable. This author has revived the ſcholaſtic way of reaſoning from theory, and of wreſting facts to make them coincide with it. His language indeed is more modiſh, but equally favourable to ſophiſtical argument, and equally proper for giving an air of plauſibility and importance to what is frivolous or unintelligible. What regard we are to pay to his profeſſion of arguing from experience has been already conſidered.

The word *metaphyſics*, according to vulgar uſe, is applied to all diſquiſitions concerning
things

things immaterial. In this fenfe the plaineft account of the faculties of the mind, and of the principles of morality and natural religion, would be termed *metaphyfics*. Such metaphyfics, however, we are fo far from defpifing or cenfuring, that we account it the fublimeft and moft ufeful part of fcience.

Thofe arguments alfo and illuftrations in the abftract philofophy, which are not obvious to ordinary underftandings, are fometimes called *metaphyfical*. But as the principles of this philofophy, however well expreffed, appear fomewhat abftrufe to one who is but a novice in the ftudy; and as very plain principles may feem intricate in an author who is inattentive to his expreffion, as the beft authors fometimes are, it would be unfair to reject, or conceive a prejudice againft, every moral doctrine that is not perfectly free from obfcurity. Yet a continued obfcurity, in matters whereof every man fhould be a competent judge, cannot fail to breed a fufpicion, either that the doctrine is faulty, or that the writer is not equal to his fubject.

The term *metaphyfical*, in thofe paffages of this book, where it is expreffive of cenfure, will be found to allude to that mode of abftract inveftigation, fo common among the fceptics and the fchoolmen, which is fupported, either wholly by an ambiguous and indefinite phrafeology, or by that in conjunction with a partial experience; and which feldom fails to lead to fuch conclufions as contradict matter of fact, or truths of indifputable authority. It is this mode of inveftigation that has introduced fo many er-

rors

rors into the moral fciences; for few, even of our moft candid moral philofophers, are entire-ly free from it. The love of fyftem, or partia-lity to a favourite opinion, not only puts a man off his guard; fo as to make him overlook in-accurate expreffions, and indefinite notions, but may fometimes occafion even a miftake of fact. When fuch miftakes are frequent, and affect the moft important truths, we muft blame the au-thor for want of candour, or want of capacity: when they are innocent, and recur but fel-dom, we ought to afcribe them to the imperfec-tion of human nature.

Inftances of this metaphyfic are fo common, that we might almoft fill a volume with a lift of them. Spinofa's pretended demonftration of the exiftence of the one great being, by which, however, he meant only the univerfe, is a me-taphyfical argument, founded in a feries of falfe or unintelligible, though plaufible, defini-tions *. BERKELEY's proof of the non-exift-ence of matter is wholly metaphyfical; and arifes chiefly from the miftake of fuppofing cer-tain words to have but one meaning, which really have two, and fometimes three. LOCKE's difcourfe againft innate ideas and principles, is likewife too metaphyfical. Some of his noti-ons on that fubject are, I believe, right; but he has not explained them with his wonted pre-cifion; and moft of his arguments are founded on an ambiguous acceptation of the words *idea* and *innate*.

The

---

* See the Appendix to vol. 1. of Chev. Ramfay's Principles of Religion.

The author of the *Fable of the Bees* feems to have carried this mode of reafoning as far as it will go.   If there had been no ambiguous words in the Englifh language, the underftanding of mankind would never have been affronted with his fyftem.   Many of our appetites become criminal only when exceffive; and we have not always names to exprefs that degree of indulgence which is confiftent with virtue.   The fhamelefs word-catcher takes advantage of this, and confounds the innocent gratification with the exceffive or criminal indulgence; calling both by the fame name, and taking it for granted, that what he proves to be the true of the one is alfo true of the other.   What is it that may not be proved by this way of arguing ? May not vice be proved to be virtue, and virtue to be vice ? May not a regard to reputation, cleanlinefs, induftry, generofity, conjugal love, be proved to be the fame with vanity, luxury, avarice, profufion, fenfuality ? May it not be proved, that private virtues are private vices ; and, confequently, that private vices are public benefits ? Such a conclufion is indeed fo eafily made out by fuch logic, that nothing but ignorance, impudence and a hard heart, is neceffary to qualify a man for making it.   If it be faid, that confiderable genius muft be employed in dreffing up thefe abfurd doctrines, fo as to render them plaufible; I would afk, who are the perfons who think them plaufible ? Never did I hear of one man of virtue or learning, who did not both deteft and defpife them.   They feem plaufible enough to gamblers, highwaymen, and *petit maitres*; but it will not

be pretended, that thofe gentlemen have leifure, inclination, or capacity, to reflect on what
they read or hear fo as to feparate truth from
falfehood.

Among metaphyfical writers, Mr, HUME
holds a diftinguifhed place.   Every part of philofophy becomes metaphyfic in his hands.   His
whole theory of the underftanding is founded on
the doctrine of impreffions and ideas, which, as
he explains it, is fo contrary to fact, that nothing but the illufion of words could make it
pafs upon any reader.   I have already given feveral inftances of this author's metaphyfical
fpirit.   I fhall give one more; which I beg
leave to confider at fome length; that I may
have an opportunity of confuting a very dangerous error, and, at the fame time, of difplaying
more minutely, than by this general defcription,
the difference between metaphyfical and philofophical inveftigation.

Does any one imagine, that moral and intellectual virtues, that juftice and genius, are virtues of the fame kind; that they are contemplated with the fame fentiments, and known to
be virtues by the fame criterion? Few, I prefume, are of this opinion; Mr HUME has
adopted it, and taken pains to prove it.   I fhall
demonftrate, that this very important error has
arifen, either from inaccurate obfervation, or
from his being impofed on by words not well
underftood, or rather from both caufes.

It is true, that juftice, great genius, and bodily ftrength, are all ufeful to the poffeffor and
to fociety; and all agreeable to, or (which in
this author's ftyle amounts to the fame things
                                         approved

approved by, every one who confiders or contemplates them. They therefore, at leaft the
two firft, completely anfwer our author's definition of virtue *.   And it would be eafy to write
a great book, to fhow the reafons why moral,
intellectual, and corporeal abilities, yield pleafure to the beholder and poffeffor, and to trace
out a number of analogies, real or verbal, fub-
fifting between them.   But this is nothing to
the purpofe : they may refemble in ten thoufand refpects, and yet differ as widely, as a
beaft or ftatue differs from a man.   Let us
trace the author's argument to its fource.

Virtue is known by a certain agreeable feeling or fentiment, arifing from the confcioufnefs
of certain affections or qualities in ourfelves, or
from the view of them in others.   Granted.
Juftice, humanity, generofity, excite approbation ;—a handfome face excites approbation ;—
great genius excites approbation : the effect or
fentiment produced is the fame in each inftance:
the object, or caufe, muft therefore, in each inftance, be of the fame kind.   This is genuine
metaphyfic: but before a man can be mifled by
it, he muft either find, on confulting his experience, that the feeling excited by the contemplation of thefe objects is the fame in each inftance; in which cafe I would fay, that his feelings

ings

---

* It is the nature, and indeed the definition, of virtue, " that
" it is a quality of the mind agreeable to, or approved by, every
" one who confiders or contemplates it."

Hume's Effays, vol. 2. p. 333. edit. 1767. Note.

Bodily qualities are excluded by this definition, but feem to be
admitted by our author in fome of his reafonings on the fubject,
as indeed upon his principles they very well may.

ings are defective, or himself an inaccurate obferver of nature :—or he muft fuppofe, that the
word *approbation*, becaufe written and pro-
nounced the fame way, does really mean the
fame thing in each of the three propofitions
above mentioned ; in which cafe, I would fay,
that his judgement and ideas are confounded by
the mere found and fhape of a word. I am
confcious, that my approbation of a fine face is
different in kind from my approbation of great
genius ; and that both are extremely different
from my approbation of juftice, humanity, and
generofity : if I call thefe three different kinds
of approbation by the fame general name, I ufe
that name in three different fignifications.
Therefore moral, intellectual, and corporeal
virtues, are not of the fame, but of different
kinds.

I confefs, fays our author, that thefe three
virtues are contemplated with three different
kinds of approbation. But the fame thing is
true of different moral virtues : piety excites
one kind of approbation, juftice another, and
compaffion a third ; the virtues of Cato excite
our efteem, thofe of Cæfar our love : if therefore piety, juftice, and compaffion, be virtues
of the fame kind, notwithftanding that they
excite different kinds of approbation, why
would juftice, genius, and beauty, be accounted virtues of different kinds * ?—This is another metaphyfical argument ; an attempt to determine by words what facts only can determine. I ftill infift on fact and experience.
                                              My

* Treatife of Human Nature, vol. 3. p. 258.

My fentiments, in regard to thefe virtues, are
fo diverfified, and in each variety fo peculiar,
that I know, and am affured, that piety, juftice, and humanity, are diftinct individual virtues of the fame kind ; and that piety, genius,
and beauty, are virtues of different kinds. Applied to each of the former qualities, the word
virtue means the fame thing; but beauty is
virtue in one fenfe, genius in another, and piety in a third.

Well, if the fentiments excited in you by
the contemplation of thefe virtues, are fo much
diverfified, and in each variety fo peculiar, you
muft be able to explain in what refpect your
approbation of intellectual virtue differs from
your approbation of moral; which I prefume
you will find no eafy tafk.—It is not fo difficult,
Sir, as you feem to apprehend. When a man
has acted generoufly or juftly, I praife him,
and think him worthy of praife and reward,
for having done his duty; when ungeneroufly
or unjuftly, I blame him, and think him worthy of blame and punifhment : but a man deferves neither punifhment nor blame for want of
beauty or of underftanding; nor reward nor
praife for being handfome or ingenious.—But
why are we thought worthy of blame and punifhment for being unjuft, and not for being
homely, or void of underftanding? The general confcience of mankind would reply, Becaufe we have it in our power to be juft, and
ought to be fo; but an idiot cannot help his
want of underftanding, nor an ugly man his
want of beauty. This our author will not allow to be a fatisfactory anfwer; becaufe, fays
he,

he, I have fhown, that free-will has no place
with regard to the actions, no more than the
qualities of men *.   What an immenfe metaphyfical labyrinth fhould we have to run through
if we were to difintangle ourfelves out of this argument in the common courfe of logic! To
fhorten the controverfy, I muft beg leave to affirm, in my turn, that our moral actions are in
our own power, though beauty and genius are
not; and to appeal, for proof of this affirmati-
on, to the fecond part of this Effay, or, rather,
to the common fenfe of mankind.

Again, " Moral diftinctions," fays Mr.
HUME. " arife from the natural diftinctions of
" pain and pleafure; and when we receive thofe
" feelings from the general confideration of
" any quality or character, we denominate it
" virtuous or vitious.   Now I believe no one
" will affert, that a quality can never produce
" pleafure or pain to the perfon who con-
" fiders it, unlefs it be perfectly volunta-
" ry in the perfon who poffeffes it †."
" ——More metaphyfic! and a fophifm too
---a *petitio principii!* Here our author endeavours to confound intellectual with moral virtue, by an argument which fuppofeth his own
theory of virtue to be true; of which theory
this confufion of the virtues is a neceffary confequence.   The reader muft fee, that this argument, if it prove any thing at all, might be
made to prove, that the fmell or beauty of a
rofe, the tafte of an apple, the hardnefs of fteel,
and the glittering of a diamond, as well as bodily

* Treatife of Human Nature, vol. 3. p. 260.
† Ibid.

dily ſtrength and great genius, are all virtue
of the ſame kind with juſtice, generoſity, and
gratitude.---Still we wander from the point.
How often muſt it be repeated, that this matter is to be determined, not by metaphyſical arguments founded on ambiguous words, but by
faĉts and experience !

"　Have I not appealed to faĉts ? he will ſay.
"　Are not all the qualities that conſtitute the
"　great man, conſtancy, fortitude, magnani-
"　mity, as involuntary and neceſſary, as the
"　qualities of the judgement and imaginati-
"　on ?*" The term *great man* is ſo very equivocal, that I will have nothing to do with it,
The vileſt ſcoundrel on earth, immediately
commences great man, when he has with im-
punity perpetrated any extraordinary aĉt of
wickedneſs ; murthered fifty thouſand men ;
robbed all the houſes of half a dozen provinces ;
or dexterouſly plundered his own country, to
defray the expence of a ruinous war, contrived
on purpoſe to ſatiate his avarice, or divert the
public attention from his blunders and villai-
nies. I ſpeak of the qualities that conſtitute the
good man, that is, of moral qualities ; and theſe,
I affirm, to be within every man's reach, though
genius and beauty are not.

"　But are not men afraid of paſſing for good-
"　natured, leſt that ſhould be taken for want of
"　underſtanding?---and do they not often
"　boaſt of more debauches than they have
"　been really engaged in, to give themſelves
"　airs of fire and ſpirit?+" Yes : fools do the
firſt,

* Treatiſe of Human Natnre, vol. 3. p. 259
+ Ibid. p. 257.

firft, to recommend themfelves to fools ; and
profligates the laft, to recommend themfelves
to profligates : but he is little acquainted with
the human heart, who does not perceive, that
fuch fentiments are affected, and contrary to
the way of thinking that is moft natural to
mankind.

    " But are you not as jealous of your charac-
" ter, with regard to fenfe and knowledge, as
" to honour and courage ?" * This queftion
ought to be addreffed to thofe in whom courage
is a virtue, and the want of it a vice: and I
am certain, that there is not in his Majefty's
fervice one officer or private man, who would
not wifh to be thought rather a valiant fol-
dier, though of no deep reach, than a very cle-
ver fellow, with the addition of an infamous
coward --- The term *honour* is of dubious import. According to the notions of thefe times,
a man may blafpheme God, fell his country,
murder his friend, pick the pocket of his fel-
low-fharper, and employ his whole life in feducing others to vice and perdition, and yet be
accounted a man of honour ; provided he be
accuftomed to fpeak certain words, wear certain cloaths, and haunt certain company. If
this be the honour alluded to by the author,
an honeft man may, for a flender confideration, renounce all pretenfions to it. But if he allude (as I rather fuppofe) to thofe qualities of
the heart and underftanding which intitle one
to general efteem and confidence, Mr. HUME
                              knows,

---

* Treatife of Human Nature, vol. 3. p. 257.

knows, that this kind of honour is dearer to a man than life.

" Well, then, temperance is a virtue in " every ftation ; yet would you not chufe to " be convicted of drunkennefs rather than of " ignorance ?*"---I have heard of a witty parfon, who, having been difmiffed for irregularities, ufed afterwards, in converfation, to fay, that he thanked God he was not cafhiered for ignorance and infufficiency, but only for vice and immorality.   According to our author's doctrine, this fpeech was neither abfurd nor profane: but I am fure the generality of mankind would be of a different opinion.   To be ignorant of what we ought to know, is to be deficient in moral virtue; to profefs to know what we are ignorant of, is falfehood, a breach of moral virtue: whether thefe vices be more or lefs atrocious than intemperance muft be determined by the circumftances of particular cafes.   To be ignorant of what we could not know, of what we do not profefs to know, and of what it is not our duty to know, is no vice at all; and a man muft have made fome progrefs in debauchery, before he can fay from ferious conviction I would rather be chargeable with intemperance, than with ignorance of this kind.

It appears, then, that our author's reafoning on the prefent fubject, is not philofophical, but what I call *metaphyfical*† ; being founded,

* See Treatife of Human Nature, vol. 3. p. 257.

† I do not contend, that this ufe of the word *metaphyfical* is
ftrictly

ed, not on fact, but on theory, and supported by ambiguous words and inaccurate experience.

The judgement of the wifer ancients in matters of morality, is doubtlefs of very great
weight, but, in oppofition to the dictates of
our own moral nature, can never preponderate;
becaufe thefe are our ultimate ftandard of moral
truth.   Mr. HUME endeavours to confirm his
theory of virtue by authorities from the ancients,
particularly the Stoics and Peripatetics. Though
he had accomplifhed this, we might have appealed from their opinion, as well as from his, to
our own feelings.   But he fails in this, as in the
other parts of his proof.

It is true, the Peripatetics and Stoics made
Prudence the firft (not the moft important) of
the cardinal virtues; becaufe they conceived it
neceffary to enable a man to act his part aright
in life, and becaufe they thought it their duty
to take every opportunity of improving their
nature: but they never faid, that an incurable
defect of underftanding is a vice, or that it is
as much our duty to be learned and ingenious,
as to be honeft and grateful.   " All the praife
of virtue confifts in action," fays Cicero†, in
name of the Stoics, when treating of this virtue of prudence.   And, when explaining the
comparative merit of the feveral claffes of moral
duty, he declares, that " All knowledge which
                                                    " is

---

ftrictly proper: I mean nothing more, than to give the reader a
notion of this particular mode of falfe reafoning; and, by fatif-
fying him that it is *not philofophical*, to guard him againft its influence.
    † De Officiis, lib. 1. cap. 6.

" is not followed by action, is unprofitable and
" imperfect, like a beginning without an end,
" or a foundation without a superstructure;
" and that the acquisition of the most sublime
" and most important science ought to be, and
" will by every good man be relinquished, when
" it interferes with the duties we owe our coun-
" try, our parents, and society*." Wisdom,
indeed, he allows to be the first and most excellent of the virtues: but the Stoics made a diftinction between Prudence and Wisdom. By
Prudence they meant that virtue which regulates our desires and aversions, and fixes them
on proper objects. Wisdom was another name
for mental perfection: it comprehended all the
virtues, the religious as well as the social and
prudential; and was equally incompatible with
vice and with error†. The wise man, the standard of Stoical excellence, was, by their own
acknowledgement, an ideal character;. the
purest virtue attainable in this life being necessarily tainted with imperfection. Hence
some have endeavoured to turn their notions
of *wisdom* into ridicule; but I think, without
reason. For is there any thing absurd or ridiculous in an artist working after a model of
such perfection as he can never hope to equal?
In the judgement of Aristotle and Bacon, the
true poet forms his imitations of nature after
a model of ideal perfection, which perhaps
hath no existence but in his own mind‡. And
are

* De Officiis, lib. 1. cap. 43. 44.
† Id. ib.
‡ Aristot. Poetica.   Bacon, De augmentis scicutiarum, lib. 2.
cap. 13.

are not Chriftians commanded to imitate the Deity himfelf, that great original and ftandard of perfection, between whom and the moft excellent of his creatures an infinite diftance muft remain for ever ‖ ?

"The ancient moralifts," fays Mr. HUME, "made no material diftinction among the different fpecies of mental endowments and defects, but treated all alike under the appellation of virtues and vices, and made them indifcriminately the objects of their moral reafonings ‡." That they confidered both intellectual and moral endowments as neceffary to the formation of a perfect character, and fometimes treated of both in one and the fame book or fyftem, and often called both by the fame general name *Virtue*, I do not deny: but that they made no *material diftinction* among them, I can by no means admit. I might here fill many a page with quotations: but a few will fuffice. "Man's virtue and vice," fays Marcus Aurelius, "confifts not in thofe affections "in which we are paffive, but in action. To "a ftone thrown upward it is no evil to fall, "nor good to have mounted†." And in another place, "The vain-glorious man placeth "his good in the action of another; the fen-"fual in his own paffive feelings the wife man "in

‖ Matth. v. 48.

‡ Hume's Effays, vol. 2. p. 387, 388.

* Οὐδὶ ἡ ἀρετὴ καὶ κακια αὐτῶ ἐν πείσει ἄλλα ἐνεργεία· τῷ ἀναῤῥιφθέντι λίθῳ οὐδὶι κακὸν τὸ κατινιχθῆναι, οὐδὶ ἀγαθὸν τὸ ἀνινιχθῆναι.

Lib. 9. *c.* 47.

" in his own action ‡." " The contemplative
" life," fays Plutarch, " when it fails to pro-
" duce the active, is unprofitable ||." " To ac-
" quire knowledge," fays Lucian, " is of no
" ufe, if we do not alfo frame our lives accord-
" ing to fomething better**." It is remarkable, that the Greek tragedians (I know not by
what authority, for Homer's idea is very different) reprefent Ulyffes as a character more diftinguifhed for political prudence or cunning,
than for ftrict moral virtue; and often place
him in fuch attitudes as make him appear odious
on this very account*. And Cicero, in his treatife of Moral Duties, often declares, that cunning, when it violates the rules of juftice, is
Vol. I.   Z   blameable

‡ Ο᾽ μὲν φιλόδοξος ἀλλοτρίαν ἐνέργειαν ἴδιον ἄγαθον ὑπολαμβάνει·
ὁ δὲ φιλήδονος, ἰδίαν πᾶσιν· ὁ δὲ νοῦν, ἔχων, ἰδίαν πρᾶξιν.
Lib. 6. *c.* 51.

|| Ο᾽ δὲ θεωρητικὸς βίος τῇ πρακτικῇ διαμαρτάνων, ἀνωφελής.
Plutarch de Educatione.

** Οὐδὲν ὄφελος ἦν ἐπίγασθαι τὰ μαθήματα, εἰ μὴ τίς ἄρα καὶ
τὸν βίον ῥυθμίζει πρὸς τὸ βέλτιον.
Lucian. Conviv.

* See particularly Sophocles, Philoct. verf. 100. and verf.
1260. I beg leave to quote a few remarkable lines. Neoptolemus
having, by the advice of Ulyffes, fraudulently got poffeffion of the
arrows of Philoctetes, repents of what he had done, and is going to reftore them. To deter him from his purpofe, Ulyffes
threatens him with the refentment of the whole Grecian army.

Neop. Σοφὸς πεφυκὼς οὐδὲν ἐξαυδᾷς σοφὸν·
Ulyf. Σὺ δ᾽ οὔτι φωνεῖς, οὔτι δρασείεις σοφὸν.
Neop. Ἀλλ᾽ εἰ δίκαια, τῶν σοφῶν κρείσσω τάδε.
Ulyf. Καὶ πῶς δίκαιον, ἃ γ᾽ ἔλαβες βουλαῖς ἐμαῖς
Πάλιν μεθεῖναι ταυτα ; *Neop.* Τὴν ἁμαρτίαν
Αἰσχρὰν ἁμαρτὼν, ἀναλαβεῖν πειράσομαι
Ulyf. Στρατὸν δ᾽ Ἀχαιῶν ἢ φοβῇ πράσσων ταδὶ ;
Neop. Ξὺν τῷ δικαίῳ τὸν σὸν οὐ ταρβῶ φόβον.   *verf.* 1279.

——Neop.

blameable and hateful†. Does Virgil confign
cripples and idiots, as well as tyrants, to Tartarus? Does he fay, that a great genius, and
handfome face, as well as a pure heart, were
the paffports to Elyfium? No. Virgil was too
good a man to injure the caufe of virtue, and
too wife to fhock common fenfe, by fo prepofterous a diftribution of reward and punifhment. The impious, the unnatural, the frau-
dulent, the avaricious; adulterers, inceftuous
perfons, traitors, corrupt judges, venal ftatef-
men, tyrants, and the minions of tyrants, are
thofe

------ *Neop*. Wife as thou art, Ulyffes,
Thou talk'ft moft idly. *Ulyf.* Wifdom is not thine,
Either in word or deed. *Neop.* Know, *to be juft*
Is better far than to be wife. *Ulyf.* But where,
Where is the juftice, thus unauthoris'd,
To give a treafure back thou oweft to me,
And to my counfels? *Neop.* I have done a wrong,
And I will try to make atonement for it.
Ulyf. Doft thou not fear the power of Greece? *Neop.* I fear
Nor Greece, nor thee, when I am doing right.
                                        FRANKLIN.
Throughout the whole play, the fire and generofity of the young
hero (fo well becoming the fon of Achilles) is finely oppofed to the
caution and craft of the politician, and forms one of the moft ftrik-
ing contrafts that can well be imagined.

† ------ Quippe cum ea (juftitia) fine prudentia fatis habeat auc-
toritatis, prudentia fine juftitia nihil valet ad faciendam fidem.
Quo enim quis verfutior et calidior eft, hoc invifior et fufpeftior,
detrafta opinione probitatis.
                            De Officiis, lib. 2. cap. 9.
Fundamentum perpetuæ commendationis et famæ eft juftitia,
fine qua nihil poteft effe laudabile.
                                        Ibid. cap. 20.
The fame doftrine is repeatedly inculcated in the third book,
and in other parts of his works, and indeed in all the good books
I am acquainted with. And in all the rational converfations I ever
witneffed, the fame doftrine was implied; nor could any man be
thought ferioufly to believe the contrary, without forfeiting the
efteem and confidence of mankind.

thofe whom he dooms to eternal mifery : and
he peoples Elyfium with the fhades of the pure
and the pious, of heroes who have died in defence of their country, of ingenious men who
have employed their talents in recommending
piety and virtue, and of all who by acts of beneficence have merited the love and gratitude of
their fellow-creatures *

Z 2   The

* Virgil. Æneid. vi. 547. --- 665. --- As the moral fentiments of nations may often be learned from their fables and traditions, as well as from their hiftory and philofophy, it will not
perhaps be deemed foreign from our defign, to give the following
brief abftract of this poet's fublime theory of future rewards and
punifhments ; the outlines of which he is known to have taken
from the Pythagoreans and Platonifts, who probably were indebted
for them to fome ancient tradition.

The fhades below are divided by Virgil into three diftricts or provinces. On this fide Styx, the fouls of thofe whofe bodies have
not been honoured with the rites of fepulture, wander about in a
melancholy condition for a hundred years, before they are permitted to pafs the river. When this period expires, or when their
bodies are buried, they are ferried over, and appear before Minos
and the other judges, who allot them fuch a manfion as their
lives on earth are found to have deferved. They who have been
of little or no ufe to mankind ; or who have not been guilty of any
very atrocious crimes ; or whofe crimes, though atrocious, were
the effects rather of an unhappy deftiny, than of wilful depravation, are difpofed of in different parts of the *regions of mourning*,
(lugentes campi), where they undergo a variety of purifying pains.
From thence, when thoroughly refined from all the remains of vice,
they pafs into Elyfium ; where they live a thoufand years in a ftate
of happinefs ; and then, after taking a draught of the waters of
oblivion, are fent back to earth to animate new bodies.—Thofe
who have been guilty of great crimes, as impiety, want of natural affection, adultery, inceft, breach of truft, fubverting the li-
berties of their country, &c. are delivered by the judge Rhada-
manthus to Tifiphone and the other furies, who fhut them up in
an immenfe dungeon of darknefs and fire, called *Tartarus*, where
their torments are unfpeakable and eternal. --- The fouls of good
men are re-united, either with the Deity himfelf, or with that
univerfal fpirit which he created in the beginning, and which ani-
mates the world ; and their fhades, ghofts, or *idola*, enjoy for ever
the repofe and pleafures of Elfiyum. Thefe fhades might be feen,
though

The Peripatetics held prudence to be an active principle diffused through the whole of moral virtue *. " None but a good man," says Ariftotle, " can be prudent;—and, a little after, " It is not poffible for a man to be " properly good without prudence, nor pru-" dent without moral virtue †." Will it yet be

though not touched; they refembled the bodies with which they had formerly been invefted ; and retained a confcioufnefs of their identity, and a remembrance of their paft life, with almoft the fame affections and character that had diftinguifhed them on earth.

On this fyftem, Virgil has founded a feries of the fublimeft defcriptions that are to be met with in poetry. Milton alone has equalled them in the firft and fecond books of Paradife Loft. Homer's *Necyomanteia*, in the eleventh of the Odyffey, has the merit of being original : but Virgil's imitation is confeffedly far fuperior. The dream of Henry, in the feventh canto of the Henriade, notwithftanding the advantages the author might have drawn from the Chriftian theology, is but a trifle, compared with the magnificent and ftupendous fcenery exhibited in the fixth book of the Æneid.

This theory of future rewards and punifhments, however imperfect, is confonant enough with the hopes and fears of men, and their natural notions of virtue and vice, to render the poet's narrative alarming and interefting in a very high degree. But were an author to adopt Mr. Hume's theory of virtue and the foul, and endeavour to fet it off in a poetical defcription, all the powers of human genius could not fave it from being ridiculous. A metaphyfician may, " blunder," for a long time, " round about " a meaning," without giving any violent fhock to an inattentive reader : but a poet, who clothes his thoughts with imagery, and illuftrates them by examples, muft come to the point at once; and, if he means to pleafe, and not difguft his readers, to move their admiration, and not their contempt, muft be careful not to contradict their natural notions, efpecially in matters of fuch deep and univerfal concern as morality and religion.

---

* —Ἀνάγκη τὴν φρόνησιν ἕξιν εἶναι—πρακτικὴν.

Ethic. ad Nicom. vi. 5.

† Ἀδύνατον φρόνιμον εἶναι μὴ ὄντα ἀγαθόν.—Οὐχ᾽ οἷον ἀγαθον εἶναι κυρίως ἄνευ φρονήσεως· οὐδὲ φρόνιμον ἄνευ τῆς ἠθικῆς ἀρετῆς.

Id. vi. 13.

See

be faid, that the ancient moralifts made no material diftinction between moral and intellectual
virtues? Is it not evident, that though they
confidered both as neceffary to the formation of
a perfect character, and fometimes difcourfed
of both in the fame treatife or fyftem, yet they
deemed the latter valuable only as means to
qualify us for the former, and infignificant,
or even odious, when they failed to anfwer
this end?

"We may," fays Mr. HUME, "by perufing
"the titles of the chapters in Ariftotle's Ethics,
"be convinced, that he ranks courage, tem-
"perance, magnificence, magnanimity, modef-
"ty, prudence, and a *manly freedom*, among
"the virtues, as well as juftice and friend-
"fhip *." True; but if our learned metaphy-
cian had extended his refearches a little beyond the *titles* of thofe chapters, he would
have found, that, in Ariftotle's judgement,
"Moral virtue is a voluntary difpofition or ha-
"bit; and that the moral approbation and dif-
"approbation are excited by thofe actions and
"affections only which are in our own pow-
"er, that is, of which the firft motion arifes
"in ourfelves, and proceeds from no extrinfic
"caufe †."

This

See the elegant paraphrafe of Andronicus the Rhodian, upon
thefe paffages.

* Hume's Effays, vol. 2. p. 388.---The term *manly freedom* does
not exprefs the meaning of the Greek ιλευθεριοτης. By this word
the philofopher denotes *that virtue which confifts in the moderate ufe
of wealth.*----περὶ χρήματα μισότης.   See Ethic. ad Nicom. lib.
4. cap. 1. 2.

† Ethic. ad Nicom. lib. 2. & 3.   Andronicus Rhodius, p. 89.
90. &c.   Edit. Cantab. 1679.

This is true philofophy, and very properly determines the degree of merit of our intellectual and conftitutional virtues. A man makes proficiency in knowledge:—if in this he has acted from a defire to improve his nature, and qualify himfelf for moral virtue, that defire, and the action confequent upon it, are virtuous, laudable, and of good defert. Is a man poffeffed of great genius?—this invefts him with dignity and diftinction, and qualifies him for noble undertakings: but this of itfelf is no moral virtue; becaufe it is not a difpofition refulting from a fpontaneous effort. Is his conftitution naturally difpofed to virtue?---he ftill has it in his power to be vicious, and therefore his virtue is meritorious; though not fo highly as that of another man, who, in fpite of outrageous appetites, and tempting circumftances, hath attained an equal degree of moral improvement. A man conftitutionally brave, generous, or grateful, commands our admiration more than another, who ftruggles to overcome the natural bafenefs of his temper. The former is a fublimer object, and may be of greater fervice to fociety; and as his virtue is fecured by conftitution as well as by inclination, we repofe in it without fear of being difappointed. Yet perhaps the latter, if his merit were equally confpicuous, would be found equally worthy of our moral approbation. Indeed, if his virtue be fo irrefolute, as to leave him wavering between good and evil, he is not intitled to praife: fuch irrefolution is criminal, becaufe he may and ought to correct it; we cannot, and we ought not to truft him,

till

till we fee a ftrong prepoffeffion eftablifhed in favour of virtue.—However, let us love virtue where-ever we find it: whether the immediate gift of Heaven, or the effect of human induftry co-operating with divine influence, it always deferves our efteem and veneration.

The reader may now form an eftimate of that author's attention, who fays, that " the anci-" ent moralifts made no material diftinction " among the different fpecies of mental endow-" ments and defects." If any one is difpofed to think, that I have made out my point, rather by inference than by direct proof, I fubmit to his confideration the following paffages, which are too plain to need a commentary.

Having propofed a general diftribution of our mental powers, (which feems to amount to this; that fome of them fit us for knowledge, and others for action,) Ariftotle proceeds in this manner. " According to this diftribution, " virtue is alfo divided into intellectual and " moral. Of the former kind are wifdom, in-" telligence, and prudence; of the latter, tem-" perance, and frugal liberality. When we " fpeak of morals, we do not fay, that a " man is wife or intelligent, but that he is " gentle or temperate. Yet we praife a wife " man in refpect of his difpofitions [or ha-" bits]; for laudable difpofitions are what we " call virtues*,"

" The

* Διορίζεται δὲ καὶ ἡ ἀρίτη κατὰ τὴν διαφόραν ταύην. λίγομεν γὰρ αὐτῶν τας μὶν διανοητίκας, τὰς δὶ ἠθικας. σοφίαν μὶν καὶ σύνισιν. καὶ φρονησιν, διανοητίκας· ἰλιυθιριότητα δὶ καὶ σωφροσηνι, ἠθικας. λίγοντὲς γὰρ πιρὶ τῦ πθους, ὰ λίγομιν ὅτι σόφος, ἤ σύνιτος, ἀλλ' ὅτι πραος ἤ σύφρων. ἰπαινῦμιν

δὶ

" The virtues of the foul," fays Cicero,
" and of its principal part the understanding,
" are various, but may be reduced to two
" kinds. The firft are thofe which Nature has
" implanted, and which are called *not voluntary*.
" The fecond kind are more properly called *vir-*
" *tues*, becaufe they depend on the will; and
" thefe, as objects of approbation, are tran-
" fcendently fuperior. Of the former kind are
" docility, memory, and all the virtues diftin-
" guifhed by the general name of genius,
" or capacity: perfons poffeffed of them are
" called ingenious. The latter clafs com-
" prehends *the great and genuine virtues*, which
" we denominate *voluntary*; as prudence, tem-
" perance, fortitude, juftice, and others of the
" fame kind*."

The word *virtue* has indeed great latitude of
fignification. It denotes any quality of a thing
tending to the happinefs of a percipient being;
it denotes that quality, or perfection of qualities,

δι καὶ τὸν σοφὸν τὴν ἕξιν, τὰς ἐξ ὧν δὲ τὰς ἰσαιότας ἀρέτας λι-
γομιν.

Ethic. ad Nicom. lib. 1. fub. fin.

* Animi autem, et ejus partis quæ princeps eft, quæque mens
nominatur, plures funt virtutes, fed duo prima genera: unum earum quæ ingenerantur fuapte natura, appellanturque non voluntariæ: alterum autem earum, que in voluntate pofitæ, magis proprie
eo nomine appellari folent; quarum eft excellens in animorum
laude præftantia. Prioris generis eft docilitas, memoria; qualia
fere omnia appellantur uno ingenii nomine; cafque virtutes qui
habent ingeniofi vocantur. Alterum autem genus eft *magnarum
verarumque virtutum*, quas appellamus voluntarias, ut prudentiam,
temperantiam, fortitudinem, juftitiam, et reliquas ejufdem generis.
---Virtutes voluntariæ proprie virtutes appellantur multumque ex-
cellunt, &c. *Cicero De Finibus, lib. 5. cap. 13. ex editione Davifii.*

ties, by which a thing is fitted to anfwer its end; fometimes it denotes power or agency in general; and fometimes any habit which improves the faculties of the human mind. In the firft three fenfes we afcribe virtue to the foul, and to the body, to brutes, and inanimate things; in the laft, to our intellectual as well as moral nature. And no doubt inftances may be found of ambiguity and want of precifion, even in the beft moralifts, from an improper ufe of this word. Yet I believe this attempt of Mr. Hume's is the firft that has been made to prove that a-mong thefe very different forts of virtue there is little or no difference.

Is it not ftrange, that a man of fcience fhould ever have taken it in his head, that the characteriftic of a genus is a fufficient defcription of a fpecies? He might as well have fup-pofed, that, becaufe perception and felf-emotion belong to animal life in general, it is therefore a fufficient definition of man, to call him a felf-moving and percipient creature: from which profound principle it clearly follows, that man is a beaft, and that a beaft is a man.

By fuch reafoning it would be eafy to prove any doctrine. The method is this: ——and I hope thofe who may hereafter chufe to aftonifh the world with a fyftem of metaphyfical para-doxes, will do me the honour to acknowledge, that I was the firft who unfolded the whole art and myftery of one branch of that manu-facture within the compafs of one fhort RE-CIPE:——Take a word (an abftract term is the moft convenient) which admits of more than one fignification; and, by the help of a predi-cate

cate

cate and copula, form a propofition, fuitable to
your fyftem, or to your humour, or to any
other thing you pleafe, except truth. When
laying down your premifes, you are to ufe the
name of the quality or fubject, in one fenfe;
and, when inferring your conclufion, in another. You are then to urge a few equivocal
facts, very flightly examined, (the more flightly
the better), as a further proof of the faid conclufion; and to fhut up all with citing fome
ancient authorities. A few occafional ftrictures
on religion as an unphilofophical thing, and a
fneer at the *Whole Duty of Man**, or any other
good book, will give your differtation what many are pleafed to call a *liberal turn*; and will go
near to convince the world, that you are a candid philofopher, a manly free-thinker, and a very
fine writer.

It is to no purpofe that our author calls this a
verbal difpute, and fometimes condefcends to
foften matters by an *almoft*, or fome fuch evafive
word. This doctrine obvioufly tends to confound all our ideas of virtue and duty, and to
make us confider ourfelves as mere machines,
acted upon by external impulfe, and not
more accountable for moral blemifhes, than
for ignorance, and want of underftanding.—
If the reader think as ferioufly of the controverfy as I do, he will pardon the length of this
digreffion.

I hope it now appears, that there is a kind of
metaphyfic, which whatever refpectable names
it may have affumed, deferves contempt or censure

---

* See Hume's Effays, vol. 2. p. 388. edit. 1767.

fure from every lover of truth. If it be detrimental to fcience, it is equally fo to the affairs
of life. Whenever one enters on bufinefs,
the metaphyfical fpirit muft be laid afide,
otherwife it will render him ridiculous, perhaps
deteftable. Sure it will not be faid, that any portion of this fpirit is neceffary to form a man for
ftations of high importance. For thefe, a turn
to metaphyfic would be an effectual difqualifica-
tion. The metaphyfician is cold, wavering,
diftruftful, and perpetually ruminates on words,
diftinctions, arguments, and fyftems. He attends to the events of life with a view chiefly
to the fyftem that happens for the time to pre-
dominate in his fancy, and to which he is anxi-
ous to reconcile every appearance. His obfervation is therefore partial and inaccurate, becaufe he contemplates Nature through the medium of his favourite theory, which is always
falfe; fo that experience, which enlarges, afcer-
tains, and methodifes, the knowledge of other
men, ferves only to heighten the natural darknefs and confufion of his. His literary ftudies
are conducted with the fame fpirit, and produce
the fame effects.——Whereas, to the admini-
ftration of great affairs, truth and fteadinefs of
principle, conftancy of mind, intuitive fagacity, extreme quicknefs in apprehending the prefent and anticipating the future, are indifpenfa-
bly neceffary. Whatever tends to weaken and
unfettle the mind, to cramp the imagination, to
fix the attention on minute and trifling objects,
and withdraw it from thofe enlarged profpects
of nature and mankind in which true genius
loves

loves to expatiate; whatever has that tendency, and furely this metaphyfic has it, is the bane of genius, and of every thing that is great in human nature.

In the lower walks of life, our theorift will be oftener the object of ridicule than of deteftation. Yet even here, the man is to be pitied, who, in matters of moment, happens to be connected with a ftanch metaphyfician. Doubts, difputes, and conjectures, will be the plague of his life. If his affociate form a fyftem of action or inaction, of doubt or confidence, he will ftick by it, however abfurd, as long as he has one verbal argument unanfwered to urge in defence of it. In accounting for the conduct of others, he will reject obvious caufes, and fet himfelf to explore fuch as are more remote and refined. Making no proper allowance for the endlefs variety of human character, he will fuppofe all men influenced, like himfelf, by fyftem and verbal argument : certain caufes, in his judgement, muft of neceffity produce certain effects; for he has twenty reafons ready to offer, by which it is demonftrable, that they cannot fail : and it is well, if experience at laft convince him, that there was a fmall verbal ambiguity in his principles, and that his views of mankind were not quite fo extenfive as they ought to have been. In a word, unlefs he be very good-natured, and of a paffive difpofition, his refinements will do more harm than even the ftiff ftupidity of an idiot. If inclined to fraud, or any fort of vice, he will never be at a lofs for an evafion; which, if it fhould not fatisfy

his

his affociate, will, however, perplex and plague him. I need not enlarge; the reader may conceive the reft. To aid his fancy, he will find fome traits of this character, in one of its moft amufing and leaft difagreeable forms, delineated with a mafterly pencil in the perfon of Walter Shandy, Efq.

It is aftonifhing to confider, how little mankind value the good within their reach, and how ardently they purfue what Nature has placed beyond it; how blindly they over-rate what they have no experience of, and how fondly they admire what they do not underftand. This verbal metaphyfic has been dignified with the name of *Science*; and verbal metaphyficians have been reputed philofophers, and men of genius.—Doubtlefs a man of genius may, by the fafhion of the times, be feduced into thefe ftudies: but that particular caft of mind which fits a man for them, and recommends them to his choice, is not genius, but a minute and feeble underftanding; capable indeed of being made, by long practice, expert in the management of words; but which never did, and never will, qualify any man for the difcovery or illuftration of fentiment. For what is genius? What, but found judgement, fenfibility of heart, and a talent for accurate and extenfive obfervation? And will found judgement prepare a man for being impofed on by words? Will fenfibility of heart render him infenfible to his own feelings, and inattentive to thofe of other men? will a talent for accurate and extenfive obfervation, make him ignorant of the real phenomena of Nature,

and,

and, confequently, incapable of detecting what is falfe or equivocal in the reprefentation of facts ? And yet, when facts are fairly and fully reprefented ; when human fentiments are ftrongly felt, and perfpicuoufly defcribed : and when the meaning of words is afcertained, and the fame words has always the fame idea annexed to it,—there is an end of metaphyfic.

A body is neither vigorous nor beautiful, in which the fize of fome members is above, and that of others below, their due proportion : every part muft have its proper fize and ftrength, otherwife the refult of the whole will be deformity and weaknefs. Neither is real genius confiftent with a difproportionate ftrength of the reafoning powers above thofe of tafte and imagination. Thofe minds in whom all the faculties are united in their due proportion, are far fuperior to the puerilities of metaphyfical fcepticifm. They truft to their own feelings, which are ftrong and decifive, and leave no room for hefitation or doubts about their authenticity. They fee through moral fubjects at one glance ; and what they fay carries both the heart and the underftanding along with it. When one has long drudged in the dull and unprofitable pages of metaphyfic, how pleafing the tranfition to a moral writer of true genius ! Would you know what that genius is, and where it may be found ? Go to Shakefpeare, to Bacon, to Johnfon, to Montefquieu, to Rouffeau * ; and when you have ftudied them, return,

if

* As feveral perfons, highly refpectable both for their talents
and

if you can, to HUME, and HOBBES, and MALE-
BRANCHE, and LEIBNITZ, and SPINOSA. If,
while you learned wifdom from the former, your
heart exulted within you, and rejoiced to contemplate the fublime and fuccefsful efforts of
human intelle&t; perhaps it may now be of ufe,

as

and principles, have defired to know my reafons for joining Rouffeau's name to thofe of Bacon, Shakefpeare, Johnfon, and Montefquieu, I beg leave to take this opportunity of explaining my
fentiments in regard to that celebrated author.

It is becaufe I confider Roufeau as *a moral writer of true genius,*
that I mention his name in this place. Senfibility of heart, a talent for extenfive and accurate obfervation, livelinefs and ardour
of fancy, and a ftyle copious, nervous and elegant, beyond that
of any other French writer,—are his diftinguifhing chara&terif-
tics. In argument he is not always equally fuccefsful, for he often miftakes declamation for proof, and hypothefis for fa&t; but
his eloquence, when addreffed to the heart, overpowers with force
irrefiftible. A greater number of important fa&ts relating to the
human mind are recorded in his works, than in all the books of
all the fceptical philofophers, ancient and modern. And he appears in general to be a friend to virtue, to mankind, to natural
religion, and fometimes to Chriftianity.

Yet none of his beft works are free from abfurdity. His reafonings, on the effe&ts of the fciences, and on the origin and progrefs
of human fociety, are diffufe, inaccurate, and often weak; much
perverted by theories of his own, as well as by too implicit an ad-
mittance of the vague affertions of travellers, and of the fyftems
and do&trines of fome favourite French philofophers; and he
feems, in thefe, and frequently too in his other writings, to confider animal pleafure and bodily accomplifhments as the happinefs
and perfe&tion of man. His plan of education, though admirable
in many parts, is in fome injudicious and dangerous, and impracticable as a whole. The chara&ter of Julia's lover is drawn with
a mafterly hand indeed, and well condu&ted throughout; but the
lady has two chara&ters, and thofe incompatible;——the wife of
Wolmar is quite a different perfon from the miftrefs of St. Preux.
Wolmar himfelf is an impoffible chara&ter; deftitute of principle,
yet of rigid virtue; deftitute of feeling, yet capable of tendernefs
and attachment; delicate in his notions of honour, yet not afhamed to marry a woman whom he knew to be to all intents and purpofes devoted to another.

Some of this author's remarks on the fpirit of Chriftianity, and
on the chara&ter of its Divine Founder, are not only excellent,

but

as a leſſon of humility, to have recourſe to the
latter, and, for a while, to behold the picture
of a ſoul wandering from thought to thought,
without knowing where to fix; and from a total want of feeling, or a total ignorance of what
it feels, miſtaking names for things, verbal
diſtinctions and analogies for real difference and
ſimilitude, and the obſcure inſinuations of a
bewildered underſtanding, puzzled with words,
and perverted with theory, for the ſentiments
of Nature, and the dictates of Reaſon. A metaphyſician,

but tranſcendently ſo; and I believe no Chriſtian ever read them
without feeling his heart warmed, and his faith confirmed. But
what he ſays,—of the abſurdities which he fancies to be contained
in the ſacred hiſtory,—of the impropriety of the evidence of miracles,—of the analogy between thoſe of Jeſus Chriſt and the
tricks of jugglers,—of the inſignificancy and impertinence of
prayer,—of the ſufficiency of human reaſon for diſcovering a complete and comfortable ſcheme of natural religion,—of the diſcou-
raging nature of the terms of ſalvation offered in the goſpel, --- of
the meaſure of evidence that ought to accompany divine revelation, (which, as he ſtates it, would be incompatible with man's free
agency and moral probation), --- what he ſays of theſe, and of
ſeveral other theological points of great importance, betrays a degree of ignorance and prejudice, of which, as a philoſopher, as a
ſcholar, and as a man, he ſhould have been utterly aſhamed. He
appears to be diſtreſſed with his doubts; and yet, without having
ever examined whether they be well or ill founded, ſcruples not to
exert all his eloquence on purpoſe to infuſe them into others: a
conduct which I muſt ever condemn, as illiberal, unjuſt, and
cruel. Had Rouſſeau ſtudied the ſcripture, and the writings of rational divines, with as much care as he ſeems to have employed in
reading the books, and liſtening to the converſation, of French
inſidels, and in attending to the unchriſtian practices and doctrines warranted by ſome eccleſiaſtical eſtabliſhments; I may venture to aſſure him, that his mind would have been much more at
eaſe, his works much more valuable, and his memory much dearer
to all good men.
Rouſſeau is, in my opinion, a great philoſophical genius, but
wild, irregular, and often ſelf-contradictory; diſpoſed, from the
faſhion of the times, and from his deſire of being reputed a bold
ſpeaker and free-thinker, to adopt the doctrines of infidelity; but
of

taphyſician, exploring the receſſes of the human heart, has juſt ſuch a chance for finding the truth, as a man with microſcopic eyes would have for finding the road.   The latter might amuſe himſelf with contemplating the various mineral ſtrata that are diffuſed along the expanſion of a needle's point; but of the face of Nature he could make nothing: he would ſtart back with horror from the caverns yawning between the mountainous grains of ſand that lie before him; but the real gulf or mountain he could not ſee at all.

Is the futility of metaphyſical ſyſtems exaggerated beyond the truth by this alluſion? Tell me, then, in which of thoſe ſyſtems I ſhall

Vol I.   A a   find

of a heart too tender, and an imagination too lively, to permit him to become a thorough-paced infidel.   Had he lived in an age leſs addicted to hypotheſis, he might have diſtinguiſhed himſelf as a moral philoſopher of the firſt rank.   What pity, that a proper ſenſe of his ſuperiority to his cotemporaries upon the continent, could not preſerve him from the contagion of their example! For, though now it is the faſhion for every French declaimer to talk of Bacon and Newton, I queſtion, whether, in any age ſince the days of Socrates, the building of fanciful theories was ſo epidemical as in the preſent.   If the men of learning formerly employed their ingenuity in defending the theories of that philoſopher by whoſe name they were ambitious to be diſtinguiſhed; they are now no leſs induſtrious in deviſing and vindicating, each man a theory of his own.

To conclude: The writings of this author, with all their imperfections, may be read by the philoſopher with advantage, as they often direct to the right obſervation and interpretation of nature; and by the Chriſtian without detriment, as the cavils they contain againſt religion are too ſlight and too paradoxical to weaken the faith of any one who is tolerably inſtructed in the principles and evidence of Chriſtianity.   To the man of taſte they can never fail to recommend themſelves, by the charms of the compoſition.

The improprieties in Rouſſeau's late conduct appear to me to have ariſen rather from bodily infirmity than from moral depravation, and conſequently to render him an object of forbearance and pity rather than of perſecution or ridicule.

find fuch a defcription of the foul of man as
would enable me to know what it is. A great
and excellent author obferves, that if all human things were to perifh except the works
of Shakefpeare, it might ftill be known from
them what fort of creature man was * : --- A
fentiment nobly imagined, and as juft as it is
fublime! Can the fame thing be faid with
truth of any one, or of all the metaphyfical
treatifes that have been written on the nature
of man ? --- If an inhabitant of another pla-
net were to read *The Treatife of Human Na-*
ture, what notions of human nature could he
gather from it ? --- That man muft believe one
thing by inftinct, and muft alfo believe the contrary by reafon : --- That the univerfe is nothing but a *heap* of perceptions without a fubftance : --- That though a man could bring himfelf to believe, yea, and have reafon to believe,
that every thing in the univerfe proceeds from
fome caufe; yet it would be unreafonable for
him to believe, that the univerfe itfelf proceeds
from a caufe :—That the foul of man is not the
fame this moment it was the laft ; that we know
not what it is; that it is not one, but many
things ; and that it is nothing at all ;—and yet,
that in this foul is the agency of all the caufes
that operate throughout the fenfible creation ;
—and yet, that in this foul there is neither power nor agency, nor any idea of either : —That
the perfection of human knowledge is to doubt:
—That man ought to believe nothing, and yet
that

* Lord Lyttleton's Dialogues of the Dead.

that man's belief ought to be influenced and determined by certain principles :—That we ought to doubt of every thing, yea of our doubts themſelves; and therefore the utmoſt that philoſophy can do, is to give a doubtful ſolution of doubtful doubts *:—That nature continually impoſes on us, and continually counteracts herſelf, by giving us ſagacity to detect the impoſture:—That we are neceſſarily and unavoidably determined to think in certain caſes after a certain manner; but that we ought not to ſubmit to this unavoidable neceſſity; and that they are fools who do ſo:—That man, in all his perceptions, actions, and volitions, is a mere paſſive machine, and has no ſeparate exiſtence of his own, being entirely made up of other things, of the exiſtence of which, however, he is by no means certain; and yet, that the nature of all things depends ſo much upon man, that two and two could not be equal to four, nor fire produce heat, nor the ſun light, without an act of the human underſtanding:—That none of our actions are in our power; that we ought to exerciſe power over our actions; and that there is no ſuch thing as power:—That body and motion may be regarded as the cauſe of thought; and that body does not exiſt :—That the univerſe exiſts in the mind; and that the mind does not exiſt: —That the human underſtanding, acting alone,

A a 2

does

---

* Strange as this expreſſion may ſeem, it is not without a precedent. The fourth ſection of Mr. Hume's *Eſſays on the Human Underſtanding* is called, *Sceptical doubts concerning the operations of the underſtanding*: and the fifth ſection bears this title, *Sceptical ſolution of theſe doubts.*

does entirely ſubvert itſelf, and prove by argument, that by argument nothing can be proved: ---Theſe are a few of the many ſublime myſteries brought to light by this great philoſopher, or plainly deducible from his principles. But theſe, however they may illuminate our terreſtrial *literati*, would convey no information to the planetary ſtranger, except perhaps, that the ſage metaphyſician knew nothing of his ſubject.

What a ſtrange detail! does not the reader exclaim? Can it be, that any man ſhould ever bring himſelf to think, or imagine that he could bring others to think ſo abſurdly! What a taſte, what a heart * muſt they poſſeſs, whoſe delight

it

---

* " A free and impartial inquiry after truth, where-ever it is
" to be found, is indeed a noble and moſt commendable diſpoſiti-
" on: a diſpoſition, which every man ought himſelf to labour af-
" ter, and to the utmoſt of his power encourage in all others. · It
" is the great foundation of all uſeful knowledge, of all true vir-
" tue, and of all ſincere religion. But when a man, in his ſearches
" into the nature of things, finds his inquiries leading him tow-
" ards ſuch notions as, if they ſhould prove true, would manifeſt-
" ly ſubvert the very eſſences of good and evil; the leaſt that a
" ſober-minded man can in ſuch a caſe poſſibly be ſuppoſed to owe
" to God, to virtue, to the dignity of a rational nature, is, that
" he ought to be in the higheſt degree fearful and ſuſpicious of
" himſelf, leſt he be led away by any prejudice, leſt he be de-
" ceived by an erroneous argument, leſt he ſuffer himſelf to
" be impoſed on by any wrong inclination. Too great an aſſur-
" ance in arguments of this nature, even though at preſent they
" ſeemed to him to be demonſtrations, ---rejoicing in the ſtrength
" of them, and taking pleaſure in the carrying of ſuch a cauſe,
" is what a good mind can never be capable of. To ſuch a per-
" ſon, the finding his own arguments unanſwerable would be the
" greateſt grief; triumphing in ſo melancholy a field would be the
" higheſt diſſatisfaction; and nothing could afford ſo pleaſing, ſo
" agreeable a diſappointment, as to find his own reaſonings ſhown
" to be inconcluſive." *Dr. S. Clarke's Remarks on a book enti-*
tled, A Philoſophical Enquiry concerning Human Liberty,——
p. 45.

" This

it is, to reprefent nature as a chaos, and man
as a monfter; to fearch for deformity and confufion, where others rejoice in the perception of
order and beauty; and to feek to imbitter the
happieft moments of human life, namely, thofe
we employ in contemplating the works of creation, and adoring their Author, by this fuggeftion, equally falfe and malevolent, that the
moral as well as material world, is nothing but
darknefs, diffonance, and perplexity!

" Where all life dies, death lives, and nature breeds
" Perverfe, all monftrous, all prodigious things,
" Abominable, unutterable, and worfe
" Than fables yet have feign'd, or fear conceiv'd!

Were this doctrine true, we fhould be little
obliged to him who gives it to the public; for
we

" This is certain (fays Shaftefbury) that it can be no great
" ftrengthening to the moral affection, no great fupport to the pure
" love of goodnefs and virtue, to fuppofe that there is neither
" goodnefs nor beauty in the WHOLE itfelf; nor any example or
" precedent of any good affection in any fuperior being.   Such
" a belief muft tend rather to the weaning the affections from any
" thing amiable or felf-worthy, and to the fuppreffing the very ha-
" bit and familiar cuftom of admiring natural beauties, or what-
" ever in the order of things is according to juft defign, harmony,
" and proportion.   For how little difpofed muft a perfon be, to
" love or admire any thing as orderly in the univerfe, who thinks
" the univerfe itfelf a pattern of diforder? How unapt to re-
" verence or refpect any particular fubordinate beauty of a *part*,
" when even the *whole* itfelf is thought to want perfection, and
" to be only a vaft and infinite deformity? --- Nothing indeed
" can be more melancholy, than the thought of living in a diftract-
" ed univerfe, from whence many ills may be fufpected, and where
" there is nothing good or lovely which prefents itfelf, nothing
" which can fatisfy in contemplation, or raife any paffion befides
" that of contempt, hatred, or diflike.   Such an opinion as this
" may by degrees imbitter the temper, and not only make the
" love of virtue to be lefs felt, but help to impair and ruin the
" very principle of virtue, to wit, natural and kind affection."

Inquiry concerning Virtue, b. 1. *p.* 3. § 3.

we could hardly imagine a greater misfortune than such a caſt of underſtanding as would make us believe it. But founded, as it is, in words miſunderſtood, and facts miſrepreſented; —ſupported, as it is, by ſophiſtry ſo egregious, and often ſo puerile, that we can hardly conceive how even the author himſelf ſhould be impoſed upon by it;---ſurely they who attempt to obtrude it on the weak and unwary, muſt have ſomething in their diſpoſition, which, to a man of a good heart, or good taſte, can never be the object of envy.

We are told, that the end of ſcepticiſm, as it was taught by Pyrrho, Sextus Empiricus, and other ancients, was to obtain *indiſturbance* *. I know not whether this be the end our modern ſceptics have in view ; if it is, the means they employ for attaining it are very prepoſterous. If the proſpect of nature exhibited in their ſyſtems produce tranquillity or indiſturbance, how dreadful muſt that tranquillity be! It is like that of a man, turned adrift amidſt a dark and tempeſtuous ocean, in a crazy ſkiff, with neither rudder nor compaſs, who, exhauſted by the agitations of deſpair, loſes at laſt all ſenſe
of

---

* Pyrrho, as he affected not to believe his ſenſes, affected alſo to be free from all paſſions and emotions : for when Anaxarchus, his maſter and fellow-traveller, happened to fall into a ditch, that worthy ſceptic paſſed on without once looking behind him ; for which indifference his beſotted maſter is ſaid to have held him in great admiration. An inſtance like this, when it occurs in hiſtory, is not leſs aſtoniſhing, than a monſtrous birth, or any other uncommon appearance; ---except we ſuppoſe theſe precious patterns of wiſdom to have played tricks with one another, to make the people ſtare. At any rate, it is ſurely unworthy of a man of honour and learning, to liſt himſelf under their banners, by reviving any of their ſilly paradoxes.

of his mifery, and becomes totally ftupid. In
fact, the only thing that can enable fceptics to
endure exiftence, is infenfibility. And how far
that is confiftent with delicacy of mind, let thofe
among them explain who are ambitious of paffing for men of tafte.

It is remarked by a very ingenious and amiable writer, that " many philofophers have been
" infidels, few men of tafte and fentiment *."
This, if I miftake not, holds equally true of
our fceptics in philofophy, and infidels in religion : and it holds true of both for the fame
reafon. The views and expectations of the infidel and fceptic are fo full of horror, that to a
man of tafte, that is, of fenfibility and imagination, they are infupportable. On the other
hand, what true religion and true philofophy
dictate of God, and providence, and man, is fo
charming, fo confonant with all the finer and
nobler feelings in human nature, that every
man of tafte who hears of it muft wifh it to be
true : and I never yet heard of one perfon of
candour, who wifhed to find the evidence of the
gofpel fatisfactory, and did not find it fo. Dull
imaginations and hard hearts can bear the
thought of endlefs confufion, of virtue depreff-
ed and vice triumphant, of an univerfe peopled
with fiends and furies, of creation annihilated, and chaos reftored, to remain a fcene of
darknefs and folitude for ever and for ever :
but it is not fo with the benevolent and tender-
hearted. Their notions are regulated by another ftandard; their hopes and fears, their joys
and forrows, are quite of a different kind.

The

* Dr. Gregory's Comparative View, p. 201. fourth edition.

The moral powers and the powers of taſte are more congenial than is commonly imagined; and he who is deſtitute of the latter will ever be found as incapable to deſcribe or judge of the former, as a man wanting the ſenſe of ſmell is to decide concerning reliſhes. Nothing is more true, than that " a little learning is a danger-" ous thing." If we are but a little acquaint-ed with one part of a complicated ſyſtem, how is it poſſible for us to judge aright, either of the nature of the whole, or of the fitneſs of that part! And a little knowledge of one ſmall part of the mental ſyſtem, is all that any man can be allowed to have, who is defective in ima-gination, ſenſibility, and the other powers of taſte. Yet, as ignorance is apt to produce te-merity, I ſhould not be ſurpriſed to find ſuch men moſt forward to attempt reducing the phi-loſophy of human nature to ſyſtem : and, if they made the attempt, I ſhould not wonder that they fell into the moſt important miſtakes. Like a ſhort-ſighted landſcape-painter, they might poſſibly delineate ſome of the largeſt and rougheſt figures with tolerable exactneſs : but of the minuter objects, ſome would wholly eſ-cape their notice, and others appear bloated and diſtorted, on which nature had beſtowed the utmoſt delicacy of colour, and harmony of proportion.

The modern ſceptical philoſophy is as corrupt a body of ſcience as ever appeared in the world. And it deſerves our notice, that the moſt conſi-derable of its adherents and promoters were more eminent for ſubtlety of reaſon, than for ſenſi-bility of taſte. We know that this was the

cafe with MALEBRANCHE, of whom Mr.
D'Alembert fays, that he could not read the moft
fublime verfes without wearinefs and difguft*.
This was alfo the cafe with another author, to
whom our fceptics are more obliged than they
feem willing to acknowledge. I mean Mr.
HOBBES; whofe tranflation of Homer bears
juft fuch a refemblance to the Iliad and Odyffey,
as a putrefying carcafe bears to a beautiful and
vigorous human body.

The philofophy of the mind, if fuch as it
ought to be, would certainly intereft us more
than any other fcience. Are the fceptical treatifes on this fubject interefting ? Do they bring
conviction to the judgement, or delight to the
fancy ? Do they either reach the heart, or feem
to proceed from it ? Do they make us better
acquainted with ourfelves, or better prepared
for the bufinefs of life ? Do they not rather in-
feeble and harrafs the foul, divert its attention
from every thing that can enlarge and improve
it, give it a difrelifh for itfelf, and for every
thing elfe, and difqualify it alike for action, and
for ufeful knowledge?

Other caufes might be affigned for the prefent
degeneracy of the moral fciences. I fhall mention one, which I the rather chufe to take notice of, and infift upon, becaufe it has been generally overlooked. DES CARTES and MALE-
BRANCHE introduced the fafhion, which continues to this day, of neglecting the ancients in
all their philofophical inquiries, We feem to
think, becaufe we are confeffedly fuperior in
                                          fome

* Effai fur le Gout.

some sciences, that we muft be so in all. But that this is a rash judgement, may easily be made appear, even on the suppofition, that human genius is nearly the same in all ages.

When accidental difcovery, long experience, or profound inveftigation, are the means of advancing a fcience, it is reafonable to expect, that the improvements of that fcience will increafe with length of time. Accordingly we find, that, in natural philofophy, natural hiftory, and some parts of mathematical learning, the moderns are far fuperior to the ancients. But the fcience of human nature, being attainable rather by intuition than by deep reafoning or nice experiment, muft depend for its cultivation upon other caufes. Different ages and nations have different cuftoms. Sometimes it is the fafhion to be referved and affected, at other times to be fimple and fincere: fometimes, therefore, it will be eafy, and at other times difficult, to gain a competent knowledge of human nature by obfervation. In the old romances, we feek for human nature in vain; the manners are all affected; prudery is the higheft, and almoft the only ornament, of the women; and a fantaftical honour of the men: but the writers adapted themfelves to the prevailing tafte, and painted the manners as they faw them. In our own country, we have feen various modes of affectation, fucceffively prevail within a few years. To fay nothing of prefent times; every body knows, how much pedantry, libertinifm, and falfe wit, contributed to difguife human nature in the laft century, And I apprehend, that in all monarchies one mode

or

or other of artificial manners muft always prevail; to the formation of which the character
of princes, the tafte of the times, and a variety
of other caufes will co-operate.

Montefquieu's opinion, that the courts of
monarchs muft always of neceffity be corrupt,
I cannot fubfcribe to: I think, that virtue may
be, and fometimes is, the principle of action,
even in the higheft offices of monarchy: my
meaning is, that under this form of government, human manners muft generally deviate,
more or lefs, from the fimplicity of nature: and
that, confequently, human fentiments muft be
of more difficult inveftigation than under fome
other forms.   In courts, it feems requifite, for
the fake of that order which is effential to dignity, to eftablifh certain punctilios in drefs,
language, and gefture: there too, the moft in-
violable fecrecy is expedient: and there, where
men are always under the eye of their fuperiors,
and for the moft part engaged in the purfuits of
ambition or intereft, a fmoothnefs of behaviour will naturally take place, which among
perfons of ordinary talents, and ordinary virtue,
muft on many occafions degenerate into hypocrify.   The cuftoms of the court are always
imitated by the higher ranks; the middle ranks
follow the higher; and the people come after
as faft as they can.   It is, however, in the laft
mentioned clafs, where nature appears with
the leaft difguife: but unhappily for moral
fcience, the vulgar are feldom objects of curiofity, either to our philofophers, or hiftorians.

The

The influence of thefe caufes, in diftinguifhing human fentiments, will, I prefume, be greater or lefs, according as the monarchy partakes
more or lefs of democratical principles.---There
is, indeed, one fet of fentiments, which monarchy and modern manners are peculiarly fitted for difclofing, I mean thofe that relate to
gallantry: and it is evident, that thefe (taking
the word Gallantry in the beft fenfe) tend in
fome refpects to render fociety comfortable, and
to enlarge the fphere of comic writing; but
whether to make the effential principles of human nature more or lefs known, might perhaps
bear a queftion.

Modern hiftory ought, on many accounts, to
intereft us more than the ancient. It defcribes
manners that are familiar to us, events whereof
we fee and feel the confequences, political efta-
blifhments on which our property and fecurity
depend, and places and perfons in which experience or tradition has already given us a concern. And yet I believe it will be acknowledged, that the ancient hiftories, particularly of
Greece and Rome, are more interefting than
thofe of latter times. In fact, the moft affecting part, both of hiftory and of poetry, is that
which beft difplays the characters, manners, and
fentiments of men. Hiftories that are deficient in this refpect, may communicate inftruction to the geographer, the warrior, the ge-
nealogift, and the politician; but will never
pleafe the general tafte, becaufe they excite no
paffion, and awaken no fympathy. Now, I
cannot help thinking, that the perfonages defcribed in modern hiftory have, with a very few
exceptions,

exceptions, a ftiffnefs and referve about them, which doth not feem to adhere to the great men of antiquity, particularly of Greece. I will not fay, that our hiftorians have lefs ability or lefs induftry; but I would fay, that democratical governments, like thofe of ancient Greece, are more favourable to fimplicity of manners, and confequently to the knowledge of the human mind, than our modern monarchies. At A-thens and Sparta, the public affemblies, the public exercifes, the regular attendance given to all the public folemnities, whether religious or civil, and other inftitutions that might be mentioned, gave the citizens many opportuni-ties of being well acquainted with one another. There the great men were not cooped up in pa- and coaches; they were almoft conftantly in the open air, and on foot. The people faw them every day, converfed with them, and ob-ferved their behaviour in the hours of relaxa-tion, as well as of bufinefs. Themiftocles could call every citizen of Athens by his name; a proof that the great men courted an univer-fal acquaintance.

No degree of genius will ever make one a proficient in the fcience of man, without accu-rate obfervation of human nature in all its va-rieties. Homer, the greateft mafter in this fcience ever known, paffed the moft of his life in travelling: his poverty, and other misfor-tunes, made him often dependent on the mean-eft, as his talents recommended him to the friendfhip of the greateft; fo that what he fays of Ulyffes may juftly be applied to himfelf, that " he vifited many ftates and nations, and
" knew

" knew the characters of many men." Virgil
had not the fame opportunities : he lived in an
age of more refinement, and was perhaps too
much converfant in courtly life, as well as too
bafhful in his deportment, and delicate in his
conftitution, to ftudy the varieties of human
nature, where in a monarchy they are moft
confpicuous, namely in the middlè and lower
ranks of mankind. Need we wonder, then,
that in the difplay of charaéter he falls fo far
fhort of his great original ? Shakefpeare was fa-
miliarly acquainted with all ranks and conditi-
ons of mēn; without which, notwithftanding
his unbounded imagination, it is not to be fuppofed, that he could have fucceeded fo well in
delineating every fpecies of human charaéter,
from the conftable to the monarch, from the
hero to the clown.   And it deferves our notice,
that, however ignorant he might be of Latin
and Greek, he was well acquainted, by tranflation, with fome of the ancients, particularly
Plutarch, whom he feems to have ftudied with
much attention, and who indeed excels all hiftorians in exhibiting lively and interefting views
of human nature.   Great viciflitudes of fortune gave Fielding an opportunity of affociating
with all claffes of men, except perhaps the higheft, whom he rarely attempts to defcribe: Swift's
way of life is well known : and I have been told,
that Congreve ufed to mingle in difguife with
the common people, and pafs whole days and
weeks among them.

   That the ancient painters and ftatuaries were
in many refpeéts fuperior to the modern, is
univerfally allowed. The monuments of their
genius

genius that ftill remain, would convince us of it, even though we were to fuppofe the accounts given by Pliny, Lucian, and other cotemporary authors, to be a little exaggerated. The uncommon fpirit and elegance of their attitudes and proportions are obvious to every eye: and a great mafter feems to think, that modern artifts, though they ought to imitate, can never hope to equal the magnificence of their ideas, or the beauty of their figures*. To account for this, we need not fuppofe, that human genius decays as the world grows older. It may be afcribed partly to the fuperior elegance of the human form in thofe days, and partly to the artifts having then better opportunities of obferving the human body, free from the incumbrances of drefs, in all the varieties of action and motion. The ancient difcipline of the Greeks and Romans, particularly the former, was admirably calculated for improving the human body in health, ftrength, fwiftnefs, flexibility, and grace. In thefe refpects, therefore, they could hardly fail to excel the moderns, whofe education and manners tend rather to enervate the body, and cramp all its faculties. And as the ancients performed many of them naked, and thought it honourable to excel in them; as their cloathing was lefs cumberfome than our Gothic apparel, and fhewed the body to more advantage; it muft be allowed that their painters and ftatuaries had better opportunities of obfervation than ours enjoy, who fee nothing but aukward and languid figures,

* Frefnoy, De Arte Graphica, lin. 190.

figures, difguifed by an unwieldy and ungrace-
ful attire*.

Will it not, then, be acknowledged, that the
ancients may have excelled the moderns in the
fcience of human nature, provided it can be
fhown, that they had better opportunities of
obferving it ? That this was the cafe, appears
from what has been already faid. And that
they really excelled us in this fcience, will not
be doubted by thofe who acknowledge their fuperiority in rhetoric and criticifm; two arts
which are founded in the philofophy of the
human mind. But a more direct proof of the
point in queftion may be had in the writings of
Homer, Plutarch, and the Socratic philofophers; which, for their admirable pictures of
human nature in its genuine fimplicity, are not
equalled by any compofitions of a later date.
Of Ariftotle I fay nothing. We are affured by
thofe who have read his works, that no author
ever underftood human nature better than he.
Fielding himfelf † pays him this compliment ;
and his teftimony will be allowed to have confiderable weight.

Let me therefore recommend it to thofe philofophers who may hereafter make human nature the fubject of their fpeculation, to ftudy
the ancients more than our modern fceptics
feem to have done. If we fet out, like the author of *The Treatife of Human Nature*, with a
fixed purpofe to advance as many paradoxes as
poffible; or with this foolifh conceit, that men
in

* See Algarotti on painting, chap. 2.
† Fielding's works, vol. 11. p. 384.   London 1766, 12mo.

in all former ages were utter ſtrangers to themſelves, and to one another; and that we are the
firſt of our ſpecies on whom Nature has beſtowed any glimmerings of diſcernment; we
may depend on it, that in proportion as our
vanity is great, our ſucceſs will be ſmall.   It
will be, like that of a muſician, who ſhould
take it in his head, that Corelli had no taſte in
counterpoint, nor Handel or Jackſon any genius for melody; of an epic poet, who ſhould
fancy, that Homer, Virgil, and Milton, were
bad writers; or of a painter, who ſhould ſuppoſe all his brethren of former times to have
been unacquainted with the colours, lineaments,
and proportions of viſible objects.

If Columbus, before he ſet out on his famous expedition to the weſtern world, had
amuſed himſelf with writing a hiſtory of the
countries he was going to viſit; would the lovers of truth, and interpreters of nature, have
received any improvement or ſatisfaction from
ſuch a ſpecimen of his ingenuity? And is not
the ſyſtem which, without regard to experience, a philoſopher frames in his cloſet, concerning the nature of man, equally frivolous?
If Columbus, in ſuch a hiſtory, had deſcribed
the Americans with two heads, cloven feet,
wings, and a ſcarlet complexion; and after vi-
ſiting them, and finding his deſcription falſe in
every particular, had yet publiſhed that deſcription to the world, affirming it to be true, and
at the ſame time acknowledging, that it did not
correſpond with his experience; I know not
whether mankind would have been moſt diſpoſed to blame his diſingenuity, to laugh at his

abfurdity, or to pity his want of underftanding.   And yet we have known a metaphyfician
contrive a fyftem of human nature, and, though
fenfible that it did not correfpond with the real
appearances of human nature, deliver it to the
world as found philofophy; we have heard this
fyftem applauded as a mafter-piece of genius;
and we have feen the experience of individuals,
the confent of nations, the accumulated wifdom
of ages, the principles of fcience, the truths of
religion, and dictates of common fenfe, facri-
ficed to this contemptible and felf-contradicto-
ry chimera.

I would further recommend it to our moral
philofophers, to ftudy themfelves with candour
and attention, and cultivate an acquaintance
with mankind, efpecially with thofe whofe manners retain moft of the truth and fimplicity of
nature.   Acquaintance with the great makes a
man of fafhion, but will not make a philofopher.   They who are ambitious to merit this
appellation, think nothing below them which
the Author of Nature has been pleafed to
create, to preferve, and to adorn.—Away with
this paffion for fyftem-building! it is pedantry:
away with this luft of paradox! it is prefumption.   Be equally afhamed of dogmatical prejudice, and fceptical incredulity; for both are as
remote from the fpirit of true philofophy, as
bullying and cowardice from true valour.

It will be faid, perhaps, that a general knowledge of man is fufficient for the philofopher;
and that this particular knowledge which we
recommend, is neceffary only for the novelift
and poet.   But let it be remembered, that many

ny important errors in moral philofophy have
arifen from the want of this particular knowledge; and that it is by too little, not by too
much experience, by fcanty, not by copious,
induction, that philofophy is corrupted.   Men
have rarely framed a fyftem, without firft confulting experience in regard to fome few obvious facts.   We are apt to be prejudiced in favour of the notions that prevail within our own
narrow circle; but we muft quit that circle, if
we would diveft ourfelves of prejudice, as we
muft go from home, if we would get rid of our
provincial accent.   " Horace afferts wifdom
" and good fenfe to be the fource and principle
" of good writing; for the attainment of
" which he prefcribes a careful ftudy of the
" Socratic, that is moral wifdom, and a tho-
" rough acquaintance with human nature, that
" great exemplar of manners, as he finely calls
" it; or, in other words, a wide extenfive
" view of real practical life.   The joint direc-
" tion of thefe two," I quote the words of an
admirable critic and moft ingenious philofopher, " as means of acquiring moral know-
" ledge, is perfectly neceffary.   For the for-
" mer, when alone, is apt to grow abftracted
" and unaffecting; the latter uninftructing
" and fuperficial.   The philofopher talks with-
" out experience, and the man of the world
" without principles.   United they fupply
" each other's defects; while the man of the
" world borrows fo much of the philofopher,
" as to be able to adjuft the feveral fenti-
" ments with precifion and exactnefs; and
" the philofopher fo much of the man of

" the world, as to copy the manners of life
" (which we can only do by experience) with
" truth and spirit. Both together furnish a
" thorough and complete comprehension of
" human life*."

That I may not be thought a blind admirer
of antiquity, I would here crave the reader's
indulgence for one short digression more, in order to put him in mind of an important error
in morals, inferred from partial and inaccurate
experience, by no less a person than Ariftotle
himself. He argues, " That men of little ge-
" nius, and great bodily ftrength, are by na-
" ture deftined to ferve, and thofe of better ca-
" pacity to command; that the natives of
" Greece, and of fome other countries, being
" fuperior in genius, have a natural right to
" empire; and that the reft of mankind, be-
" ing naturally ftupid, are deftined to labour
" and flavery †." This reafoning is now, alas!
of little advantage to Ariftotle's countrymen,
who have for many ages been doomed to that
flavery which in his judgement, Nature had
deftined them to impofe on others; and many
nations whom he would have configned to ever-
lafting ftupidity, have fhown themfelves equal
in genius to the moft exalted of human kind.
It would have been more worthy of Ariftotle,
to have inferred man's natural and univerfal
right to liberty, from that natural and univerfal
paflion with which men defire it, and from
the falutary confequences to learning, to virtue,
and

* Hurd's Commentary on Horace's Epiftle to the Pifos, p. 25.
edit. 4.
† De Republ. lib. 1. cap. 5. 6.

and to every human improvement, of which it never fails to be productive. He wanted, perhaps to devise some excuse for servitude ; a practice which, to their eternal reproach, both Greeks and Romans tolerated even in the days of their glory.

Mr. Hume argues nearly in the same manner in regard to the superiority of white men over black. " I am apt to suspect," says he, " the negroes, and in general all the other species of men, (for there are four or five different kinds), to be naturally inferior to the whites. There *never was* a civilized nation " of any other complexion than white, *nor even any individual* eminent either in action or speculation. *No* ingenious manufactures among them, *no* arts, *no* sciences. " —There are negro-slaves dispersed all over " Europe, of which *none* ever discovered " any symptoms of ingenuity*." These assertions are strong ; but I know not whether they have any thing else to recommend them.— For, first, though true, they would not prove the point in question, except it were also proved, that the Africans and Americans, even though arts and sciences were introduced among them, would still remain unsusceptible of cultivation. The inhabitants of Great Britain and France were as savage two thousand years ago, as those of Africa and America are at this day. To civilize a nation, is a work which it requires long time to accomplish. And one may as well say of an infant, that he can never become a
man,

* Hume's Essay on National Characters.

man, as of a nation now barbarous, that it never can be civilized.---Secondly, of the facts here afferted, no man could have fufficient evidence, except from a perfonal acquaintance with all the negroes that now are, or ever were, on the face of the earth. Thefe people write no hiftories; and all the reports of all the travellers that ever vifited them, will not amount to any thing like a proof of what is here affirmed.---But, thirdly, we know that thefe affertions are not true. The empires of Peru and Mexico could not have been governed, nor the metropolis of the latter built after fo fingular a manner, in the middle of a lake, without men eminent both for action and fpeculation. Every body has heard of the magnificence, good government, and ingenuity, of the ancient Peruvians. The Africans and Americans are known to have many ingenious manufactures and arts among them, which even Europeans would find it no eafy matter to imitate. Sciences indeed they have none, becaufe they have no letters; but in oratory, fome of them, particularly the Indians *of the Five Nations*, are faid to be greatly our fuperiors. It will be readily allowed, that the condition of a flave is not favourable to genius of any kind; and yet the negro-flaves difperfed over Europe, have often difcovered fymptoms of ingenuity, notwithftanding their unhappy circumftances. They become excellent handicraftfmen, and practical muficians, and indeed learn every thing their mafters are at pains to teach them, perfidy and debauchery not excepted. That a negro-flave, who can neither read nor write, nor fpeak any
European

European language, who is not permitted to
do any thing but what his master commands,
and who has not a single friend on earth, but
is universally considered and treated as if he
were of a species inferior to the human;—that
such a creature should so distinguish himself
among Europeans, as to be talked of through
the world as a man of genius, is surely no rea-
sonable expectation.   To suppose him of an inferior species, because he does not thus distinguish himself, is just as rational, as to suppose
any private European of an inferior species, because he has not raised himself to the condition
of royalty.

Had the Europeans been destitute of the arts
of writing, and working in iron, they might
have remained to this day as barbarous as the
natives of Africa and America.   Nor is the invention of these arts to be ascribed to our superior capacity.   The genius of the inventor is
not always to be estimated according to the importance of the invention.   Gunpowder, and
the mariner's compass, have produced wonderful revolutions in human affairs, and yet were
accidental discoveries.   Such, probably, were
the first essays in writing, and working in iron.
Suppose them the effects of contrivance, they
were at least contrived by a few individuals; and
if they required a superiority of understanding,
or of species, in the inventors, those inventors,
and their descendents are the only persons
who can lay claim to the honour of that superiority.

That every practice or sentiment is barbarous
which is not according to the usages of modern
Europe,

Europe, feems to be a fundamental maxim with fome of our philofophers. Their remarks often put us in mind of the fable of the man and the lion. If negroes or Indians were difpofed to recriminate; if a Lucian or a Voltaire, from the coaft of Guinea, or from *the Five Nations*, were to pay us a vifit; what a picture of European manners might he prefent to his countrymen at his return ! Nor would caricatura, or exaggeration, be neceffary to render it hideous. A plain hiftorical account of fome of our moft fafhionable duellifts, gamblers, and adulterers, (to name no more), would exhibit fpecimens of brutifh barbarity and fottifh infatuation, fuch as might vie with any that ever appeared in Kamfchatka, California, or the land of Hottentots.

The natural inferiority of negroes is a favourite topic with fome modern writers. They mean perhaps to invalidate the authority of that Book, which declares, that " Eve was " the mother of all living," and that " God " hath made of one blood all nations of men, " for to dwell on all the face of the earth."— And perhaps fome of them may have it in view to vindicate a certain barbarous piece of policy, which, though it does no honour to the Chriftian world, and is not, I believe, attended with pecuniary advantage to the commercial, has notwithftanding many patrons even in this age of light and liberty.——But Britons are famous for generofity; a virtue in which it is eafy for them to excel both the Romans and the Greeks. Let it never be faid that flavery is countenanced by the braveft and moft generous people on
earth;

earth; by a people who are animated with that heroic paſſion, the love of liberty, beyond all nations ancient or modern; and the fame of whoſe toilſome, but unwearied perſeverance, in vindicating, at the expence of life and fortune, the ſacred rights of mankind, will ſtrike terror into the hearts of ſycophants and tyrants, and excite the admiration and gratitude of all good men to the lateſt poſterity.

C H A P. III.

Conſequences of Metaphyſical Scepticiſm.

AFTER all, it will perhaps be objected to this diſcourſe, that I have laid too much ſtreſs upon the conſequences of metaphyſical abſurdity, and repreſented them as much more dangerous than they are found to be in fact. I ſhall be told, that many of the controverſies in metaphyſic are merely verbal; and the errors proceeding from them of ſo abſtract a nature, that philoſophers run little riſk, and the vulgar no riſk at all, of being influenced by them in practice. It will be ſaid, that I never heard of any man who fell a ſacrifice to BERKELEY's ſyſtem, by breaking his neck over a material precipice, which he had taken for an ideal one; nor of any Fataliſt, whoſe morals were, upon the whole, more exceptionable than thoſe of the aſſerters of free agency: in a word, that

whatever

whatever effect fuch tenets may have upon the underftanding, they feldom or never produce any fenfible effects upon the heart. In confidering this objection, I muft confine myfelf to a few topics; for the fubject to which it leads is of vaft extent. The influence of the metaphyfical fpirit upon art, fcience, manners, would furnifh matter for a large treatife. It will fuffice at prefent to fhow, that metaphyfical errors are not harmlefs, but may produce, and actually have produced, fome very important and interefting confequences.

I begin with an obfervation often made, and indeed obvious enough, namely, That happinefs is the end of our being; and that knowledge, and even truth itfelf, are valuable only as they tend to promote it. Every ufelefs ftudy is a pernicious thing; becaufe it waftes our time, and mifemploys our faculties. To prove that metaphyfical abfurdities do no good, would therefore fufficiently juftify the prefent undertaking. But it requires no deep fagacity to be able to prove a great deal more.

We acknowledge, however, that all metaphyfical errors are not equally dangerous.——— There is an obfcurity in the abftract fciences, as they are commonly taught, which is often no bad prefervative againft their influence. This obfcurity is fometimes unavoidable, on account of the infufficiency of language; fometimes it is owing to the fpiritlefs or flovenly ftyle of the writer; and fometimes it is affected; as when a philofopher, from prudential confiderations, thinks fit to difguife any occafional attack on the religion or laws of his country,

by

by some artful equivocation, in the form of allegory, dialogue, or fable. The style of *The Treatise of Human Nature* is so obscure and uninteresting, that if the author had not in his *Essays* republished the capital doctrines of that work in a more elegant style, a confutation of them would not have been very necessary: their uncouth and gloomy aspect would have deterred most people from courting their acquaintance. And, after all, though this author is one of the deadliest, he is not perhaps one of the most dangerous, enemies of religion. Bolingbroke, his inferior in subtlety, but far superior in wit and eloquence, is more dangerous, because more entertaining. So that, though the reader may be disposed to applaud the patriotism of the grand jury of Westminster, who presented the posthumous works of that Noble Lord as a public nuisance, he must be sensible, that there was no necessity for affixing any such stigma to the philosophical writings of the Scottish author. And yet it cannot be denied, that even these, notwithstanding their obscurity, have done mischief enough to make every sober-minded person earnestly wish that they had never existed.

Further, some metaphysical errors are so grosly absurd, that there is hardly a possibility of their perverting our conduct. Such, considered in itself, is the doctrine of the non-existence of matter; which no man in his senses was ever capable of believing for a single moment. Pyrrho was a vain hypocrite: he took it in his head to say, that he believed nothing, because he wanted to be taken notice of: he affected,

affected, too, to act up to this pretended difbelief; and would not of his own accord ſtep
aſide to avoid a dog, a chariot, or a precipice:
but he always took care to have ſome friends
or ſervants at hand, whoſe buſineſs it was to
keep the philoſopher out of harm's way.---
That the univerſe is nothing but a *heap* of impreſſions and ideas, is another of thoſe profound myſteries, from which we need not apprehend much danger; becauſe it is ſo abſurd,
that no words but ſuch as imply a contradiction, will fully expreſs it.   I know not whether
the abſurdity of a ſyſtem was ever before urged as an apology for its author.   But it is
better to be abſurd than miſchievous: and happy it were for the world, and much to the credit of ſome perſons now in it, if metaphyſicians were chargeable with nothing worſe than
abſurdity.

Again, certain errors in our theories of human nature, conſidered in themſelves, are in
ſome meaſure harmleſs, when the principles
that oppoſe their influence are ſtrong and active.   A gentle diſpoſition, confirmed habits of
virtue, obedience to law, a regard to order, or
even the fear of puniſhment, often prove an-
tidotes to metaphyſical poiſon.   When Fatality has theſe principles to combat, it may puzzle the judgement, but will not corrupt the
heart.   Natural inſtinct never fails to oppoſe
it; all men believe themſelves free agents, as
long at leaſt as they keep clear of metaphyſic;
nay, ſo powerful is the ſentiment of moral liberty, that I cannot think it was ever entirely
ſubdued in any rational being.   But if it were
ſubdued,

subdued, (and surely no Fatalist will acknowledge it invincible) ; if the oppofite principles
should at the fame time ceafe to act ; and if
debauchery, bad example, and licentious writings, should extinguish or weaken the fenfe of
duty ; what might not be apprehended from
men who are above law, or can fcreen themfelves from punishment ? What virtue is to be
expected from a being who believes itfelf a mere
machine ? If I were perfuaded, that the evil I
commit is impofed upon me by fatal neceffity,
I should think repentance as abfurd as Xerxes
fcourging the waves of the Hellefpont : and
be as little difpofed to form refolutions of
amendment, as to contrive fchemes for preventing the frequent eclipfes of the fatellites of Jupiter.   Every author who publifhes an effay in
behalf of Fatality, is willing to run the rifk of
bringing all men over to his opinion.   What if
this should be the confequence? If it be poffible
to make one reafonable creature a Fatalift, may
it not be poffible to make many fuch?   And
would this be a matter of little or no moment ?
It is, I think, demonftrable, that it would not.
But I have already explained myfelf on this
head.

Other metaphyfical errors there are, which,
though they do not ftrike more directly at the
foundations of virtue, are more apt to influence mankind, becaufe they are not fo vigoroufly counteracted by any particular propenfity.   What shall we fay to the theory of
Hobbes, who makes the diftinction between
vice and virtue artificial, and dependent on the
arbitrary

arbitrary laws of human governors? According to this account, no action that is commanded by a king or chief magiſtrate can be vitious, and none virtuous except warranted by that authority *.   Were this opinion univerſal, what could deter men from ſecret wickedneſs, or ſuch as is not cognizable by law? What could reſtrain governors from the utmoſt inſolence of tyranny ✝? What but a miracle could ſave the human race from perdition?

In

---

* See this doctrine of Mr. Hobbes more particularly explained, and very well confuted, by Dr. Clarke, in his *Evidences of Natural and Revealed Religion*, vol. 2. prop. 1.

✝ It is in vain to quote hiſtory to men who will not believe their own eyes; and ſuch I take all thoſe to be, who look round them in the world, and deny that the licentious theories of philoſophers have any influence on human practice.   Yet perhaps it may not be improper to lay before ſome readers the following paſſage from Plutarch's Life of Alexander, as it is elegantly tranſlated by Dr. Langhorne.

"——Alexander ſnatched a ſpear from one of the guards, and meeting Clitus,—ran him through the body.   He fell immediately to the ground, and with a diſmal groan expired.—Alexander's rage ſubſided in a moment: he came to himſelf; and ſeeing his friends ſtanding in ſilent aſtoniſhment by him, he haſtily drew the ſpear out of the dead body, and was applying it to his own throat, when his guards ſeized his hands, and carried him off by force into his chamber.   He paſſed that night and the next day in anguiſh inexpreſſible; and when he had waſted himſelf with tears and lamentations, he lay in ſpeechleſs grief, uttering only now and then a groan.   His friends, alarmed at this melancholy ſilence, forced themſelves into the room, and attempted to conſole him.   But he would liſten to none of them, except Ariſtander, who put him in mind of his dream, and the ill omen of the ſheep, *and aſſured him, that the whole was by the decree of Fate.*   As he ſeemed *a little tomforted,* Caliſthenes the philoſopher, Ariſtotle's near relation, and Anaxarchus the Abderite, were called in.   Caliſthenes began in a ſoft and tender manner, endeavouring to relieve him, without ſearching the wound.   But Anaxarchus, who had a particular walk in philoſophy, and looked upon his fellow-labourers in ſcience with contempt, cried out, on entering the room, " Is this Alexander, " upon whom the whole world have their eyes?   Can it be he who

" lies

In the preface to one of Mr. Hume's late publications, we are prefented with an elaborate panegyric on the author, " He hath ex-" erted," fays the writer of the preface, " thofe " great talents he received from Nature, and " the acquifitions he made by ftudy, in the " fearch of truth, and in promoting the good " of mankind." A noble encomium indeed ! If it be a true one, what are we to think of a Douglas, a Campbell, a Gerard, a Reid, and fome others, who have attacked feveral of Mr. Hume's opinions, and proved them to be contrary to truth, and fubverfive of the good of mankind ? I thought indeed, that the works of thefe excellent writers had given great fatisfaction to the friends of truth and virtue, and done an important fervice to fociety : but, if I believe this prefacer, I muft look on them, as well as on this attempt of my own, with deteftation and horror. But before fo great a change in my fentiments can take place, it will be neceffary that Mr. Hume prove, to my fatisfaction, that he is neither the author nor

the

" lies extended on the ground, crying like a flave in fear of the " law, and the tongues of men, *to whom he fhould himfelf be a* " *law, and the meafure of right and wrong?* What did he con-" quer for, but to rule and to command, *not fervilely to fubmit to* " *the vain opinions of men ?* Know you not, (continued he), that " Jupiter is reprefented with Themis and Juftice by his fide, to " fhow, *that whatever is done by fupreme power is right ?*" By this and other difcourfes of the fame kind, *he alleviated the king's grief indeed, but made him withal more haughty and unjuft.* At the fame time he infinuated himfelf into his favour in fo extraordinary a manner, that he could no longer bear the converfation of Callifthenes, who before was not very agreeable, on account of his aufterity."

Langborne's Plutarch, vol. 4. p. 294.

the publisher of *the Essays* that bear his name, nor of the *Treatise of Human Nature*. For I will not take it on his, nor on any man's word, that religion, both revealed and natural, and all conviction in regard to truth, are detrimental to mankind. And it is most certain, that he, if he is indeed the author of those Essays, and of that Treatise, hath exerted his great talents, and employed several years of his life, in endeavouring to persuade the world, that the fundamental doctrines of natural religion are irrational, and the proofs of revealed religion such as ought not to satisfy an impartial mind; and that there is not in any science an evidence of truth sufficient to produce certainty. Suppose these opinions established in the world, and say, if you can, that the good of mankind would be promoted by them. To me it seems impossible for society to exist under the influence of such opinions. Nor let it be thought, that we give an unfavourable view of human nature, when we insist on the necessity of good principles for the preservation of good order. Such a total subversion of human sentiment is, I believe, impossible: mankind, at their very worst, are not such monsters, as to admit it; reason, conscience, taste, habit, interest, fear, must perpetually oppose it: but the philosophy that aims at a total subversion of human sentiment is not on that account the less detestable. And yet it is said of the authors of this philosophy, that they exert their great talents in promoting the good of mankind. What an insult on human nature
and

and common fenfe! If mankind are tame enough to acquiefce in fuch an infult, and fervile enough to repiy, " It is true, we have " been much obliged to the celebrated fcep- " tics of this moft enlightened age,"—they would almoft tempt one to exprefs himfelf in the ftyle of mifanthropy, and fay, " Si po- " pulus vult decipi, decipiatur."

Every doctrine is dangerous that tends to difcredit the evidence of our fenfes, external or internal, and to fubvert the original inftinctive principles of human belief. In this refpect the moft unnatural and incomprehenfible abfurdities, fuch as the doctrine of the non-exiftence of matter, and of perceptions without a percipient fubftance, are far from being harmlefs; as they feem to lead, and actually have led, to univerfal fcepticifm; and fet an example of a method of reafoning fufficient to overturn all truth, and pervert every human faculty. In this refpect alfo we have proved the doctrine of Fatality to be of moft pernicious tendency, as it leads men to fuppofe their moral fentiments fallacious or equivocal; not to mention its influence on our notions of God, and natural religion. When a fceptic attacks one principle of common fenfe, he does in effect attack all; for if we are made diftruftful of the veracity of inftinctive conviction in one inftance, we muft, or at leaft we may, become equally diftruftful in every other. A little fcepticifm introduced into fcience will foon affimilate the whole to its own nature; the fatal fermentation, once begun, fpreads wider and

VOL. I.   C c   wider

wider every moment, 'till all the mafs be tranf-
formed into rottennefs and poifon.

There is no exaggeration here. The prefent
ftate of the abftract fciences is a melancholy
proof, that what I fay is true. This is called
the age of reafon and philofophy; and this is
the age of avowed and dogmatical Atheifm.
Sceptics have at laft grown weary of doubting;
and have now difcovered by the force of their
great talents, that one thing at leaft is certain,
namely, that God, and religion, and immortality, are empty founds. This is the final triumph of our fo much boafted philofophic fpirit ;
thefe are the limits of the dominion of error,
beyond which we can hardly conceive it poffible for human fophiftry to penetrate. Exult,
O Metaphyfic, at the confummation of thy
glories. More thou canft not hope, more thou
canft not defire. Fall down, ye mortals, and
acknowledge the ftupendous bleffing : adore
thofe men of *great talents*, thofe daring fpirits,
thofe patterns of modefty, gentlenefs, and candour, thofe prodigies of genius, thofe heroes
in beneficence, who have thus laboured—to
ftrip you of every rational confolation, and to
make your condition ten thoufand times worfe
than that of the beafts that perifh.

Why can I not exprefs myfelf with lefs
warmth ! Why can I not devife an apology for
thefe philofophers, to fcreen them from this
dreadful imputation of being the enemies and
plagues of mankind !—Perhaps they do not
themfelves believe their own tenets, but pub-
lifh them only as the means of getting a name
                                    and

and a fortune. But I hope this is not the cafe;
God forbid that it fhould! for then the enor-
mity of their guilt would furpafs all power of
language; we could only gaze at it and trem-
ble.   Compared with fuch wickednefs, the
crimes of the thief, the robber, the incendiary,
would almoft difappear. Thefe facrifice the fortunes or the lives of fome of their fellow-creatures, to their own neceffity or outrageous appetite : but thofe would run the hazard of fa-
crificing, to their own avarice or vanity, the
happinefs of mankind, both here and hereafter.   No; I cannot fuppofe it : the heart of
man, however depraved, is not capable of fuch
malignity.---Perhaps they do not forefee the
confequences of their doctrines. BERKELEY
moft certainly did not.——But BERKELEY
did not attack the religion of his country, did
not feek to undermine the foundations of virtue, did not preach or recommend Atheifm.
He erred; and who is free from error? but his
intentions were irreproachable ; and his conduct
as a man, and a Chriftian, did honour to human nature.---Perhaps our modern fceptics
are ignorant, that, without the belief of a
God, and the hope of immortality, the mife-
ries of human life would often be infupportable.   But can I fuppofe them in a ftate of total ftupidity, utter ftrangers to the human heart,
and to human affairs? Sure they would not
thank me for fuch a fuppofition. Yet this I
muft fuppofe, or I muft believe them to be
moft perfidious and cruel.

Careffed by thofe who call themfelves the
great, ingroffed by the formalities and foppe-

ries of life, intoxicated with vanity, pampered
with adulation, diffipated in the tumult of bufinefs, or amidft the viciffitudes of folly, they
perhaps have little need, and little relifh, for
the confolations of religion.   But let them
know, that, in the folitary fcenes of life, there
is many an honeft and tender heart pining
with incurable anguifh, pierced with the fharp-
eft fting of difappointment, bereft of friends,
chilled with poverty, rackcd with difeafe,
fcourged by the oppreffor ; whom nothing but
truft in Providence, and the hope of a future
retribution, could preferve from the agonies of
defpair.   And do they, with facrilegious hands,
attempt to violate this laft refuge of the miferable, and to rob them of the only comfort that
had furvived the ravages of misfortuns, malice,
and tyranny ! Did it ever happen, that the influence of their execrable tenets difturbed the
tranquillity of virtuous retirement, deepened
the gloom of human diftrefs, or aggravated the
horrors of the grave ? Is it poffible, that this
may have happened in many inftances ? Is it
probable, that this hath happened, or may happen, in one fingle inftance ?---Ye traitors to
human kind, how can ye anfwer for it to your
own hearts ! Surely every fpark of your generofity is extinguifhed for ever, if this confideration do not awaken in you the keeneft remorfe, and make you wifh in bitternefs of
foul——But I remonftrate in vain.   Could I
inforce the prefent topic by an appeal to your
vanity, I might perhaps make fome impreffion :
but to plead with you on the principles of benevolence or generofity, is to addrefs you in
language ye do not, or will not, underftand.
                                      But

But let not the lovers of truth be difcouraged. Atheifm cannot be of long continuance, nor is there any danger of its becoming univerfal. The influence of fome confpicuous characters has brought it too much into fafhion; which, in a thoughtlefs and profligate age, it is no diffi- cult matter to accomplifh. But when men have retrieved the powers of ferious reflection, they will find it a frightful phantom; and the mind will return gladly and eagerly to its old endearments. One thing we certainly know : the fafhion of fceptical fyftems foon paffeth away. Thofe unnatural productions, the vile effufion of a hard heart, that miftakes its own reftleff- nefs for the activity of genius, and its own captioufnefs for fagacity of underftanding, may, like other monfters, pleafe a while by their fin- gularity ; but the charm is foon over : and the fucceeding age will be aftonifhed to hear, that their forefathers were deluded, or amufed, with fuch fooleries. The meafure of Scepticifm feems indeed to be full ; it is time for Truth to vindicate her rights, and we truft they fhall yet be completely vindicated. Such are the hopes and the earneft wifhes of one, who has feldom made controverfy his ftudy, who never took pleafure in argumentation, and who dif- claims all ambition of being reputed a fubtle difputant; but who, as a friend to human na- ture, would account it his honour to be in- ftrumental in promoting, though by means unpleafant to himfelf, the caufe of virtue and true fcience, and in bringing to contempt that fceptical fophiftry which is equally fubverfive of both.

POST-

P O S T S C R I P T.

November, 1770.

To read and criticife the modern fyftems of fcepticifm, is fo difagreeable a tafk, that nothing but a regard to duty could ever have determined me to engage in it. I found in them neither inftruction nor amufement; I wrote againft them with all the difguft that one feels in wrangling with an unrealonable adverfary; and I publifhed what I had written, with the certain profpect of raifing enemies, and with fuch an opinion of my performance, as allowed me not to entertain any fanguine hope of fuccefs. I thought it however poffible, nay, and probable too, that this book might do good. I knew that it contained fome matters of importance, which, if I was not able to fet them in the beft light, might however, by my means, be fuggefted to others more capable to do them juftice.

Since thefe papers were firft publifhed, I have laid myfelf out to obtain information of what has been faid of them, both by their friends, and by their enemies; hoping to profit by the cenfures of the latter, as well as by the admonitions of the former. I do not hear, that

any

any perfon has accufed me of mifconceiving or
mifreprefenting my adverfaries doctrine. Again
and again have I requefted it of thofe whom I
know to be mafters of the whole controverfy,
to give me their thoughts freely on this point;
and they have repeatedly told me, that, in
their judgement, nothing of this kind can be
laid to my charge.

Moft of the objections that have been made,
I had forefeen, and, as I thought, fufficiently
obviated by occafional remarks in the courfe of
the effay. But, in regard to fome of them, I
find it neceffary now to be more particular. I
wifh to give the fulleft fatisfaction to every candid mind: and I am fure I do not, on thefe
fubjects, entertain a fingle thought which I
need be afhamed or afraid to lay before the
public.

I have been blamed for entering fo warmly
into this controverfy. In order to prepoffefs
the minds of thofe who had not read this performance, with an unfavourable opinion of it,
and of its author, infinuations have been made,
and carefully propagated, that it treats only
of fome abftrufe points of fpeculative metaphyfics; which, however, I am accufed of having
difcuffed, or attempted to difcufs, with all the
zeal of a bigot, indulging myfelf in an indecent vehemence of language, and uttering rancorous invectives againft thofe who differ from
me in opinion. Much, on this occafion, has
been faid in praife of moderation and fcepticifm; moderation, the fource of candour,
good-breeding, and good-nature; and fcepticifm, the child of impartiality, and the parent
of

of humility. When men believe with full conviction, nothing, it feems, is to be expected from them but bigotry and bitternefs; when they fuffer themfelves in their inquiries to be warmed with affection, they are philofophers no longer, but revilers and enthufiafts!---If this were a juft account of the matter and manner of *the Effay on Truth*, I fhould not have the face even to attempt an apology; for were any perfon guilty of the fault here complained of, I myfelf fhould certainly be one of the firft to condemn him.

In the whole circle of human fciences, real or pretended, there is not any thing to be found which I think more perfectly contemptible, than the fpeculative metaphyfics of the moderns. It is indeed a moft wretched medley of ill-digefted notions, indiftinct perceptions, inaccurate obfervations, perverted language, and fophiftical argument; diftinguifhing where there is no difference, and confounding where there is no fimilitude; feigning difficulties where it cannot find them, and overlooking them when real. I know no end that the ftudy of fuch jargon can anfwer, except to harden and ftupify the heart, bewilder the underftanding, four the temper, and habituate the mind to irrefolution, captioufnefs, and falfehood. For ftudies of this fort I have neither time nor inclination, I have neither head nor heart. To enter into them at all, is foolifh; to enter into them with warmth, ridiculous; but to treat thofe with any bitternefs, whofe judgements concerning them may differ from ours, is in a very high degree odious and criminal.

minal. Thus far, then, my adverfaries and I are agreed. Had the fceptical philofophers confined themfelves to thofe inoffenfive wrang-lings that fhow only the fubtlety and captiouf-nefs of the difputant, but affect not the princi-ples of human conduct, they never would have found an opponent in me. My paffion for writ-ing is not ftrong; and my love of controver-fy fo weak, that, if it could always be avoided with a fafe confcience, I would never engage in it at all. But when doctrines are publifhed fubverfive of morality and religion, doctrines of which I perceive and have it in my power to expofe the abfurdity, my duty to the public forbids me to be filent; efpecially when I fee, that, by the influence of fafhion, folly, or more criminal caufes, thofe doctrines fpread wider and wider every day, diffufing ignorance, mifery, and licentioufnefs, where-ever they pre vail. Let us oppofe the torrent, though we fhould not be able to check it. The zeal and example of the weak have often roufed to ac-tion, and to victory, the flumbering virtue of the ftrong.

I likewife agree with my adverfaries in this, that fcepticifm, where it tends to make men well-bred, and good-natured, and to rid them of pedantry and petulance, without doing indi-viduals or fociety any harm, is an excellent thing. And fome forts of fcepticifm there are, that really have this tendency. In philofophy, in hiftory, in politics, yea, and even in theolo-gy itfelf, there are many points of doubtful difputation, in regard to which a man's judge-ment may lean to either of the fides, or hang
                                                    wavering

wavering between them, without the leaft inconvenience to himfelf, or others. Whether
pure fpace exifts, or how we come to form an
idea of it; whether all the objects of human
reafon may be fairly reduced to Ariftotle's ten
categories; whether Hannibal, when he paffed
the Alps, had any vinegar in his camp; whether Richard III. was as remarkable for cruelty and a hump-back, as is commonly believed;
whether Mary Queen of Scotland married Both-
well from inclination, or from the neceffity of
her affairs; whether the earth is better peopled
now than it was in ancient times; whether
public prayers fhould be recited from memory, or read:—in regard to thefe, and fuch like
queftions, a little fcepticifm may be very fafe
and very proper, and I will never think the
worfe of a man for differing from me in
opinion. And if ever it fhould be my chance
to engage in controverfy on fuch queftions, I
here *pledge myfelf to the public*, (abfit invidia
verbo!), that I will conduct the whole affair
with the moft exemplary coolnefs of blood,
and lenity of language. I have obferved, that
ftrong conviction is more apt to breed ftrife, in
matters of little moment, than in fubjects of
high importance. Not to mention (what I
would willingly forget) the fcandalous contefts
that have prevailed in the Chriftian world about
trifling ceremonies and points of doctrine, I
need only put the reader in mind of thofe
learned critics and annotators, Salmafius, Val-
la, and Scaliger who in their fquabbles about
words, gave fcope to fuch rancorous animofity,
and virulent abufe, as is altogether without example.

ample. In every cafe where dogmatical belief tends to harden the heart, or to breed prejudices incompatible with candour, humanity, and the love of truth, all good men will be careful to cultivate moderation and diffidence.

But there are other points, in regard to which a ftrong conviction produces the beft effects, and doubt and hefitation the worft: and thefe are the points that our fceptics labour to fubvert, and I to eftablifh. That the human foul is a real and permanent fubftance, that God exifts, that virtue and vice are diftinctly and effentially different, that there is fuch a thing as truth, and that man in many cafes is capable of difcovering it, are fome of the principles which this book is intended to vindicate from the objections of fcepticifm. Attempts have been made to perfuade us, that there is no evidence of truth in any fcience; that the human underftanding ought not to believe any thing, but rather to remain in perpetual fufpenfe between oppofite opinions; that it is unreafonable to believe the Deity to be perfectly wife and good, or even to exift; that the foul of man has nothing permanent in its nature, nor indeed any kind of exiftence diftinct from its prefent perceptions, which are continually changing, and will foon be at an end; and that moral diftinctions are ambiguous. This fcepticifm, the reader will obferve, is totally fubverfive of fcience, morality and religion, both natural and revealed. And this is the fcepticifm which I am blamed for having oppofed with warmth and earneftnefs.

I de-

I defire to know, what good effects this fcepticifm is likely to produce? " It humbles," we
are told, " our pride of underftanding." Indeed! and are they to be confidered as patterns
of humility, who fet the wifdom of all former
ages at nought, bid defiance to the common
fenfe of mankind, and fay to the wifeft and beft
men that ever did honour to our nature, Ye are
fools or hypocrites; we only are candid, honeft, and fagacious! Is this humility! Should
I be humble, if I were to fpeak and act in this
manner! Every man of fenfe would pronounce
me loft to all fhame, an apoftate from truth
and virtue, an enemy to human kind; and
my own confcience would juftify the cenfure.

And fo it feems that pride of underftanding
is infeparable from the difpofition of thofe
who believe, that they have a foul, that there
is a God, that virtue and vice are effentially
different, and that men are in fome cafes
permitted to difcern the difference between
truth and falfehood! Yet the gofpel requires or
fuppofes the belief of all thefe points: the
gofpel alfo commands us to be humble: and
the fpirit and influence of the gofpel have produced the moft perfect examples of that virtue
that ever appeared among men. A believer
may be proud: but it is neither his belief, nor
what he believes, that can make him fo; for
both ought to teach him humility. To call in
queftion, and labour to fubvert, thofe firft
principles of fcience, morality, and religion,
which all the rational part of mankind acknowledge, is indeed an indication of a prefumptuous

ous underſtanding: but does the ſceptic lay this to the charge of the believer? I have heard of a thief, when cloſe purſued, turning on his purſuers, and charging them with robbery: but I do not think the example worthy a philo-ſopher's imitation.

The prevention of bigotry is ſaid to be ano-ther of the bleſſed effects of this modern ſcep-ticiſm. And indeed, if ſceptics would act con-ſiſtently with their own principles, there would be ground for the remark: for a man who believes nothing at all, cannot be ſaid to be blindly attached to any opinion, except per-haps this one, that nothing is to be believed; in which, however, if he have any regard to uniformity of character, he will take care not to be dogmatical. But it is well known to all who have had any opportunity of obſerving his conduct, that the ſceptic rejects thoſe opi-nions only which the reſt of mankind admit: for that, in regard to his own paradoxes, he is as dogmatical as other people. An ingeni-ous author has therefore, with good reaſon, made it one of the articles of the Infidel's creed, That, " he believes in all unbelief *." Though a late writer is a perfect ſceptic in regard to the exiſtence of his ſoul and body, he is cer-tain, that men have no idea of power: though he has many doubts and difficulties about the evidence of mathematical truth, he is quite poſi-tive, that his ſoul is not the ſame thing to-day it was yeſterday: and though he affirms, that it is by an act of the human underſtanding,
that

* Connoiſſeur, No. 9.

that two and two have come to be equal to four; yet he cannot allow, that to fteal or to abftain from ftealing, to act or to ceafe from action, is in the power of any man. In reading fceptical books, I have often found, that the ftrength of the author's attachment to his paradox, is in proportion to its abfurdity. If it deviates but a little from common opinion, he gives himfelf but little trouble about it; if it be inconfiftent with univerfal belief, he condefcends to argue the matter, and to bring what with him paffes for a proof of it; if it be fuch as no man ever did or could believe, he is ftill more conceited of his proof, and calls it a demonftration; but if it is inconceivable, it is a wonder if he does not take it for granted. Thus, that our idea of extenfion is extended, is inconceivable; and in the *Treatife of Human Nature* feems to be taken for granted: that matter exifts only in the mind that perceives it, is what no man ever did or could believe; and the author of the *Treatife concerning the Principles of Human Knowledge* has favoured the world with what paffes among the fafhionable metaphyficians for a demonftration of it: that moral and intellectual virtues are upon the fame footing, is inconfiftent with univerfal belief: and a famous author has argued the matter at large, and would fain perfuade us, that he has proved it; though I do not recollect, that he triumphs in this proof as fo irrefiftible, as thofe by which he conceives himfelf to have annihilated the idea of power, and exploded the permanency of percipient fubftances. I will not fay, however, that this gradation

dation holds univerfally. Sceptics, it muft be
owned, bear a right zealous attachment to all
their abfurdities, both greater and lefs.   If they
are moft warmly interefted in behalf of the
former, it is, I fuppofe, beeaufe they have had
the fagacity to forefee, that thofe would ftand
moft in need of protection.

We fee now how far fcepticifm may be faid
to prevent bigotry.   It prevents all bigotry, and
all ftrong attachment on the fide of truth and
common fenfe ; but in behalf of its own paradoxes, it eftablifhes bigotry the moft implicit
and the moft obftinate.   It is true, that fceptics fometimes tell us, that, however pofitive-
ly they may aflert their doctrines, they would
not have us think them pofitive aflertors of any
doctrine.   Sextus Empiricus has done this; and
fome too, if I miftake not, of our modern
Pyrrhonifts.   But common readers are not capable of fuch exquifite refinement, as to believe their author to be in earneft, and at the
fame time not in earneft; as to believe, that
when he afferts fome points with diffidence, and
others with the utmoft confidence, he holds himfelf to be equally diffident of all.

There is but one way in which it is poffible
for a fceptic to fatisfy us, that he is equally
doubtful of all doctrines.   He muft affert nothing, lay down no principles,, contradict none
of the opinions of other people, and advance
none of his own : in a word, he muft confine
his doubts to his own breaft, at leaft the grounds
of his doubts ; or propofe them modeftly and
privately, not with a view to make us change
our mind, but only to fhew his own diffidence.

For from the moment that he attempts to obtrude them on the public, or on any individual,
or even to reprefent the opinions of others as
lefs probable than his own, he commences a
dogmatift; and is to be accounted more or lefs
prefumptuous, according as his doctrine is
more or lefs repugnant to common fenfe, and
himfelf more or lefs induftrious to recommend it.

Though he were to content himfelf with urging objections, without feeking to lay down
any principle of his own, which however is a
degree of moderation that no fceptic ever yet
arrived at, we would not on that account pronounce him an inoffenfive man. If his objections have ever weakened the moral or religious
belief of any one perfon, he has injured that
perfon in his deareft and moft important con-
cerns. They who know the value of true religion, and have had any opportunity of obferving its effects on themfelves or others, need
not be told, how dreadful to a fenfible mind it
is, to be ftaggered in its faith by the cavils
of the Infidel. Every perfon of common humanity, who knows any thing of the heart
of man, would fhudder at the thought of in-
fufing fcepticifm into the pious Chriftian. Suppofe the Chriftian to retain his faith, in fpite
of all objections; yet the confutation of thefe
cannot fail to diftrefs him; and a habit of
doubting, once begun, may, to the lateft hour
of his life, prove fatal to his peace of mind.
Let no one miftake or mifreprefent me : I am
not fpeaking of thofe points of doctrine which
rational believers allow to be indifferent : I

fpeak

speak of those great and most essential articles of faith; the existence of a Deity, infinitely wise, beneficent, and powerful; the certainty of a future state of retribution; and the divine authority of the gospel. These are the articles which some late authors labour with all their might to overturn; and these are the articles which every person who loves virtue and mankind, would wish to see ardently and zealously defended. Is it bigotry to believe these sublime truths with full assurance of faith? I glory in such bigotry: I would not part with it for a thousand worlds: I congratulate the man who is possessed of it; for, amidst all the vicissitudes and calamities of the present state, that man enjoys a fund of consolation, of which it is not in the power of fortune to deprive him. Calamities, did I say? The evils of a very short life will not be accounted such by him who has a near and certain prospect of a happy eternity.---Will it be said, that the firm belief of these divine truths did ever give rise to ill-nature or persecution? It will not be said, by any person who is acquainted with history, or the human mind. Of such belief, when sincere, and undebased by criminal passions, meekness, benevolence, and forgiveness, are the natural and necessary effects. There is not a book on earth so favourable to all the kind, and all the sublime affections, or so unfriendly to hatred and persecution, to tyranny, injustice, and every sort of malevolence, as that very gospel against which our sceptics entertain such a rancorous antipathy. Of this they cannot be ignorant, if they have ever read it; for it

VOL. I.   D d   breathes

breathes nothing throughout, but mercy, benevolence, and peace. If they have not read
it, they and their prejudices are as contemptible, as any thing so hateful can be: if they
have, their pretended concern for the rights of
mankind is all hypocrify and a lie. Nor need
they attempt to frame an answer to this accufation, till they have proved, that the morality
of the gofpel is faulty or imperfect: that virtue
is not useful to individuals, nor beneficial to
fociety; that the evils of life are moft effectually alleviated by the extinction of hope; that
annihilation is a more encouraging profpect to
virtue, than the certain view of eternal happinefs; that nothing is a greater check to vice,
than a firm perfuafion that no punifhment
awaits it; and that it is a confideration full of
mifery to a good man, when weeping on the
grave of a beloved friend, to reflect, that they
fhall foon meet again in a better ftate, never
to part any more.

I wonder at thofe men who charge upon
Chriftianity all the evils that fuperftition, avarice, fenfuality, and the love of power, have
introduced into the Chriftian world; and then
fuppofe, that thefe evils are to be prevented,
not by fuppreffing criminal paffions, but by
extirpating Chriftianity, or weakening its influence. In fact, our religion fupplies the only effectual means of fuppreffing thefe paffions,
and fo preventing the mifchief complained of;
and this it will ever be more or lefs powerful
to accomplifh, according as its influence over
the minds of men is greater or lefs; and greater or lefs will its influence be, according as its
doctrines

doctrines are more or lefs firmly believed. It was not becaufe they were Chriftians, but becaufe they were covetous and cruel, that the firft invaders of America perpetrated thofe diabolical cruelties in Peru and Mexico, the narrative of which is infupportable to humanity. Had they been Chriftians in any thing but in name, they would have loved their neighbour as themfelves; and no man who loves his neighbour as himfelf, will ever cut his throat, or roaft him alive, in order to get at his money.

If zeal be warrantable on any occafion, it muft be fo in the prefent controverfy: for I know of no doctrines more important in themfelves, or more affecting to a fenfible mind, than thofe which the fcepticifm I controvert tends to overturn. But why, it may be faid, fhould zeal be warrantable on any occafion? The anfwer is eafy: Becaufe on fome occafions it is decent and natural. When a man is deeply interefted in his fubject, it is not natural for him to keep up the appearance of as much coolnefs, as if he were difputing about an indifferent matter: and whatever is not natural is offenfive. Were he to hear his deareft friends branded with the appellation of knaves and ruffians, would it be natural, would it be decent, for him to preferve the fame indifference in his look, and foftnefs in his manner, as if he were inveftigating a truth in conic fections, arguing about the caufe of the Aurora Borealis, or fettling a point of ancient hiftory? Ought he not to fhow, by the fharpnefs as well as by the folidity of his reply, that he not only difavows, but detefts the accufation? Is there a

man

man whofe indignation would not kindle at fuch
an infult? Is there a man who would be fo
much overawed by any antagonift, as to conceal his indignation? Of fuch a man I fhall
only fay, that I would not chufe him for my
friend. When our fubject lies near our heart,
our language muft be animated, or it will be
worfe than lifelefs; it will be affected and hypocritical. Now what fubject can lie nearer
the heart of a Chriftian, or of a man, than the
exiftence and perfections of God, and the immortality of the human foul? If he cannot,
if he ought not, to hear with patience the blaf-
phemies uttered by unthinking profligates in
their common converfation, with what temper
of mind will he liften or reply to the cool, in-
fidious, and envenomed impieties of the deliberate Atheift! --- Fy on it! that I fhould need
to write fo long an apology for being an enemy to Atheifm and nonfenfe!

    " But why engage in the controverfy at all?
" Let the Infidel do his worft, and heap
" fophifm on fophifm, and rail, and blaf-
" pheme as long as he pleafes; if your religi-
" on be from God, or founded in reafon, it
" cannot be overthrown. Why then give your-
" felf or others any trouble with your attempts
" to fupport a caufe, againft which it is faid
" that hell itfelf fhall not prevail?"—This objection has been made, and urged too with confidence. It has juft as much weight as the following. Why enact laws againft, or inflict
punifhment upon murderers? Let them do
their worft, and ftab, and ftrangle, and poifon, as much as they pleafe, they will never be
able

able to accomplifh the final extermination of
the human fpecies, nor perhaps to depopulate
a fingle province. --- Such idle talk deferves no
anfwer, or but a very fhort one. We do believe, and therefore we rejoice, that our religion fhall flourifh in fpite of all the fophiftry of
malevolent men.   But is their fophiftry the lefs
wicked on that account ? Does it not deferve to
be punifhed with' ridicule and confutation ?
Have we reafon to hope, that a miracle will
be wrought to fave any individual from infidelity, or even any believer from thofe doubts
and apprehenfions which the writings of infidels are intended to raife ? And is it not worth
our while, is it not our duty, ought it not to
be our inclination, to endeavour to prevent
fuch a calamity? Nor let us imagine that this
is the bufinefs of the clergy alone.   They, no
doubt, are beft qualified for this fervice ; but
we of the laity who believe the gofpel, are under the fame obligation to wifh well, and, according to our ability, to do good to our fellow-creatures.   For my own part, though the
writing of this book had been a work of much
greater difficulty than I found it to be, I would
have chearfully undertaken it, in the hope of
being inftrumental in reclaiming even a fingle
fceptic from his unhappy prejudices, or in preferving even a fingle believer from the horrors
of fcepticifm.   Tell me not, that thofe horrors
have no exiftence.   I know the contrary.   Tell
me not, that the good ends propofed can never
in any degree be accomplifhed by performances
of this kind.   Of this too I know the contrary.

Sup-

Suppofe a fet of men, fubjects of the Britifh government, to publifh books fetting forth, That liberty, both civil and religious, is an abfurdity; that trial by juries, the *Habeas Corpus* act, magna charta, and the Proteftant religion, are intolerable nuifances; and that Popery, defpotifm, and the inquifition, ought immediately to be eftablifhed throughout the Britifh empire; fuppofe them to exhort their countrymen to overturn, or at leaft to difregard, our excellent laws and conftitution, and make a tender of their fouls and confciences to the Pope, and of their lives and fortunes to the King of France; --- and fuppofe them to write fo cautioufly as to efcape the cenfure of the law, and yet with plaufibility fufficient to feduce many, and give rife to much diffatisfaction, difcord, and licentious practice, equally fatal to the happinefs of individuals and to the public peace; --- With what temper would an Englifhman of fenfe and fpirit fet about confuting their principles? Would it be decent, or even pardonable, to handle fuch a fubject with coolnefs, or to behave with complaifance towards fuch adverfaries? Suppofe them to have fpecious qualities, and to pafs with their own party for men of candour, genius, and learning; yet the lover of liberty and mankind would not, I prefume, be difpofed to pay them any exceffive compliments on that account, or on any other. But fuppofe thefe political apoftates to appear, in the courfe of the controverfy, chargeable with ignorance and fophiftical reafoning, with evafive and quibbling refinements,

with

with misreprefentation of common facts, and misapprehenfion. of common language, more attached to hypothefis than to the truth, preferring their own conceits to the common fenfe of mankind, and feeking to gratify their own exorbitant vanity and luft of paradox, though at the expence of the happinefs of millions : --- with what face could their moft implicit admirers complain of the feverity of that antagonift who fhould treat both them and their principles with contempt and indignation? with what face urge in their defence, that though perhaps fomewhat blameable on the prefent occafion, they and their works were notwithftanding intitled to univerfal efteem, and the moft refpectful ufage, on account of their fkill in mufic, architecture, geometry, and the Greek and Latin tongues! On this account, would they be in any lefs degree the pefts of fociety, or the enemies of mankind? would their falfe reafoning be lefs fophiftical, their prefumption lefs arrogant, or their malevolence lefs atrocious? Do not the men who, like Alexander, Machiavel, and the author of La Pucelle d'Orleans, employ their great talents in deftroying and corrupting mankind, aggravate all their other crimes by the dreadful addition of ingratitude and breach of truft? And are not their characters, for this very reafon, the more obnoxious to univerfal abhorrence? An illiterate blockhead in the Robinhood Tavern, blafpheming the Saviour of mankind, or labouring to confound the diftinctions of vice and virtue, is a wicked wretch, no doubt: but his
wickednefs

wickednefs admits of fome fhadow of excufe, he might plead his ignorance, his ftupidity; and the ftill more profligate lives and princi- ples of thofe whom the world, by a prepof- terous figure of fpeech, is pleafed to call his betters: but the men of parts and learning, who join in the fame infernal cry, are criminals of a higher order; for in their defence nothing can be pleaded that will not aggravate their guilt.

My defign in this book was, to give others the very fame notions of the fceptical philofo- phy that I myfelf entertain; which I could not have done, if I had not taken the liberty to de- liver my thoughts plainly and without referve. And truly I faw no reafon for being more indul- gent to the writings of fceptics, than to thofe of other men. The tafte of the public requires not any fuch extraordinary condefcenfion. If ever it fhould, which is not probable, we may then think it prudent to comply; but, as we fcorn, in matters of fuch moment, to exprefs ourfelves by halves, we will then alfo throw pen and ink afide, never to be refumed until we again find, that we may with fafety write, and be honeft at the fame time.

Infidels take it upon them to treat religion and its friends with opprobrious language, mifreprefentation, undeferved ridicule, and di- vers other forts of abufe. Some of them affert, with the moft dogmatical affurance, what they know to be contrary to the common fenfe of mankind. All this paffes for wit, and elo- quence, and liberal inquiry, and a manly fpi- rit,

rit. But whenever the friends of truth efpoufe, with warmth, that caufe which they know to be agreeable to common fenfe and univerfal opinion, this is called *bigotry :* and whenever the Chriftian vindicates, with earneftnefs, thofe principles which he believes to be of the higheft importance, and which he knows to be eflential to the happinefs of man, immediately he is charged with want of moderation, want of temper, enthufiafm, and the fpirit of perfecution. Far be it from the lover of truth to imitate thofe authors in mifreprefentation, or in endeavouring to expofe their adverfaries to unmerited ridicule. But if a man were to obtain a patent for vending poifon, it would be very hard to deny his neighbour the privilege of felling the antidote. If their zeal in fpreading and recommending their doctrines be fuffered to pafs without cenfure, our zeal in vindicating ours has at leaft as good a title to pafs uncenfured. If this is not allowed, I muft fuppofe, that the prefent race of infidels, like the *jure divino* kings, imagine themfelves invefted with fome peculiar fanctity of character; that whatever they are pleafed to fay is to be received as law ; and that to contradict their will, or even addrefs them without proftration, is indecent and criminal. I know not whence it is that they affume thefe airs of fuperiority. Is it from the high rank fome of them hold in the world of letters ? I would have them know, that it is but a fhort time fince that high rank was either yielded to, or claimed by, fuch perfons. Spinoza, Hobbes, Collins, Woolfton, and

and the reft of that tribe, were within thefe forty or fifty years accounted a very contemptible brotherhood. The great geniufes of the laft age treated them with little ceremony; and would not, I fuppofe, were they now alive, pay more refpeft to imitators, that they did to the original authors. If the enemies of our religion would profit by experience, they might learn, from the fate of fome of their moft renowned brethren, that infidelity, however fafhionable and lucrative, is not the moft convenient field for a fuccefsful difplay of genius. Ever fince Voltaire, ftimulated by avarice, and other dotages incident to unprincipled old age, formed the fcheme of turning a penny by writing againft the Chriftian religion, he has dwindled from a genius of no common magnitude into a paltry book-maker; and now thinks he does great and terrible things, by retailing the crude and long-exploded notions of the free-thinkers of the laft age, which, when feafoned with a few miftakes, mifreprefentations, and ribaldries of his own, form fuch a mefs of falfehood, impiety, obfcenity, and other abominable ingredients, as nothing but the monftrous maw of an illiterate infidel can either digeft or endure. Several of our famous fceptics have lived to fee the greateft part of their profane tenets confuted. I hope, and earneftly wifh, that they may live to make a full recantation. Some of them muft have known, and many of them might have known, that their tenets were confuted before they adopted them: yet did they
adopt

adopt them notwithftanding, and difplay them
to the world with as much confidence as if
nothing had ever been advanced on the other
fide.   So have I feen a tefty and ftubborn dogmatift, when all his arguments were anfwered,
and all his invention exhaufted, comfort himfelf at laft with fimply repeating his former
pofitions at the end of each new remonftrance
from the adverfary.

They who are converfant in the works of
the fceptical philofophers, know very well,
that thofe gentlemen do not always maintain
that moderation of ftyle which might be expected from perfons of their profeffion; and
if I thought my conduct in this refpect need-
ed to be, or could be, juftified by fuch a precedent, I might plead even their example as
my apology.   But I difclaim every plea that
fuch a precedent could afford me : I write not
in the fpirit of retaliation; and when I find
myfelf inclined to be an imitator, I will look
out for other models.   Indeed it is hardly to
be fuppofed, that I would take thofe for my
pattern, whofe principles and projects are fo
directly oppofite to mine.   Their writings tend
to fubvert the foundations of human knowledge, to poifon the fources of human happinefs, and to overturn that religion which the
beft and wifeft men have believed to be of divine original, and which every good man, who
underftands it, muft reverence as the greateft
bleffing ever conferred upon the human race.
I write with a view to counteract thefe tenden-
cies, by vindicating fome fundamental articles
of

of religion and fcience from the fceptical objections, and by fhowing, that no man can
attempt to difprove the firft principles of
knowledge without contradicting himfelf.   To
the common fenfe of mankind, they fcruple
not to oppofe their own conceits, as if they
judged thefe to be more worthy of credit than
any other authority, human or divine.   I urge
nothing with any degree of confidence or fer-
vour, in which I have not good reafon to think
myfelf warranted by the common fenfe of mankind.   Does their caufe, then, or does mine,
deferve the warmeft attachment ? Have they,
or have I, the moft need to guard againft
vehemence of expreffion * ? As certainly as
the happinefs of mankind is a defirable object,
fo certainly is my caufe good, and theirs
evil.

To conclude : Liberty of fpeech and writing is one of thofe high privileges that diftinguifh Great Britain from all other nations.
Every good fubject wifhes, that it may be preferved to the lateft pofterity : and would be
                                   forry

* " There is no fatisfying the demands of falfe delicacy,"
fays an elegant and pious author, " becaufe they are not regulat-
" ed by any fixed ftandard.   But a man of candour and judge-
" ment will allow, that the bafhful timidity practifed by thofe
" who put themfelves on a level with the adverfaries of religion,
" would ill become one who, declining all difputes, afferts pri-
" mary truths on the authority of common fenfe ; and that who-
" ever pleads the caufe of religion in this way, has a right to af-
" fume a firmer tone, and to pronounce with a more decifive air,
" not upon the ftrength of his own judgement, but on the re-
" verence due from all mankind to the tribunal to which he
" appeals."
                    Ofwald's Appeal in behalf of religion, p. 14.

forry to fee the civil power interpofe to check the progrefs of rational inquiry. Nay, when inquiry ceafes to be rational, and becomes both whimfical and pernicious, advancing as far as fome late authors have carried it, to controvert the firft principles of knowledge, morality, and religion: and confequently the fundamental laws of the Britifh government, and of all well-regulated fociety; even then, it muft do more hurt than good to oppofe it with the arm of flefh. For perfecution and punifh- ment for the fake of opinion, feldom fail to ftrengthen the party they are intended to fup- prefs; and when opinions are combated by fuch weapons only, (which would probably be the cafe if the law were to interpofe), a fufpicion arifes in the minds of men, that no other weapons are to be had; and therefore that the fectary, though deftitute of power, is not wanting in argument. Let opinions then be combated by reafon, and let ridicule be employed to expofe nonfenfe. And to keep our licentious authors in awe, and to make it their intereft to think before they write, to examine facts before they draw inferences, to read books before they criticife them, and to ftudy both fides of a queftion before they take it upon them to give judgement, it would not be amifs, if their vices and follies, as authors, were fometimes chaftifed by a fatirical feverity of expreffion. This is a proper punifhment for their fault; this punifhment they certain- ly deferve; and this it is not beneath the dig- nity of a philofopher, or divine, or any man who loves God and his fellow-creatures, to in- flict.

flict. Milton, Locke, Cudworth, Sidney, Tillotſon, and ſeveral of the greateſt and beſt writers of the preſent age, have ſet the example; and have, I doubt not, done good by their nervous and animated expreſſion, as well as by the ſolidity of their arguments.— This puniſhment, if inflicted with diſcretion, might teach our licentious authors ſomething of modeſty, and of deference to the judgement of mankind; and, it is to be hoped, would in time bring down that ſpirit of preſumption, and affected ſuperiority, which hath of late diſtinguiſhed their writings, and contributed, more perhaps than all their ſubtlety and ſophiſtry, to the ſeduction of the ignorant, the unwary, and the faſhionable. It is true, the beſt of cauſes may be pleaded with an exceſs of warmth; as when the advocate is ſo blinded by his zeal, as to loſe ſight of his argument; or as when, in order to render his adverſaries odious, he alludes to ſuch particulars of their character or private hiſtory as are not to be gathered from their writings. The former fault never fails to injure the cauſe which the writer means to defend: the latter which is properly termed *perſonal abuſe*, is in itſelf ſo hateful, that every perſon of common prudence would be inclined to avoid it for his own ſake, even though he were not reſtrained by more weighty motives. If an author's writings be ſubverſive of virtue, and dangerous to private happineſs, and the public good, we ought to hold them in deteſtation, and, in order to counteract their baneful tendency, to

endeavour

endeavour to render them deteftable in the eyes
of others ; thus far we act the part of honeft
men, and good citizens : but with his private
hiftory we have no concern ; nor with his character, except fo far as he has thought proper
to fubmit to the public judgement, by difplaying it in his works. When thefe are of that
peculiar fort, that we cannot expofe them in
their proper colours, without reflecting on
his abilities and moral character, we ought by
no means to facrifice our love of truth and mankind to a complaifance, which, if we are what
we pretend to be, and ought to be, would be
hypocritical at beft, as well as mockery of the
public, and treachery to our caufe. The good
of fociety is always to be confidered as a matter of higher importance than the gratification
of an author's vanity. If he does not think of
this in time, and take care that the latter be
confiftent with the former, he has himfelf to
blame for all the confequences. The feverity
of Collier's attack upon the ftage, in the end
of the laft century, was, even in the judgement of one * who thought it exceffive, and
who will not be fufpected of partiality to that
author's doctrine, productive of very good effects ; as it obliged the fucceeding dramatic poets to curb that propenfion to indecency, which
had carried fome of their predeceffors fo far beyond the bounds of good tafte and good manners. If we are not permitted to anfwer the
objections of the infidel as plainly, and with
as little referve, as he makes them, we engage
him

* Colley Cibber. See his Apology, vol. i. p. 201.

him on unequal terms. And many will be
difpofed to think moft favourably of that caufe,
whofe adherents difplay the greateft ardour;
and fome, perhaps, may be tempted to impute
to timidity, or to a fecret diffidence of our principles, what might have been owing to a much
more pardonable weaknefs.

For my own part, though I have always
been, and fhall always be, happy in applaud-
ing excellence where-ever I find it; yet neither
the pomp of wealth nor the dignity of office,
neither the frown of the great nor the fneer of
the fafhionable, neither the fciolift's clamour
nor the profligate's refentment, fhall ever footh
or frighten me into an admiration, real or pretended, of impious tenets, fophiftical reafoning, or that paltry metaphyfic with which literature has been fo difgraced and peftered of late
years. I am not fo much addicted to controverfy, as ever to enter into any but what I judge
to be of very great importance; and into fuch
controverfy I cannot, I will not, enter with
coldnefs and unconcern. If I fhould, I might
pleafe a party, but I muft offend the public; I
might efcape the cenfure of thofe whofe praife
I would not value, but I fhould juftly forfeit
the efteem of good men, and incur the difapprobation of my own confcience.

END OF THE FIRST VOLUME.

www.ingramcontent.com/pod-product-compliance
Lightning Source LLC
Chambersburg PA
CBHW021336110726
47900CB00005B/1490